The Rev. Dom Benedict Steuart is a monk of St. Michael's Abbey, Farnborough. He is of Scottish descent from the well known family the Steuarts of Ballechin, Perthshire. From 1929 to 1937 he was Prior of Prinknash Abbey, Gloucestershire, and became in 1948 the first Superior of the restored pre-Reformation Priory of Pluscarden in Moray.

The author designed this book as a 'text-book' on the history of Christian worship.

It sets out the teaching and opinions of the accepted authorities on liturgical studies. It will therefore be of use to many people who, while interested in liturgical matters, are themselves unable to undertake a serious study of the subject, and will help to familiarize them with the latest conclusions of scholarly research

ther be unknown or unavail-
circumstances in which they

dict Steuart explains in his
the meaning of the two chief
virtue of religion: Sacrifice
The first part of the book,
s of the institution by Christ
velopment of the Christian
Holy Eucharist. The
s on the Christian liturgy
Eastern forms, but deals
h the Roman Rite which is
ly the only usage of the
ch, and especially with the
on of the 'canon' of the
In the second part, Prayer,
e origin and growth of the
of the Church for every day
rtant section of the day—
ice. He gives an explana-
ristian Year dedicated to
work of Jesus Christ and
Him, and brings out the
racter of Christian worship

J. B. O'Connell writes in
"He covers the entire
al study . . . his book is
ed with interesting and
on."

THE DEVELOPMENT OF
CHRISTIAN WORSHIP

TO
DOM BEDE GRIFFITHS, O.S.B.
FRATER FRATRI,
GRATO CORDE
ET AMANTI

We are indebted to Messrs. A. & C. Black Ltd. for permission to include material from THE SHAPE OF THE LITURGY by Dom Gregory Dix.

THE DEVELOPMENT OF
CHRISTIAN WORSHIP

An Outline of Liturgical History

DOM BENEDICT STEUART

Monk of St. Michael's Abbey
Farnborough, Hants

With a Foreword by
THE REV. J. B. O'CONNELL

LONGMANS GREEN AND CO
LONDON · NEW YORK · TORONTO

LONGMANS, GREEN AND CO LTD
6 & 7 CLIFFORD STREET LONDON W I
ALSO AT MELBOURNE AND CAPE TOWN
LONGMANS, GREEN AND CO INC
55 FIFTH AVENUE NEW YORK 3
LONGMANS, GREEN AND CO
215 VICTORIA STREET TORONTO I
ORIENT LONGMANS LTD
BOMBAY CALCUTTA MADRAS

First published 1953

Nihil obstat

DANIEL DUIVESTEIJN, S.T.D.
CENSOR DEPUTATUS.

Imprimatur

E. MORROGH BERNARD
VIC. GEN.

Westmonasterii, die 11a Julii 1953

PRINTED AND BOUND IN GREAT BRITAIN BY
HAZELL WATSON AND VINEY LTD
AYLESBURY AND LONDON

CONTENTS

PART II

PRAYER: The Divine Office

APPENDICES

FOREWORD

"THE end of the last century and the beginning of the present have seen an unprecedented revival of liturgical studies, due in part to the admirable initiative of a number of individuals, but especially to the devoted zeal of certain monasteries of the renowned Benedictine Order", wrote Pope Pius XII, in his Encyclical *Mediator Dei* (1947),[1] the great charter of the "liturgical movement". "The laudable and useful spirit of emulation thus aroused"—continued the Holy Father—"not only in many parts of Europe but also overseas, has yielded a salutary harvest in the field of sacred study with a wider knowledge and deeper understanding of the liturgical rites of the Eastern and the Western Church; and it has also proved beneficial to the spiritual life of many Christians. . . . This Apostolic See . . . has at all times endeavoured to inspire the faithful under its charge with a sound and active liturgical sense". Further on in the same Encyclical,[2] Pius XII wrote: "To go back in mind and heart to the sources of the sacred Liturgy is wise and praiseworthy. The study of liturgical origins enables us to understand better the significance of festivals and the meaning of liturgical forms and ceremonies".

Dom Benedict Steuart in his book *The Development of Christian Worship* has gone back, as the Pope recommended, and has provided us with an excellent 'outline of liturgical history', to cite the sub-title of the work.

It is of paramount importance to know something of the history of the Liturgy that is ours, for only by a competent knowledge of the origins of our rites can we attain to a true understanding of the real meaning of the prayers and actions of the Sacred Liturgy. For too long have these prayers and ceremonies been 'explained' by a priori theories, culminating very often in the merely fanciful. History is a valuable corrective of speculation, of subjective hypotheses, and the only really

---

[1] "Christian Worship" (C.T.S. version of the Encyclical translated by Mgr G. D. Smith, D.D.) § 5.
[2] Ibid. § 66.

sound knowledge of the Roman rite must be based on a historical foundation, on the rock of historical fact.

The examination of the origins of our Liturgy is not mere 'archaeologism'; it has a very practical bearing on our personal worship, for the Liturgy is not a dead thing—a museum piece—but an organism. It is a life-stream into which we must plunge our own little acts of worship that they may mingle with, and be transformed by, the great river of the divine worship of the Mystical Body of Christ.

Much labour has been devoted for the past half-century to the history of the development of Christian worship, and it is engaging ever more the attention of scholars, under the aegis of the Church, indeed in obedience to the bidding of successive Popes. Our knowledge of this development has advanced by leaps and bounds, but much of this knowledge is contained in long and expensive books, most of them not in English, and in monographs on special points published in learned journals, accessible to but few. The results of the work of experts over a long period need to be collected, co-ordinated, epitomised and set forth in English, in simple form, for the benefit of the many. A work of *vulgarisation* is needed and this Dom Benedict has given us.

He covers the entire field of liturgical study, consulting not only the rites of the Western Church but also those of the East. He gives us the latest information about the discoveries and views of liturgical savants—and his own views, too—on various obscure points, and on matters that are still under discussion. His book is indeed crammed with interesting and useful information. May it be widely read and contribute, in full measure, to the greater appreciation of, and ever more active participation in, the Sacred Liturgy.

J. B. O'CONNELL.

PREFACE

THE following pages have been written in order to gather together the results of recent work by authoritative writers on the history of the Liturgy—both abroad and in this country—for the sake of those people who, while anxious to know more about the meaning and history of the worship of the Church, are unable, for one reason or another, to take up a really serious study of the matter. Among such people are, for instance, busy parish priests, religious occupied with teaching or other absorbing work, and lay folk who, in these days of 'liturgical movements' of one kind or another, are tending more and more to take an interest in liturgical matters from both the practical and historical points of view, but are in most cases unable to find time to look it up for themselves. What seems to be much needed, nowadays, is some kind of text-book on the history and explanation of the Liturgy—that is, the Mass, Divine Offices and the Sacraments—and no such book (by a Catholic writer, at least) exists in this country as yet. Abroad, liturgical literature is intended rather for *savants* of the same type as the writers themselves; or else the language in which it is written (Italian, German or French) restricts such literature to a limited number. There are, however, English translations of the liturgical writings of the late Dom Fernand Cabrol, Abbot of Farnborough, which are widely read. A Catholic text-book on Christian worship (to use a term less technical-sounding than the somewhat controversial word 'liturgy') would also be welcomed perhaps by novice-masters and mistresses as a help in the instruction of their novices—especially in the case of those religious orders in which liturgical worship is a feature of the daily life. The writer, in offering *The Development of Christian Worship* as a humble attempt to provide a text-book on this subject, founded upon the authority of the learned authors abroad and in England whose works are quoted or referred to in these pages, may be allowed, perhaps, to make a modest claim that what he has written here is also the result of a considerable number of years spent in the personal study of these questions—years of a life, too, which may with truth be said to be founded upon the Liturgy.

Among books dealing with the Liturgy in our own country, the writer wishes to refer especially to a recent work called *The Shape of the Liturgy*,[1] by Dom Gregory Dix of the Anglican Abbey of Nashdom (Dacre Press, Westminster, 1945). This book, as its author says, was written primarily by an Anglican for Anglicans, and deals with certain difficult problems in the Church of England. But apart from the especially Anglican elements of the book, it provides a real summing up, and also development, of the most recent liturgical study and, to a great extent, continues the work begun by that great liturgical scholar, the late Edmund Bishop, particularly in what concerns the Roman rite, the canon of the Mass and so on. The question of the Roman canon, in fact, so long regarded as almost insoluble, is set forth, and to a great extent 'cleared up', by Dom Gregory Dix in a most refreshingly simple and straightforward manner—in strong contrast to the innumerable complicated and often contradictory theories put forward by one writer after another. On the whole, *The Shape of the Liturgy* has been very favourably reviewed by the Catholic Press. A well-known Catholic priest, writing in the liturgical review *Magnificat*, says that: "In the view of the present writer, perhaps Fr. Dix's signal contribution to liturgical study is that he has driven us back behind the great fourth-century liturgies and forced every honest scholar to think out his position again."[2] In the *Eastern Churches Quarterly* for October–December 1945,[3] a reviewer of the Orthodox Church, in an interesting appreciation, declares that Dom Dix's book—in spite of certain shortcomings (especially in connection with the Eastern liturgies)—is worthy of taking the place in these days of Mgr. Duchesne's well-known book, *Origines du Culte Chrétien*—in its English translation known as *Christian Worship*.[4]

---

[1] 'Dix', in footnotes or in notes in the text, refers always to *The Shape of the Liturgy*. References to other works of this author give the titles in full.

[2] *The Shape of the Liturgy*: a review by the Rev. J. D. Crichton—in *Magnificat*, No. 3, p. 7, Spring, 1946.

[3] Published in London by Geo. E. J. Coldwell, Ltd., 17, Red Lion Square, Holborn, W.C.1—edited at St. Augustine's Abbey, Ramsgate.

[4] London: S.P.C.K., fifth edit., 1919; reprinted (latest reprint) 1949, with additional notes and corrections.

Since these words were written the death of the author of
The Shape of the Liturgy has deprived liturgical scholarship of one
of its most prominent exponents. Dom Gregory Dix died on
May 12th, 1952, after a long illness bravely borne. He had
hoped to live until he had finished one more book on his
special subject, but it was not to be.

In spite of this loss to liturgical study, the words of the Rev.
J. D. Crichton, quoted a few lines back, remain true—Dom
Gregory Dix's "signal contribution to liturgical study" will
not cease to have its effect.

There are a number of other books on liturgical matters by
Anglican authorities in this country and, besides, many articles
in such well-known reviews as *The Journal of Theological Studies*
and in Catholic reviews such as *The Downside Review*, and also
in those which are especially concerned with liturgical studies—
e.g. *Liturgy* (the quarterly magazine of the Society of St.
Gregory); *Magnificat; Pax*, the quarterly magazine of the
Benedictines of Prinknash Abbey, Gloucester and its dependent
monasteries at Farnborough, Hants and Pluscarden in Scotland. In the United States there is the wide-spread liturgical
magazine *Orates Fratres*,[1] published by St. John's Abbey,
Collegeville, Minn. It would take too long to attempt to discuss
all these works in detail, but among books on liturgical history
we must mention here especially *The Early History of the
Liturgy*, by J. H. Srawley, D.D., which is of quite special
importance and authority. This book was originally published
in 1913, but has recently been revised and partly rewritten and
republished in 1947 (Cambridge University Press).

Besides his own book, Canon Srawley contributed an essay
on the history and development of the Communion Service in
a former book called *Liturgy and Worship*, containing a series of
essays on the Anglican Book of Common Prayer, edited by
W. K. Lowther Clarke, D.D., with the assistance of Charles
Harris, D.D. (London: S.P.C.K., 1932). These essays involve a
considerable amount of work on the early history and development of the Liturgy in general. Canon Srawley's contribution
is found in Part II, pp. 302–73—*The Holy Communion Service*.

---

[1] This review has recently altered its title, and is now known as *Worship* (published by The Liturgical Press, Collegeville, Minnesota, U.S.A.).

There are also the well-known liturgical works of the late venerable and learned Bishop of Truro, the Right Reverend Walter Howard Frere, C.R.

Two quite recent and important books by a Catholic writer must also be recommended here. These are: (i) *The Rites of Eastern Christendom* (two vols., Catholic Book Agency, Rome, 1947) and (ii) 'The Rites of Western Christendom' (12 chapters of extant rites and Roman Variants, and a number of appendices of obsolete usages—not yet published), by Archdale A. King. An earlier work by the same writer is called *Notes on the Catholic Liturgies* (one vol., Longmans, 1930).[1]

Among articles deserving particular attention are those written, both in *The Journal of Theological Studies* and in Catholic reviews, by the late H. Codrington, whose death a few years ago was a real loss to liturgical studies. References, too, that will always be found helpful, and even necessary, will be those made to the learned and even now 'up-to-date' writings of that 'Master' of liturgical history, Mr. Edmund Bishop, especially to his final summary of liturgical study, *Liturgica Historica* (Oxford: Clarendon Press, 1918). Abroad, there is the work carried out by another great authority on liturgical matters whose recent death has left a void in liturgical studies, the learned Benedictine monk of Maria Laach in Germany, Dom Odo Casel, O.S.B. Dom Casel's special contribution to the study of the Liturgy is found in his *Le Mystère du Culte dans le Christianisme* (the French Translation of the original German work, 1944, by Dom J. Hild, O.S.B., monk of Clervaux Abbey in the Grand Duchy of Luxembourg[2]—which might be 'Englished' as: 'The Mystery of Christian Worship'). In this book, and in all his writings, Dom Odo Casel insisted upon the fact that the Christian religion and its form of worship is a 'mystery', using that word in its ancient and religious meaning found in the Liturgy, not merely in the sense of something 'hidden' and 'mysterious', but in the sense

[1] There has just been published a pamphlet entitled *The Western Liturgy and its History: Some Reflections on Recent Studies*, by Theodor Klauser (Professor of Church History in the University of Bonn), translated into English by F. L. Cross, Lady Margaret Professor of Divinity in the University of Oxford and Canon of Christchurch. (London: A. R. Mowbray & Co., Ltd., 1952.)

[2] Lex Orandi, 6, etc.: Les Editions du Cerf, 29, boulevard Latour-Maubourg, Paris VII; also Blackfriars Publications, Oxford agents for the Editions du Cerf.

given to the word by St. Paul—namely, the accomplishment
of an eternal plan in the mind of God by means of an *action*
which, proceeding from Him and from all eternity, is now
realised in time. In connection with this is another work by
the French Oratorian, the Rev. Louis Bouyer: *Le Mystère
Pascal* ('The Mystery of Easter') (Les Editions du Cerf-Lex
Orandi, 4–29, 1947). This book—as the sub-title tells us—is
primarily a series of meditations on the Liturgy of the three
last days of Holy Week. But these excellent and most helpful
meditations are founded on deeply interesting studies of
liturgical history, and on innumerable references to the writings
of the Fathers and others. An English translation appeared
in 1949—*The Paschal Mystery*, by Louis Bouyer, Oratorian,
translated by Sister M. Benoit, R.S.M. (London: Allen &
Unwin, Ltd., 1949). Again, in liturgical work abroad, there is
that being carried on in the Abbey of Mont César, Louvain, in
Belgium, by the Abbot, the Right Reverend Dom B. Capelle,
by Dom B. Botte and other monks, in *Textes et Études liturgiques: Les Questions liturgiques et paroissiales, etc.*

With regard to the historical aspect of Christian worship and
the need of a text-book on the subject for Catholics in our own
country, there is a well-known theological axiom: *Nil volitum
quin præcognitum* ('Nothing is *desired* unless it be *known* first'). In
order to really love and appreciate the Liturgy of the Church
as it deserves; in order to really *desire* to take part in it—that is,
by an active sharing in the celebration of the Holy Sacrifice of
the Mass and (where possible) in that of the Divine Office, and
also, it may be added, in order to take part in or make use of
the Sacraments of the Church as she herself intends us to—it is
necessary, or at least a very great help, to *know* something about
the origin and development of the prayers that are said and the
ceremonial actions that are carried out. In other words, it is
necessary, or very helpful, to find an answer to the 'why and
wherefore', and even to the 'when', of the various elements of
Christian worship. But the historical study of the liturgy should
not be a mere delving into the past—a 'dry-as-dust' gathering
together of things which have happened long ago. The rites
and ceremonies of the Christian religion are not, as in the case
of the old religions of the pagan world, mere ritual acts handed

down from time immemorial, and objects of a superstitious reverence simply because they were so old—because they had 'always been done'. Christian rites and ceremonies are true expressions of its teaching and worship; they really mean something, and that meaning has lasted throughout the ages of the Church's life, and will last until the end of time itself.

I cannot end this Preface without attempting to express my gratitude for, and appreciation of, the kind help given to me and the interest shown in the work, which has made it possible for me to get this book into shape.

First my gratitude and appreciation are due to my Abbot— the Right Reverend Dom Wilfrid Upson, Abbot of Prinknash Abbey—who gave his ready permission for the work, and continued to show his fatherly interest in it and his satisfaction when it was accepted by Messrs. Longmans, Green & Co., for publication; then to the one to whom I have ventured to dedicate the book—Dom Bede Griffiths—to whom, when he was Prior of Farnborough Abbey, I owe the very idea of writing the book at all and who continued to encourage me in spite of initial difficulties; and in his turn, to the present Prior of Farnborough, the Very Reverend Dom Basil Robinson, whose help and unfailing support have been invaluable to me. I owe next special thanks to my friends: to the Rev. J. B. O'Connell— well known as the author of important and useful works on liturgical matters—who has kindly agreed to write the Foreword, and who took the trouble of reading my MS. through, and offered many valuable suggestions and corrections; to my friend also, Mr. Archdale A. King, author of several important works on the history of the Liturgy, whose judgment and opinion—the results of his wide knowledge on the question—have been of immense help to me. Mr. King, too, was kind enough to read through my MS. and to help with useful suggestions. And another kind friend, the Rev. Ronald Pilkington (now at Westminster Cathedral; formerly Professor of Liturgy at the Diocesan Seminary in Florence, Italy) has helped me in the same way and given useful advice.

Finally, I would like to mention here the name of my brother, Father Robert H. J. Steuart, S.J., who died on July 9th, 1948 (the feast of the English martyrs, SS. John Fisher and Thomas More). A writer of great distinction himself, he was always interested in the attempts of others of lesser importance and learning. He was always especially—and really—interested in my own 'attempts'—articles in magazines and so forth—and really took trouble over them. He and I discussed the idea of this book together, and I know how interested he would have been in it all had I been able to show him my MS. before his death, and how delighted he would have been to hear of its acceptance for publication—as much, indeed, as if it had been his own work.

In connection with him, I cannot but conclude with the name of our mutual friend, Miss Katharine Kendall, the author of his recently written Life—*Father Steuart: Priest of the Society of Jesus. A Study of His Life and Teaching*, by Katharine Kendall, with a Foreword by Francis C. Devas, S.J. (Burns, Oates & Washbourne, Ltd., 28, Ashley Place, London, S.W.1, 1950), whose constant friendly interest and advice have been of very great help to me.

BENEDICT STEUART, O.S.B.

Feast of the Holy Guardian Angels,
  October 2nd, 1952.

NOTE.—On p. 128 (towards the end of Chapter VI, 'The Roman Canon') there is mention of a most important work on the Mass-liturgy by a German Jesuit, called *Missarum Solemnia*. It was only after the completion of my book that I was able to obtain the French translation of Part I—*Tome premier* (the second and succeeding parts still await (February 1952) translation. (See reference and full title in Chapter VI, p. 128.)

INTRODUCTION

SACRIFICE AND PRAYER

THE real, substantial importance of the Christian Liturgy and of the 'Liturgical Movement' of the present day lies simply in the fact that the Liturgy is the worship of the Blessed Trinity by Christ Our Lord Himself, in person, and by His mystical Body, the Church which is the 'whole Christ', as St. Augustine says in his treatise on Psalm lxxiv, 4. This idea is repeated in his *Ennarationes in Psalmos,* and in his 'sermons' also.[1]

The word 'liturgy' is derived from the Greek word *leiturgia,* which means 'public work' or 'service'. Originally referring to service owed to the state by its members, the word has come to refer exclusively to 'divine service', that is, the public or social worship of God. Public, social worship is found in all forms of religion and from the earliest periods of human history, for man is a 'social animal' with regard to his religion as in all else that concerns human life.

From the philosophical and theological points of view, God has an absolute right to the worship of human society as well as to that of each individual composing it, since He is the Creator and Lord of the former as well as of the latter. Besides this, God has a right, not only to the interior adoration of each and of all in general, but also to the *exterior expression* of this adoration—through the body, in words, actions, signs and ceremonies. He has, in fact, a right to the worship of the 'whole man'—body and soul. Worship of God, individual and social, finds its expression in two ways—in *prayer* and *sacrifice.*

Prayer means the intercourse of mind, heart and, in fact, the whole of man's soul with God—this is interior or 'mental' prayer. 'Vocal' prayer includes the use of the voice and other exercises of the body. *Purely mental* prayer cannot be public or social, but is entirely personal.

---

[1] The full words are: "When Christ hath begun to dwell in man's heart by faith . . . there is made up the whole Christ, the Head and the Body, and out of many One." (*An Augustine Synthesis*: arranged by Erich Przywara, S.J. (London: Sheed & Ward, 1936. p. 228).

Sacrifice might be loosely described as the fulfilment in act of the dispositions expressed mentally and vocally in prayer. It is the pledge and proof of the reality and sincerity of the 'religious attitude', and it is the supreme and all-embracing act of the virtue of religion. Sacrifice can be offered to God alone, as the Beginning and the End of all life. As the internal and external recognition of that fact, sacrifice consists in the offering and entire surrender—the *consecration* or *devotion*—of life to God. The intention and desire of the offerer (individual or society, nation or family) to perform this sacred act is the *interior sacrifice*, the 'soul' of the *exterior sacrifice* without which this latter would be mere formalism.[1] The exterior act of sacrifice, in the Religion of Israel and in all other known religions, consisted principally in the ceremonial offering of a living creature of some description—the 'victim'. This word is derived from the Latin *victima*, and it is interesting to note that the word *victima* is cognate with the Gothic word *weihan*, which means 'to consecrate' (*weihs* = 'holy').[2] This fact fits in, too, with the word 'sacrifice', itself derived from the Latin *sacrum facere*—to 'make holy', to 'consecrate'. For far too long the real substantial meaning of sacrifice has lain hidden under the general belief that the word signified the *destruction* of life in token of the supreme power of God over all existence— especially in connection with reparation for sin in order to obtain reconciliation with an offended Deity. The fact that living victims were killed and, in part at least, burned, and other offerings of inanimate articles (food and drink, etc., also included in sacrificial worship) were usually burned or destroyed in some way, led to this notion of the *destruction* of life instead of its *consecration*—the latter, surely, far more con-sonant with God's honour and majesty than the former, for God neither destroys nor desires the destruction of anything that He has made. The fact, however, that life can be con-secrated and offered to God only *through* death or surrender in some form is a valuable lesson to be kept in mind. This fact is

---

[1] In his *De civitate Dei*, St. Augustine says: "*visible sacrifice* is the *sacrament*, that is, the sacred sign of the invisible sacrifice." (*De Civ. Dei X* = V: *Summa Theol.*, 2-2, 85, 2; 38, 22, 2, C).

[2] See *The New English Dictionary*, by E. A. Baker, M.A., D.Lit. (Odhams Press, Ltd., London, 1932.)

the result of sin, and it entered into all forms of sacrifice, even those offered entirely in adoration or as signifying peace and union with God.

Properly speaking, man should have offered his own life to its Maker. But, since on account of sin as we have just seen above, life can be offered to Him only through death and suffering, and since this would mean that man must take his own life or that of some fellow creature in his place, God decreed that some substitute for human life should be the victim of sacrifice. This was usually a domestic animal—as more representative of human life than any wild animal[1]— and also of other (inanimate) kinds of food, especially the universal food and drink—bread and wine.

The classic example of the 'substitute sacrifice' in the Old Testament is the sacrifice of a ram offered by Abraham in place of his son Isaac (Gen. xxii. 1–13). In pagan religions, however, human sacrifice was often offered, even in comparatively civilised nations.

In the revealed ritual code of Israel in Leviticus and Deuteronomy, we find especial emphasis laid upon the offering of the victim's blood—which act was reserved to the priest alone, though any other, a levite or the 'lay' offerer himself, might actually *kill* the victim. The blood poured out upon or around the altar by the priest represented the victim's life and that of the offerer—as the text says: "the life of the flesh is in the blood and I have given it to you, that you may make atonement with it upon the altar for your souls" (Levit. xvii. 11). This consecrated blood 'made atonement' (i.e. effected a reunion, an 'at-one-ment') with God for the sinful or otherwise unworthy life of the offerer, as it was the offering of a more worthy and pleasing gift of an, at least ritually, 'pure and unblemished' life. Even in those sacrifices offered expressly in reparation for sin in general or for some 'trespass' in particular, the slaying, outpouring of blood and burning in the altar fire were not regarded as *punishments*—either of the victim, which was

[1] In the primitive stages of the human race, however, before men possessed flocks and herds or any settled dwelling-place, sacrifices of the first wild animal killed in hunting, and of the first examples of wild fruit and other 'growing things' plucked for use as food, are found. See *The Religion of Earliest Man*, by Rev. W. Schmidt. S.V.D. (London: C.T.S., R.102, p. 5.)

'holy' and 'consecrated' and so in no sense needed 'punishment', or even of the sinful offerer; it was all simply the unavoidable result of the sin of the First Man which had been inherited by his descendants and which made all approach to God difficult and painful.

With regard to the meaning underlying the ritual burning of the victim or other offerings, in whole or in part, the daily morning and evening sacrifice of incense in the Temple at Jerusalem really provides the best explanation. No one would be likely to suggest that the burning of precious gums on the altar of incense in the Holy Place was intended to *destroy* them. On the contrary, the burning effected their sublimation—producing the sweet-smelling smoke which ascended to heaven (in the words of Holy Writ) 'as a sweet savour before the Lord'. The latter words were applied also to all sacrificial burnings, but in the case of ordinary sacrifices (especially those of animal victims) the words were merely symbolical; the 'sweet savour' was realised in the literal sense only in the offering of incense; the 'sweet savour' in other sacrifices implied that they were *acceptable* to God through the intentions of those who offered them.

These symbolical sacrifices of the Old Law, and to a certain extent those of pagan religions also, were summed up and transcended in the One Sacrifice of the New Law. Jesus Christ Our Lord offered His own life upon the Cross, to make real 'at-one-ment' between His Heavenly Father and all mankind. The perfect life of the Perfect Man (officially) 'consecrated' in sacrifice gave infinite pleasure to the Father and made complete reparation for the evil of sin. The sufferings and death freely undergone in this sacrifice and suffered on behalf of all men gave complete satisfaction for all sins against God. This supreme Sacrifice offered *once* in blood upon the cross is offered *continually* upon the altars of the Church in the Sacrifice bequeathed to her by her Divine Head at the Last Supper, 'on the day before He suffered'. In this unbloody Sacrifice we have the most complete and most perfect example of 'consecration'—*sacrum facere*—that could be imagined. The Church, fulfilling the command of her Master, makes her offering of bread and wine, representing the life, both spiritual and temporal, of her children, and representing, too, the 'Holy Bread of everlasting life' and the 'Chalice of salvation', the true supports of all life. By means of the power entrusted to her priests by her Master, the consecration of these offerings not only renders them sacred in the official or ritual sense, but changes them *substantially* into the Body and Blood of the Victim of Calvary whose one act of self-oblation is thus brought from eternity into time until the end of time.[1]

Besides sacrifice and prayer—the Holy Mass and the Divine Office—the sacraments and, in a lesser degree, what are known as 'sacramentals' must be included in the Liturgy. The Christian religion is founded on the sacramental system, the Incarnation of the Second Person of the Blessed Trinity being the Supreme Sacrament—using that word in a wider sense. In the strict, official sense a sacrament (in the words of the Catholic penny Catechism) is 'An outward sign of inward grace, ordained by Jesus Christ, by which grace is given to our souls'. In the wider sense, the word 'sacramental' can be given to any external signs of higher things. For example, the external rites and ceremonies of sacrifice are the sacramental indications of the interior meaning of the act. As we saw on p. xx of this *Introduction*, St. Augustine tells us plainly that the "visible sacrifice is the *sacrament*, that is, the *sacred sign* of the invisible sacrifice".

In the strict, official sense a sacrament is an outward sign of grace given to man's soul, but it is not merely a sign, a symbol of God's gift. A sacrament is an 'effective sign'—that is, it really produces the grace in the soul—provided that neither the person receiving nor the one dispensing the sacrament puts any obstacle in the way. A sacrament is a *human* act (though a supernatural one), it is not a magical performance. In the sacrament of baptism, for instance, pouring water on the recipient's head while pronouncing the words "I baptise thee

---

[1] See *The Christian Sacrifice*, by Canon Eugène Masure, translated by Dom Illtyd Trethowan, Monk of Downside Abbey (London: Burns, Oates & Washbourne, Ltd., 1943); also 'The Mass: Sacramental Immolation', by Canon E. Masure, in *The Downside Review*, July 1947, p. 195; and, 'The Theology of the Mass and the Liturgical Datum', by Dom Sebastian Moore, in *The Downside Review*, Winter, 1950, pp. 31–44, and Spring, 1952, pp. 119–34. See also Dom Trethowan's recently published book, *Christ in the Liturgy* (London: Sheed & Ward, 1951). A splendid statement of the nature and history of the Christian Liturgy.

in the name of the Father, the Son and the Holy Ghost"
really brings about in the baptised person the spiritual washing
of the soul from the stain of original sin and of any sins
committed since birth. Baptism is the first of the seven Sacraments: Baptism, Confirmation, Holy Eucharist, Penance,
Matrimony, Holy Orders and the Last Anointing (Extreme
Unction is the usual 'Latinised' form in which the name is
expressed). Baptism incorporates (literally 'embodies') the
recipient into the Mystical Body of Christ—that is, the Church.
The act of Baptism is often called 'christening', or 'to christen'
—that is, it makes the recipient 'another Christ', as Tertullian
tells us that all Christians are by their very vocation. But the
Holy Eucharist is the greatest and highest of the seven, for not
only Divine grace is given to the soul, but the Author of all
grace, Jesus Christ Himself, who is really and actually present
under the outward signs or forms of bread and wine. Our
Saviour is present in this Sacrament, in order to be offered in
sacrifice by His Church—the sacramental offering of the
Sacrifice offered in blood and death upon the Cross. Through
this sacramental Sacrifice—as its result—He gives His Body
and Blood to all as the Food and Drink of the spiritual life.

The chief difference between a sacrifice and a sacrament is
that in the former man offers something to God, and this is
true also of prayer, in which man offers to God the homage
due to Him and recognises Him as worshipful, and as the source
of life and of all that is needed in life. In the latter it is *God*
who offers something to *man*: Christening in Baptism; its full
development and settlement in Confirmation; the 'consecration' of the natural contract of matrimony which makes it a
living copy of the union between the soul and Our Lord; a
share in His own Priesthood in Holy Orders; forgiveness of
sins committed since Baptism in the Sacrament of Penance; a
share in the Sacrifice of Redemption and nourishment of the
soul in the Holy Eucharist. Finally, in the Last Anointing,
God sometimes restores health, but always strengthens His
servant for the journey of death and, by the anointing with
consecrated oil, cures each member of the body that has
perhaps been used in sin—in look, hearing, speech, touch or
step.

All the Sacraments are connected with and depend upon that Sacrament which is known distinctively as 'the Blessed Sacrament'. Each of the other Sacraments is a means of applying to all men, and in all ages of the world, the saving effects of the Redemption. In the Holy Eucharist we have *the Work of the Redemption itself*: as the secret prayer at the offertory in the Mass of the ninth Sunday after Pentecost expresses it: "Grant, we pray thee, Lord, that we may worthily and often take part in these mysteries, for each and every offering of this memorial sacrifice *carries on the work of our redemption.*"[1]

Sacramentals were originally so-called, either because of their connection with the Sacraments[2] or their resemblance to or analogy with them. Now, however, the term indicates only those rites and ceremonies instituted by the Church in the course of ages and which bear a certain resemblance to the Sacraments instituted by Our Lord Himself.

The seven Sacraments produce—each in its own way— what is called sanctifying grace in the recipient's soul; that is, the free gift (*gratia*) from God to man of holiness and the means to preserve and develop it. But the sacramentals, not being immediately 'ordained' by Jesus Christ, are simply helps for obtaining special graces. One example is the blessing of holy water on Sundays and its sprinkling upon the congregation before the public Mass, in cathedrals, collegiate and parish churches, and also the general use of holy water in churches and houses: making the sign of the cross with the finger dipped in holy water and so on.[3] Then certain devotional objects are included among sacramentals—for example: holy pictures, ikons, medals, the rosary, scapulars—and many others. All these offer the means of obtaining spiritual help in one way or another. Also, as is shown by long experience, they can serve as 'arms' to be used against the attacks of Satan and his fallen angels.

[1] The Latin text is as follows: *Concede nobis, quæsumus, Domine, hæc digne frequentare mysteria: quia quoties huius hostiæ commemoratio celebratur, opus nostræ redemptionis exercetur.*

[2] The rites and ceremonies of administration, etc. Although Christ instituted each of the seven Sacraments directly, He left the rites and ceremonies to the authority of His Church to develop in the course of time.

[3] Other important 'sacramentals' are the solemn blessing of ashes on Ash Wednesday, of palms on Palm Sunday, and of Candles on Candlemas Day (February 2nd).

With regard to sacrifice and prayer: the Christian Liturgy comprises two distinct public services—the Holy Sacrifice of the Mass, of which we have just spoken above, and the Divine Office. The Mass includes a number of prayers as well as ceremonial actions; but the Divine Office forms besides an ordered system of public, corporate prayer at stated times of the day. We read in the Acts of the Apostles that the disciples went up to the Temple to pray, according to the Jewish custom, at the ninth hour of the day—about 3 p.m. of our time. This was, at that period, the hour of the daily evening sacrifice offered in the Temple. In earlier times the daily sacrifices had been offered at sunrise and sunset respectively. It is not till the fourth century of the Christian era that we find official corporate prayer fully developed and distinct from the Holy Eucharist and private prayer. It is then found in two forms: the 'Ecclesiastical Office'—public prayer carried out by the clergy and their congregations; and the 'Monastic Office'—the family prayer of the 'Ascetics', both men and women; monks and nuns, as we should call them to-day. Quite distinct at first, these two offices gradually influenced each other in one way or another, and were finally welded into the 'Divine Office', the solemn, corporate prayer of the whole Church. The Monastic Office, although it has preserved certain characteristics of its own distinct from that of the clergy in general, is now included in the Public Prayer of the whole Church, carried out officially in the name and with the authority of the Church.

PART I

SACRIFICE : THE HOLY EUCHARIST

CHAPTER I

THE INSTITUTION OF THE HOLY EUCHARIST AND THE EARLY FORMATION OF THE LITURGY

THE Institution of the Holy Eucharist by Our Lord at the Last Supper is described in the Synoptic Gospels; St. John does not record it, although he speaks of the Last Supper and the washing of the feet of the disciples by Our Lord, His discourse to them and His prayer for them—and the going forth to the Garden of Gethsemane (John xiii.–xviii.). The Synoptic Gospels tell us that Our Lord, after the Supper with His disciples, took bread and wine, blessed God, 'giving thanks' over them and declaring that they were now His Body and Blood, commanded His disciples to repeat what He had done 'in memory' of Him; broke the consecrated bread and distributed it, together with the chalice of consecrated wine, to the disciples (Matt. xxvi. 17–30; Mark xiv. 12–26; Luke xxii. 7–21). St. Luke is the only Evangelist who gives the words used by Our Lord after the words of institution. These are: "Do this for a commemoration of Me." Students are not agreed as to the exact nature of the supper which preceded the institution of the Holy Eucharist—that is, as to whether it was the actual paschal supper after the sacrifice of the paschal lamb in the Temple court; whether it was an anticipation of that supper, before the actual day of the Passover, or, finally, whether it was simply one of the ordinary Jewish 'family meals'. These latter also had a religious—even a sacrificial—character, e.g. the *kiddush* and the *chaburah* (or *haburah*). The former was held on the eve of the Sabbath day; the latter was a meal shared by a company of friends—the name being derived from *chaber* or *haber*, a friend or comrade. (See *The Early Eucharist*, by Felix L. Cirlot (London: S.P.C.K., 1939, chap. i); also *The Apostolic Tradition of St. Hippolytus*, edited by Dom Gregory Dix (London: S.P.C.K., 1937, pp. 73 *et seq.*); *The Shape of the Liturgy*—by the same author (Dacre Press, Westminster, 1945, pp. 50 *et seq.*); also *Études Bibliques: L'Évangile de Jesus Christ*, by the Rév. Père M. J. Lagrange, O.P. (Paris: Lecoffre, 1929).) Dom Gregory Dix considers that the institution of the Holy Eucharist took place during a chaburah meal, but in the latest edition of his work—*The Early History of the Liturgy*—Canon J. H. Srawley discusses the matter and comes to the conclusion that one must deny "anything so formal" as the chaburah in this case.[1] (See p. 3.) But it is a fact that the Last Supper, whatever its *actual* nature, was regarded by the disciples and early Christians as the Christian fulfilment of the paschal sacrifice and feast.

All Jewish meals consisted of the following elements: (*a*) a preliminary informal course eaten *seated*, in which everyone blessed the food and drink for himself; (*b*) the formal meal taken *reclining*, which opened with the blessing and breaking of the bread by one 'leader' for all present; (*c*) at the conclusion, the 'grace-after-meals', called the 'food blessing'—also said by the leader for all present. On simple occasions the 'food blessing' was merely said without any accompanying ceremony, but on special, joyful occasions it was said over a common cup, known as the 'cup of blessing' or 'of the blessing'. No former cup was thus blessed by *one* person for the whole group. (*d*) Finally, came, in some cases, the cup called the 'kiddush-cup', blessed with a double blessing—'of the wine' and 'of the day'. This, too, was a 'common' cup and was blessed by one person. (*The Early Eucharist*, by F. L. Cirlot, p. 13.)

Taking this description as the 'scheme' of the Last Supper, the consecration of the bread would have taken place at the blessing and breaking of the bread by the host—in this case, Our Lord Himself—and after the preliminary informal course. The meal proper then followed, and the consecration of the wine would have been during the grace-after-meals or 'food blessing'. As this Supper was a special occasion of joy (in the institution of the Holy Eucharist), there was a cup of blessing —which fully justified its title in its result; that is, the change of ordinary wine into the Precious Blood of Our Saviour

---

[1] See also 'The Last Supper', by Joachim Jeremias, in *Journal of Theological Studies*, January–April 1949, pp. 1–10, in favour of the Last Supper as the Passover meal.

(1 Cor. x. 16—where St. Paul uses explicitly the term 'cup of blessing' in speaking of the Eucharist). In Matthew and Mark the consecration of the bread is not clearly stated to have taken place at the *beginning* of the Supper and that of the wine *after* it, but St. Luke, after mentioning the first cup of wine before the supper proper began, speaks of the consecration of the bread, and then goes on: "in like manner the chalice, *after He had supped*, etc." (Luke xxii. 17–20). The first cup was probably that of the preliminary course of the meal, and Our Lord, no doubt, blessed this cup only for Himself, that is it was His own personal 'grace', but He would have passed the wine (not the *cup* from which He Himself drank) round the disciples. St. Paul, too, in the above quotation expressly states that Our Lord blessed the chalice (in which blessing He changed the wine into His own Blood) "after supper". There would then have been quite a long time between the two consecrations and communions. The whole rite ended, after the communion of the chalice, with the singing of the hymn (Matt. xxvi. 30; Mark xiv. 26), and the usual hand-washing. After the Crucifixion, if at first the Holy Eucharist was celebrated during or after the usual evening meal, this order would, no doubt, have been adhered to by the disciples. But when—perhaps on account of the troubles and lack of reverence spoken of by St. Paul in 1 Cor. xi. 17–34—this connection between the ordinary meal and the Eucharist which had been continued at first, owing perhaps to the desire to follow Our Lord's example as closely as possible, was given up, we find that the usual time was in the early morning, in honour of the Resurrection.[1] Some authorities consider that the above quotation from 1 Corinthians refers to a special meal before the Eucharist introduced by the early Church, named the 'agape', that is, 'love-feast' (from the Greek word meaning 'love'), which was continued during the early centuries, in memory of the Last Supper. But the whole question of the agape is still very much disputed,

---

[1] See St. Paul's Epistles to the Churches, Vol. III of the New Testament in the *Westminster Version of the Sacred Scriptures*, etc. (Longmans, 1927, 48, footnote on verses 21 and 22); also 'L'Église ancienne, a-t-elle connu la messe de soir?' by Dom Eloi Dekkers, O.S.B. (Steenbrugge, Belgium) in *Miscellanea Liturgica in honorem, L. Cuniberti Mohlberg, O.S.B.*, Vol. I. (Edizioni Liturgiche, Roma, Via Pompeo Magno 21, 1948).

and liturgical authorities do not agree about its true character
nor the method of usage. In any case, the agape was never a
universal custom, and, in fact, at Rome was never accepted as
a liturgical ceremony, but only tolerated as a 'private devotion' (Dix, *The Apostolic Tradition of St. Hippolytus*, pp. 45 and
83). When the meal before the Eucharist was given up, the
short blessing of the bread—the usual grace *before* meals—was
dropped, and the long blessing of the wine (the usual grace
after meals) became the long, uninterrupted 'Eucharistic
[thanksgiving] Prayer'. Besides the words of blessing and
thanksgiving in this prayer, there were the words used by Our
Lord at the Last Supper—known as 'the Words of Institution'
or 'of Consecration': "This is My Body", etc.; "This is My
Blood", etc. These words are found in all liturgies, Eastern and
Western—except in one Liturgy as used by an heretical Body,
of which we shall speak later. In the Eastern liturgies, the
words of Our Lord are taken from 1 Cor. xi. 23: "the Lord
Jesus, *the same night in which He was betrayed*, took bread", etc.
(in Latin: *in qua nocte tradebatur*); in the Western liturgies, the
Roman and almost certainly the Gallican, the words are: "Who,
the day before He suffered, took Bread", etc. (in Latin: *Qui pridie
quam pateretur*). The origin of these latter words is unknown. In
the Spanish Liturgy (the same, practically, as the Gallican), the
Eastern form was used, and still is now at Toledo. But this seems
to be the result of later Eastern influence—as in so many cases
in the 'Gallican family'—and the fact remains that the prayer
immediately after the consecration is nearly always preceded
in the MSS. by the rubric: *Post Pridie* ('after [the words] the
day before', etc.), which seems to indicate naturally that this
was the original form.

With regard to blessing in the Holy Eucharist, we have to
keep always in mind the Jewish conception of the meaning of
blessing. A Jewish blessing did not ask God to bless the food (or
whatever was to be blessed); it blessed *God*—for the food, etc.,
provided by Him. Thanksgiving, blessing, praising, all meant
the same to the Jew. To bless God was the way to 'free'
the food for human use or consumption—for to eat or use anything without first blessing God over it would have been a theft
on man's part of what really belonged to God—a sacrilege. So,

the idea of sacrifice—that is, of declaring that all creation belongs first to its Creator—entered into the whole of life and among all ancient nations, pagan as well as Jewish. (See *The Early Eucharist*, by F. L. Cirlot, p. 14.)

THE PREPARATORY SERVICE: Quite early in the history of the Church, the Eucharist Sacrifice was celebrated after a service of readings from Holy Scripture, chanting of psalms and recitation of intercessory prayers. This service was almost certainly derived (but also *adapted*) from the weekly service held by the Jews in the synagogue. This preparatory service was not at first considered to be a necessary part of the Holy Eucharist. The latter was often celebrated without it, and, on the other hand, the service itself was sometimes celebrated alone as complete in itself. As we shall see, the service thus celebrated alone was probably the origin of the Divine Office of the Christian Church. But little by little the two distinct services tended to fuse into one.

Of this Christian adaptation of the Jewish synagogue service and its connection with the Holy Sacrifice, we have a possible *indication*, even as early as the Acts of the Apostles—in chap. xx, 7-12. Here it is said that on the "first day of the week" (already tending to take the place of the Jewish sabbath) the disciples were "assembled to break bread"; St. Paul "discoursed with them, being to depart on the morrow, and he continued his speech until midnight" (7 and 8). Nothing is said, it is true, as to any readings from Scripture—unless it might be presumed, fairly reasonably, that the Apostle's discourse implies that reading, or took its place to a certain extent. The extreme length of this discourse, coupled with the heat of the "great number of lamps in the upper chamber", led to the disastrous fall "from the third loft down" of poor Eutyches, unwisely sitting in the window, and to the miracle worked by the Preacher—and so we come to the "breaking of bread" (11), which almost certainly means the Holy Eucharist.

This preparatory service is *officially* described for the first time in the second century, by St. Justin Martyr, in his Apology. It was known by a title which sounds nowadays very 'Protestant', the 'meeting'—in Greek, *synaxis* or *syneleusis*.

This meeting became, later on, the principal service on what were known as 'aliturgical' days—that is, certain days of the week on which the Holy Sacrifice (the 'Liturgy' in the full sense) was not celebrated. This word 'aliturgical' is equivalent to '*non-liturgical*'—the 'a' being what is known as the Greek 'alpha privative' (that is, the 'depriving A'), which, when used in certain cases at the beginning of a word, implied the negative or opposite—as in the case above, 'aliturgical'. An example of the old aliturgical service is still to be found in the Roman rite, in the Mass of the Pre-sanctified celebrated on Good Friday—that is, as far as the 'bidding prayers' or 'solemn collects' after the Passion, inclusive.

The preparatory service was derived from the old synagogue service on the Sabbath (Saturday). Besides this, shorter services were held also, on Tuesday and Thursday, and these latter days were fast-days.[1]

It may then be of interest to give an outline of the synagogue service in the time of Our Lord—as far as it is possible to reconstruct it now.

THE SYNAGOGUE SERVICE IN THE TIME OF OUR LORD: The Rev. W. O. E. Oesterley gives a description of the synagogue service in early times (as far as it can be gathered) in his book *The Psalms in the Jewish Church* (London: Skeffingtons, 1910, chap. viii, p. 144). While the Temple was the place of worship *par excellence*—in the daily morning and evening sacrifices, and also in prayer and praise, the chanting of the psalms during the sacrifices (special psalms being assigned to each day of the week) —and while the original object of the synagogue was to be a place of teaching and instruction about Holy Scripture, it tended to become, especially in places far distant from Jerusalem, a place of public worship also, and prayer gradually became a substitute for sacrifice. The service held both evening and morning on the Sabbath (Saturday) and on the Tuesdays and Thursdays was as follows:

(i) The 'offering of prayer' (the *Shema*, consisting of the following parts of Scripture: Deut. vi. 4–9; xi. 13–21; Num. xv.

---

[1] Hence the Pharisee in the Gospel declares that he fasts "twice in the week" (Luke xviii. 10–12).

37-41). To these passages were attached certain 'Benedictions', followed by more prayer.

(ii) The reading of the Law (the *Torah*).

(iii) The *Tepilla* or *Shemoneh Esreh*—that is, the 'Eighteen Benedictions'.

(iv) The reading of the Prophets—known as the *Haptarah*, that is, the 'Conclusion'.

(v) A sermon or exhortation based upon what had been read.

(vi) The 'Offering of Praise', which was probably introduced by the chanting of 'Holy, Holy, Holy' (Isaias vi. 3)[1] and of Ezechiel iii. 12.

(vii) Then—again, *probably*—the chanting of the psalm appointed for the day in the Temple, at the end of the morning and evening sacrifices.

(viii) The 'Aaronic Blessing' (Num. vi. 24-6), with the response, 'amen', from the congregation.

This is the service which seems to have formed the basis of the Christian synaxis or service preparatory to the Eucharistic Sacrifice, and also of the synaxis or 'meeting' in itself alone, on 'aliturgical days', and which formed the beginnings of the 'Divine Office'. The Christian service, however, did not follow the Jewish example slavishly in everything. The reading of the law, for example, was given up quite early and, in later times, that of the Prophets did not always form an element in the reading, the Epistles and, especially, the Gospels gradually taking its place as these came to be written.[2]

EUCHARISTIC SACRIFICIAL RITES: There are three chief elements in the Rite of the Holy Eucharistic—which are found in all liturgies, Eastern and Western. These are: (i) 'Taking' bread and wine—in order to set them apart for special use; (ii) 'Giving thanks' over the bread and wine; (iii) 'Communion'—that is,

---

[1] From this, some liturgical writers (e.g. the late regretted Dom Odo Casel of the Abbey of Maria Laach) consider that the threefold *Sanctus* of the Eucharistic Liturgy was derived directly from Jewish usage, and is therefore a 'primitive' element of the Liturgy. But there is no certainty with regard to its use in the synagogue-service, at the time of early Christian developments.

[2] This word 'gospel' is old Saxon English, from 'god' (that is, 'good') and 'spell' (a 'story', 'tale' or 'account' of some new thing). The Latinised Greek word 'evangelium' means 'the good news'.

eating and drinking the 'eucharistised' (consecrated)[1] bread and
wine, and so entering into communion with Christ and all the
members of His Mystical Body, the Church.

No. i developed into the 'offertory', which in some places became a very long and intricate ceremony. No. ii developed into
the long, undivided 'Eucharistic—i.e. "thanksgiving"—Prayer'
which was called the 'anaphora' (offering) in the East; in the
West, the 'canon', that is 'rule', from the Greek word meaning a
'ruler' or any straight rod or bar and so, metaphorically, a 'rule'
or standard of excellence, direction, etc. At first, this latter name
was given to the whole Eucharistic Prayer, but later, the first
part up to the threefold *Sanctus* (when introduced into the
Liturgy) was called the *præfatio* (i.e. the 'preface', introduction
or preparation), the word 'canon' being reserved for the consecratory portion, after the *Sanctus*. The Eucharistic Prayer—in
both Eastern and Western liturgies—besides the introductory
acts of thanksgiving to God for all His benefits to mankind—
Creation, Incarnation and Redemption—contained a reference
to the Last Supper, and also the actual words used by Our Lord
in instituting the Eucharist (hence known as the 'words of institution'), and also His words *after* the Institution, commanding
the disciples to: "Do this as a memorial [or 'in commemoration'] of me." These words in some places (not everywhere) developed into what is called the *anamnesis* ('memorial'), a prayer
founded on the above words of Our Saviour, and referring besides to His Passion, Death, Resurrection and Ascension. In
other places, however, only a prayer of oblation of the consecrated offerings is found in this place. No. iii—at first very simple—the giving by celebrant and deacons of the Bread and
Wine (after their own communions) to all present, was preceded
by the 'Breaking of Bread' (in Latin, the *fractio*), which enabled
it to be divided among all the communicants, and which actually was the earliest name given to the Holy Sacrifice. Among
the Jews, the expression 'breaking bread' or 'to break bread'
was the general term for any meal, religious or profane. It was
always the duty of the host to break the bread and distribute it
among his guests—as we have seen with regard to the Last Sup-

---

[1] Literally, the 'thanksgiven' bread and wine—the offerings over which the
thanksgiving prayer (or Eucharistic prayer) had been pronounced.

per. This action signified friendship, union and peace between all who were to partake of the broken bread. Among both the Jews and all ancient nations, even pagan, all meals among family or friends had a sacrificial character. Every meal included the preliminary offering to God, or the gods, of the life of those present and of food and drink, its support in recognition of the dependence of both upon the Divine bounty.

OTHER NAMES: The title 'The Mysteries' was used also—especially in Rome. This title, taken, externally, from that of the secret rites in the Greek 'mystery-religions', was actually realised in the fullest and deepest sense in the Christian 'Secret Rite'. The Holy Sacrifice was at first offered in secret in the catacombs, owing to the persecution of the Roman Imperial authorities, but in the deeper meaning of the word the Eucharist is the 'Mystery of mysteries'—in the words of the Roman Mass to this day it is called the 'Mystery of faith'. For the whole question of the 'Christian Mystery', see *Le Mystère du Culte* and *Le Mémorial du Seigneur dans la Liturgie de l'Antiquité Chrétienne* (Les Editions du Cerf, Paris; issued in England by Blackfriars Publications, Oxford). These two works in French are translations of the original German of the author, the late Dom Odo Casel, O.S.B., of Maria Laach Abbey, by Dom J. Hild, O.S.B., of Clervaux Abbey in the Grand Duchy of Luxembourg, and they give a wonderful and striking explanation of the Christian idea of the 'Divine Mystery', from both the historical and spiritual points of view.

In the Eastern Churches, the Holy Sacrifice was, and still is, called the 'Divine Liturgy', for the Holy Sacrifice sums up in itself the full significance of that word which means, as we have seen, 'public, social work' or 'service'—in the Christian sense the service rendered by man to God. The name given by St. Benedict in his Holy Rule to the Liturgy in the wide sense—'the Work of God' (*opus Dei*)—is realised again most fully in the Holy Eucharist—the 'work' of sacrifice offered by the God-Man Himself. (*The Rule of St. Benedict*, chaps. xvi and xliii.) In the Western Church, the word 'liturgy' usually includes, as well as the Holy Eucharist, the other Sacraments and the Divine Office. The usual name for the Holy Sacrifice in the Western

Church is the 'Mass'. This word, in Latin *missa*, is derived from the Latin form of dismissal at the end of the Holy Sacrifice recited by the deacon: *Ite missa est*—the word *missa* is late Latin for *missio* ('go, it is the dismissal'—that is, the end). This dismissal was also pronounced by the deacon at the end of the synaxis—not only when it was celebrated apart from the Eucharist, but even when the latter followed it immediately. This dismissal concerned those not yet baptised (the 'catechumens', still under instruction), or others who, for some reason, were unable to take full part in the Sacrifice. In the sixth century, St. Gregory the Great mentions in his *Dialogues* what seems to be a relic of the first dismissal. In the second book, which gives the life of St. Benedict, he speaks in chap. xxiii of two nuns whom the patriarch of monks had threatened to excommunicate on account of their uncharitable treatment of their unfortunate 'man of business'. A few days after his reprimand, both the nuns died and were buried in the church which they attended. While Mass was being celebrated there, the deacon—in the words of St. Gregory—"according to custom, cried aloud: 'if there be anyone who does not communicate, let that person depart' " (*si quis non communicet, det locum*). The former nurse of the two nuns, who was in the habit of making an offering of bread and wine for them at Mass, saw them both arise from their tombs and go out of the church at the above words of dismissal. St. Gregory does not say at what precise *moment* of the Mass this dismissal was pronounced, but it seems most probable that it took place after the chanting of the Gospel —at the end, that is, of the preliminary synaxis and before the beginning of the Holy Sacrifice itself.[1]

Various additions made after the words *Ite missa est* during the Middle Ages have deprived them of their original significance. Sometimes their place is taken by other forms of dismissal—for example, when the *Gloria in excelsis* is not said, the form of dismissal is: *Benedicamus Domino* ('let us bless the Lord'), and in a requiem Mass for the dead, it is *Requiescant in pace* ('May they [the dead] rest in peace'). The reason for the latter is easy to

---

[1] At this period, this first dismissal may have been a relic of that of the penitents in the earlier Liturgy, dismissed with the catechumens and others excluded from assistance at the Sacrifice. This particular dismissal seems to have remained in use much longer than any of the others.

see, but the reason for *Benedicamus Domino* is not so clear. It has been suggested that, originally, these words were chanted during Lent when Mass was followed almost immediately by Vespers, so as to allow those present to break their fast (which lasted till after Vespers) as soon as possible. As the people were not expected to leave the church till the end of the latter office, the deacon exhorted them to stay and 'bless the Lord'. Others—for instance, the late Dom Cabrol, Abbot of Farnborough—consider that, at first, both forms—*Ite missa est* and *Benedicamus Domino*—were always chanted at the end of Mass, the second form being a reminder of the ever-present duty of praising God, even when the *official* acts were over.

Even to-day the memory of two dismissals during Mass is found in the rubrical expression sometimes used to indicate that some special ceremony—an ordination, religious profession, etc.—is to take place during Mass. This expression is: *inter missarum solemnia* (literally—'at the time of the solemnities of Masses'); that is, the two solemn Masses—of 'the catechumens' and 'of the faithful'; the synaxis and the Eucharist respectively. Ceremonies such as the two mentioned above usually take place after the Gospel and before the Offertory.[1]

EARLY TEXTS AND LITURGIES: Up till about A.D. 140, the only references to the Christian Liturgy since the time of the Apostles are found in the letter written by St. Clement of Rome to the Corinthians (A.D. 96), the letter of Pliny (Caius Plinius Cæcilius), the Governor of Bithynia, a Roman province in Asia Minor, to the Emperor Trajan (A.D. 112), and in a document known by the Greek title *Didache* ('teaching'; the full title is *The Teaching of the Apostles*). In Clement's letter are found certain words and phrases which occur in the liturgies of a later period, and the whole of his letter bears the character of a liturgical 'Eucharistic Prayer'—but this does not mean that it was necessarily the reproduction of an already fixed form. Pliny's letter provides a

---

[1] Fr. Jungmann, in his book *Missarum Solemnia* (referred to at the end of the Preface and also towards the end of Chapter VI on the Roman canon), shows that the dismissal *Ite missa est* was considered from the earliest times to include a form—or at least the *notion*—of a blessing granted by the Church to all present at the Mass who were about to depart (*Missarum Solemnia. Tome premier. Deuxième Partie*, i, pp. 218, 220).

non-Christian's description of Christian ceremonies in the second century. One rite is described as the meeting 'before day-break' to sing a hymn 'to Christ as God'; the other as a meeting later in the day, to eat food, which is declared to be 'common and harmless'—'common', i.e. 'ordinary' food such as bread and wine, the practically universal type of human food and drink in all ages—and 'harmless', i.e. not a feast of gorging and drunkenness, as so often among the pagan Romans.

THE 'CHURCH ORDERS': The *Didache* is probably the earliest example of a class of liturgical literature known as 'Church Orders'—i.e. documents purporting to have been composed by the Apostles themselves and laying down laws, rules, examples —the 'order' of rites and ceremonies to be observed by clergy and laity. These documents were invented in Syria and Egypt, and "*there alone* that literature took firm root, and there alone it continued to be valued long after the rest of Christendom had forgotten it". (See *The Apostolic Tradition of St. Hippolytus*, pp. xlvi–xlix.) It seems that the *Didache* was probably written towards the end of the second century (*c.* A.D. 190, cf. Dix, above). Its interest lies principally in the fact that it gives what appears to be an example of the combined agape and Eucharist. But liturgical authorities are not agreed as to its real character— though most of them do agree that it was never actually in use in any Church of the East. It follows, apparently, the usual type of Jewish meals, described on p. 3 and following.

Besides the *Didache*, the other Church Orders are: *The Apostolic Church Order*, derived partly from the *Didache*, and dating from the fourth century, but also from other sources which date from the third century. The later and more developed ones are: *The Canons of Hippolytus; Egyptian Church Order; Ethiopic Church Order; Verona Latin Fragments; Constitutions through Hippolytus; The Testament of Our Lord; The Apostolic Constitutions; The Arabic Didascalia* ('teaching'). These documents arose probably during the third and fourth centuries, each of them to a certain extent adapting and revising the contents of those earlier than itself. It seems that—except perhaps in the case of the *Testament of Our Lord*, which is one of the latest and may come from Asia Minor—all these writings are certainly of Syrian or Egyptian origin. *The Canons of Hippolytus* and other writings attributed to him are made up out of a third-century document actually written in Greek at Rome by Hippolytus—who was a bishop and for a time anti-pope in opposition to the real Pope, St. Callistus; both were born in the second century. This document written by Hippolytus himself is called *The Apostolic Tradition*—not as being written by any Apostle, for St. Hippolytus (who, in spite of having been an anti-pope, was afterwards martyred and canonised by 'Vox populi') lays no such claim—but as laying down what its author considered to be the true, apostolic, traditional organisation and ceremonies of the Roman Church, in contradistinction to those in use under the authority of St. Callistus.

THE APOSTOLIC TRADITION: This was written about A.D. 215, and it seems correct to say that the result of comparing it with the information given us by other and earlier Christian writers makes it very probable that the Eucharistic Liturgy described in it is a true example of what it claims to be: "The usages which he [Hippolytus] describes having *a surprising number of contacts with those referred to by other early writers.*" (*The Apostolic Tradition of St. Hippolytus*, pp. xxxvii and xxxviii—the latter page gives a discussion of Hippolytus and his connection with the more ancient Roman traditions). This is especially interesting and important, as Hippolytus provides a text of a Eucharistic Liturgy —including the consecration of a bishop and other directions concerning the Liturgy—to which we shall return. The title and contents of *The Apostolic Tradition* led to its inclusion in the pseudo-apostolic literature of the Church Orders. But it entered among these only towards the very end of the series, when they had already taken on the character of works composed from many different sources, rather than that of original productions.

The strange inclusion of a really *Western* document among Eastern liturgical literature was owing to the steady search for older matter of this kind which was going on in Syria in the later fourth century—as an effort to uphold the importance and authenticity of a type of literature that was really dying out. The inclusion of *The Apostolic Tradition* among the Church

Orders is, as a matter of fact, a very fortunate thing, for it has preserved it for us and made a correct edition of the original document possible in these days. This is especially valuable as—apart from Hippolytus' own followers—this work of his does not appear to have had any general lasting influence on the Western Church. The original Greek text is no longer extant; there are only later versions and adaptations in Latin and in Eastern languages. But the original text has been restored, so far as this is possible at present, and translated into English by Dom Gregory Dix in the work above referred to.

THE APOSTOLIC CONSTITUTIONS AND THE TESTAMENT OF OUR LORD: These two documents are of far fuller character than earlier documents of this kind. *The Apostolic Constitutions* may be regarded as the climax (in importance) of the Church Orders, and *The Testament* as actually the last of them all. Both *The Apostolic Constitutions* and *The Testament*, as well as other Church Orders, contain interpolations from the *Apostolic Tradition*. *The Testament* (c. A.D. 350—some think it is more probably of fifth-century origin), which originated somewhere between Asia Minor, Syria and Egypt, made use of a very good text of *The Apostolic Tradition*. While a great deal of his own composition has been added by the author, he nevertheless "has succeeded", says Dom Dix, "in treating his source with remarkable respect". (*The Apostolic Tradition of St. Hippolytus*, p. lxvii). In fact, *The Testament* gives the whole Liturgy of Hippolytus in a better text than in any of the other Church Orders.

THE EARLIEST OFFICIAL ACCOUNTS OF THE LITURGY:
I. *In the West:* Apart from the outlines in the Synoptic Gospels, the earliest full description of the Christian Liturgy is found in the First Apology of St. Justin Martyr (c. A.D. 140), written to the Roman Emperor Antoninus Pius. This description is evidently that of the contemporary Liturgy in use in Rome and elsewhere in Italy. St. Justin gives two descriptions: one of the Liturgy following immediately after a baptism; the other of the ordinary Sunday use.

The first begins with the Kiss of Peace, which takes place just before the offerings of bread and wine are brought to the altar (what we should now call the 'offertory'), and does not include any preliminary service of readings from Scripture. The second description, however, *does* describe this preliminary service. In those days, when the Liturgy followed after a baptism—or an ordination (as in the Liturgy of *The Apostolic Tradition*)—the preliminary service was, apparently, omitted altogether, its place being supplied by the administration of the Sacrament of Baptism or Holy Orders. The Sunday Liturgy is described as follows:

(*a*) *The Lessons:* These, according to St. Justin, were taken from "the memoirs of the Apostles"—this would seem to be a general description without details regarding the exact nature or order of the various lessons, and, no doubt, including the epistles and gospels. The 'writings of the prophets' (lessons from the Old Testament) are also mentioned; again the exact order is not given.

(*b*) *The Sermon:* This was an instruction based upon the Scripture lessons, and was given by the 'president' of the assembly.

(*c*) *The Prayers and the Kiss of Peace:* The Prayers were those later known as the 'intercessions'—or 'prayers of the faithful'—which really formed the conclusion of the synaxis, but which in later times, after the complete fusion of synaxis and Eucharist, came to be regarded as the first part of the latter service.

(*d*) *The Kiss of Peace:* This was the original beginning of the Eucharist. It was followed by what later developed into the 'offertory'. The deacons, after spreading a cloth on the altar, brought the offerings of bread and wine, presented by the faithful, to the altar, and a little water was mingled with the wine.

(*e*) *The Eucharistic Prayer:* A long, solemn prayer of 'praise and glory to the Father of all through the name of the Son and the Holy Spirit' and 'giving thanks [in Greek, *eucharistein*] at great length'. In the second description, instead of the above last words—'at great length'—St. Justin says: 'according to his [the president's] ability'. This suggests, perhaps, extempore prayer. The people answered at the end: *amen.*

(*f*) *The Communion of Celebrant, Deacons and People:* Communion in both kinds was administered to all present by the deacons, and the deacons also took the sacred Species to those unable to take part in the Sacrifice.

St. Justin goes on to state that the bread and wine of the Liturgy were received "as the Body and Blood of Christ".

There seem to have been no prayers of thanksgiving after communion, and that ceremony alone brought the whole rite to an end.

Justin does not give any text of this Liturgy described by him, but it is interesting to note that the text supplied by St. Hippolytus in his *Apostolic Tradition* fits the order of Justin's description perfectly.

St. Justin's is the earliest account of the Liturgy in the West. Besides being probably the Liturgy as used in the West—and especially in Rome and its dependencies during the second century—Justin's descriptions give us those elements which are found in practically all known forms of the Eucharistic Liturgy.

We have said that *The Apostolic Tradition* of Hippolytus provides us with a text which exactly fits the description given by St. Justin: we give here a short sketch of this text.

The Liturgy follows immediately after the consecration of a bishop and the latter's reception of the Kiss of Peace from everyone. The deacons then "bring the oblations, and he [the bishop] with all the presbyters laying his hand on the oblation shall say, giving thanks [*euchariston*]: 'The Lord be with you', etc., and the long undivided Eucharistic Prayer begins with the words: 'We render thanks unto thee, O God, through thy beloved Child Jesus Christ' " (see *The Apostolic Tradition of St. Hippolytus*, pp. 6–11). There is no *Sanctus*—the Eucharistic Prayer is entirely undivided, and after the thanksgivings leads up to the words of institution and ends with a very short *anamnesis*—that is, the prayer developing the words of our Lord to His disciples: "Do this as a memorial of me"—and including an oblation of the consecrated Gifts. This is followed finally by an invocation[1] of the Holy Ghost and a prayer for all "who partake, to be united [to Thee]", concluding with the doxology of the same type as in the actual Roman Mass: ". . . that we may praise and glorify

---

[1] The question whether this invocation really belongs to the Liturgy as written by Hippolytus, or whether it is a later interpolation, is much discussed by the authorities. (See *The Apostolic Tradition of Hippolytus*, pp. 75–9.)

Thee through Thy [Beloved] Child Jesus through whom glory and honour be unto Thee with the Holy Spirit in Thy holy Church now and for ever and world without end. Amen."

ANOTHER EARLY DOCUMENT: This is found in the Western Church in the work entitled *De Sacramentis Libri Sex* ('Concerning the Sacraments, in Six Books'). This document was written by St. Ambrose, Bishop of Milan (A.D. 374–97). At first his authorship was disputed, but in recent times it has been practically established by the late Dom R. Hugh Connolly, monk of Downside, in two 'Papers' published by the Alden Press in 1942. (See also *The Early History of the Liturgy*, by J. H. Srawley, D.D. (Cambridge, Second Edition, 1947, p. 155 and p. 164—footnote 5).) In Book IV, chap. iv of the *De Sacramentis* there is a treatise on the Holy Eucharist, in which the author shows that Our Saviour is the author (*auctor*) of all the sacraments and so of the Sacrament of the Eucharist, and he refers to parts of the Liturgy to establish what he says. As regards the earlier part, the Saint says that here all is carried out by the priest as a human being: "Praises are offered [*deferuntur*] to God; prayer [*oratio*] is besought [*petitur*] for the people, for kings, for the rest [*pro ceteris*]." The 'praises offered to God' would seem to be the series of praise and thanksgiving for all His benefits to mankind with which the old eucharistic prayers always began. Hence, the 'prayers' for the people, kings and 'the rest' were, perhaps, the Ambrosian equivalents of the Roman *Memento* (of the living), the *Communicantes* and the *Hanc igitur*; in other words, these prayers appear to have been recited within the Eucharistic Prayer and were apparently not the old 'Prayers of the faithful' recited after the Gospel. The *exact* position in the Eucharistic Prayer, however, is not clear, as St. Ambrose says nothing about the chant of the *Sanctus*—which, when introduced into the Prayer, divided it into two distinct parts ('preface' and 'canon'). The 'praises offered to God' cannot be the *Sanctus* itself, as some liturgical writers have suggested, for St. Ambrose, as Dix points out, declares that they were said by the priest—"For everything which is said before is spoken by the priest: praises are offered to God", etc.[1]—and the *Sanctus* when

[1] Dix, *The Shape of the Liturgy*, p. 539.

introduced was chanted only by choir and congregation, and the priest waited in silence until they had finished chanting before starting the canon. Hence, it would appear that the *Sanctus* had not yet become part of the Eucharistic Prayer at Milan. In chap. v of the *De Sacramentis*, St. Ambrose quotes prayers from the consecratory portion of the canon, which lead up to and follow the words of Christ Himself. These prayers are very similar to those of the Roman Canon, probably because the two rites were fundamentally the same in spite of certain elements of the Ambrosian rite, showing interpolations from the Gallican rite where this differs from Rome. Having spoken of those parts of the Mass said by the priest 'as a man', St. Ambrose goes on to show that "when it comes to making [or 'bringing about'—*ut conficiatur*] the venerable sacrament, the priest no longer uses his own words but the words of Christ". Then come the texts of the above-mentioned prayers (which seem to be earlier forms of those in the Roman Canon) one leading up to the words of Christ; and one after the consecration.

In the latter the three prayers of the Roman Canon are, in St. Ambrose's description, united in one form, and the order of meaning is slightly different.

TWO EARLY EUCHARISTIC PRAYERS: Somewhat later than the *De Sacramentis* are two interesting examples of the early Western Eucharistic prayer. These were discovered, in the fragments of a work by a Western Arian heretic in North Italy, by Cardinal Mai, and published by him in 1827. The date of the texts themselves, unfortunately, is uncertain, but it seems probable that it falls between A.D. 380 and 450. The prayers in themselves are, however, much older than the MSS. The special interest of these texts is that the second of the two (which is more complete than the first) provides the example of an undivided Eucharistic Prayer—leading up to the consecration without the interruption of, or any reference to, the *Sanctus*. The last clause, too, of this prayer recalls very closely the *Te igitur* clause of the Roman Canon—as far as the words in which the gifts are offered to God. This prayer, in fact, passes at once from the thanksgivings of the first part (which again provide at least a relic of the old thanksgiving series) to petitions for the acceptance of the sacrificial offerings (Srawley, p. 165, edit. 1947; Dix, pp. 539 ff.). In his book, *The Shape of the Liturgy*, Dom Gregory Dix gives the whole of each text in English, and in two footnotes the Latin, taken from *Scriptorum Veterum Nova Collectio, III* (1828), Fragm. vii, p. 223. We shall return to these ancient prayers, and in greater detail, when speaking of the Roman Canon.

THE LETTER OF INNOCENT I: Finally, in the year 416 Pope St. Innocent I wrote a letter to Decentius, Bishop of Eugubium (now Gubbio) in Central Italy, in answer to certain liturgical questions made to him by the bishop. These concerned especially two matters: first, the position in the Mass for the recital of the names of those who had presented offerings of bread and wine for the Sacrifice; second, the position of the ceremonial Kiss of Peace. Both these ceremonies were in earlier positions in the rite of Gubbio—that is, in general, the Western rite outside Rome—than in this latter.

II. *In the East:* The earliest official written Liturgy—the earliest, too, from every point of view—is found in the *euchologion* (literally 'prayer-book', the Greek equivalent of the Western 'sacramentary') of Sarapion, who was Bishop of Thmuis in Egypt in the Nile Delta, about A.D. 337–9. This bishop was the personal friend of St. Athanasius.

The *euchologion*, as said above, was in the Eastern Churches practically equivalent to the 'sacramentary' (in Latin, *sacramentarium* or *liber sacramentorum*, i.e. 'book of the sacraments') of the Western Church. The sacramentary was not only the earliest form of 'Mass Book' in the West; it contained, besides the prayers of the Mass proper to the celebrant, all that is now divided among several other books—the pontifical, the ritual, etc.; as, in fact, its very title—'book of the sacraments'—makes clear. Sarapion's book, written about A.D. 350–6—he appears to have written the *whole* of it himself—was, as it would be called in the West in these days, his 'pontifical'—that is, it was intended primarily for the use of a bishop. It contains thirty prayers divided into six sections: 1 to 6: the prayers of the Liturgy beginning with a prayer entitled 'The Prayer of Oblation of Sarapion the Bishop'—in Greek, *Euché Prosphorou*; this was the Eucharistic Prayer, the sacrificial prayer; it contains the consecration of the offerings of bread and wine and the blessing of oil and water—for the sick; 7 to 11: baptismal prayers; 12 to 14: ordination prayers; for bishops, priests and deacons—nothing is said about sub-deacons or readers, although they are mentioned in the 'prayers before the Oblation' (No. 25); 15 to 17: the blessing of oils and of bread and water, for the healing and use of the sick; 18: prayer for one to be buried; 19 to 30: 'prayers before the Oblation'. At the end of this last section is a rubric—very unusual at this period: "All these prayers are performed before the Oblation prayer" (that is, the Eucharistic Prayer). This rubric is of great importance with regard to the original position of these prayers—usually called the great or, as Edmund Bishop preferred to say: *general* intercessions.[1]

In 1907 three pages of papyrus on which were written what appeared to be parts of the Alexandrian (Egyptian) Liturgy were discovered by Flinders Petrie and W. Crum in the ruins of a Coptic monastery at Der-Balizeh in Upper Egypt. These writings, which were said at first to be of either sixteenth- or seventeenth-century date, have recently been closely inspected by Mr. C. H. Roberts, in the Bodleian Library, "with dramatic results". Mr. Roberts and Dom Capelle, Abbot of Louvain, consider that these fragments are parts of a *euchologion*, but a collection of prayers and not a unitary liturgy; "The prayers may therefore be of various provenance and date, but 'several elements may be of considerable antiquity'."[2]

What is especially interesting is that there is a fully developed invocation of the Holy Ghost *before* the Words of Institution, immediately after the *Sanctus* of the Eucharistic Prayer (anaphora). But whether this was the only invocation in the Liturgy or whether there was another after the Consecration also, it is not possible to decide, as the manuscript ends with the first part of the *anamnesis*.

---

[1] *Bishop Sarapion's Prayer-Book*, translated by John Wordsworth, Bishop of Salisbury (London: S.P.C.K., 2nd edition, 1910); *The Early History of the Liturgy*, by J. H. Srawley, D.D. (Cambridge: Second Edition, 1947, pp. 50 *et seq.*); *Florilegium Patristicum* (MCMXXXV, Fasciculum VII, Pars I, pp. 48 *et seq.*).

[2] See review in *The Downside Review*, Autumn 1949, pp. 452-4; *An Early Euchologion: The Der-Balizeh Papyrus*, enlarged and re-edited by C. H. Roberts and Dom B. Capelle, pp. 72 (Bureaux du Muséon, 7, Mont Saint-Antoine, 1949).

Another ancient Egyptian liturgical fragment was found in 1928, by M. Andrieu and P. Collomp, in the Library of Strasbourg University. This fragment contains a part of the Greek Liturgy of St. Mark, which consists of a portion of the great intercession. In the extant texts of the actual Liturgy of St. Mark, the intercessions come in the middle of the anaphora *before* the *Sanctus*—a position found only in this particular Liturgy. Apparently this fragment belongs to the fourth century, and so shows an earlier and simpler form of the Liturgy—in fact, it is the earliest known example of it so far, for all extant texts are of the twelfth century.

FULLY DEVELOPED LITURGIES: The fundamental division of the Eucharistic liturgies is into Eastern and Western, and each of these is subdivided into various 'families', those of the Eastern rites being far more numerous than those of the Western. The Eastern liturgies may be broadly divided into *West Syrian*, originating at Antioch; *East Syrian*, which arose in Persia and which is usually known as the 'Nestorian Liturgy',[1] as that heresy has found its home in Persia. Then, we have the *Alexandrian* or *Egyptian* Liturgy—called 'Alexandrian' because it originated in the Patriarchal see of Alexandria. All these liturgies are called after various saints—St. John Chrysostom, St. Basil, St. Mark, SS. Addai and Mari, St. James. But such titles are mere *dedications*; the various saints were not the actual authors of the liturgies called after them, any more than the Apostles were the actual authors of the *Teaching of the Apostles* (the *Didache*) or of the other Church Orders dedicated to them. The names and descriptions of all these liturgies will be found in *Liturgies Eastern and Western*, Vol. I: 'Eastern Liturgies' (the only volume existing), by F. E. Brightman (Oxford, 1896); *An Introduction to the Study of Eastern Liturgies*, by Père S. Salaville, A.A., translated by The Very Reverend Monsignor J. M. T. Barton, D.D. (Sands, 1938); *The Early History of the Liturgy*, by J. H. Srawley, D.D. (Second Edition, Cambridge University Press, 1947); *The Rites of Eastern Christendom* (2 vols.),

[1] This Liturgy is also used by the Chaldeans (Persian Christians reunited with Rome), and also by the Catholic Malankarese in India. This East Syrian rite is officially called 'the Liturgy of SS. Addai and Mari' (founders of the Churches of Edessa and Seleucia), and it possesses some very ancient characteristics.

by Archdale A. King (Catholic Book Agency, Rome, 1947 and 1948)—also, in his earlier book, *Notes on the Catholic Liturgies*, Longmans, 1930. There are also three books by the Rev. Adrian Fortescue: *The Orthodox Eastern Church* (C.T.S., London, 1929); *The Lesser Eastern Churches* (C.T.S., 1913); *The Uniate Eastern Churches* (Burns, Oates & Washbourne, Ltd., 1923).

Besides these, we have later books by Donald Attwater: *The Catholic Eastern Churches* and *The Dissident Eastern Churches*— both published by the Bruce Publishing Company, Milwaukee, Wisconsin, U.S.A., the first in 1935, the second in 1937. Both these books are full of information and have excellent pictures and photographs.

As a matter of fact, in the course of time the Liturgy of St. Chrysostom—usually known as the Byzantine Liturgy from the older name of Constantinople—Byzantium—superseded almost entirely the other national or local rites throughout the Orthodox Eastern Church subject to the Patriarch of Byzantium. The Nestorians, however, and the Chaldeans still use their own Liturgy untouched by Byzantine influences, and the same is true of the Syrian Jacobites and the subjects of the famous convert bishop, Mar Ivanios, the Malankarese, in India. With regard to the Egyptian rite: the Monophysite heretics of Egypt known as 'Copts' (this title is probably a corruption and adaptation of the Greek word for Egypt—*Aiguptos*) still use a Liturgy which, although known as the Liturgy of St. Cyril (of Alexandria) is really the Liturgy of St. Mark translated into the Coptic language, the ancient language of Egypt. The Ethiopian or Abyssinian Church[1] also makes use of this Liturgy, and it is an interesting fact that in connection with it, an anaphora is used which is simply that written by St. Hippolytus of Rome in his *Apostolic Tradition*. This is the only example of a living use of this ancient form of the Roman Liturgy. Its preservation in the East is the result of the circulation of its text in the churches of Syria and Egypt, in which regions, as we have seen above, the literature known as 'Church Orders' arose. (See p. xlix. to p. li.)

THE WESTERN LITURGIES: These can be divided into only two clearly known types—viz. (i) *the Roman rite*; (ii) *the Gallican*

---

[1] Abyssinia—the country ruled by the Emperor Haile Selassie.

rite. Liturgists speak also of the *Mozarabic* or *Spanish rite*, the *African rite* and the *Celtic rite*, but the Mozarabic rite, except for a few unimportant local differences, is substantially of the same type as the Gallican (it is uncertain which of them is the mother, which the daughter). The Celtic rite, too, appears to be merely, like the Spanish rite, the Gallican rite with unimportant local differences. As for the African rite, not very much is known about it.

The Roman rite was followed in Rome and in most of the rest of Italy; the Gallican rite was observed in Gaul—that is, France and parts of Germany, and in some parts of Italy also; the Mozarabic rite—which, as we have seen, was substantially the same as the Gallican rite—was used in Spain. The 'Celtic rite' was used in Scotland and Ireland, and for a time in parts of England also. With regard to the 'African rite', although, as Dr. Srawley says: "We have no such liturgical forms as are available for the history of the liturgy in Egypt and Syria. . . . the fragmentary notices of Tertullian, Cyprian [Bishop of Carthage], Optatus [Bishop of Milevis in Numidia in the fourth century] and Augustine enable us to reconstruct very fairly the scheme of the liturgy, and supply us with occasional notices of some of the shorter liturgical formulæ which were current" (Srawley, chap. vi, 'The Liturgy in Africa', p. 120). Besides these examples of the Western rite, we must also mention that of Milan, also known as the 'Ambrosian rite', as it was attributed to the great Bishop of Milan in A.D. 397, St. Ambrose. This rite possesses both Gallican and Roman features, and its original character is still disputed; that is, whether it should be considered as *substantially* Roman or *substantially* Gallican. The former view seems to be the most likely. Eventually, as in the Eastern Empire the Byzantine Liturgy ousted all the other and much older rites of the various Eastern Churches, so also in the West the Roman rite gradually supplanted the other Western rites, even those of Gaul and Spain. These latter, however, survived to a certain extent in some prayers and ceremonies—not only in France and other places, not only in some religious orders (e.g. Carthusian, Dominican and in the old Carmelite rite now observed by the Calced Carmelites only), but even in Rome itself. The Roman rite, in fact, is no longer the 'pure' rite of the city of Rome—as Edmund Bishop has pointed out in his 'Genius of the Roman Rite' (see his *Liturgica Historica* (Oxford: Clarendon Press, 1918, pp. 1–19)).

THE ROMAN SACRAMENTARIES: As we have seen, the earliest written form of the Roman rite is found in *The Apostolic Tradition of St. Hippolytus* in the third century. The earliest fully *official* texts are the *Leonine Sacramentary* (sixth century; attributed to St. Leo the Great, A.D. 440–61); the *Gelasian Sacramentary* (seventh century; attributed to St. Gelasius I, A.D. 492–6)—this latter sacramentary is based probably on the Pope's own work, and also gives us probably the Roman liturgy of his time, or of at least the sixth century; the *Gregorian Sacramentary*—this text is of eighth-century date; it is ascribed to St. Gregory the Great (A.D. 590–604), and probably does give substantially his revision of the Roman rite in the sixth century. The Leonine Sacramentary (which is not complete and does not contain the canon of the Mass) has been explained by some as being probably a private collection of liturgical prayers and not an official Mass book. Of recent times, however, the tendency is to dispute this view and to look on the Leonine Sacramentary as an official—if incomplete—sacramentary. (See *Liturgica Historica*, pp. 39–115; and also Dix, pp. 563–73, and especially p. 567, concerning the character of the Leonine Sacramentary).[1] There are modern editions of all three Sacramentaries: *The Gregorian Sacramentary* (*G.S. Under Charles the Great*), edited by H. A. Wilson, M.A. (London: Henry Bradshaw Society, 1915); *The Gelasian Sacramentary* (*Liber Sacramentorum Romanæ Ecclesiæ*), edited by H. A. Wilson (Oxford, 1894); *The Leonine Sacramentary* (*Sacramentarium Leonianum*), edited by the Rev. C. Lett-Feltoe, B.D. (Cambridge, 1896).

THE ORDINES ROMANI: Besides the sacramentaries, there are other ancient documents which provide further knowledge about the later development of the Roman rite—the *Ordines*

---

[1] Père Jungmann, however, believes that it *is* a 'private collection', but, he thinks, undertaken in order to prepare for an 'official edition' for liturgical use (*Missarum Solemnia*. Vol. I, Part I, n. 7).

Romani. These are what we should call ceremonials, giving the order (hence the name *ordo*, 'order, series, list') of the ceremonies to be observed in celebrating the liturgy of the Mass. They were the necessary accompaniments of the sacramentary, since the latter gave only the words of the prayers, blessings and consecrations, without any directions as to carrying out the different rites and ceremonies. The late Dom Pierre de Puniet, of the French Congregation, says in his book on the Roman pontifical: "They are wholly Roman in origin; in fact, the earliest of them do not take any account of any ceremonies except those performed by the supreme Pontiff in person."[1] Dom de Puniet goes on to show how the *Ordines* soon became models for the pontifical ceremonies carried out by all bishops, and spread, together with the sacramentary, to France, Germany and England. The *Ordines* outside Rome came inevitably under foreign influences, which led to modifications—incorporated, finally, in the Roman Liturgy itself. In the *Ordines* were regulated the ceremonies of the Mass, baptism, ordinations, the dedication of churches, etc. Usually they did not contain the actual formulæ and rubrics which were reserved for the sacramentary, but only the 'ordering' in detail of the rites and ceremonies. Some, however, of these *Ordines* were introduced into the sacramentary in the case of baptism and penance, for example, in the Gelasian sacramentary of the seventh and eighth centuries. The best and most complete series of the *Ordines Romani* is contained in Migne, *P.L.*, t. lxxviii (reproduced from Mabillon, *Musæum Italicum*, t. ii). The latest and best edition of the *Ordines* is found in *Les Ordines Romani du haut moyen age*, by M. Andrieu (Louvain, 1931). There are fifteen documents of different periods. The most ancient are: No. I (*Ordo Romanus Primus*—at least, parts 1 to 21); No. VII and No. VIII—these are of the seventh and eighth centuries; Nos. II, III and IX are of the ninth century at the earliest; and Nos. IV, V, VI and X are of the eleventh. The last five are (according to Dom de Puniet) of the fifteenth century, but according to later writers they are of somewhat earlier date than that. In his *Christian Worship: its Origin and*

---

[1] *The Roman Pontifical: A History and Commentary*, by Dom Pierre de Puniet, Monk of Oosterhout (Holland), (English Translation: Longmans, 1932, pp. 25 et seq.).

Evolution (London: S.P.C.K., 1903—English translation of the original French work) Mgr. Duchesne gives on p. 455, Appendix I, the text of the 'Ordo of S. Amand', belonging to the ninth century. The *Ordo Romanus Primus* gives a description of the papal Solemn Mass of the eighth—and probably of the seventh century also; the 'Ordo of S. Amand' gives the same, but with some slight additions added in the ninth century. From these *Ordines*, together with the sacramentaries, we get the Pontifical —the "Bishop's Book" (as Abbot Justin McCann, of Ampleforth Abbey, calls it in his introduction to the translation of Dom Pierre de Puniet's *The Roman Pontifical*)[1]—"which gives precise formularies and precise directions for some of the chief functions which appertain to the office of a bishop—a bishop of the Roman Rite".

THE ROMAN MISSAL: As we have it now it is a very composite book, made up of a number of books, formerly quite distinct— the sacramentary, the ordo, the lectionary (with the lessons from the Old and New Testaments), the evangeliary (containing the four gospels), and the antiphonary, in which latter were contained the various chants of the Mass. In the Eastern (Byzantine) Churches, this combination of the various liturgical books has never taken place. There are still separate books— the *euchologion* (from two Greek words—*euche*, prayer and *logion*, word; that is, 'form of prayer'), the Eastern equivalent of the Western sacramentary, and separate books containing the lessons, epistles, gospels and chants, each series in a different book.

The earliest witness to the Gallican rite is found at the end of the third century or beginning of the fourth. This witness is concerned especially with the Spanish or Mozarabic form of the rite, and is found in the Council of Elvira in Spain in A.D. 305 or 306, in a decree concerning the recitation of the names of those who had made offerings of bread and wine at the offertory of the Mass. This recitation was to be made aloud, during the offertory, when the oblations of bread and wine were actually presented by the people. (See *The Diptychs*, by Edmund Bishop, Appendix III in *The Liturgical Homilies of Narsai*, edited by Dom R. H. Connolly (Cambridge, 1909).)

[1] *The Roman Pontifical* (Longmans, London, 1932, p. viii).

THE GALLICAN TEXTS: These date from the seventh century and they are:

1. *The Missale Gothicum*: This is really a sacramentary, not a missal in the later sense—in spite of its title—and it is French not Spanish. What the word 'Gothicum' signifies is not clear.

2. *The Sacramentarium Gallicanum* (really a missal)—this is generally known as the 'Bobbio Missal' as it was found by Dom Mabillon at Bobbio in North Italy, and, in spite of its name (given it by Mabillon), it is *Irish* in origin and character but of the Gallican type.

3. *Missale Gallicanum Vetus* (like the *Missale Gothicum,* really a sacramentary). There is also a collection of Gallican Masses in a MS. of the seventh century, published in 1850 by Herr Mone; a description purporting to be of the Gallican Liturgy, in two letters formerly ascribed to St. Germanus of Paris (555–76), but no historical reliance can be placed upon this text with regard to the Gallican Liturgy in general, as it is now shown to be *not* really the work of St. Germanus, but of much later date. The contemporary treatise of St. Isidore of Seville, *De Officiis Ecclesiasticis,* gives a very different impression of the nature of the Gallican Liturgy of that time. These so-called letters of St. Germanus probably refer to some local and temporary customs in connection with that Liturgy. (See article 'S. Germain de Paris', by Dom André Wilmart, in *Dictionnaire d'Archéologie Chrétienne et de Liturgie* (Vol. VI, G–Hyp).

Of the Mozarabic Liturgy—the only example of the Gallican type that has left any more or less complete texts—the earliest account (as we have seen above with regard to the Gallican rite in general) is at the beginning of the fourth century. The name 'Mozarabic' is derived originally from the use of this rite by the Christians in Spain, who were in the Moorish dominions and who were known as 'Mozarabes' or 'Muzarabes'. The derivation of these words is uncertain, but the best theory is that the origin is 'Musta'rab', which means a naturalised Arab or one who had adopted Arab nationality or customs. This term applied only to the persons using the Liturgy and not to the Liturgy itself, which shows no sign of Arab influence. (See article 'Mozarabic', by Henry Jenner, in *Catholic Encyclopædia*, Vol. X.) Texts of the Mozarabic Liturgy are found edited by the late

Dom Marius Férotin, of Farnborough Abbey, in *Monumenta Liturgica Ecclesiastica*, Vols. V and VI (edited at Farnborough). The principal MS., discovered by Dom Férotin himself in a chemist's shop in Spain (where it served to wrap up parcels!), is the *Liber Ordinum*, which contains, after a calendar and a few pages of less important items, a series of forms for the blessing of oil, salt and water, an order of baptism with the rites of making a catechumen, various ordination services (clerk, sacristan, librarian, sub-deacon, deacon, archdeacon, 'primiverius', priest and abbot—but none for the usual minor orders nor for the consecration of a bishop).[1]

PRINTED EDITIONS

These are: (i) *Missale Mixtum*—edited by Cardinal Ximenes (Toledo, 1500), and re-edited by Alex. Lesley (Rome, 1755); also edited by Cardinal Lorenzana (with Lesley's notes) (Rome, 1804).

(ii) Lesley's edition, in Migne, *P.L.*, lxxxv (Paris, 1850).

(iii) *Missa Omnium Offerentium*, edited by Lorenzana (Toledo, 1875). "In 1936, there were nine priests of this rite, attached to the chapel in Toledo Cathedral, eight of these were martyred by the Reds in that year, the ninth died soon after, presumably from shock. This took place on July 22nd, 1936. There were then no priests who followed the Mozarabic rite. On December 15th, 1940, the rite was revived—and four new chaplains and two *beneficiados* ['beneficiaries'] were appointed. The rite was learnt afresh in the Abbey of Silos, where the late Dom Germanos Prado was a monk, very cognisant of things Mozarabic"—from a note sent to the writer in 1944 by Archdale King, author of *Notes on the Catholic Liturgies* (Longmans, 1930, and other, more recent, liturgical books, referred to in our Preface).

The earliest texts of the Ambrosian rite (by some liturgists regarded as Gallican in origin)—apart from the fragments in the *De Sacramentis* of St. Ambrose (see pp. 19 & 20)— are of the tenth and eleventh centuries. The earliest *evidence* of this liturgy—again apart from the *De Sacramentis* and other

---

[1] See 'The Mozarabic and Ambrosian Rites', by W. C. Bishop, M.A., in *Alcuin Club Tracts*, XV. (A. R. Mowbray & Co., London, 1924); see also article, cited above, in *Catholic Encyclopædia*, X, list of MSS., etc.

writings of St. Ambrose, and also apart from those of St. Augustine—is of the ninth century.

THE CELTIC RITE: This rite seems to have been of the Gallican type, but with features introduced from many other places than Gaul. It was in use in Ireland, Cornwall, Wales and Scotland, and (before the introduction of the Roman rite by St. Augustine of Canterbury) in England also. It was in use, too, in those parts of the Continent inhabited by Celts, e.g. Brittany. In this latter place, the Celtic rite lasted till A.D. 817; in Scotland till the eleventh century—when the Queen, St. Margaret, brought in the Roman rite; in Ireland till the beginning of the twelfth century—the Roman rite being then introduced by Gilbert Bishop of Limerick and Papal Legate. The texts are: (i) *The Bobbio Missal* (seventh century)[1] which, as above, though not written in Ireland, seems to be entirely Irish in character[2]; (ii) *The Missal of Rheinau* (end of the eighth or beginning of the ninth century); (iii) *The Stowe Missal* (tenth century), discovered in the eighteenth century by John Grace of Nenagh. Its title is due to the fact that it was put in the library of the Duke of Buckingham at Stowe; (iv) *Sacramentary of S. Gall* (eighth century); (v) *Sacramentary of Cambrai* (eighth and ninth centuries), and various fragments containing collections of collects, hymns, canticles, versicles and responsories of the seventh and eighth centuries.

All these texts show a Gallican rite very much mixed with Roman elements, especially in the Canon of the Mass. In Scotland the only text of the Celtic rite is the *Book of Deer* (i.e. of the Monastery of Deer, in Buchan). It is now at Cambridge. (See *Catholic Encyclopædia*, III, 'Celtic Rite,' by Henry Jenner.)

THE AFRICAN RITE (North Africa): There are no existing texts, as in the case of the Egyptian Liturgy; nor is there any formal treatise on the subject. All that exist are fragmentary notices in the writings of Tertullian, St. Cyprian, St. Augustine

---

[1] *The Sacramentarium Gallicanum* (see p. 29).
[2] See article 'Bobbio Manuscrits' and also 'Misselde' in *Dictionnaire d'Archéologie*, T. 2, p. 1, by Dom A. Wilmart; and his 'Notice du Missel de Bobbio', in *The Bobbio Missal* (Henry Bradshaw Society, Vol. LXI, London, 1924).

and Optatus, from which only a general idea of the form of the Liturgy in Africa can be gathered.

(i) For Tertullian, see his *Apologia* c. 39, and *De Anima*, c. 9; *De Oratione*, c. 1, 4; *De Corona*, c. 3; *Ad Uxorem*, ii. 4, etc.; for St. Cyprian, see his *Epistola*, xxxviii (xxxiii), xxxix (xxxiv); see also *The Early History of the Liturgy*, by J. H. Srawley—the new edition of 1947—concerning the Liturgy in Africa (pp. 120–49); the articles under *Afrique* (liturgies, etc.) and *Alexandrie* (liturgie, etc.) in the *Dictionnaire d'Archéologie*, I. The chief interest of the African rite is the fact that it was used in Latin before the Roman rite, which latter was celebrated in Greek until about the third to fourth century. Thus, it is possible that much of the Latin text used later at Rome was derived from the African rite.

In spite of certain external differences between the various rites—Roman, Ambrosian (or Milanese), Gallican, Spanish (or Mozarabic), Celtic and African—they never developed into distinct 'liturgies' in the same sense as did the many rites of the Eastern Churches. It is, in fact, a mistake to read back into the fifth or sixth—or even into the seventh or eighth—centuries, the far later conception of special, distinct rites, each providing the *consciousness* of such differences and leading to a kind of rivalry between them. In the earliest times there was no idea at all of different 'rites' or 'liturgies'—even in the East—there was simply 'the Liturgy', which was *fundamentally* the same everywhere. But each local church developed its own traditional customs in the manner of celebrating this 'one Liturgy', and such customs were freely revised, improved or added to as appeared good to each local church and later to each *national* church. In the course of the sixth and seventh centuries these local differences tended to become real distinctions, and so, in the West, we arrive at distinct 'rites'—of Rome, Gaul, Spain and Milan.

CHAPTER II

THE INTRODUCTORY SERVICE AND THE EUCHARIST IN EAST AND WEST

WE have seen that the Liturgy of the Holy Eucharist is composed of two originally quite distinct services, each of which at first could be celebrated without the other. We have also seen that the first service, known in Greek as the *synaxis*—the 'meeting'—was derived from the service held by the Jews in their synagogues on the Sabbath day and (in a shorter form) on Mondays and Thursdays as well, but in Christian hands it was adapted to their own special circumstances and was not a mere 'copy'. This adaptation was concerned first with the lessons or readings from Holy Scripture. The synagogue practice was to read the Books of Holy Writ in the following order of importance —first the Law (the Heptateuch), then the Prophets and then other books. In the Christian meeting the Old Testament books were still read first, but as of *lesser* importance and leading up to those of the New Testament—Epistles, Acts and, as the summing-up of all, the Gospel. Secondly, the series of prayers of intercession for all classes were recited at the end of the whole service—after the Gospel, but in the synagogue service of to-day similar prayers are said at the *beginning*. If this latter was the case, too, in the time of Our Lord and of the early Church, the Christian position would be another example of independent adaptation. But it is possible that it was the later Jews who changed the position of the prayers in the synagogue and that the Christian Church kept the original place. If, however, this latter position of the prayers was really due to Christianity, the change was made probably because the preparatory service, as a public meeting, was open to all who cared to attend—Jews, pagans—anyone interested in Christianity. All such people could be admitted to listen to the readings from Holy Writ and to the sermons and teaching connected with them, since the Church considered that she had a general duty to preach the Gospel 'to every creature' and to witness to the truth before all men. United *prayer*, however, was possible only for those actually united in the one faith of Jesus Christ. Now, up till the end of the preparatory service there was no prayer of any kind; only instruction, since the prayers were at the end of the whole service. Those who did not share in the one faith were asked to depart by means of a form of 'dismissal', and then the disciples of Christ could join together in prayer for all—for those who had just departed as well as for themselves.

THE LESSONS: In the early Church there were usually three lessons from Holy Scripture: a lesson from the Prophets or other book of the Old Testament; another from the Epistles or Acts, and finally the solemn reading of the Gospel—the 'Law of Christ'—which among Christians took the place of importance given in the synagogue to the Law of Moses. Between or after these lessons, psalms were chanted, as in the synagogue.

The lessons were not read in an ordinary reading voice—as one person may read aloud to another—but were "chanted with a simple inflection, partly that they [the lessons] might be heard more easily, partly to give them solemnity" (Dix, p. 39). This was the usual custom in the synagogues, except in small country places. The psalms and canticles, between the lessons, were real 'responsories', in the original sense of that word—that is, they were *responses*, 'answers' to the lessons which they followed. They were also in a sense themselves lessons (from the psalter), chanted for their own sake and not merely to fill up time while something else was being carried out—as, for example, were the later chants of the Mass—the introit, offertory and communion anthems. The responsories were sung by one singer with simple refrains chanted by the congregation at stated moments. This form of chant was to become known as 'responsorial chant'—as opposed to 'antiphonal chant', which was introduced later and in which the verses of the psalms were sung by two alternate choirs or choruses. In the synagogue, the cantor made use of the cry 'hallelujah' ('Praise be to God') as a signal for the people's refrain in the psalmody. It seems that the Christian use of 'alleluia' in the psalmody of the liturgy is derived from this custom. In later times it became practically a chant in itself, with verses added from the psalms. (See Dix, pp. 39 and 40.) After the gospel came:

THE SERMON: This was the special office of the bishop; it was his 'liturgy' ('public work') in this service, as the consecration and offering of the bread and wine was his 'liturgy' in the Eucharistic sacrifice. The bishop preached seated in the episcopal *cathedra*, the throne which gave its name to the episcopal church itself—the 'cathedral'. As in the case of individual celebrations of the Holy Sacrifice by simple priests, that of preaching by simple priests came into use much later in the history of the Church. (See St. Irenaeus, *c.* A.D. 180–200 *Adversus Hæreseos*, I, x, 2, on the bishop's supreme right to preach.)

THE DISMISSALS: Towards the end of the service but before the series of intercessory prayers which formed its actual conclusion, those who were not members of the Church, Jews, pagans and also even those who were 'on the way' but had not yet been admitted (the later catechumens), were asked to leave the meeting in various forms of dismissal. This dismissal was of course specially insisted upon when the meeting was followed by the Holy Eucharist.

THE CATECHUMENATE: This came into being in both Eastern and Western Churches towards the end of the second century. The word 'catechumen' is derived from the Greek *catecheo*—'to teach by word of mouth'. The catechumenate was the state of those 'being taught'. The same Greek term provides us with the word 'catechism'—the 'treatise of instruction'. The catechumenate formed quite a long period of preparation for baptism in which the catechumen not only followed a course of instruction in the faith, but also went through a series of ceremonies which are now all united in the solemn rite of baptism as usually given to adults.

The introductory service has sometimes been called in the West the 'Mass of the catechumens', as the latter were allowed to assist only at that part of the service during their catechumenate. In the same way, the title of 'Mass of the Faithful' was given to the actual service of the Mass, beginning now with the intercessions after the Gospel. Even after these two Masses had been finally welded into one service, the distinction between them remained quite evident, and so remains even at the present day. This is especially so in a solemn Pontifical Mass; that is, a solemn Mass celebrated by a bishop or other prelate having the right to 'pontificalia', the celebrating prelate remaining at his throne or fald-stool for the first part of the Mass, up till after the Gospel. A relic of the dismissals, too, is still found in the Roman rite in the words at the end of the Mass: *Ite missa est*—'go, it is the dismissal' (*missa* being late Latin for *missio*, 'sending away, discharge, dismissal'). The word *missa*, moreover—although it was the name of a very unimportant ceremony—has become the usual title of the Holy Sacrifice itself, and so has acquired a specially sacred character and meaning.

THE PRAYERS OF INTERCESSION: First the catechumens were dismissed, after any others who also had to be dismissed—Jews, pagans, Christian penitents, etc.—and after being told by the deacon to 'bow down their heads' for the bishop's blessing. This latter was given in the form of a prayer—as were all early liturgical blessings. Then came the intercessions for all classes (the only *individuals* admitted here much later being the Pope and the Emperor), which now had become the 'Prayers of the Faithful' and formed the beginning of the 'Mass of the Faithful', instead of being, as formerly, the conclusion of the 'Mass of the Catechumens', even when followed by the Holy Eucharist.

The favourite title for these prayers among liturgical scholars is the 'Great Intercession'. Edmund Bishop preferred, as much more accurate, the expression 'the *General* Intercession', meaning that the intercessions were made as he puts it—"for all sorts and conditions". They were said, not only for the different members of the 'Christian Priesthood'—bishops, the various orders of the clergy, the faithful laity and the catechumens— but also for pagans and Jews and for all those who were sick or in any need or trouble. Curiously enough in our eyes to-day there were no public intercessions for the dead. Prayer for the dead was not of course excluded—every Mass was offered for 'the quick and dead'—but the latter were not mentioned 'liturgically'. The Liturgy was concerned primarily and externally with the living members of the Universal Church in *each local church* (diocese, as we should say now).

The General Intercessions were of the ancient collect-form, which originally was used in the Eastern Churches as in those of the West, but was superseded later in the East by the litany form of prayer.

The full collect-form was as follows: the object or intention of the prayer and an exhortation to the faithful present to pray, was announced by the celebrant—perhaps originally by the deacon. This latter then gave the signal for prayer—saying, if it were a penitential season: *flectamus genua* ('let us bend the knees'), and all then prayed in silence—on their knees, if it were a penitential season, but on other occasions and especially in Easter-tide, standing in honour of the Resurrection. After a pause of some length for this silent 'common prayer', the subdeacon—at least in later ages, but perhaps originally the deacon—gave the signal to rise if all were kneeling, in the words: *levate* ('arise'). If they were standing in silent prayer, no doubt the celebrant simply began the prayer aloud at his own discretion. This prayer aloud was the summing-up by the celebrant (usually a bishop) of all the petitions of the congregation —in the Roman Mass in the characteristic Roman short, terse and expressive form. If kneeling for the silent prayers, *all* alike arose to listen to and join in the celebrant's prayer of summing-up, because: "the corporate prayer of the Church is a priestly act, to be done in the priestly posture for prayer standing. Therefore *all*, not the celebrant only, rose for the concluding collect" (Dix, p. 42). The best example of these collects is found in:

THE GOOD FRIDAY SERVICE (Roman rite): This service, from the first of the two lessons up till the end of the *orationes solemnes* ('solemn prayers'), after the Passion, gives us a perfect picture of the ancient aliturgical synaxis. The rest of the Good Friday service is a development of another ancient ceremony of the Roman rite—communion in the species of bread only, apart from the Holy Sacrifice, with the *Pater noster* as the only accompanying prayer and an 'ablution' of unconsecrated wine and water. The procession from the 'Altar of repose', the chants and the incensing and additional ceremonies are all of later date. In the *orationes solemnes* of Good Friday there is first the *præfatio* or *monitio* ('preface' or 'announcement'); that is, the long exhortation of the celebrant to the people, beginning *Oremus, dilectissimi nobis* ('Let us pray, most beloved'); the deacon then chants: *flectamus genua* ('Let us bend the knees') for the silent prayer, but now, immediately, the sub-deacon chants: *levate* ('arise'). Thus, the congregation in these days only has time to make a rapid genuflection, and no time at all for any silent prayer. Nevertheless, the standing and kneeling are at least *signs* of the congregation's union with the celebrant in the general intercessions. In their present form these Good Friday collects date probably from the fourth or fifth century, but they also probably follow very closely the earlier type of intercessory prayer. The exhortation was called *præfatio* ('preface'), as preparing the way for the prayer itself, known as *oratio* (literally 'speech' or 'announcement' or, again, 'declaration'). There are several other cases in the Roman rite of survivals of this full form of the collect; the latter title, by the way, was never accepted at Rome; it was in use in the Gallican rite, where the full collect-form existed up till the end. In the canon of the present Roman Mass, the celebrant addresses the people before the *Pater noster*, with the words *Oremus: præceptis salutaribus moniti et Divina institutione formati; audemus dicere: Pater noster, etc*. ('Let us pray: instructed by saving precepts and taught by Divine example, we make bold to say: Our Father', etc.). In this particular case, the Our Father, chanted immediately, takes the place of the silent prayer. It was probably originally chanted at Rome as in Gaul, by all the people together with the celebrant, and so was the 'general' prayer' of all. The *Pater* is followed by the collect beginning *Libera nos* ('Deliver us, O Lord'), but now recited secretly—except in the Mass of the Presanctified on Good Friday. Better examples of the collect preceded by the long *præfatio* occur in the Ordination Masses. But in all other cases the 'preface' has been reduced to the word: *oremus* ('let us pray')—an example, as the author of *The Shape of the Liturgy* puts it, of the "different genius of the two Western liturgical rites, Italian and Franco-Spanish"—the former cutting down the lengthy 'prefaces' to one simple, expressive term; the other tending to make them even more lengthy—"some Mozarabic *præfationes* are fifty or sixty lines long" (Dix, p. 489).

THE INTERCESSIONS IN THE EAST: In the East the collect-form of 'the Prayers' was replaced by the litany-form—introduced from Antioch during the fourth century. The word 'litany' comes from the Greek *litaneuo*, which means to pray in a supplicating, entreating manner—with great force! The litany was composed of a series of petitions or intercessions for various classes of people or for various needs or intentions, pronounced in a few short words by the deacon, the people responding aloud to each petition with the words *Kyrie eleison* (the Latinised orthography of these Greek words—meaning 'Lord, have mercy' —turns the second, *long* 'e' into an 'i'). There was no interval of silent prayer as in the collect. At the end, the celebrant summed up the whole series of petitions in a prayer which was formerly chanted aloud, but is now said secretly. As the author of *The Shape of the Liturgy* truly says, the litany has become a kind of dialogue between deacon and congregation—the former having the 'lion's share'—while the celebrant *sings* only the doxology at the end, the celebrant's prayer being said secretly *during* the chanting of the litany instead of at the end. This method of silent recitation by the celebrant, while prayers are being chanted aloud by the deacon and the people, is a special feature now of the Eastern liturgies, but originally each section of the 'Christian priesthood' exercised its own special function and took its own part in the offering of the Holy Sacrifice. Nevertheless, although the celebrant in the Eastern liturgies now says the closing prayer of the litany secretly, and while the latter is still in process, the prayer is not looked upon as his private devotion. Many other prayers in the Liturgy which are now recited privately are of their very nature really public. With regard to this, we have the criticism of *The Shape of the Liturgy* in *The Eastern Churches Quarterly* (October–December 1945, pp. 170–200), in which the critic declares (in denial of Dom Dix's statements to the contrary) that the deacon's exhortations *are* really 'exhortations' addressed to the people, not prayers addressed

to God, and that the people reply by the recital of the words
Kyrie eleison—which *are* addressed directly to God. Thus, he
says, the people's part is not reduced to mere 'chorus'; but it is
still true, in spite of this, that the people's part in intercessory
prayer is at least more *evident*, though not more audible, in
the collect than in the litany. It seems probable that the litany
and its methods of recital are due to the introduction in Syria,
in the later fourth century, of the sanctuary-veil; that is, a
curtain drawn in front of the entrance to the sanctuary. This
curtain hid the celebrant and the altar altogether from the
sight of the congregation during the greater part of the Liturgy,[1]
and so the deacon was obliged to act as a 'link' between them
both, and also to act as the people's guide in taking part in the
Liturgy. The litany form of prayer appeared for the first time,
fully developed, in the north Syrian rite known as the *Apostolic
Constitutions* (viii, *c.* A.D. 370; see Dix, p. 477). In the East this
new form of prayer took the place of the old series of collects,
but the collect-form still 'shows up' in the Egyptian Liturgy to
a certain extent.

SPECIAL INTEREST AND IMPORTANCE OF INTERCESSORY
PRAYERS: This lies in the fact that these prayers are examples
of the way in which public intercessions were made in early
times—namely, by a *corporate* act in which the whole Church
took part, each 'order'—bishops or priests, deacons, lay-folk—
actively carrying out their own distinct function in the Mystical
Body of Christ. This public intercession, too, was made, not
only for the local community and its members present at the
Liturgy nor only for the Church in general, but also for the
whole world outside the Church. By the middle of the fourth
century, which was in a special sense the period of far-reaching
liturgical changes, developments and the disappearance of some
earlier and even universal customs, this form of intercessory
prayer was beginning to disappear also. With its disappearance

---

[1] This separation of sanctuary from nave was still more effectively carried out
in yet later times by the erection of the screen known as the *ikonostasis* (literally
'picture-stand'). This screen is made of marble or wood, solid except for three
doors which can be closed. As the name indicates, its chief purpose is to
support the many 'ikons' or sacred pictures which are heaped upon it in Byzantine
churches, but, in effect, it forms a complete barrier between sanctuary and nave.

or modification, the litany had a good deal to do. It was during this century that the intercessions in the Eastern liturgies were transferred from the end of the preparatory service (or beginning of the Eucharist) to a position within the anaphora— usually after the consecration, but the exact place differs according to the different national rites of the East. The change, too, involved one of two results—either the *duplication* of the series of intercessions—one series remaining in its original position, the other entering the anaphora—or else it simply involved the *shifting* of the series of prayers from after the Gospel to the anaphora, and so the complete abandonment of any form of intercession in the original place. In the West—both at Rome and elsewhere—the intercessions about this period were dropped altogether in the ordinary Masses, being reserved for very special occasions, e.g. at Rome, the Wednesday and Friday of Holy Week. Later, the Wednesday intercessions were dropped also—when on that day the Holy Sacrifice came to be celebrated regularly, instead of only the introductory service as still on Good Friday. In the Gallican and Spanish rites, and in the Ambrosian rite as well, the intercessions were reserved, as at Rome, for Holy Week only, but on Holy Saturday in all these three rites. In the Gallican and Spanish rites, however, the old place of the prayers after the Gospel was taken in everyday use by a *litany* of intercessions of the Eastern type. In the Ambrosian rite a litany of this type is also found, but in a much earlier position—*at the beginning of the Mass*, after the 'ingressa', the equivalent of the Roman 'introit'—that is, the psalm and antiphon chanted during the entrance of the celebrant and sacred ministers into the sanctuary to begin the Mass. The threefold *Kyrie eleison*, chanted in the Ambrosian rite after the Gospel (there is also a threefold *Kyrie* after the communion), is not a relic of a litany, according to Dom Gregory Dix, but a form of hymn (Dix, pp. 461, 462 and footnote 1 on the latter page). In the Roman rite, too, the place of the intercessions of the synaxis was taken by a litany of the same Eastern form, but for the same series of intentions as the former collect-type. The litany, as in the case of the Ambrosian rite, was put at the very beginning of the Mass, after the introit. In the Roman rite this litany was recited in every Mass, but at Milan only on the Sundays of Lent. It is important to remember that in the West, the old intercessions were *not* moved from the first service to the Eucharistic Prayer, as in the East, but *suppressed altogether* except on the special occasions mentioned. The fact that, both in Rome and at Milan, the litanies which, to a certain extent, took their place in the early part of the ordinary Mass were recited at the beginning of the whole service is probably the result of the complete fusion of the preliminary service and Eucharist at that period into one undivided service. In the case of the Roman Mass, the ninefold *Kyrie* recited to-day at the beginning of every Mass is really a relic of the litany described above, as we shall see farther on.

We must mention here two occasions when the connection between the intercessions and the synaxis of pre-Nicene days was not observed. In the liturgy as described by both Justin and Hippolytus when celebrated after baptism and confirmation, the intercessory prayers were recited between the administration of the two sacraments and the celebration of the Eucharist, although there had been no preliminary service.[1] In *The Apostolic Tradition*, as we have seen, there is another example of the liturgy without the introductory service—in the case of the consecration of a bishop (pp. 2–11). In this case the 'Prayers' were not said—precisely because there had been no such service, and they were still looked upon as its conclusion—being *distinct* from the Eucharist, even when celebrated just before it. The prayers, on the other hand, were recited at the baptismal liturgy; the reason being, probably, to allow the newly baptised to take part at once in the privilege of the 'order' to which they had just been admitted—the 'order of layfolk', the 'Holy People of God' in the Mystical Body of Christ—the privilege, that is, of joining in common or corporate prayer. Before their Baptism, catechumens prayed 'by themselves apart from the faithful', and after the prayer they did not receive or give the Kiss of Peace, 'for their kiss is not yet pure' (*The Apostolic Tradition of St. Hippolytus*, p. 29). After the prayers of the catechumens, special prayer was said *for* them, they were blessed and then dismissed.

[1] Justin: *Apologia*, i, 65; Hippolytus: *The Apostolic Tradition*, xxii, 5, p. 39— see pp. 33–9 for the whole ceremony of baptism, etc.

THE EUCHARIST AND THE AGAPE: The development of the ceremonies and prayers of the actual Sacrifice leads us back to the question of the agape once more. A recent liturgical scholar, Dom Eloi Dekkers, O.S.B., monk of the Abbey of Steenbrugge in Belgium, maintains that in spite of the fact that the Holy Eucharist was instituted during a meal and in the evening, there does not seem to have been any desire among the first Christians to reproduce the actual circumstances of the Last Supper in detail. According to this writer, it appears that very early if not from the *beginning*, in the newly founded Church, the Holy Sacrifice was celebrated in the early morning of the 'first Day of the week' (Sunday), and that this day and time were chosen in honour of the Resurrection of Our Lord.[1] The agape, says this writer, was celebrated in the evening, but there is no indication of any immediate connection with the Eucharist in the early Church. St. Paul, in his first Epistle to the Corinthians, is probably not speaking of the agape, followed by the Eucharist, but of the Eucharist alone and of the danger of turning the Holy Sacrifice itself into a means of eating and drinking—in fact, into an ordinary meal (1 Cor. xi. 17–34). It seems, however, that in this particular case the Eucharist *was* celebrated in the evening, though this is not explicitly stated. It is also possible that if it was in the evening the Apostle was objecting to this very attempt to imitate Our Lord's action in too material a manner. In the account of the Eucharist celebrated by him at Troas (at which his too lengthy sermon brought about the death of the drowsy Eutychus and the subsequent miracle of his restoration to life by the Apostle), the Holy Sacrifice was offered after midnight—that is, in the early morning of the 'first day of the week' which, according to Jewish reckoning, had *begun* on the evening of the Saturday (Acts xx. 7–12).

DEVELOPMENTS IN THE EUCHARISTIC LITURGY are concerned with: (i) The Offertory; (ii) the Eucharistic Prayer; (iii) the Fraction, that is the ritual breaking of bread; (iv) the communion of celebrant, ministers and congregation.

[1] 'L'Église ancienne, a-t-elle connu la messe du soir?' See p. 5.

THE OFFERTORY: In later days this was the development of the original simple acts of spreading a linen cloth over the altar and laying out on it the bread and wine later provided by the people assisting.[1] Each person brought a little of both for himself or herself. Offerings, too, of oil, milk, vegetables, fruit, cheese and even flowers were often added to the essential oblations of bread and wine. (See *Apostolic Tradition*, pp. 10 and 11, Nos. v and vi; also p. 53, No. xxviii, and p. 55.) Such offerings were placed upon or beside the altar, and were blessed after the consecration of the bread and wine with a special blessing, which exists at the end of the Roman Canon to this day in the words: *per quem hæc omnia*, etc. This is still the moment in the Roman rite for the consecration of the oil of the sick on Maundy Thursday. But, as will be shown farther on, the above words in earliest times probably referred *directly* and *primarily* to the consecrated Bread and Wine themselves.

While it was the people who brought the offerings of bread and wine for the sacrifice and who presented their offerings in the 'place of meeting' (private room in a dwelling-house, basilica, chapel, etc.), it is not very clear as to *how* the presentation was carried out. Was it a ceremonial act at the altar, or were the offerings given up to the proper authorities in what we should now call the sacristy, and afterwards taken to the altar by the deacons without any special ceremonial connecting them directly with the offerers? Whatever was the fact in the earliest times, the solemn ceremonial offering by the people at the time of the offertory became the usual custom in Rome, and is fully described in the eighth-century *Ordo Romanus Primus*. At Rome, too, this ceremonial offering by the members of the congregation was kept up, at least on certain great feasts, till towards the end of the Middle Ages. The provision of the bread and wine for the Sacrifice was considered as the 'liturgy' of the faithful laity—as Dom Gregory Dix puts it: "The communicant *brings* (*prosenegkein*) the *prosphora* ('offering'); the deacon 'presents' it or 'brings it up' (*anapherein*); the bishop 'offers' it (*prospherein*)" (Dix, pp. 111 *et seq.*). The gifts thus providing the

---

[1] The Prayer-book of Sarapion gives us the earliest evidence in Egypt of the custom for each member of the congregation to bring his or her own *prosphera* ('offerings') of bread and a flask of wine. The evidence occurs in the prayer for 'those who had offered the oblations' (*prosphera*), at the end of the anaphora.

matter of the Eucharist were "at all points 'the gifts of thy holy church'" presented for use at the altar by each 'order' according to its own special 'liturgy'—that is, public office or duty. Above all, the bishop's 'liturgy' was the ritual sacrificial oblation of the gifts which, in the Person of Christ Himself, he would bless and consecrate and so transform them into the only 'acceptable oblation' of His sacred Body and Blood. As Dom Dix again says: "The whole rite was a true corporate offering by the church, in its hierarchical completeness, of the church in its organic unity" (Dix, p. 117). But, again, this undoubted truth does not supply us with a clear notion as to the *way* in which the corporate act of the offering was actually carried out in the earliest periods.

In the fourth century and onwards, there was an important difference between Eastern and Western customs. In the East the people took their offerings to the sacristy before the Liturgy began, and the deacons brought them from the sacristy to the altar when they were needed at the offertory. This practice led to the preliminary service known as the *prothesis* ('setting forth' or 'placing before') in the side chapel or at the side-table in the sanctuary (both also called *prothesis*), and to the solemn procession with the offerings, treated with great reverence, known as the 'Great Entrance'. In the West in Rome the people brought their offerings of bread and wine to the chancel rail or colonnade,[1] laid the bread on a dish held by a deacon and poured the wine into a large two-handled chalice held by another deacon. These deacons then took the offerings to the altar, and the bishop advanced and laid his hands upon them and so 'offered' them as high priest of the Christian priesthood. It seems, at least in our present knowledge of liturgical history, impossible to decide which use is more ancient or whether perhaps both existed side by side from the beginning. According to the Abbot of Louvain, Dom Bernard Capelle, and others, the ceremonial offering by the people at Mass in the West started in Rome as a local practice in the fourth century, and

---

[1] This colonnade was a later development of the low wall and metal grating, called *cancelli* (from which is derived the English word 'chancel'), which separated the tribunal in the apse of the lay basilica from the main part—the 'bar' as it would be called in English—and, when the basilica became a Christian church, the sanctuary from the nave.

the Eastern practice described above was the original practice
of the whole pre-Nicene Church. But—to quote Dom Gregory
Dix again—"We have no evidence at all anywhere from the
pre-Nicene period as to how the layman's oblation came into
the hands of the deacons," apart from a passage from the
Syrian Church Order known as the *Didascalia* (*c.* A.D. 250)
which speaks of the deacons standing—one by the oblations,
the other by the door—to observe those who come in (Dix,
p. 122), which suggests that at that period the later practice
of the Eastern rites already existed, at least in Syria.

THE EUCHARISTIC PRAYER: This was originally one undivided
prayer, beginning with a series of thanksgivings offered to God
for His benefits to mankind—the Creation, Incarnation, Redemption—leading up to the Last Supper, and so to the consecration of the offerings of bread and wine. But later on this
one prayer was practically divided into two parts, both in the
East and West, by the introduction of the *Sanctus*—the words
'Holy, Holy, Holy, Lord God of Hosts', taken from the prophecy
of Isaias vi. 3. The 'Thanksgiving Prayer' itself was probably
derived from, or rather adapted from, the long thanksgiving
prayer recited at the end of all Jewish meals—the 'grace after
meat'—rather than from a combination of the two shorter
prayers—one for the blessing of the bread, the other for that of
the wine—as suggested by Dr. Cirlot, in his *The Early Eucharist*
(see p. 4). According to Dom Dix, these latter prayers appear
in the agape but not in the Eucharist. The long 'grace' at the
end of Jewish meals was always looked upon as *the* blessing—of
all that had gone before it. It was, moreover, the special
blessing for what was actually known as 'the cup of blessing',
and which is spoken of by St. Paul in referring to the Holy
Eucharist (1 Cor. x. 16). Thus in the Lord's Supper this
blessing became the 'prayer of blessing or thanksgiving'—the
'Eucharist'—and it was pronounced over both bread and wine
together.

The word 'eucharist' (from the Greek *eucharistia*, meaning
'thanks') became the usual title of the Christian Sacrifice. It is
simply the Greek translation of the Hebrew word *berakah*—
'blessing' or 'thanksgiving', for to a Jew the two things were one

and the same—to 'give thanks' to God was to 'bless' Him, to declare Him to be 'blessed' and to 'praise' Him. To do this *over* any objects—that is, to declare God to be blessed over them —was, in effect, to bless such objects themselves.

Another name for the Holy Sacrifice was *eulogia*—also a Greek word meaning 'blessing', and this word, too, could be used as a translation of *berakah*. *Eucharistia* was used when the emphasis was laid upon *God* to whom one gave thanks; *eulogia* when the emphasis was rather upon the *thing* for which thanks was given to Him (Dix, p. 79).

In the Jewish meal—whatever its precise nature or the particular occasion on which it took place—the president of the meal invited the guests to join in the 'grace', in words which were probably the source of the opening words of the Christian Eucharistic Prayer. The Jewish words were as follows: "Let us give thanks to the Lord our God"—and those present "gave their assent". We do not know in what formula they gave this assent, but the traditional Christian response to the celebrant's exhortation at the Eucharist—"It is meet and just"—seems to be Jewish in character and may be descended from the old Jewish words. The Jewish thanksgiving prayer, too, ended with a doxology. This word, from the Greek, means an expression glorifying somebody or something—in this case, the Name of God. From this notion comes that of the Christian doxology at the end of the Eucharistic Prayer, which is found in analogous terms in all rites, Eastern and Western. In the Roman rite we have *Per ipsum et cum ipso et in ipso est tibi Deo Patri omnipotenti, in unitate Spiritus sancti, omnis honor et gloria.*[1] To this doxology— which sums up the whole meaning and effect of the Mass in a few words—those present answered *amen*, the Hebrew response meaning 'so be it', in sign of faith and acceptance.

THE FRACTION: The breaking of bread at meals and at the Eucharist was originally merely the practical means of distributing it among a number of people. It had no symbolical meaning—except in so far as it was a sign of hospitality, the host offering his guests the bread which he had provided for

---

[1] "Through Him and with Him and in Him all honour and glory is given to Thee, O God the Father Almighty, in the unity of the Holy Spirit."

them. In the early Eucharistic service, the consecrated bread
was broken immediately after consecration, as communion followed at once; there were, at first, no distinct prayers of oblation after the consecration and no Lord's Prayer. All this is
clear from Justin and (a little later on) from Hippolytus also.
The symbolic notion, however, of breaking the bread to represent the 'breaking' of Our Lord's Body upon the Cross was
introduced, later on, into the Liturgy. To justify it there is the
reading of 1 Cor. x. 24: "This is my Body which is *broken* for
you." In the Vulgate the words are: *hoc est corpus meum, quod
pro vobis tradetur*—"which shall be *delivered* for you". Fr. Lattey
in Vol. III of the *Westminster Version of the Sacred Scriptures* (*The
New Testament*: 'St. Paul's Epistle to the Churches, 1 Corinthians', p. 49) translates: "This is my body *on your behalf*", saying
in a note that the words "which shall be *delivered* for you" are
perhaps due to the influence of Matt. xxvi. 26; Luke xxii. 19,
but in any case they have "too little support to be trusted". The
other reading "which is *broken for you*", is better supported, but
not strongly enough to be adopted in preference to the one
which he has adopted—perhaps an abbreviation of a phrase
such as that in Luke xxii. 19—"which is *being given* for you—on
your behalf". In any case, such words point clearly to the
offering of a sacrifice at the Last Supper.

THE COMMUNION AND CONCLUSION: In the pre-Nicene
Church it appears to have been the custom for all to receive
communion standing—as is still the custom in the Eastern
Churches. The Jews *sat* to eat the bread at their religious
meals, but *stood* to drink from the 'cup of blessing'.

As we have seen, the consecration of the bread was later on
united directly with that of the wine, both consecrations being
effected in the one prayer of thanksgiving. As it was the Jewish
custom to stand when reciting the *berakah* (thanksgiving), this
affected the reception of the bread as well as that of the cup.
The psalm sung at the end of the Jewish religious meals is found
at the end of the agape—not of the Eucharist which ended at
once with the communion, no need being felt for any special
thanksgiving after it, since the Eucharistic Prayer was *the*
thanksgiving of the whole rite. Special thanksgiving after com-

munion was not admitted till the Church had lost all contact with the Jewish origins of the Eucharistic rite, that is, only during the fourth century, when it began to make its appearance in the Syrian and Egyptian liturgies. Even then it was very short—a mere section added to the 'Eucharistic Action', which really ended in the communion, as its climax. In the pre-Nicene Church, a single sentence of dismissal probably said by the deacon seems to have been the only element that followed the communion. Portions of the consecrated bread were taken home by the faithful for their communions on the days when the Liturgy was not celebrated, and the deacons—after the third century, their assistants the acolytes—also carried such portions to all those who had been unable, for any reason, to take part in the public Liturgy. The deacons—in later times again the acolytes—carried portions of the bread consecrated at the solemn Mass, celebrated by the Pope or by other bishops in their own dioceses to priests celebrating Mass elsewhere. These portions were placed by each priest in the chalice at the fraction, and this was done as a sign of the union between the Pope (or bishop) and his priests in the one Sacrifice of which Pope (or bishop) was the 'high priest', the principal celebrant by right of his 'order', or office, in the Church.

LATER DEVELOPMENTS: While it is true that at first the communion of all present marked the end of the whole service, the necessary 'clearing up' took place at the end in public and before all present. As at the beginning of the Eucharist, the altar was covered with its linen cloth and the bread and wine were laid upon it in paten and chalice in the presence of all taking part in the Sacrifice; so at the end the cleansing of these vessels and the removal of the cloth from the altar took place in the presence of all, before they were dismissed. This remained the practice in the West, even when a formal thanksgiving after communion had been introduced, and it remains so to-day in the Roman Mass, both in the full ceremonial of 'High Mass' and in the simple rite of 'Low Mass'. In the former the sub-deacon cleanses the chalice and takes it with the paten, covered with the 'chalice-veil', to the credence table; in the latter it is the priest himself who cleanses and covers the chalice. In both

High and Low Mass, the priest now drinks the 'ablutions' ('washings', 'cleansings') of wine and water with which the chalice has been cleansed—formerly these 'ablutions' were poured away into the 'piscina' (a Latin word originally meaning a tank for keeping fish); that is, the drain made in the wall for this purpose, and usually on the Epistle side of the altar.

THE KISS OF PEACE: The kiss was originally given at the very beginning of the Eucharist—after the intercessions (when there was a preliminary service, as was usually the case). The kiss was given in all the Eastern liturgies at this part of the rite, and it is still so given—more or less. In the Western rite as described by both Justin and Hippolytus, the kiss was given in this place, and it seems to have been the liturgical tradition that it should occur at this point. Before joining in the sacrifice the matter of which (the bread and wine) they had themselves provided, the faithful present exchanged this sign of Christian unity and charity, receiving it through the chief celebrant from the altar; that is, from Christ Himself, Victim and 'altar' of His own sacrifice. Nothing is heard about the position of the kiss again till about two hundred years after Hippolytus, and then its position at Rome is just before the communion. Some writers on the Liturgy suggest that in the beginnings the kiss was given in all, or practically all, liturgies, in *both* places since it is equally appropriate in each. Before the offertory (to use the later term for convenience' sake), the kiss expressed the more ancient idea of charity and union between the *offerers* (or at least *providers*) of the sacrificial elements; before communion, the kiss was the greeting of mutual charity between those about to be fed with the same Food and Drink—Body and Blood of the Divine Victim—in the sacrificial Banquet, the true agape or 'love-feast'. Those who uphold the two places for the kiss as the ancient custom in all liturgies, consider that East and West independently dropped one or other of the two according to the prevalent attitude of each. But it is perhaps more likely that there was at first only the one position at the beginning of the Eucharistic rite, and that the position before communion was new and really contrary to primitive usage. The author of *The Shape of the Liturgy*, however, points out that this change was "the *only* change [as distinct from *insertions*] in the primitive order of the liturgy which the Roman rite has ever undergone". He adds that in the change in position of the *Pax*, Rome was probably following an innovation *first* admitted into the African Churches. The position just before communion is, in fact, attested in that country, at the end of the fourth century, by St. Augustine in his *Epistola* (lix (cxl), ix); *Sermo* vi. The adoption of this custom by Rome was probably, it seems, made not long before A.D. 416, since at this date the matter is mentioned by Pope Innocent I, in his letter to Bishop Decentius of Gubbio. The position before the offertory was still the custom in the church of Gubbio and in other Italian Churches outside Rome (Dix, p. 108). In the Eastern Churches the kiss is now placed after the developed rites of the offertory instead of being at the very beginning of the Eucharist proper. This slight change was first made at Jerusalem, later on at Antioch and at Constantinople, and then, during the fifth or sixth century, all over the East except in the Coptic and Abyssinian rites, in both of which it is still in the early position—the only existing examples of this primitive practice. The reviewer of *The Shape of the Liturgy*—in *The Eastern Churches Quarterly*, already referred to in the Preface—maintains that in spite of this the Kiss of Peace still holds the ancient position in the Eastern rites—that is, just before the beginning of the *anaphora*, but that this fact has been obscured by the introduction of the Creed and the various ceremonies of the offertory *before* the kiss is given. In the Western rites of Gaul and Spain the kiss was, as at Gubbio, at the beginning of the Eucharist, but in the Eastern position *after* the offertory prayers and ceremonies, which had been adopted, together with a certain number of other Eastern practices, probably in the sixth century. In Spain this may have been the result of the temporary occupation by Byzantine forces under Justinian (Dix, p. 109); in Gaul, on account of the close association also with the Byzantine Court and the Western Court of the two Empires. The predecessor of St. Ambrose as Bishop of Milan was an Arian called Auxentius, and so had special sympathy with the East, the home of Arianism. In the church of Gubbio and other Italian churches, apart from that of Rome, the kiss remained in the primitive position *before* any offertory prayers. At Milan the Roman position had been adopted before the ninth century, but to the present day the deacon in the Milanese rite still chants *Pacem habete* ('have peace [with one another]') just before the offertory. In the Celtic rite the kiss was also in the Roman position, and there is no tradition as to the date of its adoption.

THE LORD'S PRAYER; THE PATER NOSTER: The view that the Lord's Prayer is a primitive and universal element of the Eucharistic Liturgy is no longer held as certain by liturgical authorities, as there are early examples of its absence from some liturgies Eastern and Western. In the East it is absent from the Apostolic Constitutions or Clementine Liturgy—so-called as it was probably put together by a learned writer of the fourth century generally believed to be the interpolator of the Epistles of St. Ignatius of Antioch, and who made use also of the Epistle of St. Clement of Rome to the Corinthians. It is true that this liturgy was never *in use* as a liturgy, but is merely a compilation of liturgical formulæ made by the above inter-polater of St. Ignatius' Epistles, but it is, nevertheless, based upon the Syrian type of the Liturgy at the end of the fourth or beginning of the fifth century, and is in fact the earliest written account of it. The first evidence for the use of the Lord's Prayer towards the end of the anaphora or Eucharistic Prayer is given by St. Cyril of Jerusalem (A.D. 348). St. John Chrysostom does not speak of it at Antioch a generation later, so even in St. Cyril's time it could not have been a widespread custom (Dix, p. 130). It is absent again in the early form of the Egyptian rite given us in the Liturgy of Sarapion.[1]

In the West St. Ambrose speaks of the *Pater* in his *De Sacramentis* (iv. 24—not vi. 24, as given by Dix in the 1945 edition of *The Shape of the Liturgy*, p. 131), about A.D. 395 at Milan. In Africa, early in the fifth century, St. Augustine says: "The whole of this petition" [that is, the Eucharistic Prayer—which the Saint describes as: 'the prayers made when the elements are blessed and consecrated, and broken for distribution'] "*almost*

---

[1] It is true that in a 'rubric' Sarapion says: "After *the prayer* [comes] the fraction", etc., but this probably refers to the Eucharistic Prayer itself; there is nothing to indicate that it was the Lord's Prayer

the whole Church concludes with the Lord's Prayer" (*Epist.* 59 and also *Epist.* 149, 16; see, besides, Dix, p. 131; Srawley, 1947 edition, p. 143. Italics mine). Notice here that the Saint says: '*almost the whole* Church'—not the '*whole* Church', absolutely speaking. The chief exception of which St. Augustine was thinking here was perhaps the Roman Church—where the Lord's Prayer seems to have been introduced only in St. Gregory the Great's time (*c.* A.D. 595, Dix, p. 131—and in a footnote giving reference to the writings of the above Saint—*Epist.* ix. 12—in which he speaks of the Lord's Prayer at Mass; see also John the Deacon, *Vita Greg*, ii, 20). It seems curious to us that Our Lord's own prayer given to His disciples at their request, "Lord, teach us to pray" (Luke xi. 1), should ever have been absent from His act of sacrifice—the summary of all prayer. Probably the explanation lies in the emphasis then placed upon the Eucharistic Prayer itself as containing all necessary for that Act. The *Pater* is not mentioned by St. Justin in his two descriptions of the Liturgy, nor by St. Hippolytus in the text of his *Apostolic Tradition*. As we shall see, it appears probable that St. Gregory the Great himself actually introduced the *Pater* into the later Roman rite. Up till fairly recently, he was considered to have only *moved* it from just before the communion to immediately after the doxology of the Canon—its present place.

CHAPTER III

THE FUSION OF INTRODUCTORY SERVICE AND EUCHARIST IN ROME

THE union between the two services, the Synaxis or 'Mass of the catechumens' and the Eucharist or 'Mass of the Faithful', was not a conscious or deliberate act of ecclesiastical authority —or conscious and deliberate in any way. It just 'happened', as so many other developments or changes in the history of the Liturgy. In fact, we must free our minds from the subconscious idea of a species of 'congregation of rites' introducing and deciding the various elements of the Liturgy. As a matter of fact, such developments and changes were usually brought about by the Christian people itself in various places and according to various circumstances, and later on were accepted and established by authority. The union of preparatory service and Eucharist during the fourth–fifth centuries was due, to a great extent, to the growing infrequence of lay-communion and the consequently gradual cessation of the offerings of bread and wine made by the laity during the Liturgy. Besides this, there was the gradual disappearance of catechumens, penitents and so on, as 'official' persons to be ceremonially legislated for and publicly dismissed from the church at special points of the service. All this helped to obscure the distinction between the two services, and to make each simply a part of one whole, at which *all* could be present. At the same time the real distinction between the two was not altogether lost. It is still evident to-day, and especially in the Western Church. In the latter it is seen most clearly in a pontifical Mass; that is, a Mass celebrated by a bishop or other prelate possessing the right or privilege of *pontificalia*.[1] In a pontifical Mass the celebrant goes to the altar—to *remain* there—only at the offertory. The first part of the Mass (the old Synaxis), apart from the prayers at the foot of the altar and the incensing of the altar at the

---

[1] That is, the use of mitre, dalmatic and tunicle, buskins and sandals, as well as the chasuble.

beginning—all of late introduction—takes place entirely at the throne.

THE DISMISSALS ABANDONED: These were given up in Rome probably during the sixth century, but survived in South Italy to a later date. (See on p. 12 the description in *The Dialogues of St. Gregory the Great*, ii. 23, of what seems to have been a survival of the dismissal of penitents.) In Gaul the dismissal of the cate-chumens lasted until at least the eighth century in some places, and it is still found in the Mozarabic books, together with the dismissal of the penitents.[1] The Dismissals are still found in the Eastern liturgies, and the deacon still announces them. But no one goes out; they are a mere relic of past usage; a formula without effect.

In most places the fusion of Introductory Service and Eucha-rist took place very gradually, and even while it was taking place, either of the two services was occasionally celebrated without the other. This is especially the case with regard to the Introductory, the 'aliturgical', Service, of which we have al-ready spoken, and which continued in some places—e.g. Rome—on Wednesdays and Fridays. These days were next re-duced to the Wednesday and Friday of Holy Week only and finally to Good Friday and Palm Sunday, and communion from the Blessed Sacrament reserved from Maundy Thursday Mass together with an ablution of unconsecrated wine was added on Good Friday. This communion (originally, no doubt, for all present but now allowed only to the celebrant) is accompanied by the recitation of the *Pater noster* with its little 'preface' and following prayer, *Libera nos*, also recited aloud. All this is probably a relic of the pre-Nicene method of receiving com-munion outside the Holy Sacrifice—which at first took place only in private homes. It was transferred to parish and other churches, perhaps during the fifth century, when 'domestic reservation' was being given up (Dix pp. 440 and 441). In the East the 'aliturgical Liturgy', accompanied by the communion of the reserved Sacrament, but for the ministers and laity as

---

[1] See *The Mozarabic and Ambrosian Rites*, by W. C. Bishop, M.A. Edited from his papers by C. L. Feltoe, D.D., in *Alcuin Club Tracts*, XV. (A. R. Mowbray & Co., London and Oxford, 1924, p. 30.)

well as the celebrant, became the custom on the weekdays of
Lent. During this season the full Liturgy is celebrated only on
Saturdays and Sundays.

THE EUCHARIST WITHOUT PREPARATORY SERVICE: This seems
to have disappeared everywhere in the East after *c.* A.D. 500,
but in the West it lasted longer in some places, on Maundy
Thursday alone. The choice of this day was in order to provide
for a special reminder of the Institution of the Holy Eucharist
at the Last Supper, and the Mass was therefore celebrated in
the evening. In some churches *three* Masses were celebrated on
Maundy Thursday: one for the reconciliation of the penitents
in the morning; one for the consecration of the Holy Oils, at
midday; the third in memory of the Last Supper, in the evening. At the first Mass the preparatory service was omitted—the
long rite of the reconciliation of penitents taking its place. The
second Mass was preceded by that service, in the usual way.
The third Mass, like the first, was celebrated without it, beginning at the offertory. No more is heard of all this after the
ninth century.

It is uncertain whether or not there were three Masses on
Maundy Thursday in Rome, as the texts for these Masses in the
Gelasian Sacramentary do not seem to be Roman in origin,
but to have been taken from other parts of Italy—or even from
France.[1] The formulæ for the Blessing of the Holy Oils in this
Sacramentary are of Roman origin, but these Roman prayers
are for only *one* Mass on the day.[2]

LATEST EVIDENCE FOR THE EUCHARIST WITHOUT INTRO-
DUCTORY IN THE WEST: This seems to occur in a 'most ancient
Roman Ordo', as Dom Martène calls it in his *Antiq. Eccles.
Rit.* iv. 5. This Ordo contains three Masses for Maundy Thursday as in the Gelasian Sacramentary, but its origin and antiquity are now disputed. In a footnote on p. 441 of *The Shape of
the Liturgy*, Dom Gregory Dix, however, says: "Whatever its
origin, this document is the latest evidence I have found for the
celebration in the West of the eucharist without a synaxis." The

---

[1] See *Gelasian Sacramentary*, Ed. H. A. Wilson, pp. 63–73.
[2] Ibid., pp. 48 *et seq.*

celebration of more than one Mass on the same day, as in this case, seems to have started at Jerusalem, where there were two on Maundy Thursday and in separate churches, when the famous Spanish abbess, Etheria or Egeria, paid her visit to the Holy Places in A.D. 385, of which she has given such a living and also amusing description in her *Peregrinatio* ('pilgrimage'). This 'Pilgrimage' was discovered by J. F. Gamurrini (Rome, 1887), and the text is printed by Duchesne. (See the English translation in his *Christian Worship*, pp. 541 ff. (London: S.P.C.K., 1949 (re-print)); an English translation of the *Peregrinatio* was also made separately by Mrs. McClure and C. L. Feltoe (S.P.C.K.).) At first this pilgrim was thought to have been Silvia of Aquitaine, sister of the imperial minister, Rufinus, but her name is now known to have been Etheria or Egeria. She was probably the abbess or superioress of a community of Spanish nuns.

To return for a moment to the synaxis without the Eucharist. In the Byzantine rite besides the Liturgy of the Pre-sanctified already spoken of there is another example of this synaxis without the Eucharist—but also without the communion which *is* given in the Pre-sanctified Liturgy. This is a service called the 'typica' (i.e. 'type' or 'figure'), which is recited usually after the office of Sext, and in which, besides the parts evidently taken from the Eucharistic Liturgy, are also certain elements taken from Vespers. The parts taken from the Liturgy are the Epistle and Gospel of the day and the *apolusis*— that is, the 'dismissal' of the people at the conclusion of the act of worship. As the Ven. J. Norman, M.A., says, describing this office in his *Handbook to the Christian Liturgy* (London: S.P.C.K., 1944, pp. 129, 130): "Its structure suggests that it was formed for use on days on which the liturgy was not celebrated, and used as a substitute for it; later the portions which were not already in the liturgy were placed there at the beginning.... The *typika* is, indeed, *almost the liturgy without the Anaphora*" (italics mine).

SPECIAL ADDITIONS: The result of the fusion of Preliminary Service and Eucharist led, in the former, to an introduction as the principal new feature. The pre-Nicene service began at once with the lessons without even a greeting and response—as the Mass of the Pre-sanctified in the Roman rite does to this day—and in this latter not even the titles of the lessons are announced. Besides the introduction, there was also the addition of special prayers and of chants while certain actions were taking place.

THE INTRODUCTION: In the East the introduction may be divided into three forms, which took shape during the fourth–fifth centuries. In the West there was only one form which, while differing from any of the three Eastern forms, was influenced to a certain extent by them, and it also partly borrowed from them. The three Eastern forms are:

(i) In the liturgies of *Mesopotamia* and *East Syria* and of *Armenia*. In these parts of the world the inhabitants regarded what we usually call 'the east' as the 'west', compared with their own positions.

(ii) In the *Egyptian* or *Alexandrian Liturgy*.

(iii) In the *Greek Liturgy*—in Jerusalem, Antioch and Constantinople (Byzantium). The Western introduction is of more immediate interest to us for, as we have seen, there is plenty of literature about the Eastern rites, and texts, too, of the actual liturgies themselves, but there is not so much about the Western rite—even that of Rome; the Western introduction is, besides, much less complicated than the Eastern.

THE ROMAN INTRODUCTION: This consisted of:

(i) The *introit*—the chant of a psalm with an antiphon repeated after each verse. The title is taken from the Latin *introitus*—'entrance'—as the psalm was chanted during the entrance of the celebrant and ministers from the *secretarium* (the sacristy as we should say now) into the church.

(ii) *A litany*—of prayers for all the intentions of the old intercessory prayers formerly recited after the Gospel; later, this long litany was replaced by the Greek words *Kyrie eleison* and *Christe eleison* ('Lord have mercy, Christ have mercy).

(iii) *A hymn*—the *Gloria in excelsis*—followed by the greeting *Dominus vobiscum* ('The Lord be with you') and the response—

et cum spiritu tuo ('And with thy spirit'—a Hebrew form of reply, meaning 'and with you also'). The greeting *Pax vobis* ('Peace be with you') was reserved for bishops, and in later times for other prelates also, on certain days.

(iv) The *introductory prayer*, often called now the *collect* (from the late Latin word *collecta*—earlier form, *collectio*—'a gathering together'). In the Roman texts the name of this prayer is *oratio* ('a speech' or 'address'—in the case of prayer—made to God); the title *collectio* ('collect') is, as we shall see, really a Gallican term.

The above form of introduction in general was derived structurally from the Greek form (iii, above)—except the *oratio*, which was taken probably from the Egyptian rite (ii). It appears that from *c*. A.D. 430–45 there were very close relations between Rome and Alexandria, and there are other cases of liturgical connections between the two rites. According to the *Liber Pontificalis* (a series of lives of the Popes and their acts, the earliest part of which was compiled under Boniface II, A.D. 530–2[1]), it was Pope Celestine I (A.D. 422–82) who ordered the antiphonal singing of psalms before the sacrifice by all—"which used not to be done, but only the epistle of blessed Paul used to be read and the holy gospel". Up till this command of Pope Celestine, the only chants from the psalms in the Liturgy, both Eastern and Western, were the responsory psalms between the Scripture lessons, which come down from the use of the Jewish synagogue and belong to the earliest stage of the Liturgy. Neither was there originally any prayer before the lessons; the service began—as we have seen, it still does on Good Friday—with the lessons.

INTRODUCTION OF THE LITANY: This was almost certainly brought into the Mass by Pope Gelasius I (A.D. 494–6), and in order to take the place of the old intercessory collects said after the Gospel—originally as the end of the synaxis. It has been pointed out by Dom Capelle, Abbot of Louvain, that down to the time of Gelasius the intercessions are frequently spoken of at Rome as coming at the end of the synaxis and in the old

---

[1] See *The Catholic Encyclopædia*, Vol. IX, article 'Liber Pontificalis,' by J. P. Kirsch.

collect-form. After this Pope's time, however, they completely disappear except in Holy Week. (See *Revue d'histoire ecclésiastique*, xxxv, 1939, pp. 22 *et seq.*; see also *The Shape of the Liturgy*, p. 453, text and footnotes.) The text of the Latin litany introduced into the Roman Mass is given us by Alcuin, Abbot of St. Martin's Abbey at Tours and 'Master' of Charlemagne's palace (born *c.* A.D. 735—died 804). He restored the Roman rite in Gaul. This litany preserved by Alcuin is called *Deprecatio quam Papa Gelasius pro universali Ecclesia constituit canendam esse* ('The intercession which Pope Gelasius ordained to be sung for the universal Church'). (*P.L.* ci, vol. ii., col. 560-89—see Appendix III in this book for the full text). Although this litany is evidently based upon an Eastern model, Edmund Bishop has shown that it is nevertheless of "local Roman manufacture in the details of the phrasing, and that there is reason to accept the attribution to Gelasius" (*Journal of Theological Studies*, xii, 1911, pp. 407 *et seq.*; quoted in footnote 4, by Dix, p. 453). The petitions of the litany are for the same purposes as in the older form of intercessions—except that prayer for the dead, which was not in the old form, is included in the litany. Its position at the very beginning of the Eucharist seems to be the result of the fusion of two formerly distinct rites into one undivided service. But besides the resumption of the old intercessory collects on Good Friday at the end of the aliturgical synaxis (now somewhat obscured by the addition of the procession, the celebrant's communion and other ceremonies), there is a possible relic of these older intercessions in the *Te igitur* prayer at the beginning of the Roman Canon, after the *Sanctus*.[1] There is a very short prayer for the Church, the Pope (local bishop elsewhere than Rome) and for all 'orthodox supporters' of the Catholic Faith. These latter words almost certainly mean other Catholic *bishops*, besides the Pope and the local bishop; they can hardly refer to the faithful in general, as these have already been mentioned in the prayer for the Church. As the words of

---

[1] On pp. 171 and 505 in *The Shape of the Liturgy*, Dix refers to what he calls, on the latter page, the "(much less developed) intercession for the church" in the *Te igitur* and compares it with the analogous position of intercessions and diptychs in the Alexandrian rite—but in this rite they occur *before* the *Sanctus*. This slight difference between the two rites is probably simply due to the chant of the *Sanctus* being a later interpolation in the Eucharistic Prayer, and having no very certain position within it in the various liturgies.

this particular 'mention' (it is hardly long enough to be called a prayer) are almost exactly the same as those used in the prayer for the Church in the Good Friday intercessions, it is at least possible that this part of the *Te igitur* was introduced (perhaps, again, by Gelasius) when the fashion was coming in (in the East) of having the intercessions in that part of the Mass. The Roman practical spirit is in evidence again—as in the case of the *præfatio* of the collect (e.g. the *Oremus dilectissimi* of the Good Friday examples), reduced to the one word *oremus*. We have seen that in the East the intercessions found their way into the anaphora, and usually after the Words of Institution, before or after the Invocation of the Holy Ghost. If the prayers for Church and Pope, etc., in the *Te igitur* are really a condensed form of intercessions, their position is nearer to that of the Egyptian rite than to that of the other Eastern rites. In the Egyptian rite (the Liturgy of St. Mark), the intercessions (which still possess certain interesting remnants of the collect-form) are recited in the middle of the anaphora *before* the *Sanctus*, and so cause an interruption in the Eucharistic Prayer.

Dom Gregory Dix also agrees with those who consider that the litany at the beginning of the Roman Mass was inserted by Pope Gelasius, and he adds, in a footnote, that the last reference to the old intercessions after the Gospel was in the time of the immediate predecessor of Gelasius—Felix III (A.D. 487–8). (Cf. A. Thiel, *Epistulæ Rom. Pont. genuinæ*. Braunsberg, 1868, i. 263; Dix, p. 453 and footnotes.) The petitions were made by the deacon or by the choir; the responses of the people were made in the Latin words: *Domine exaudi et miserere* ('Lord hear and be merciful'). But St. Gregory the Great, in a letter to the Bishop of Syracuse, shows that the Greek form *Kyrie eleison* ('Lord, have mercy') was in use in his time, and he denies the 'accusation' that it was he himself who had introduced these words (and in general the customs of Constantinople) into the Western rite.

St. Gregory the Great and the Kyrie Eleison: The Saint declares that the Roman use of *Kyrie eleison* was really different from the Byzantine use. He says: "We neither used to say nor do we say *Kyrie eleison* as it is said among the Greeks.

For among them, all [the congregation] sing it together [as a response to the deacon]. But with us something is sung by the choir"—that is, no doubt, the petitions or some of those included in the Gelasian litany—"and the people answer it (*a populo respondetur*). And *Christe eleison* ['Christ have mercy'] which is never sung by the Greeks is [at Rome] sung as many times. But on non-festal days we omit certain things usually sung [i.e. the petitions(?)—the 'something is sung' of the above words] and sing only *Kyrie eleison* and *Christe eleison*, so that we may spend somewhat longer on these words of supplication" (*Epist.* ix. 12 (ed. Ben.)—A.D. 598).[1] These words seem to mean (though it is not absolutely certain) that on festal days, in St. Gregory's time, the litany—probably that of Gelasius unless a change had been made in or about the sixth century—was sung in full. But on ordinary ('non-festal') days the Pope had introduced the custom of singing *Kyrie* and *Christe eleison* without the litany, where formerly this litany had been entirely omitted and the collect had followed immediately after the introit. The Gelasian Sacramentary, when directing the omission of the preliminary service on Maundy Thursday in the Mass for the reconciliation of the penitents, says that on this day there was to be no introit nor greeting (the *Gloria in excelsis* would be omitted in any case, as it was a non-festal Mass), but the service was to begin at once with the prayers for the penitents (*Gelasian Sacramentary*, ed. Wilson, p. 63). At the baptismal Mass on the Paschal Vigil (Holy Saturday), however, the litany is ordered, and the *Gloria*, too, is sung. There seems no reason to doubt that St. Gregory, in introducing this chant of *Kyrie* and *Christe eleison* alone, also fixed the number at nine, though there is again no direct evidence. This novelty of using the response, *Kyrie*, etc., as a chant *in place of* the litany on non-festal days soon became the accepted custom on all days, and the litany disappeared altogether— except on Holy Saturday. On this occasion the names of the saints have been added to the litany, and the ninefold *Kyrie* and *Christe eleison* are put at the end instead of being used as formerly as the response of the people *throughout* the litany.

---

[1] 'As many times'—*totidem vicibus*; but now, *Christe eleison* is said only three times, *Kyrie eleison*, six.

The litany, too (with the above addition of the saints), is said or sung on the Rogation days and in ordination Masses. In these two latter cases, however, the position of the litany is not quite the same: in the Rogation Mass it is sung during the procession before the Mass, and it is followed by the introit and also the usual ninefold *Kyrie*. In an ordination Mass—that is, when all the orders are given at the same Mass—the litany is sung just before the epistle, after the minor orders have been conferred. If deacons alone are ordained, *after* the epistle; if only priests are to be ordained, the litany is also sung after the epistle.

While the *Deprecatio Gelasii* contained the same series of petitions as in the old intercessory prayers (represented still in the 'solemn collects' of Good Friday), there is also the interesting addition of the *petition for the faithful departed*—which does not occur in any of the old intercessions at the end of the synaxis. In his brochure, *The Saints of the Canon of the Mass*, Fr. V. L. Kennedy, C.S.B., says himself that this is "a type of prayer found nowhere else in the diaconal litanies of the West". But his claim that the reason for its place in Gelasius' litany was "to replace the intercessions for the dead which was *found* [italics mine] in the old Roman *Oratio communis*", etc., is not correct, for as already pointed out there was no liturgical intercession for the dead in the early Church. Fr. Kennedy, however, does make it clear that in the introduction of this litany into the Roman Mass, "we have the explanation for the disappearance of the 'oratio communis' or 'oratio fidelium' in its full form from the Roman Mass". Up till lately its disappearance was considered to be due to 'some unknown reason'. But the fact is that it was simply *replaced* by a diaconal litany, so common in the East, and in the new form was placed at the beginning of the Mass, no doubt because "the gradual Christianization of Rome had broken down the old rigid divisions between the Mass of the Catechumens and the Mass of the Faithful" (pp. 33 and 34; see also footnote referring to the article 'Germain de Paris' in *D.C.A.L.*, Vol. I, col. 1075).

Thus the old prayers of intercession disappeared from the Mass at Rome in favour of a litany of Eastern type, as they were also replaced, but still *in the old position*, after the Gospel, in the Gallican and Mozarabic rites, and, in turn, the litany introduced by Pope Gelasius was replaced by the nine *Kyries* introduced on non-festal days by Pope Gregory. These latter can still be regarded as an 'intercession'—but in a very general sense, since they do not include any special petitions, as in the old forms.

THE LITANY AT JERUSALEM: The fact that a litany at the beginning of the Liturgy is found in the East only at Jerusalem, seems to indicate that this practice actually *started* at Jerusalem. From there it may have spread to Antioch, Egypt and the West, as local Jerusalem customs seem to have done so often. In the Egyptian Liturgy of St. Mark, before its 'Byzantinisation' (eighth–eleventh centuries), there are three prayers in the place of a litany at the beginning which are known as the 'Great Prayers'. The unusual position of the litany in the Liturgy of Jerusalem—so entirely different from all other Eastern rites—is perhaps due to the fact that when litanies were introduced into the Eastern rites, during the fifth century, as substitutes for the old Prayers of the Faithful after the Gospel, the Church of Jerusalem had long before this transferred these prayers from that position to within the anaphora (after the consecration), and as there was no reason for inserting a litany after the Gospel, the position at the very beginning of the Liturgy was chosen. When the other Eastern rites moved on their intercessions from after the Gospel to the anaphora, they moved them on in the new litany-form. At Rome, St. Gelasius, apparently desiring to get rid of the old methods of intercessory prayer, adopted the Eastern litany, taking exactly the same means of inserting the latter into the Mass as at Jerusalem; that is, at the beginning of the whole service.

NO HYMN BEFORE THE TIME OF POPE CELESTINE I: Before his time, nothing at all preceded the lections—neither introit, litany, hymn nor collect, and even after Celestine's introduction of the introit the latter was the only item of the Roman 'Introduction', according to the *Liber Pontificalis*. But again, Rome followed an Eastern custom. Constantinople had introduced the *Trisagion* (the threefold *Sanctus* in Greek) between the entrance chant and the lections before A.D. 450, and

Antioch, and probably Jerusalem, did the same before *c.* A.D. 470. It was not, however, till A.D. 498–514 that Pope Symmachus: "Ordained that on every Sunday and Martyr's feast the hymn 'Glory be to God on high' should be said" (*Liber Pontificalis*, edited Duchesne, I, 263). In the footnote in Dix, p. 456, the author shows that this authority is wrong in saying that earlier it was the Pope Telesphorus (martyred *c.* A.D. 130) who ordained that the *Gloria* should be sung on Christmas night only, since this feast did not come into being in Rome until a century and a half *after* Telesphorus, and, in any case, it was connected with Easter much more closely than with Christmas at Rome.

THE GLORIA IN SYRIA AND ASIA MINOR: It was used there in the fourth–fifth centuries and is said to have been brought into the West by St. Hilary of Poitiers (*c.* A.D. 363), who had heard it while banished to the East (Dix, p. 456). The *Gloria* apparently arose in the third, or even as early as the second, century. In pre-Nicene days it was used as a 'hymn of dawn', and so found its way into the morning office of *Orthros* ('Daybreak') in the Eastern Churches—an office equivalent to the Western offices of Matins and Lauds together. In the above Eastern office the *Gloria* forms a greater doxology at the end of the psalms. In the Roman Church the *Benedictus* ('Song of Zachary') seems always to have been used in this place and so the *Gloria* was free for use at the beginning of Mass, when the idea of such a hymn came in from the East. But it did not become—any more than did the litany—a *constant* feature of the Mass, as it was in the East. The litany was not used at the beginning of the Liturgy in the East—except in the Liturgy of Jerusalem. In the other liturgies it replaced the older collect-form of the intercessions after the Gospel.[1] At Rome the *Gloria* was reserved for Christmas and certain other great feasts, and at first only in the solemn Mass celebrated by the Pope and other bishops. Simple priests were allowed to make use of it only on Easter Day. During the eleventh or twelfth

---

[1] No doubt the same usage in the Gallican and Mozarabic rites, already mentioned farther back, is another example of that imitation of the East so common in the rites of the West.

century the use of the *Gloria* became customary on all Sundays and feast-days and could be used by all priests.

THE GREETING AND FIRST PRAYER: In the earliest form of the preliminary service we have said that neither greeting nor prayer existed at the beginning of the service. This simple beginning is asserted to have been the case, by the *Liber Pontificalis*, even as late as in the time of Pope Celestine (*c.* A.D. 430), but it seems probable that both greeting and prayer were inserted not very much later than that date. The introduction of a prayer in this place seems to have been owing to Egyptian influence—as suggested farther back.[1] In the Egyptian rite the greeting (in both Greek and Coptic) is 'Peace to all'; in the Roman it is *Dominus vobiscum* ('The Lord be with you' or *Pax vobis*—'Peace be unto you'). These were recited immediately before the first lesson and were connected with it. In the Byzantine rite (Constantinople) the greeting was chanted immediately after the entrance. At Milan the greeting—*Dominus vobiscum*, without *Oremus*—was chanted before the first prayer (called *super populum*—'over the people'), which preceded the first lesson. But in the other Western rites (Gallican and Mozarabic) the greeting without any prayer came immediately before the lessons till later in their history. Thus it seems likely that the Roman collect (to give it the now accepted title, apart from the liturgical text) was derived from the Egyptian prayer, at least as far as its *position* in the Mass is concerned. This arrangement in the Egyptian rite seems to have been an independent, local arrangement. In Sarapion's *Euchologion* (the earliest form of the Egyptian liturgy) the synaxis begins with a prayer entitled 'First Prayer of the Lord's [Day]', and this prayer comes just before the lessons, and is, in fact, a petition for grace to interpret the Scriptures. (Dix, pp. 446 and 447.) As Dix puts it, this prayer is "by its position, the earliest 'collect' we possess". He says also that at first sight a prayer in such a position seems to be completely opposed to the accepted rule that no corporate prayer should be made in the presence

---

[1] This suggestion made by Dix, in his book quoted in these pages, is denied by the author of *Missarum Solemnia*, who upholds the connection between collect and litany or *Kyrie eleison*. (*Tome Deuxième*: French transl. p. 11, footnote 17. Paris, 1952.)

of the catechumens and others who were not yet members of the Faithful. But it is possible that, as it was a prayer *for* those present at the Liturgy rather than *with* them (that is, one in which they took an active part), it was not considered to be a transgression of the rule.

The chief difference between the Roman and Egyptian collect is that the former is variable, according to feasts or liturgical seasons, and seems to have been so from its introduction into the Liturgy. The latter, however, was always invariable. The Roman collect *may* have begun life as invariable like the Egyptian, and have become variable only with the development of the liturgical year; but there is no evidence of this.

That the Roman rite may have taken the introductory collect from Egypt would not be surprising, for there are so many other striking points of resemblance between the two rites. For example, in the Egyptian liturgy the anaphora begins with the greeting: 'The Lord be [always] with you', instead of the usual longer form of the other Eastern rites, and these words, except for the one word 'always', are the same as the Roman form: *Dominus vobiscum* ('The Lord be with you'). The Egyptian rite, it is true, later on adopted the Byzantine form of entrance, but without losing its own peculiarity, the collect.

Some liturgical writers have taken it for granted that because the *oratio* or collect came immediately after the litany before the hymn (the *Gloria in excelsis*) was introduced, the collect was originally the 'summing-up' prayer of the litany, and that the insertion of the *Gloria* between litany and collect is a mistake, owing to a lack of knowledge of the older ways.[1] Others think that this is not the case, but that the collect was really connected with the lessons and not with the litany, and the insertion of the *Gloria* between it and the litany is more correctly regarded as *proof* that it had nothing to do with the latter.

Besides the collect, we find, about this period, the introduction of three other similar prayers in the Roman rite and in the other Western rites also.

THE PRAYER AFTER THE GOSPEL: This was a prayer of the same type as the *oratio* or collect, and it was placed after the

---

[1] See *ante*, reference to *Missarum Solemnia*.

Gospel—that is, after the intercessions, as long as these were still in their original place there. It seems to have formed the opening prayer to the Eucharist proper.[1] It was peculiar to the Western rite, and none of the Eastern rites had anything like it. The best examples of this prayer are found in the Ambrosian rite (in which it is still used in every Mass) and in the MSS. of the Gallican and Mozarabic rites. In the Roman rite there is no direct mention of such a prayer, but what seems to be an actual relic of it exists in the *Dominus vobiscum* and *Oremus* sung or said in every Mass after the Gospel (or creed, when this is said), but which is now followed only by the offertory anthem and not by any prayer. In his edition of the Gelasian Sacramentary, Mr. H. A. Wilson says that this Sacramentary (which is of earlier date than the Gregorian) generally · gives *two* prayers before the lessons, while the Gregorian never provides more than one. Mr. Wilson continues: "in every case, the later Gregorian Sacramentary leaves out the *second* of the two collects. This seems to show that the two collects in the Gelasian Sacramentary were not two collects before the Epistle, but that the second was the prayer after the Gospel, which disappeared in the Gregorian—leaving the *Dominus vobiscum* and *Oremus* behind" (*The Gelasian Sacramentary* (Oxford: The Clarendon Press, 1894) p. lxxiv—in a footnote). Dom Gregory Dix also takes this view, and says that a certain number of these second collects in the Gelasian are actually to be found in the Milanese rite as *orationes super sindonem*, the latter being the special title given to this prayer in the Milanese rite. The title *oratio super sindonem* means 'the prayer over the linen cloth', that is the 'corporal' spread on the altar at the offertory, on which the chalice and host were placed.[2] The Rev. V. L. Kennedy, C.S.B.(Toronto), in an article entitled, 'The Two Collects of the Gelasian' in *Miscellanea Liturgica in honorem L. Cuniberti Mohlberg, O.S.B.*, Vol. I (Edizioni Liturgiche, Roma, 1948), makes a different suggestion. He says that: "the normal pre-Gregorian Mass involved two readings before the Gospel and that each was preceded by a prayer". He thinks that the

---

[1] As distinguished from the preliminary service (synaxis).

[2] The word *sindon* is of Greek origin, and means fine linen or muslin. In the Ambrosian rite there is no *oremus* before the prayer—nor before *any* of the collects in that rite.

introduction of the *Gloria in excelsis* led to the exclusion of the
first lesson with its prayer, but only to moving the first responsory psalm after the first lesson to its present place after
the *second* lesson, so that there were now two responsories (the
gradual and alleluia or tract) after this lesson. Fr. Kennedy
gives an example of the old use from the Gelasian Sacramentary
in the Good Friday Mass of the Presanctified. In this Sacramentary the rubric on Good Friday orders the collect *Deus a
quo et Iudas* (preceded by *Oremus, flectamus genua* and *levate*—'Let
us pray; let us bend the knees; arise') at the very beginning,
before the first lesson. After the lesson and its responsory, follows *Oremus*, etc., and another collect, which begins *Deus quo
peccati veteris hereditarium mortem*; then the second lesson and
responsory; the Passion and the intercessions. According to the
writer, this rubric explains the two prayers in the Gelasian
Sacramentary in ordinary Masses.

Fr. Kennedy mentions the view already referred to, held
by others[1] and originally suggested by Edmund Bishop in his
'Genius of the Roman Rite', namely that the second of the two
Gelasian collects is the Roman equivalent of the Ambrosian
oratio super sindonem; but he says of it: "Unfortunately there is
no corroborative evidence from Rome itself, save the presence
of the two collects in the Gelasian and the survival of the greeting and the *oremus* before the offertory." He refers to an article
entitled 'Le Pape Gélase et la Messe Romaine' in the *Revue
d'Histoire Ecclésiastique*, 35 (1939), 31, which upholds the view
originally put forth by the Abbé Duchesne in his *Christian
Worship*, chap. vi, 'The Roman Mass,' p. 172 (S.P.C.K., 1949,
last reprint), namely that the above *Dominus vobiscum* and
Oremus after the Gospel is a survival of the intercessions. But
the objection against this theory is that there is no *Dominus
vobiscum* (and apparently never was) before these intercessory
prayers. It seems that *Dominus vobiscum* presupposes a beginning
of some description, whereas the intercessions were really the
end of the original service, and their form was not changed
when they came to be regarded as a part of the Eucharist

---

[1] See Dix, pp. 488 ff. This writer calls it 'The Prayer of the Day' as it varied with
the days, feasts, etc., and was in this very similar to the collect at the beginning of
Mass.

proper, since this rite *began* with the Kiss of Peace. In the Ambrosian rite the *Oratio super sindonem* marks the beginning of the Eucharist—as the first prayer before the lessons—called, in the Ambrosian rite, the *Oratio super populum* ('prayer over the people')—marks the beginning of the whole united service. Finally, it may also be pointed out that the Gelasian Sacramentary is, to a certain extent, gallicanised and the two prayers on Good Friday—one of which, as we have seen, is said in the Mass of the Presanctified of the revised Roman Missal—are decidedly Gallican in character and are not in the typical Roman short and terse style. The idea of the 'Prayer of the Day' as the explanation of the second of the Gelasian collects seems, on the whole, the most likely one, and it is strengthened by the existence, not only of the *Oratio super sindonem* in the Milanese rite, but of precisely similar prayers (different, however, in style from either the Roman or Milanese forms) in the Gallican and Spanish rites, found in the same place in the Mass; that is, after the Gospel. These prayers, too, were considered to be the *first prayer* of the Eucharist proper. As to the reason for the disappearance of the prayer from the Roman rite, this may be another example of the practical nature of the Roman liturgy, opposing the *un*-practical nature of two prayers fulfilling the same purpose—especially after synaxis and Eucharist had been welded together into one service which needed only one beginning. In the Ambrosian rite, to this day the two prayers (*Oratio super populum* and *Super sindonem*) are almost indistinguishable in character. Years ago, in an article in the *Dublin Review*, Father Lucas, S.J., suggested that the prayer after the Gospel had not been completely *dropped*, but had merely *moved back*, before the epistle, to serve as the opening of the now united service. The special interest of the 'prayer of the day' is double: first, as being common to all the Western rites and absent from all the Eastern rites; secondly, from its position between the synaxis and Eucharist and before the offertory, it appears that its introduction must go back to the period before the union of the two services, but (since it was variable) after the development of the liturgical year. The author of *The Shape of the Liturgy* suggests "round about A.D. 420–30" as a probable date (Dix, p. 492).

THE LATER CHANTS OF THE ROMAN MASS: The primitive chants between the lessons were reduced to two in the later Roman rite—the 'gradual' and 'Alleluia' or 'Tract' (in penitential seasons). The name 'gradual' (in Latin, *graduale*) was given to the first responsory, as it was sung—at first by deacons, later by special cantors—from the steps (in Latin *gradus*) of the pulpit called *ambo* (from the Greek *anabaino*, meaning to go up) from which the lessons were read in the Roman basilica,[1] that is the churches in Rome, either halls of justice converted into churches, or built in the same style as these halls. We have already seen in Chapter II, pp. 34 and 35, that the Alleluia (in Hebrew, *hallelujah*), originally used in the synagogue by the cantor as the signal for the people to join in the refrain during the psalmody, became in Christian use a distinct chant like that of the gradual, verses from the psalms being added to the word *alleluia*. These verses from the psalms in the Roman rite may have been taken from the Byzantine liturgy during the seventh century. This latter rite began to reduce the number of lessons from three to two (by suppressing the first, from the Old Testament) in the fifth century, and in the late fifth or early sixth centuries, Rome also reduced its lessons in general to two, although the old number of three was kept up for Ember Wednesdays and two other Wednesdays in Lent, and on Ember Saturdays there are even six lessons (counting the epistle) besides the Gospel. Sometimes (e.g. on the week-days of Lent) the one lesson before the Gospel is from the Old Testament, the epistle or other New Testament lesson in this case being dropped. While three was originally the normal number for the lessons in the East, there were and still are, as with the Copts, examples in some of the Eastern rites of a larger number. Although the alleluia seems to have always been a part of the first responsory (gradual) and not a separate chant moved after the gradual when the first lesson was discarded, this *was* done in the case of the tract which was always separate from the gradual and, according to Dix, possibly the oldest Christian form of the psalmody used between the

---

[1] A Greek word meaning 'kingly' or 'royal hall'; then applied to any fine building.

lessons.[1] After the development of the alleluia-verse, the tract was regarded as penitential in character, and so was laid down for use during Lent when the joyful alleluia was forbidden: *these chants are 'primitive' elements of the liturgy*; but besides the introit already mentioned, two other chants were introduced in the Roman rite and other Western rites and in the Eastern as well. One was sung while the bread and wine was being collected and taken to the altar, this chant being known as the 'offertory' (in Latin, *Offertorium*); the second was sung while the people were receiving communion, this chant being also called 'communion' (*Communio*). The introit—which was introduced probably earlier than the other two—consisted of the chant of a whole psalm with an antiphon, a Greek word meaning 'to answer', and so, in singing, alternate chants. The antiphon as a distinct thing in itself was a verse from the psalms or from other parts of Holy Scripture, which was sung before the psalm, repeated after each verse, and at the end, before and after the *Gloria Patri* ('Glory be to the Father', etc.), when this doxology was introduced into the psalmody. This method of chanting the psalms was very similar to the responsorial method spoken of farther back. The difference between the two seems to have been that in the responsory the refrain was not repeated *in full* each time, but, alternately, the whole verse and only a few words of it. In the psalm with an antiphon, the latter was repeated in full each time. In later times the introit was reduced to an antiphon followed by one verse of a psalm, the *Gloria Patri* and the antiphon repeated; in mediæval rites the antiphon was still repeated before and after the Gloria, as in early days. The offertory-chant was originally a responsory, like the older chants between the lessons, but it was reduced later to an antiphon without even the verse of a psalm—except in Requiem Masses, in which, though not taken from the psalms, the offertory is responsorial *in form*. The chant sung during the communion of the congregation was like the introit, a psalm with antiphon, and has also been reduced to a mere antiphon or anthem. It is now chanted *after* the communion. All these

---

[1] In the Good Friday Liturgy there are *two* tracts—one after each lesson before the Passion. The title 'tract' (in Latin, *tractus*) is from the Latin word *traho—ĕre—tractum*—'drawn out'—because this chant was sung by one singer alone, and without repetitions.

reductions were due both to the shortening of the procession into the church, and to the gradual lessening and final disappearance of the offering by the congregation (and also of less frequent communions), especially during solemn Mass.[1]

OTHER PRAYERS INTRODUCED: Besides the 'collect' and the 'prayer of the day', we have about the same period three others: the prayer at the offertory called *Secreta* ('secret') in the Gelasian Sacramentary; *Oratio super oblata* ('prayer over the offerings') in the Gregorian Sacramentary,; the prayer of thanksgiving after communion, called *Postcommunio*—no doubt originally it was entitled *Oratio post communionem* ('prayer after communion')—and, finally, the prayer now used only on weekdays in Lent, after the postcommunion, called *Oratio super populum* ('prayer over the people', formerly also *ad plebem*—'addressed to the people'). This title is the same as that used in the Ambrosian rite for the first prayer of the Mass, before the lessons, but the Roman prayer is quite different in meaning and origin.

All these prayers are really outward special insistences upon elements already included in the Eucharistic Prayer as a whole, viz. the *offering* of the bread and wine for the Sacrifice; *thanksgiving* for the sacred food and drink; the *blessing* bestowed upon all who assisted in the Sacrifice.

The Secret: This prayer, which indicates the offerings of the Church for use in the Sacrifice, is distinguished from the other prayers of the collect-form by the fact that it possesses neither *Dominus vobiscum* nor *Oremus*, and that it is,[2] and apparently always was, recited secretly, hence its name. It is true that before the prayer the celebrant turns to the people and says *aloud* (but not *chanting*) the words *Orate fratres* ('Pray, brethren'); the continuing words *ut meum ac vestrum sacrificium acceptabile fiat apud Deum Patrem omnipotentem* ('that my sacrifice and yours may prove acceptable in the eyes of God the almighty Father') being

---

[1] It might be added: owing to the introduction of 'low Mass', in which there was no ceremonial offering by the people and during which it was customary to receive communion—when there were any communicants.

[2] Fr. Jungmann considers that the *Dominus vobiscum* and *Oremus* after the Gospel belong to the secret (formerly, he says, chanted aloud), and that the long separation between them is a 'relic' of the silent prayer of the people.

recited secretly. But these words are not—as has been suggested—a form of *Præfatio* to the secret, like those of the Good Friday Intercessions (the *Oremus dilectissimi*). Originally only the two words, now pronounced aloud, *Orate fratres*, were said, and they were always *said*, not sung, and in a voice only loud enough to be heard by those near the altar. They seem to have been addressed originally by the chief celebrant of the Mass to the concelebrating clergy standing around the altar. They were, no doubt, a 'call to prayer'—more earnest and more united prayer—as the most sacred moment of the Mass, the canon and consecration, was approaching. The other words of this 'address' and the response (made by the subdeacon at High Mass and the server at Low Mass) were added during the Middle Ages. The silent recital of the secret was, perhaps, also partly due to the length of the offertory responsory (later antiphon); it may be again, that a feeling of the respect owing to the Eucharistic Prayer (which the secret merely *emphasised* but could not replace) kept the latter 'secret'. It has been suggested, however, that the title *Secreta* does not mean 'secret' in the sense of 'hidden' or 'silent', but really means 'set apart'. This is the *primary* meaning of the Latin word (derived from *secerno-ĕre*: 'to separate, set apart'), and secret in the sense of 'concealment' is only the secondary meaning. The former full title, then, might perhaps have been *Oratio super oblata secreta* ('prayer over the offerings set apart')—thus combining the two names found separately in the two sacramentaries.[1]

THE POSTCOMMUNION PRAYER AND THE 'PRAYER OVER THE PEOPLE': We take these two prayers together. The 'Prayer over the people' came into being *before* the postcommunion, but it was finally ousted from the everyday Mass by the latter; it is now found only in the Lenten weekday Masses. This prayer 'over the people' has always been a difficulty to liturgical scholars, and has had many and not always very helpful explanations. It is now usually explained as being the original Roman blessing at the end of the Mass—which in early days was not a mere blessing with the sign of the cross and pronunciation of the

---

[1] But see *Missarum Solemnia* (French translation, *Tome Deuxième* p. 369. 8. *La Secrète, et seq.*, see also p. 254. 10. *La Prière Ecclésiale, et seq.*).

names of the Blessed Trinity, but was a liturgical prayer, *oratio*, 'collect'—like the other prayers of the Mass described above. The author of *The Shape of the Liturgy*, while he agrees that this prayer was the original blessing in the Roman Mass, maintains that it was not at first at the very end of the service, but was placed just before the communion. This was the place for the blessing in the other Western rites—the Gallican, Spanish, Italian (outside Rome) and African—and, indeed, in all rites, Eastern also—by the end of the fourth century. He shows, too, that the blessing in this position in the Roman Mass is actually mentioned by a Roman writer in the late fourth century (*c.* 385). This writer was known as 'Ambrosiaster' (i.e. pseudo-Ambrose), because his commentary on the Pauline Epistles, from which he omitted Hebrews, was at first ascribed to St. Ambrose and included among his writings. His real name is not certain, but Dom Germain Morin, O.S.B., suggests that he was a distinguished layman of consular dignity, called by the resounding names—Decimus Hilarianus Hilarius! (See the *Catholic Encyclopædia*, Vol. I, A–Assize; article 'Ambrosiaster', by Francis J. Schaefer). Ambrosiaster says: "The priests, whom we call bishops,[1] have a form drawn up and handed down to them in solemn words, and they bless men by applying this to them—and though a man be holy, yet he bends his head to receive the blessing' (Ambrosiaster: *Quæst.* 109; see Dix, p. 518). The *Oratio super populum* or *ad plebem* is preceded, not only by the usual *Oremus* of all such prayers, but also by the proclamation (sung by the deacon at High Mass): *Humiliate capita vestra Deo* ('Bow down your heads to God'), and these words are at least suggested by Ambrosiaster when he says: "and though a man be holy, yet he *bends his head* to receive the blessing"; the Roman words are also analogous to those used by the deacon before the communion blessing in some of the Eastern rites to-day. Dix says, too: "The fact that the Roman rite in the fifth century always had a blessing before communion appears to be certain." In a footnote on this page he refers us to Dom Ménard's note on the 'Gregorian Sacramentary' (*M.P.L.*, lxxviii, 286–8; Dix, p. 518). The posi-

---

[1] This blessing was reserved for bishops—who were still the usual celebrants of the Mass at this period.

tion of this 'prayer over the people' after the postcommunion prayer instead of before communion (as we find it now on Lenten ferias), may have been due to the introduction of the postcommunion—sometime during the fifth century. Formerly, the 'prayer over the people' before communion had been the last prayer of the Mass, for the latter ended with the general communion which was not followed by any other prayer. But when the special prayer of thanksgiving after communion was introduced, it may have seemed more fitting that the solemn blessing should now be placed after the thanksgiving prayer, and so conclude the whole service. The fact, too, that many of the 'prayers over the people' were hardly distinguishable from the postcommunion prayers—only a certain number of these prayers express clearly the notion of blessing—may have led to their being dropped altogether in the everyday Mass, as being practically redundant. The survival in the Lenten weekday Masses is another example, as Dix puts it, that Lent is "a season when archaisms are apt to survive in all rites" (Dix, p. 521).

A SUMMARY OF THE ROMAN MASS RITE: For clearness' sake we give here an outline of the above study of Roman liturgical history:

(i) *The Introit*: A psalm with antiphon sung during the entry of the officiating clergy (introduced by Pope Celestine I, A.D. 422–82).

(ii) (*a*) *The Litany*: A series of petitions for 'all sorts and conditions' of people; based on an Eastern form, but of 'local (Roman) manufacture'. (Almost certainly introduced by Pope St. Gelasius I, A.D. 494–6.)

(*b*) *The Ninefold 'Kyrie Eleison'*: These Greek words were repeated thus: *Kyrie eleison* three times; *Christe eleison*, three times; *Kyrie eleison*, again three times. These ejaculations took the place of the long litany, at least on feast-days, in the time of St. Gregory the Great (A.D. 540–604). It was St. Gregory, probably, who finally suppressed the long litany, and who ordered the number nine.

(iii) *The 'Gloria in Excelsis'*: This hymn is of Eastern origin, and used in the East in the Divine Office, not in the Eucharistic Liturgy. It was introduced by Pope Symmachus (A.D. 498–

514), to be used on Sundays and certain feasts. At first used only in papal or episcopal Masses; simple priests were allowed to use it only on Easter Day till the eleventh century, when it became customary on all Sundays and feasts.[1]

(iv) *The Greeting and Collect*: This was probably due to Egyptian influence (close relations existed between Rome and Alexandria from A.D. 430 to 435); this latter Liturgy is the only Eastern one with greeting and prayer in this position—before and connected with the lessons. The Egyptian prayer is invariable; the Roman collect variable—apparently from the beginning. This was due to the development of the liturgical year. Name 'collect' not Roman—found in Gallican rite. Roman term in Latin is *oratio*—literally a 'speech' or 'address'.

In the 'Mass of the Presanctified' on Good Friday in the Roman rite, the service still begins immediately with the lessons; the collect before the second lesson was probably a later introduction from the Gallican rite; its style is Gallican.

(v) *Psalmody between the Lessons*: This is 'primitive'—derived from the Jewish synagogue-service. There were certain changes and developments, however, in later times—e.g. two chants formerly sung separately, one after each of the two lessons before the Gospel, came to be sung together after the one lesson (Epistle or other New Testament or Old Testament lesson), the first (always from the Old Testament) being dropped in ordinary Mass in Roman rite, though retained on certain days (e.g. the lesson before the Epistle on Ember Wednesdays and five lessons before the Epistle on Ember Saturdays and the Vigil of Pentecost). The usual number of three lessons in the Mass before the Gospel was first reduced to two in the Church of Constantinople in the fifth century, and Rome followed this example in the late fifth or sixth centuries. In other Eastern and Western rites the first of the three usual lessons was discarded later than the above dates, but not everywhere. The first chant was called 'gradual' because sung on the steps (*gradus*) of the *ambo*—the pulpit in which the lessons were chanted; the 'Alleluia' chant: originally the word *Alleluia* (in Hebrew, *halle-*

---

[1] Although a development of the 'Song of the Angels' at Our Lord's birth at Bethlehem, the *Gloria* was always more closely connected with Easter than with Christmas at Rome—since the latter feast was not introduced till fairly late, i.e. in A.D. 354—though observed elsewhere in the Western Church.

lujah), simply the signal for the refrain (chanted by the people) which was given by the cantor; later it became a separate chant with verses from the psalms attached to it—probably introduced in the seventh century, and possibly from Byzantine custom (three *alleluias* sung after two psalm-verses following the epistle). A chant of several verses of psalms, called *prokeimenon* ('set before'), is sung *before* the epistle—probably the relic of the responsory after the former first lesson from the Old Testament, and so equivalent to the Roman gradual.

The tract, so-called probably because it was sung slowly and protractedly by one singer, was perhaps the oldest form of psalmody used between the lessons. Later (after the development of the *alleluia* and the introduction of the Lenten season) it became the accepted form for penitential times.[1]

(vi) *The 'Prayer of the Day'*: This is a convenient title, suggested by Dom Gregory Dix, for an otherwise nameless prayer (i.e. nameless in the Roman rite), which probably followed the *Dominus vobiscum* and *Oremus* still sung or said after the Gospel or creed in the Roman Mass—but which is now followed only by the offertory anthem. The latter is not a 'prayer' in the technical sense and so there is no connection at all between them. Such a prayer is still in use in the Ambrosian rite, and there it is called *Oratio super sindonem* ('the prayer over the linen cloth', i.e. the corporal—it is said just after spreading the latter on the altar). It seems to have been a special feature of the Western rite: it is not found in any of the Eastern liturgies.

Its disuse in the later Roman rite (there is a trace of it still in the Gelasian Sacramentary) was quite likely due to the fusion of synaxis and Eucharist into one service, and the introduction of the prayer at the beginning, before the lessons. The Prayer of the Day had been the first prayer of the Eucharist, when this was still distinct from the synaxis; after the union between the two its place was filled by the collect before the lessons, and so it became redundant.

(vii) *The Offertory Anthem* (in Latin, *Offertorium*): This chant, like the introit (and also the communion anthem) is one of the later introductions and was introduced to 'fill up time' while

---

[1] The tract is now always sung in alternate verses by each side of the choir—or by cantors and choir.

something else was being done—in this case while the people were bringing their offerings of bread and wine to the sanctuary entrance. It is first mentioned by St. Augustine in Africa (*Retractationes*, II, 11 and 17). It was originally a responsorial chant, but afterwards was reduced to an antiphon or anthem. The responsorial form is still used in Requiem Masses, although the text is not taken from the psalms. The offertory was probably adopted in Rome (together with the communion anthem) in the fifth century—later than the introit, however (Dix, pp. 492 and 493 *et seq.*).

(viii) *The Offertory Prayer* (in Latin, *Oratio super oblata*, 'prayer over the offerings' or *Secreta*): At first, in pre-Nicene days, the action of placing the offerings upon the altar and then at once reciting the full Eucharistic Prayer over them was considered enough. The offertory and postcommunion prayers (like the prayer of the day and the collect before the lessons) are, as it were, clearer expressions and insistences upon the elements contained or implied in the one Eucharistic Prayer.

The term *Secreta* (in English, 'secret') seems to mean simply a 'prayer said secretly'—because of the long offering by the people and the chant of the anthem while it was taking place. There is no *Dominus vobiscum* or *Oremus*—these words which, as we have seen, come after the Gospel or creed have another explanation—and in any case they are separated from the secret by the offertory anthem. The secret, like the collect (*oratio*), is variable according to the feast or liturgical season. The address—*Orate fratres*—made by the celebrant aloud but not chanted, before the secret, was originally made by the Pope or bishop to the concelebrating clergy standing round the altar and so pronounced in a low voice, for them alone. Next came the preface and canon (which are treated in a separate chapter); then we have the communion anthem (in Latin, *Communio*)—the same type of chant as the offertory anthem and introduced about the same date.

(ix) *The Postcommunio and the Oratio super populum*: It seems certain that in the fifth century there was in the Roman rite, as in the other rites, Eastern and Western, a prayer of blessing pronounced by the celebrating bishop over the people just before communion. This prayer was preceded by a proclamation addressed to the people by the deacon 'to bow down their heads before God'. Such a prayer of blessing still exists in the Roman rite, but only in the weekday Masses in Lent, and then, at the very end of Mass, after the postcommunion. This change of place was perhaps due to the introduction—towards the end of the fifth century—of the special prayer for thanksgiving after communion, the *Postcommunio*,[1] and so the Prayer over the people became the final blessing of the Mass. But as it often was a kind of second thanksgiving prayer after communion, it was dropped as redundant and later its place as a blessing was taken by the actual form now used—no longer a complete 'prayer', as were the ancient forms of blessing. The Lenten 'prayer over the people' is preceded by the 'proclamation' chanted by the deacon—or at Low Mass said by the priest himself—which is identical with that used in the fifth century—at least in meaning (Dix, p. 518).

THE BLESSING AT THE END: Now consists in the sign of the cross made over the congregation with the accompanying words: *Benedicat vos omnipotens Deus: Pater et Filius et Spiritus sánctus* ('May almighty God, Father, Son and Holy Ghost, bless you'). It was derived from the blessing given by the Pope as he passed through the basilica after the solemn Mass, in the eighth century. The blessing is only *recited* by a priest even at High Mass, but is *sung* by a bishop—with mitre and pastoral staff. A metropolitan gives the blessing with *uncovered* head and his cross is held before him.

---

[1] No doubt, as remarked farther back, the original full title of this prayer was *oratio post communionem* ('prayer after communion'). In Latin, 'communio' should really be 'communio*nem*'—in the accusative case following the word *post* ('after').

CHAPTER IV

THE COMPLETED RITE IN OTHER PARTS OF THE WEST

THAT venerable and learned monk of Solesmes, Dom Paul Cagin, always maintained that the Gallican and Spanish (Mozarabic) rites were really earlier forms of the Western Liturgy from which the Roman rite of the seventh (or, perhaps, sixth) century, found in the Gelasian Sacramentary, was a later departure; and he upheld this view with much learning.[1] It must be remembered, however, that the existing texts of these rites are not earlier than the sixth century, and they therefore give us a form of the liturgy which is as much a later development as that of the Roman sacramentaries. It is true, nevertheless, that these rites have preserved certain ancient features more faithfully than the Roman rite—although the really ancient features of the latter still underlie the later additions, and can still be discovered and separated from these additions. Besides the comparatively late date of the Gallican and Spanish texts, there is also the fact that both rites have borrowed certain elements from Eastern rites—so much so that the author of *Christian Worship* (the English translation of *Les Origines du Culte Chrétien*), the learned Mgr. Duchesne, considered that the two rites were simply Eastern liturgies introduced into the West. This theory is no longer held by any liturgical authority; the Gallican and Mozarabic rites seem to be essentially Western in character,

---

[1] In a work entitled, *Te Deum ou Illatio* (Solesmes, 1906)—this title should be translated, *Te Deum—hymn or Illatio*—the latter being the name for the Eucharistic Prayer in the Mozarabic rite—Dom Cagin maintained the theory that the *Te Deum* was not an ordinary hymn, but an early form of the Eucharistic Prayer. This theory was strongly contested by Dom Germain Morin of Maredsous in Belgium, at the time. To-day it is interesting to see that in a fairly recent pamphlet— *Eucharistic Consecration in the Primitive Church* (London: 1948, S.P.C.K.), the author, G. A. Michell, seems to regard the *Te Deum*—if not in itself a form of Eucharistic Prayer, at least as founded upon and adapted from the early Western Prayer, and as giving an example of the combination of the older form with its long series of thanksgivings and the later form with its 'preface' and threefold *Sanctus*—a combination which, he believes, took place towards the end of the fourth century and which finally led to the abandonment of the thanksgiving series. (See pp. 31 and 32.)

and the Eastern elements are simply the results of later local contacts with the East—and the same applies to the Eastern features in the Ambrosian rite. This latter rite is still considered by some authorities to be essentially Gallican (in the above sense), with Roman additions. By others it is regarded, on the contrary, as being essentially Roman in character, with later Gallican interpolations. The rite followed in North Italy and in Celtic countries, and also in Africa, together with those of Gaul (that is, France, Switzerland and part of Germany—this latter was the real 'Gallican rite' in the literal sense and not in the really incorrect 'extended sense' used by Dom Cagin and others) and in Spain, are all local forms of one 'Western rite'. The Roman and Ambrosian or Milanese rites (the latter is probably an early type of the former) are also local forms of this Western rite. But it is an undoubted fact that the Roman rite—especially as regards the Canon (and on this point the Ambrosian rite also)—remains somewhat of a puzzle. The differences between it and its Ambrosian 'brother-rite' and all other Western rites are not only very marked, but there is also absolutely no evidence obtainable as yet as to *how* or *why* or *when* these differences came about. Nevertheless, great advance has been made of late years in the explanation of its history and in 'clearing out' later additions from the more primitive elements—especially, again, in the Canon.

The Introduction in the Developed Gallican Rite: The account given by Pseudo-Germanus of Paris is not to be relied on—at least, as far as the general use is concerned; it probably applies to certain special places and at a late date.

The developed introduction was as follows: (i) an entrance-chant taken from the East—the *Trisagion* ('The Threefold Holy': 'Holy God, Holy Strong One, Holy Immortal One, have mercy on us')—which is used in the Roman rite only on Good Friday during the Adoration of the Cross. (ii) *Kyrie eleison* chanted three times, and as a chant, not as a litany. Dix suggests that possibly St. Gregory the Great, when he introduced the ninefold *Kyrie* and *Christe eleison* into the Roman Mass in place of the long litany put in by St. Gelasius, may have got the idea from the above arrangement in the Gallican rites, and therefore have intended to bring in a 'chant' as in Gaul, rather than a short form of litany. He points out, too, that as a matter of fact the Greek *Kyrie eleison* was not the response of the people in Gelasius' litany, but the Latin form *Domine miserere*. Dom Gregory Dix insists, too, in another place, that a true litany implies a series of petitions in short form given out by celebrant or deacon to which the congregation reply with *Kyrie eleison* or some such short cry of appeal to God. He deplores the loose way in which the word litany is used in the case of prayers, which are not true litanies at all—for example, the 'Solemn Prayers' (*Orationes solemnes*), after the Passion in the Good Friday Mass of the Presanctified. In these prayers the people's part, apart from the *Amen*, was prayer in complete *silence* and the *præfatio* (a species of proclamation announced by the celebrant) was of some length—in fact, the 'collect', an entirely different type of prayer. (iii) Next came the canticle *Benedictus*[1] (Luke i 68–79). (iv) The *Greeting* and *Collect*. After this collect came the *lessons* with their responsory-psalms. Before the earlier chants described above had been introduced, the synaxis began with the lessons themselves, and the number of these latter was very varied, as there was no special rule. But in time—that is, towards the end of the fourth century—the number three became usual: Old Testament; Epistles or Acts; Gospel. In Spain and Gaul, instead of the Old Testament lessons, one taken from 'acts' of the martyrs was read on their feast-days. A responsory taken from the psalms was sung, in Gaul apparently, between the second lesson and the Gospel, the first two lessons having no responsory between them.[2]

THE GALLICAN EUCHARIST: This began, as probably in Rome in early times and as at Milan even at the present day, with the 'prayer of the day'—originally the first prayer of the Mass. In the Gallican rite, and originally in the Spanish, the full 'collect-type' of prayer is found—including the *præfatio* or admonition by the celebrant to the congregation to pray for

[1] The *Benedictus* takes the place of the Roman *Gloria in excelsis* as the hymn before the collect; in the sixth century the *Gloria* was used at Lauds—exact contrary to Roman usage, in short (Dix, p. 467.)

[2] After the Gospel, a litany, called *prex* ('the prayer') was chanted 'for all sorts and conditions'. This litany of Eastern character had ousted the old intercessory collects relegated to Holy Week.

certain intentions laid down; the silent prayer of the congregation, followed by the 'summing-up' prayer of the celebrant. In the Gallican Mass the rubric indicates the *Præfatio Missæ* ('preface *of the Mass*'—as this prayer was reckoned as the first, in *dignity* at least, after others had been added before it); then, after the silent prayer of the people, *Collectio sequitur* ('the collect'—i.e. the prayer proper—'follows'). The full, original title is given in the Gallican texts, though *collectio* afterwards degenerated into *collecta*). In the Spanish rite the titles were: *Missa*—for the *Præfatio* and *Alia oratio* ('another prayer') instead of *Collectio*. The first title is a 'corruption' of the full title, *Præfatio missæ*; the second is due to the fact that in later times the *Præfatio* often became itself a prayer, its ancient signification and the ancient character of a collect being forgotten. This change took place in the case of the other liturgical collects also. In the Spanish rite most of the *præfationes* have been dropped altogether. After the above prayer followed the recitation of the 'Names'—that is, of those who had presented offerings of bread and wine for the Mass and, in later days, also of the dead—the 'waiting ones' (*pausantium*); this part of the Mass will be treated in detail in Chapter VII. Then came a rubric, *post nomina* ('after the names'), indicating the *Præfatio* of the following collect called *Ad pacem* ('with regard to—or for—peace'), as this prayer was the preparation for giving the Kiss of Peace. It also often included mention of the offerings of bread and wine. Later the rubric *post nomina* became the title of the *Præfatio*— now changed into a prayer, as in the case of the following collect. Then began the 'Eucharistic Prayer', called, in the Gallican rites, *Immolatio* ('sacrifice'). This was the equivalent of the Roman *Præfatio* ('preface'), leading up to the threefold *Sanctus* and the Canon. After the *Sanctus* in the Gallican Mass, came a prayer usually beginning with the words: *Vere sanctus, vere benedictus Filius tuus, Dominus noster Jesus Christus*, etc., linking up the *Immolatio* and *Sanctus* with the consecratory portion. The prayer itself was usually fairly short and leading directly to the words of institution. These in the texts are of the Eastern form—*in qua nocte tradebatur* ('in the same night in which He was betrayed'), but this seems to have been merely another example of the Gallican and Mozarabic tendency to borrow from the Eastern rites, for the prayer following the account of the institution is often preceded by a rubric *post pridie* ('After [the words:] on the day before [He suffered]'), a clear sign of the original usage. This prayer, *Post pridie*,[1] ends with a text just before the Breaking of Bread closely resembling that in the Roman Canon: *Per quem hæc omnia*, etc. (which will be discussed in full in a later chapter); a chant called *confractorium* was sung during the Fraction, replaced on certain days by the Creed. The Bread was broken during the Creed—when the latter was sung. The Fraction was very elaborate and highly developed. The Lord's Prayer followed immediately, preceded by a little *Præfatio*, and followed by a prayer beginning with the words *Libera nos*—or words to that effect.

Next came the blessing prayer before Communion preceded by an admonition from the deacon to the people to bow down for it—there was a special form of blessing for a bishop. After this blessing came the communion of celebrant and people. A chant was sung during the celebrant's communion and, after that of the people, a thanksgiving collect was chanted. This collect was called *Consummatio Missæ* ('consummation' or 'completion' of the Mass), and was preceded by an admonition called *Postcommunionem* (perhaps this also was the original arrangement of the Roman prayer after communion). Between the *Præfatio* and the collect itself was the silent prayer of the congregation.

The Mass ended with a dismissal pronounced by the deacon after the celebrant had said *Dominus sit semper vobiscum* and the people had responded *et cum spiritu tuo*. The Gallican form of this dismissal is not known; it may have been as in the Stowe Missal: *Missa acta est in pace* ('The Mass is enacted [i.e. 'completed'] in peace').

All the prayers, and, in fact, almost every part of the Mass, were variable in the Gallican and Spanish rites, and they changed almost every day. Both this variability and the length of the prayers were developed to an exaggerated extent, some of the *præfationes* to the collects being really long theological treatises, and the same is true of even the actual prayers them-

[1] This is a prayer of oblation. It sometimes includes an 'invocation' of the Holy Ghost and originally a prayer for communicants also.

selves. This is very marked in comparison with the sober dignity
of the Roman collects. In the latter rite the variability is reduced to a comparatively small number of formulas, and in the
case of the Canon is reserved for a few parts only and for special
occasions (e.g. Easter, Pentecost). In the Roman collect, too,
the *Præfatio* was quite early reduced to the one word *Oremus* ('let
us pray'), except in the case of the old form of intercessions still
found on Good Friday, and in the ordination Masses.

THE COMPLETED RITE AT MILAN: The Ambrosian rite at
Milan closely resembles that of Rome, differences being found
chiefly in the names or terms used for the same types of prayers
and chants. It is *still in use*, unlike the Gallican rites.[1]

The Introductory Chant: This is an *antiphon* usually taken from
the psalms. But this antiphon has no added verse or verses, nor
Gloria Patri, as in the Roman rite. The title is *Ingressa* ('entrance'); then, on the Sundays of Lent, comes a litany of
Eastern type chanted by the deacon and answered by the people with the words *Domine miserere*, followed immediately by
Dominus vobiscum. There are two forms of litany in use: one on
the first, third and fifth Sundays, the other on the second and
fourth. On other days the *Gloria in excelsis* is chanted in this
place. After the latter, or after the litany, *Kyrie eleison* is sung
three times—but as a *chant* and not in any way connected with
a litany.

The Greeting—Dominus vobiscum: This is followed immediately,
and without *Oremus*, by a prayer called: *Oratio super populum*
('prayer over the people'). This prayer is analogous to the
Roman *Oratio* before the epistle, and not to the prayer of the
above name recited in the Roman rite in ferial Masses of Lent,
after the Postcommunion. The greeting *Dominus vobiscum* is
used about ten times during the Mass, but the celebrant never
turns to the people when chanting or reciting it, and *Oremus* is
never used at all.[2] This rite, in fact, has gone one step farther
than the Roman rite: not only is the *Præfatio* of the old form of
the collect reduced to the mere word *Oremus* as in Rome, but
even that word itself is suppressed.

---

[1] The Spanish rite *is* used still, but only in one special chapel at Toledo.

[2] See Dix, p. 491. It is said here that 'Let us pray' (*oremus*) is said before the
'prayer of the day' (at Milan, called *Oratio super sindonem*), but this is a mistake.

On many days of the year there are two lessons before the Gospel: the first is usually taken from the Prophets or other parts of the Old Testament, but on Sundays in Eastertide from the Acts of the Apostles, and on some saints' feasts from the life of the saint. Each lesson is preceded by a special blessing given by the celebrant at the request of the reader—for the epistle the subdeacon first sings the title and *then* asks for the blessing. After the first lesson is sung a responsory called *Psalmellus* ('little psalm'), usually consisting of one or two verses from the psalms; the epistle is followed by *Hallelujah* with a verse—again usually taken from the psalms. On solemn days the word *Hallelujah* is doubled. In Lent and other penitential seasons this joyful chant is replaced by a chant called *cantus* ('chant') resembling the Roman tract. On some solemn feasts (e.g. Christmas and Epiphany) a chant, called *Antiphona ante Evangelium* ('Antiphon before the Gospel'), is sung after the *Hallelujah*. The blessing for the Gospel is given to the deacon by the celebrant after the former has sung *Dominus vobiscum* and has announced the Gospel. After the Gospel the celebrant chants: *Dominus vobiscum* again, and *Kyrie eleison* (except in a Requiem Mass) is sung three times; then again comes *Dominus vobiscum* and the *Oratio super sindonem* ('the prayer over the linen cloth'—i.e. the corporal, now already spread on the altar). Then the *Antiphona post Evangelium* ('antiphon after the Gospel') is sung—it is analogous to the Roman *Offertorium* ('offertory chant'). After the preparation of the bread and wine, which takes place during this chant, another chant, formerly called *Offerenda* but now, as in Rome, *Offertorium*, is sung. The two chants were once sung in immediate succession, but are now separated by the private offertory prayers (of mediæval introduction), said by the celebrant. After the first chant—the *Antiphona post Evangelium*—the deacon, turning to the people, sings *Pacem habete* ('May you have peace'). The people now reply: *Ad te Domine* ('To Thee, O Lord'), which hardly makes sense, but formerly the deacon also sang: *Erigite vos ad orationem* ('Rise up for prayer'); that is, for 'the prayer for peace' and for giving the *Kiss of Peace*, which originally took place here, the more primitive position. As we have seen, it was given *originally*, even before the bread and wine were brought to the altar (cf. the Liturgy described by St. Justin (see pp. 16 to 18). The Kiss of Peace is given now at Milan before communion, as in the Roman rite. The offerings of bread and wine by two old men and two old women (representatives of the School of St. Ambrose, which consists of ten old men and ten old women known as the *Vecchioni*) are made at this moment in the metropolitan church— as in ancient times in Rome and elsewhere. Their offerings are received by the celebrant and sacred ministers at the entrance of the sanctuary. Three altar-breads and one silver vessel of white wine are presented by each old man and old woman. The incensing of the *oblata* and the altar follows; then the Creed is chanted and is followed by *Dominus vobiscum* and the *Oratio super oblata* ('prayer over the offerings')—equivalent to the Roman *Secreta* (actually called, as we have seen, by the above name in the Gregorian Sacramentary), but at Milan said aloud. The Canon—except for certain minor differences in the wording[1]—is the same as in the Roman rite. The prayer after the *Pater noster*, which begins with the word *Libera* as in the Roman rite, is chanted or recited aloud in all Masses. Before the *Pater* and during the Fraction a chant called *confractorium* is sung. The *Agnus Dei* is said only in Requiem Masses. A chant called *Transitorium* (literally 'a passage through') is sung after communion—formerly during it; this is usually taken from the Gospel texts of the day. Then comes the *Oratio post communionem* ('prayer after communion')—this was perhaps the original form of the title in the Roman rite, later shortened into *post-communio*. After the prayer, *Dominus vobiscum* is said, and then *Kyrie eleison* recited three times. The dismissals follow; these are: *Benedicat et exaudiat nos Deus* ('May God bless and hear us'), *Amen; Procedamus cum pace* ('Let us go forth with peace'); *Benedicamus Domino—Deo gratias* ('Let us bless the Lord— Thanks be to God')—the celebrant then says the prayer *Placeat*, as in the Roman rite, but addressed to *Deus* ('God') instead of *Sancta Trinitas* ('Holy Trinity'). Then the Blessing is given as in the Roman Mass. The Last Gospel, of St. John, was introduced in 1560, and *ordered* by the Council of Milan in 1576.

[1] For example, the wording of the *Qui pridie*, introducing the consecration, is always that which is used in the Roman rite only on Maundy Thursday.

THE AFRICAN AND CELTIC RITES are known of only in scattered accounts—especially in the case of the former. But they are both evidently forms of the general Western rite. When we begin to hear much about the Celtic rite in Scotland and Ireland, it is a 'conflation' between the so-called Gallican rite and the later Roman rite. In the African rite we know that— usually if not always—there were two lessons before the Gospel and psalms were chanted in between. Even in Augustine's time nothing is said about any kind of 'entrance chant', like the Roman introit—although chants during the offertory and communion are mentioned. There seem, also, to have been intercessory prayers after the Gospel. But the chief points of interest are first that, in the African rite, the names of dead individuals and a mention of the dead in general apparently both occurred during the Eucharistic Prayer, and that this was the case even as early as the second century.[1] Secondly, the position in Africa of both the Kiss of Peace and the *Pater noster*. The latter was recited after the Fraction; the former was given immediately after the recitation of the *Pater*, and was preceded by the salutation *Pax vobiscum* ('Peace be with you'). The kiss was followed by the blessing of the people before communion, as in the Gallican and Spanish rites, and formerly in the Roman rite also. This position of the Kiss of Peace in Africa and the similar position in Rome is different from the other Western and all the Eastern rites. In both the Gallican and Spanish rites the kiss was given at the beginning of the actual Eucharist—just before the offertory, and in the Eastern rites it is still placed before the anaphora. In the Roman rite, described by St. Justin, the kiss was given before the offerings were placed upon the altar, just after the intercessory prayers with which the preliminary synaxis concluded. It is not possible to decide which Church—the Roman or the African—influenced the other as to the positions of the kiss and the *Pater noster*.

---

[1] The names of *living* persons were not recited in Africa, either in the earlier period or in Augustine's time. It is not really clear—especially in what St. Augustine says about the names of the dead—whether those of any individual persons were mentioned, or whether only *certain names of special persons*—bishops, nuns (*sanctimoniales*)—were so mentioned. (See Dix, pp. 498 and 499; Srawley, p. 137.)

CHAPTER V

THE EUCHARISTIC PRAYER: PREFACE, SANCTUS AND CANON

THE Eucharistic Prayer was the bishop's special 'liturgy', as the normal celebrant surrounded by his priests as concelebrants and assisted by his deacons. The concelebration of the simple priests who shared in the full priesthood of the bishop did not apparently consist, in primitive times, of an active participation in the words and ceremonies of the liturgy, but simply in the presence near the altar as official witnesses to the bishop's sacrificial action—sharing in it by their presence and consent. But in *The Apostolic Tradition* the presbyters are more active: it is said, speaking of the Fraction during the Sunday Stational Mass in the third century: "And the presbyters also shall break the bread. And whenever the deacon approaches the presbyter he shall hold out his [vessel] and the presbyter shall himself take and deliver to the people with his hand." Some MSS. of *The Tradition* read 'robe' instead of 'vessel' here—which does not make sense. This is probably a mistake due to a confusion between the words for 'vessel' and 'dress', which are rather alike in Arabic—one of the texts is written in this language. The 'vessel' held by the deacon before the presbyter would seem, according to the editor of *The Tradition*, to refer to "a practice ascribed by the *Liber Pontificalis* (not necessarily rightly) to the institution of Pope Zephyrinus (A.D. 198–217), by which, at the Papal liturgy the concelebrating presbyters actually consecrated not on the altar with the Pope, but on glass patens held before them by the deacons". He adds that this custom was probably necessitated by the small size of the altars at that period—"two or three feet square only". In the eighth century, as we know from the *Ordo Romanus Primus*, linen corporals were used by the concelebrants instead of the glass patens (*The Apostolic Tradition of St. Hippolytus*, edited by Dom Gregory Dix, 1937, p. 44, E. 2 and p. 82, No. xxiv: 'The Stational Mass'). From the above it seems, then, that active concelebration had 'come in' in Hippolytus' time; that is, in the early third century. This active concelebration of Pope, bishops and priests lasted in Rome—at least on certain great feasts—till about the thirteenth century. In the Eastern Churches, both Orthodox and in union with Rome, concelebration is still frequently practised; for example, when a bishop celebrates pontifically, and also when several priests, or at least two, wish to celebrate at the same time where (as is usually the case) there is only one altar in the church.[1]

The oldest specimens actually existing of the Eucharistic Prayer are those of Rome, Alexandria and Antioch—the three most important Sees in pre-Nicene times. Those of North Africa, Spain and Gaul in the West, and of the churches of the Balkans and of Asia Minor in the East, were of equal antiquity, but unfortunately no texts have survived from pre-Nicene times—or from any period justifying a comparison with the three principal texts mentioned above. Nevertheless, it seems safe to say that they were all *fundamentally* alike everywhere, although certain phrases and external elements varied according to the different localities. As the author of *The Shape of the Liturgy* puts it: "Diversity of form and a fundamental identity of meaning seem to have been the mark of the old local traditions everywhere" (Dix, p. 157).

THE EARLIEST SOURCES OF INFORMATION: In the West—at Rome—(apart from the descriptions given by St. Justin in his *Apologia*) there is the text of the liturgy in the *Apostolic Tradition of St. Hippolytus* (*c.* A.D. 215). In the East the oldest source is found in Egypt—in the liturgy written by Bishop Sarapion of Thmuis. This liturgy was found in a MS. of the eleventh century, but the text itself dates from the *fourth century* (probably before A.D. 350). It seems certain that it is only a revision of an older Egyptian text, the form of which can be gathered to a certain extent from a comparison with passages concerning the Liturgy in third-century Egyptian writers (Dix, p. 162).

---

[1] Concelebration is an outward witness to the unity of the Christian Priesthood of the clergy. In it the act of consecration is carried out *personally* by each individual priest, but *all together*, at one and the same time, pronouncing the words together aloud. This latter is done only by the uniates (see *Catholic Encyclopædia*, Vol. IV, p. 190, article "Concelebration").

THE SYRIAN FORM OF EASTERN LITURGIES: This is divided
into (i) the *old rite* used in the Church of Antioch—of which very
little is known; (ii) the other early West Syrian rites; (iii) the
East Syrian rite, of which the centre was Edessa, and which
consists of the liturgies used by the Nestorians and Chaldeans;
(iv) the South Syrian rite of Jerusalem.

The Eucharistic Prayer—or 'Prayer of Oblation' as it is
called in Sarapion's Liturgy—was everywhere originally one
undivided prayer. It led from the initial series of thanksgivings
for the Divine goodness to man, up to certain petitions based,
as it were, upon the acts of thanksgiving which had been
offered first as in duty bound—*Vere dignum et justum est* ('it is
truly fitting and just'), as the Western rite has it. The *duty* of
thanksgiving thus carried out provided the *right* to make petitions to God. The petitions were concerned primarily with the
acceptance by God of the offerings made to Him by the Church,
and for their change from mere bread and wine into the Body
and Blood of His Son Jesus Christ—true victim of the sacrifice. Then, in return for this supreme act of worship, the prayer
asked that the offerers be admitted to union with God in
Christ through the consecrated offerings. At the conclusion of
the Prayer, the celebrants, ministers (deacons, acolytes, etc.)
and members of the congregation partook of the sacred food
and drink. In this undivided prayer was the complete expression of the sacrifice instituted by Our Saviour at the Last
Supper. But the textual oneness of the Prayer was gradually
obscured to a great extent by its practical division into two distinct portions, owing to the introduction of the chant of the
threefold *Sanctus*. Most liturgical authorities now consider this
chant to be of fairly late introduction, and not an original
element of the Eucharistic Prayer. It is true that Dom Odo
Casel of Maria Laach Abbey (whose recent death, referred to
in the Preface, has meant so great a loss to liturgical studies)
considered that the *Sanctus* in the Eucharistic Prayer was probably derived immediately from the use of the Jewish synagogue.[1] But this use of the *Sanctus* in the synagogue service, and

---

[1] See his book in the French translation, *Le Mémorial du Seigneur dans la Liturgie
de l'Antiquité Chrétienne: Lex Orandi.* (Les Editions du Cerf. Obtainable from Blackfriars Publications, agents for Les Editions du Cerf, Oxford.)

the form of the service itself in general at this period, is very uncertain. In the Eastern liturgies the separation of the Prayer by the *Sanctus* into two parts is less evident than in the Western rite—that is, in that of Rome—for in the other Western rites (Gallican and Mozarabic) the division of the Prayer as found in the sixth-century texts resembles more or less closely that in the Eastern rites. In both the Gallican and Spanish forms the second part of the Prayer, after the *Sanctus*, usually starts with words directly taken from the *Sanctus*—e.g. *Vere sanctus, vere benedictus*, etc. ('truly holy, truly blessed', etc.). . . .

In the Roman rite, however, there is no apparent connection at all between the first part called the 'Preface' (in Latin, *Præfatio*, before) and the second part after the *Sanctus*, known as the 'Canon'. With regard to the names of these two parts of the Prayer, Dom Bernard Botte, O.S.B., says in his *Le Canon de la Messe Romaine* that the word *Præfatio*, translated in English preface, does not mean a preface in the sense of an 'introduction' to or 'preparation' for what follows (in this case, the Canon). Both titles—Preface and Canon—were formerly each ascribed to the whole Prayer. For example: *Canon actionis*—that is, the 'rule of the [sacrificial] action'—and *Præfatio*, which latter, says Dom Botte, does not refer to time but indicates that the formula is a *solemn address* made 'before'—that is, 'in the presence of'—the Christian assembly. According to Dom Gregory Dix, however, the word *Præfatio* should be understood also in the sense of time, a 'preparation for' or 'introduction to' as above; not, however, an introduction to the Canon, but to the *Sanctus* itself, up to which it leads.[1]

INTRODUCTION OF THE SANCTUS: This introduction led to the first part of the Prayer being transformed from a series of thanksgivings to God for all His mercies into an introduction— a 'preface'—to the praises of the angelic choirs and the union of the Church therewith; the earlier series, derived from Jewish custom, being almost entirely suppressed. This development brought about a substantial change everywhere in the very nature of the great Act of Thanksgiving—leaving in the Western

[1] The word *Præfatio*, as a matter of fact, seems to have been, at least in some cases, applied only to the opening 'invitation' to the prayer: *Sursum corda*, etc., up to *gratias agamus*, etc. In this case the word would mean 'introduction'.

rites only a short allusion to the thanksgiving at the start. This is very evident in the prefaces of the Roman missal. Most of these begin: *Vere dignum et justum est . . . nos tibi semper et ubique gratias agere* ('It is truly meet and just . . . that we should at all times and in all places, give thanks to Thee'), but they go on immediately to speak of the particular feast or liturgical season being kept on that day.[1] In the East, there are no 'proper' prefaces for feast-days or liturgical seasons, the anaphora (which term includes both preface and canon) is always the same in each Liturgy, and the thanksgiving series has kept nearer to its earlier form. Sarapion's Prayer, however, is an exception to this: not only are the thanksgiving series omitted, but the very word 'thanksgiving' itself is absent and the first section of the Prayer has become a kind of theological hymn leading up to what is now a preface to the threefold *Sanctus*. This second section of the first part of the Prayer closely resembles that of the later Egyptian (Alexandrian) rite, and can be traced, according to Dix, in the writings of Origen at Alexandria (*c*. A.D. 230), and he therefore maintains that in this rite we have the earliest certain evidence of the use of the *Sanctus* in the Liturgy. The earlier existing quotations of the Angelic Hymn—that is, quotations from Holy Scripture, e.g. by St. Clement of Rome and Tertullian—do not necessarily imply that the threefold *Sanctus* was actually in use in the Mass Liturgy. We have already seen that there is no trace of it in Hippolytus' Liturgy, nor is there any in some other early liturgical documents, and St. Justin does not mention it in his description of the Western rite in his time. This would seem to indicate that the *Sanctus as an element of the Eucharistic Prayer* originated in the Alexandrian Church some time before A.D. 230. From there it appears to have spread, first to other Egyptian churches, and finally all over both East and West (Dix, p. 165). If this is really the fact—and there seems to be good reason for it—the *Sanctus* and its 'preface' were introduced from Alexandria first of all into Sarapion's Liturgy—it is not possible to say exactly when. In Sarapion the first part of the Prayer—

---

[1] In the proper preface of Apostles the note of thanksgiving has now completely disappeared. This, however, seems to be accidental; there are early texts of the preface, in which the usual full form is found (cf. *The Clergy Review*, July 1941, p. 62. (London: Burns, Oates & Washbourne, Ltd.)).

that originally given up to the various thanksgiving clauses—is much longer than it is in Hippolytus' Liturgy.

THE PREFACE AN INTRODUCTION TO THE SANCTUS: This special explanation of the word 'preface' certainly makes the whole question of the development of the Eucharistic Prayer much easier to follow. According to this point of view there is in Hippolytus' Prayer no preface at all. It has preserved the original form more closely: it is one undivided prayer. On the other hand, we do not find the long series of thanksgivings, but a thanksgiving through Jesus Christ, for His work in Creation, the Incarnation and the Redemption, leading up to the account of the Last Supper and the Institution of the Holy Eucharist. The Prayer ends with a 'statement' of the Church's act in following His example: "doing *therefore*[1] the *anamnesis* ('memorial') of His death and resurrection, we offer to Thee the bread and the cup, making *eucharist* ('thanksgiving') to Thee". (See *The Apostolic Tradition of St. Hippolytus*, pp. 8 and 9.) In Sarapion's Liturgy the introduction of the preface and *Sanctus* from Alexandria destroyed the original opening with the thanksgiving series, and the same effect is found substantially in the Roman rite. In Sarapion's Prayer the gap was filled up by the 'theological hymn' already referred to above (Dix, p. 163), but at Rome the gap was not filled up at all. From this it seems that the preface and *Sanctus* should not be looked upon as a development of the old thanksgiving series, but, rather, as an *alternative* to them—an alternative that has ended in taking their place altogether. It is only in the East, in the Antiochene type of the Liturgy, that a successful attempt has been made to unite both thanksgivings and preface by putting the preface and *Sanctus before* the older Antiochene thanksgiving series. Even in this case, instead of the words 'give thanks' at the beginning of the Prayer, we find: 'Holy art Thou', etc.

THE SANCTUS, AT FIRST THE CLIMAX OF THE PRAYER: It seems probable that, at Alexandria, these two new elements of

[1] This portion with its 'therefore' is equivalent to the *Te igitur* ('Thee, *therefore*') clause in the Roman Prayer. The word 'therefore' in both cases connects the thanksgivings with offering the gifts and with petition about them.

the Eucharistic Prayer were first introduced as the *conclusion* of the whole Prayer. Hence, preface and *Sanctus* (strange as this must seem to us now) would have been chanted *after the consecration*, as the climax of the doxology with which the Eucharistic Prayer came to an end. But in Syria, in those rites in which the thanksgiving, series was retained, the preface and *Sanctus* were placed, as said above, *before* the series. Where the series had been dropped altogether—as at Jerusalem—preface and *Sanctus* simply took their place. Hence, in the fourth century they appear for the first time as an 'introduction' (a 'preface' in *that* sense of the term) to the consecratory portion of the anaphora. In the Western rites this arrangement appears during the fifth–sixth centuries.

PREFACE AND SANCTUS IN THE ROMAN AND OTHER WESTERN RITES: In all these other rites—as in the Roman rite itself—the Eucharistic Prayer begins with only a few words of thanksgiving in quite general terms; there is no 'thanksgiving *series*'. These few words, too, on feast-days and on other special occasions, lead up to the commemoration of the feast or liturgical period, or other occasion. After this the preface turns to the Church's worship of God on earth, which she shares with the angels, and so to the threefold *Sanctus*: 'Holy, holy, holy', etc. Thus it appears, according to Dix, that in all the Western rites—Roman, Milanese, Gallican and Spanish—the preface and *Sanctus* ousted the long series of thanksgiving of the early Eucharistic Prayer, at some period between Hippolytus (*c.* A.D. 200) and S. Gregory I (*c.* A.D. 600), at the latest. It appears also that the insertion of preface and *Sanctus* in the Roman and other Western rites is another example of 'importation' from Syria. This is supported by the fact that, in the Egyptian rite and in all the Greek Liturgies and in Greek writers, generally speaking, the *Sanctus* runs as follows: 'Holy, holy, holy Lord of Sabaoth'—following the text of Isaias vi. 3; it is only in the Syriac liturgies that the form 'Lord *God* of Sabaoth' is found. But this latter form is found also in *all* the Western rites.

PREFACE AND SANCTUS NOT IN ALL MASSES: From the Council of Vaison in the south of France, which was held in A.D. 529, we find in the third canon a decree that in future the threefold *Sanctus* is to be sung or said in *all* Masses—'whether these are early masses (*matutinis*) or in Lent or in those which are offered for the commemoration of the dead . . . in that arrangement (*eo ordine*) in which it is now said at public masses'. Thus it appears that while the *Sanctus* was part of the rite in southern France, it was at first customary to leave it out in Requiem Masses, in times of penance, and also in 'low' or 'private' Masses, as we should say now. The *Sanctus* was then reserved for any public Mass, 'High Mass' as we say now. It appears, too, that since the chief purpose of the Council of Vaison was in this, as in other matters, to bring the southern French customs into conformity with those usual in the West elsewhere, and especially in the Apostolic See of Rome (but without in any way attempting to *abolish* the Gallican rite), it follows that the use of the *Sanctus* at all Masses was already the custom in that city. But this seems to have been "a recent modification [at Rome] of a previous practice of using the *Sanctus* only at the 'stational' liturgy on Sundays and saints' days", says Dom Gregory Dix, but he adds that "on this we have no Roman evidence" (Dix, pp. 538 and 539). The exact date of the first adoption of the *Sanctus* in the Roman and other Western rites is uncertain: there is no mention of it in St. Ambrose's description of the Mass at Milan, just before A.D. 400. It is true that the saint refers to the words of Isaias in his prophecy, vi. 3, and he speaks of the Cherubim and Seraphim or the Seraphim alone, "with unwearying voices [*indefessis vocibus*] praising and saying, Holy, Holy, Holy". He also quotes the actual text of Isaias, in which the words *indefessis vocibus* ('unwearying voices') do not occur (Srawley, pp. 152 and 153. Edition 1947). But these references do not *necessarily* imply the use of this chant of praise in the Liturgy, and St. Ambrose does not make any direct reference to the latter, as would surely be likely if the *Sanctus* had been an element in the Mass Liturgy in his time. St. Augustine in Africa (*c.* A.D. 430) does not speak of the *Sanctus* either, nor again, in A.D. 415, does Pope St. Innocent I, in his famous letter to Decentius, Bishop of *Eugubium* (Gubbio). The fact that these three saints were writing explicitly about the Mass Liturgy (and also explicitly about that very part of the Mass

in which the *Sanctus* now occurs) seems to make it at least probable that the chant had not yet been introduced, for such an
important element of the Liturgy—and one, too, which was at
first chanted by the whole congregation)—could hardly have
been left on one side without any reference to it at all. It seems
then at least probable that it did not find its way into the
Liturgy until towards the end of the fifth century, or even not
till the century after.

Two Early Latin Eucharistic Prayers: In 1827 Cardinal
Mai (then not yet a cardinal) published the two Latin Eucharistic Prayers which he had discovered in a Milanese MS., fragments of a controversial work written by an Arian writer. This
writer made use of the two prayers, as, in his own view, wit-
nessing to his argument that Catholics, in practice, subordinate
the Son to the Father just as much as Arians themselves do.
This misuse by a heretic of liturgical texts has had an important result with regard to the history of the Liturgy; for it has
preserved for future centuries what might otherwise have been
completely lost. These two prayers provide examples of the
Eucharistic Prayer in the West before the introduction of the
Sanctus. But, says Dix—and with reason—they "have been
unaccountably neglected by all the liturgists of the nineteenth and
twentieth centuries" (italics mine). In his recent re-edition
of his book *The Early History of the Liturgy* (2nd edition, 1947),
Dr. J. H. Srawley does, however, make a short reference to
"some north Italian prayers" in chap. vii, p. 150, and on p.
165 he gives a short description of the prayers themselves, in
which he points out that one of the fragments, in the last
clause, "recalls the *Te igitur* of the Roman Canon", and he
declares that "the important feature is that it passes at once
from the thanksgiving to the prayer . . . without any intervention of the *Sanctus*". He adds: "Similarly in the Roman
Canon the *Te igitur* forms a natural sequence to the Preface,
and suggests that the *Sanctus* and the clauses leading up to it
are a later insertion" (Srawley, pp. 151 and 165). In the article
on Cardinal Angelo Mai in the *Catholic Encyclopædia* (Vol. IX,
p. 538, 1913), while a long list of the immense number of
palæographical discoveries made by him from 1811 to 1858 are

given, there is no reference of any kind to the discovery of these two liturgical texts. In *The Sacramentary* of Cardinal Schuster (Vol. I, pp. 271 and 272 (London: Burns, Oates & Washbourne, Ltd., 1924—English translation)) the author speaks of this "fragment of an ancient Preface [*sic*]", and says that it "seems to refer (without the interpolation of any Trisagion [the 'Three-fold-Sanctus'] between the Preface and the Canon) to the opening . . . *Te igitur* . . ." The source of these prayers is given by Dix as follows: *A. Mai. Scriptorum Veterum Nova Collectio,* t. iii (1827), pt. ii, pp. 208, *et seq.*[1] It is true, as Dix himself points out, that the date of these two interesting relics of the early Western Prayer can be fixed only vaguely between *c.* A.D. 380 and 450—or even a little later. Nevertheless, they have some importance in the question of the connection between preface and *Sanctus* and the absence of the latter in earlier times. The texts of both prayers are given by Dix on p. 540—in an English translation. The Latin text is given in footnote 1 on the same page. These texts probably belong to North Italy, as suggested by Cardinal Mai. The Arian writer who made use of them evidently had possession of the sacramentary of the local church. Both the prayers are clearly related to the Roman Eucharistic Prayer, and may be looked on as examples of the general Western rite still in use at that period in parts of Italy. They bear much the same relation to the later Roman rite as the Liturgy of Sarapion bears to the later Egyptian Liturgy—as an example of the latter before the influence of other important Eastern Churches had interfered with local traditions.

The first of these two Latin prayers is probably older than the second. Unfortunately, it is also much less complete. But even the second prayer has lost its ending, stopping short just at the important point leading to the consecration.

Both prayers begin with the traditional opening words of the Eucharistic Prayer, and both show at least an indication of the old series of thanksgivings. In the fuller prayer the thanksgivings are concerned, like the Prayer in Hippolytus' Liturgy, with the

[1] Srawley gives this a little differently, viz.: Mai, *Scriptorum Veterum Nova Collectio*, iii. (1828), Fragm. vii, p. 223 (*The Early History of the Liturgy.* (Cambridge, 1947, p. 165)).

Incarnation, Passion and Redemption of our Lord, leading up to the Eucharistic Sacrifice. Although the first prayer is a mere fragment, it nevertheless says enough to give a fairly clear idea of its character. It declares that while "it is right and just, proper and just" (*Dignum et iustum est; æquum et iustum est*) that we should "above all things give thanks to thee, holy Lord, Father almighty", there is no other means to do this, to pray or to offer sacrifice to God except through "Him whom Thou hast sent unto us"—here the text breaks off. But from these few words, and from the fuller of the two prayers, we can gather how the first would probably continue if complete.

In this longer prayer, as both Dix and Srawley point out, we find quite a close resemblance to the Canon of the actual Roman rite—almost, in fact, identity. For example, the prayer, after thanking God for His mercy and 'loving-kindness', passes on to beg Him to "hold accepted this sacrifice *which we offer unto Thee* . . . through Jesus Christ our Lord and God: *through whom we pray and beseech*" . . . here the text breaks off suddenly. The above words (in Latin, *petentes . . . acceptum ferre sacrificium istud quod tibi offerimus . . . per Iesum Xstum Dnm et Deum nostrum: per quem petimus et rogamus*) are very similar to those in the Roman Canon, though not in quite the same positions in the respective prayers. But, as both Srawley and Dix say, speaking of these two ancient Prayers, the important point is that the more complete of the two, besides the resemblance to the *Te igitur* section of the preface and Canon, passes immediately from thanksgivings to a prayer for the acceptance of the offerings of the Church "without any intervention of the *Sanctus* and the clauses leading up to it", and that this suggests that the *Sanctus* and the preliminary clauses are a later insertion (Srawley, p. 165; Dix, p. 541).

These two prayers are of the same type as that in Hippolytus' Liturgy, and, as we have just seen, are related with the Roman Canon, but as Dix says: "probably as 'brothers' rather than as ancestors".

In the longer of the two prayers we have an equivalent to the *Te igitur* section of the Roman Prayer, but in this equivalent there is no kind of 'intercession' for the Church, Pope and bishop as in the Roman Canon, nor is there anything approaching the prayer for the living (*memento*) or the commemoration of the saints (*communicantes*); this text is concerned only with the Sacrifice and its acceptance by God from those who offer it.[1]

THE DIFFICULTY OF THE TE IGITUR CLAUSE: In the Roman Canon we have the following: *Te igitur clementissime Pater, per Jesum Christum filium tuum Dominum nostrum, supplices te rogamus ac petimus ut accepta habeas et benedicas hæc dona, hæc munera, hæc sancta sacrificia illibata . . . quæ tibi offerimus*—("And so, through Jesus Christ, thy son, Our Lord, we humbly pray [*rogamus*] and beseech [*petimus*] thee, most gracious Father, to accept and bless these presents [*dona*], these dutiful offerings [*munera*], these holy, unblemished sacrificial gifts which we offer thee"). The word *igitur* ('therefore' or 'and so', 'accordingly') has been considered to be an almost insurmountable difficulty. To what exactly does it refer? It has no apparent connection with the preceding preface nor with the *Sanctus*. In the older forms of the Roman prayer, however, this would have been no difficulty: the connection between the words *Te igitur* and the thanksgiving series at the beginning would, no doubt, have been quite evident and clear. In his edition of *The Apostolic Tradition of St. Hippolytus* Dix says that the Eucharistic Prayer is "modelled strictly on those old Jewish 'eucharistic' prayers of which many examples are to be found in the Old Testament, e.g. those ascribed to Solomon (2 Chron. vi. 4), Ezra (Neh. ix. 5 *et seq.*), Judas the Maccabee (1 Macc. iv. 30) and others".[2] Such prayers always, it seems, follow the same lines: first there is a series of thanksgivings, usually in the form of *blessing* God for all His mercies in the past. Secondly, these blessings lead up to and *justify* certain petitions which are generally introduced by the words 'now therefore'—that is, "as we have thanked and praised (or 'blessed') Thee for Thy past gifts, we now venture to ask for more"! In the Christian Eucharistic Prayer the chief petition is for the acceptance of the Sacrifice offered through the Church by Our Lord's own command, and for all who partake in it. In Hippolytus' prayer the word 'therefore' comes towards the end of the prayer: "doing *therefore* the anamnesis" (in his

---

[1] For the full texts of these two prayers, see Appendix V, p. 271.
[2] *The Apostolic Tradition of St. Hippolytus*, pp. xl and xli, and footnote on p. xli.

translation Dom Gregory Dix uses this term untranslated, to insist on the meaning underlying it—much deeper and more expressive than the usual word 'being mindful' or 'remembering'). In the Latin text the words are: *memores, igitur*—'the memory'; that is, 'of His death and resurrection'. The Greek words are *memnemenoi toinun* (see *The Apostolic Tradition of St. Hippolytus*, p. xii, footnote). In the text of this page Dix points out that: "It is important to note that of over sixty early liturgies, *one* only, that of Sarapion, has not this arrangement." In the two Italian prayers spoken of previously there is no 'therefore' clause—that is, the *word* 'therefore' (or other similar word) is not actually used; the *idea*, however, is expressed in the whole text of the longer prayer, and one can gather it from even the few words of the shorter one. In the longer prayer, too, we have only a relic of the old thanksgiving series. In the Apostolic Tradition Liturgy the thanksgiving contains four items: thanksgiving for the creation effected through the Word of God and His action in the Incarnation, in the Passion, at the Last Supper—in that order. All the early liturgies, it seems, follow this arrangement. The Last Supper is put *after* instead of before the Passion (its historical position) because the Institution of the Eucharistic Sacrifice took place at the Last Supper, which is therefore the "supreme *Justification* for the communion-petitions about to follow" (Dix, *The Apostolic Tradition of St. Hippolytus*, p. xli—text and third footnote).

In the Roman prayer as we have it and as it was in the eighth century (and probably in the two earlier centuries, also), the '*Te igitur*—clause' is analogous to the above words in Hippolytus—although they come in an earlier place—that is, the words as far as *hæc dona, hæc munera, hæc sancta sacrificia illibata* [*in primis*] *quæ tibi offerimus* ('these presents, these dutiful gifts, these holy unblemished sacrificial offerings which [in the first place] we offer thee'). We put the words *in primis* or *imprimis* ('in the first place') in square brackets, as the mention of the Church, Pope, bishop, for all of whom the gifts are offered 'in the first place', is almost certainly of late introduction in this place. The *Te igitur* then marks the transition from thanksgiving to petition, or rather did so in the early Roman prayer. A striking example supporting this (but one which seems to have escaped most liturgical scholars) exists in the 'Eucharistic' prayer used in cathedrals for—

THE BLESSING OF THE HOLY OILS ON MAUNDY THURSDAY: The very words *Te igitur* are found in the prayer which does not contain the *Sanctus* nor any other kind of interruption, and so the *Te igitur* in this case really marks the transition between thanksgiving and petition. The text of this prayer is as follows:[1]

Vere dignum et justum est, æquum et salutare nos tibi semper et ubique gratias agere: Domine sancte, Pater omnipotens, æterne Deus: Qui in principio, inter cetera bonitatis tuæ munera, terram producere fructifera ligna iussisti, inter quæ huius pinguissimi liquoris ministræ olivæ nascerentur, quarum fructus sacro chrismati deserviret [here follows mention of Our Lord's 'consecration' by the Holy Ghost at His Baptism in the Jordan].... *Te igitur* deprecamur, Domine sancte, Pater omnipotens, æterne Deus: per eumdem Jesum Christum Filium tuum, Dominum nostrum, ut huius creaturæ pinguedinem sanctificare tua benedictione digneris, ut sancti Spiritus ei adminiscere virtutem, etc.

It is truly meet and just, right and availing unto salvation, that we should at all times and in all places give thanks unto thee, O holy Lord, Father almighty, eternal God: who in the beginning, among other gifts of thy goodness, didst command the earth to bring forth fruitful trees, amongst which sprang forth the ministers of this most strengthening liquid of the olive tree, whereof the fruit serveth for the sacred chrism. . . . *We therefore* entreat thee, O holy Lord, almighty Father, eternal God, through the same Jesus Christ thy Son our Lord, that thou wouldest deign to sanctify by thy blessing, the fruitfulness of this creature and that thou wouldest add thereto the strength of the Holy Spirit, etc.

THE EXSULTET: There are, too, several other examples in the Roman rite of the word *igitur* used to express the transition from thanksgiving to petition. These are found in the solemn

---

[1] The writer owes the above indication to the author of *The Shape of the Liturgy*— in a private letter dated September 30th, 1939.

Eucharistic Prayer, used on Holy Saturday in inaugurating the paschal candle. This prayer is preceded by the *Exsultet*—which is a kind of introduction to the actual prayer. The latter begins, as usual, with the words *Vere dignum et justum est*, and, after expressing the reasons for thanking God and 'proclaiming' (*personare*) Him and His Divine Son, there are a number of sentences beginning with the word *igitur*. The one that most closely resembles the *Te igitur* clause in the canon of the Mass is as follows: *In huius igitur noctis gratia, suscipe, sancte Pater incensi huius sacrificium vespertinum: quod tibi in hac cerei oblatione solemni . . . sacrosancta redit Ecclesia.* After having 'proclaimed' the goodness and mercy of God comes this petition, in virtue of the above duty thus carried out, that He may accept the offering of the burning candle.[1]

The above view of the original signification of the *Te igitur* (that is, of the word *igitur* especially) was also supported by that learned liturgical scholar, the late H. W. Codrington—quite independently of Dom Gregory Dix—in an article entitled 'Some Liturgical Notes' on the *Liber Ordinum* of the Mozarabic rite edited by the late Dom Marius Férotin of Farnborough Abbey; pp. 321–2 in the *Downside Review* (April 1941, p. 195). He says in this article that "the '*Te igitur*' takes up the '*Vere dignum et justum est*' and the thanksgiving" (p. 197); that it is a connecting-link between the first and second parts of the Eucharistic Prayer. He goes on to show that there was once another formula in the place now held by the *Te igitur*, which is found in the Mozarabic rite. This is a prayer "reproducing or based on an old form of the Roman Canon and corresponding with the Gregorian Canon from the 'Te igitur' up to and inclusive of 'Quam oblationem' [and it] appears [in Mozarabic books] as a 'Post Pridie' [the title of the prayer immediately following the consecration] in a Mass 'for those who on feasts of martyrs, offer their vows to God'." As Mr. Codrington goes on to say, the fact that this prayer is

---

[1] The English is: "In the grace, *therefore*, of this night, accept O Holy Father the evening sacrifice of this burning light: which Holy Church renders unto Thee in the solemn offering of this candle." The Latin word *incensi* refers to the lighted candle, not to the five grains of incense—which, through a 'happy fault' were introduced into the ceremony by misunderstanding the word *incensi* as meaning 'the sacrifice of this *incense*' instead of 'this *lighted candle*'—or 'this *light*'.

placed after the consecration in the Mozarabic Mass is no proof or even probability that it was ever in this position in Rome. This remark refers, no doubt, to the theories maintained by a certain school of liturgical studies, that the Roman Canon has undergone a continual series of upheavals involving changes before and after consecration. The above-mentioned Mozarabic prayer closely resembles the Roman *Te igitur* clause, but instead of those words it begins—*Per quem* ('through Whom'— that is, Our Lord) and continues: *Te petimus et rogamus, Pater, ut accepta habeas . . . hec [hæc] sacrificia inlibata quæ tibi in primis . . . offerimus*, etc. Mr. Codrington goes on (again independently of Dom Dix) to refer to the use of the *Te igitur* in the blessing of chrism on Maundy Thursday. With all this he compares other analogous words; for example, *'idcirco' huic famulo* ('*For this reason*, to this [Thy] servant') in the consecration of a bishop, and also *'qua propter' infirmitati quoque nostræ* ('*wherefore*, unto our infirmity also') in the ordination of a priest, and, again, *In huius 'igitur' noctis gratia* ('in the grace, *therefore*, of this night') of the Eucharistic Prayer on Holy Saturday. Mr. Codrington sums up: "All these [that is, the ordination prayers and that on Holy Saturday] are constructed on the model of the old Eucharistic Prayer which is followed even more closely by the BLESSING OF THE FONT.[1] 'Te igitur' thus marks the transition from the thanksgiving and the causes thereof to the consequent prayer [of petition]." So far as the sense goes, it repeats the 'Et ideo' or the equivalent of these words in the preface, and possibly it (the phrase *Te igitur*) "took the place of these before the introduction of the 'sanctus' with its preliminary clauses." According to Mr. Codrington, too, the *Sanctus* was introduced into the Eucharistic Prayer later in the West than in the East, and later still in Rome.

SUMMARY: In the earliest form of the Eucharistic Prayer we have:

(i) *The 'Naming of God'*—that is, the pronunciation of the

---

[1] In this Eucharistic Prayer the phrase is, first: 'procul *ergo* hinc, iubente te, Domine, omnis spiritus immundus abscedat' ('let all unclean spirits, *therefore*, at thy command, Lord, withdraw hence, afar off'); secondly: *'unde* benedico te, creatura aquæ' ('*Therefore*—*unde*—'I bless thee, creature of water'). The above phrases follow after a long series of thanksgivings and blessings offered to God.

Divine Name—always a very solemn act with the Jews and with the early Christians, too.

(ii) *A series of thanksgivings* to God for:

(*a*) The Creation.

(*b*) The Incarnation and Redemption.

(*c*) The New Covenant in Christ.

(*d*) 'Taking bread', etc.—that is, the account of the Last Supper, with the repetition of Our Lord's own act of thanksgiving.

(iii) *A series of petitions*—chiefly concerning the acceptance by God from the Church of the sacrifice of thanksgiving, based upon and consequent to the praise and thanks offered *first* to God and usually connected with it by some such phrase as 'therefore' or 'and so'. Thus, in the supreme type of all prayer—the Lord's Prayer—due honour is first paid to God in the words: "hallowed be Thy name; Thy kingdom come, Thy will be done", before the petitions: "give us this day our daily bread; forgive us our trespasses".

(iv) *The Consecration* with the repetition of Our Lord's own action and Words of Institution at the Last Supper: the great Act of Sacrifice whereby the offerings of the Church were changed into the Offering (by Our Lord Himself) of His own Body and Blood.

(v) *The 'Glorifying of the Name'*—like the 'Naming of God' at the beginning of the prayer, but now made over the consecrated elements on the altar. This act, too, was derived from Jewish custom. It led up to (vi) *The final 'Doxology'* which ended the Eucharistic Prayer, summing up its whole meaning and significance.

(vii) *The Communion followed*—of celebrant and concelebrants, ministers and people. This was carried out at first, without any special prayers or ceremonies, either before or after the Communion. The whole rite was completed by what may be summed up under the term 'the ablutions'; that is, the consumption by celebrant or deacons of anything remaining of the consecrated Bread or Wine, the cleansing of chalice and paten and the removal of the altar cloth.

THE ORIGINAL SERIES OF THANKSGIVINGS: This leading up to Our Lord's own act of thanksgiving at the Last Supper, has left visible traces in the Egyptian Liturgy of St. Mark. It seems probable, as stated farther back, that it was in the Egyptian (or Alexandrian) Liturgy that the threefold *Sanctus* first found a place, and that it was placed originally at the very end of the Eucharistic Prayer as the conclusion of the Doxology. The anaphora of the Liturgy of St. Mark now begins as follows:

(i) The 'Naming of God'.

(ii) Thanksgiving for Creation, and then the prayer turns at once to what Dix calls 'the preface of the *Sanctus*', leaving aside altogether the rest of the old thanksgiving series. This Egyptian preface is now also interrupted in the very middle by the series of intercessions and diptychs for the living and the dead. These, since its introduction in this position, are followed by the threefold *Sanctus*. In the Alexandrian Liturgy, then, only the first of the thanksgiving series survives, but probably a full series of thanksgiving—for Incarnation, etc., etc.—existed in earlier times, and the words which now follow immediately after the thanksgiving for Creation would originally have been at the *end* of the Eucharistic Prayer, carrying on the Doxology and glorifying the Name, for which purpose they were evidently intended; the words are: "Thou didst make all things by Thy wisdom, Thy true light, Thy Son our Lord and Saviour Jesus Christ." These words are the normal introduction to a concluding doxology, which then continues: "that we may praise and glorify Thee through Thy servant, Jesus Christ, through Whom honour and glory be unto Thee with the Holy Spirit, in Thy holy Church, now and for ever and world without end, for Thou art far above every name that is named". These words would have led up to the final climax: "Holy, holy, holy, Lord of Sabaoth; full is the heaven and earth of Thy glory"; to which the people would then have answered: "As it was and is and shall be unto generations of generations and world without end. Amen." These latter words are still the answer of the people at the end of the Eucharistic Prayer, as it is found in the actual manuscripts[1]; but now a long section of the prayer divides the *Sanctus* from their response and does not in itself lead up to this particular response.

---

[1] In Sarapion, St. Mark and other forms of this rite.

THE EUCHARISTIC PRAYER AND THE WORDS OF INSTITUTION: With regard to the original outline and character of the Eucharistic Prayer, the author of *The Shape of the Liturgy* holds views which are not altogether in keeping with traditional Catholic teaching. He apparently favours the idea that in the early days of Christianity the Thanksgiving Prayer, in itself and *as such*, was probably considered to be enough to bring about the Presence of the Divine Victim and to carry out the sacrificial act, without necessarily any direct reference to the Last Supper or any repetition of Our Lord's words at the Supper: "This is my Body"—"this is my Blood", and without any reference to His admonition to His disciples to: "Do this for a commemoration of Me" (Luke xxii. 19). It is no doubt a fact that, during the course of ages, the simple Prayer of Thanksgiving used at the Last Supper, of the same type and character as the prayers used by the Jews at their religious meals, developed considerably and was adapted in form to different places, times and peoples. But it must have contained from the very beginning some kind of reference to the Last Supper (the actual occasion of its institution as the central act of Christian worship), and some kind of repetition of Our Saviour's own solemn 'Words of Institution', and of His equally solemn admonition to His immediate disciples, who were to be witnesses to His action for the Church all over the world. There is only one example in existence of an ancient Liturgy without such a reference and repetition. This is the Liturgy in normal use in the East Syrian Church of Persia—better known as the Nestorian Church, so-called after the heresiarch Nestorius, Patriarch of Constantinople (A.D. 428) and composed of his followers. The Liturgy to which we refer here is the Liturgy of SS. Addai and Mari, reputed founders of the Church of Edessa and apostles of the East Syrians and Persia; the Liturgy is also called 'of the Apostles'. The anaphora of this Liturgy, as we have said, does not contain the Words of Institution, nor is there any direct reference to the Last Supper, and neither seem to have ever formed a part of the text as it now stands. But apart from the fact that this Liturgy is connected with a notoriously heretical section of Eastern Christianity, whose heresy, moreover, is concerned especially with the Person of Our Lord, there is the further fact that no really early example of the text is extant. Hence, it is possible—even probable—that the existing texts have been altered or are deficient. It has been suggested, also, that it was never intended for use as a liturgy but that it is a relic of an ancient custom, similar to the agape.

'Religious meals' of this type were based upon the Liturgy and contained a form of thanksgiving over the bread and wine (or, perhaps, over bread alone), and served as a 'memorial' of the Holy Eucharist. But there was no consecration of the bread and wine (where both were used) and no sacrificial character. (See 'Some Flaws in the Shape of the Liturgy' by Maurice Bévenot, S.J., in *The Month* for January–February 1946, No. 949, lxxxii, 50–57; also 'The Shape of the Liturgy: A Review,' by the Rev. J. D. Crichton, in *Magnificat*, Spring 1946, No. 3, iv, 1–7.) It is certainly true that in those early times there was no very clear notion with regard to the exact 'moment of consecration'; probably the whole of the Eucharistic Prayer was vaguely considered as being consecratory without fixing upon any particular 'moment'. Nevertheless, it is hardly possible to believe that Our Lord's own words at the Last Supper, recorded by the Synoptic Gospels, would have been regarded as of such slight importance that they could be put into the Liturgy or left out of it merely at choice. The Rev. J. D. Crichton, in the review mentioned above, says of the notion that the thanksgiving and the accompanying ceremonial alone sufficed: "We cannot agree that the rite, the mere action performs the liturgy . . . Fr. Dix's view that it does not matter whether there is a form or not seems to be a novelty. We will insist that *even liturgically* a rite without the words of institution is defective" (pp. 3 and 4—italics mine). Fr. Crichton adds that Dom Gregory Dix's contention that St. Cyril of Jerusalem does not mention the words of institution at all in his Catechetical Discourses (xxiii) on the Liturgy is no evidence that he considered the Invocation of the Holy Ghost alone to be sufficient for consecration. Also, as a matter of fact, it is not really correct to give the impression that the saint does not mention the words of institution at all; he actually *does* speak of them in his previous Discourse (xxii), and so it was not necessary to repeat them in the later one. In his book, *The Early History of the Liturgy* (edition 1947), Dr. Srawley says on p. 76: "From the *Sanctus* Cyril passes on to the Invocation without mentioning any further thanksgiving or the recital of the institution. There is . . . a parallel omission in the case of the people's offering. This renders highly improbable the suggestion (Dix, p. 198) that at Jerusalem, in the time of Cyril, where liturgical development in other respects had reached such an advanced stage, these features of the rite were absent. Cyril had already expounded the narrative of the institution in the preceding *Catechesis* [xxii]." Dr. Srawley, at the same time, does admit that for Cyril, "the ground of the consecration of the elements is the operation of the Holy Spirit" (Srawley, p. 77). St. Cyril of Jerusalem lived in *c.* A.D. 315–86, and the date of his *Catecheses* was probably A.D. 347. At the same time, while all that has been said above about the words of institution and the reference to the Last Supper as original elements of the Eucharistic Liturgy represents the most usual theological opinion, we must mention here the attitude taken in a recent article on the Eucharist and the agape in a French liturgical magazine. After speaking of the early form of the Eucharistic Prayer and its connection with the Jewish *berakah* (thanksgiving prayer), without doubt used by Our Lord Himself at the Last Supper, the author says: "It is undoubtedly possible that the primitive Eucharist contained, at least in some places, an explicit reference to the Last Supper on Maundy Thursday. The 'discourse and prayer coming from Jesus' who, in the words of St. Justin, 'eucharistises', that is, consecrates ordinary bread and wine, would certainly seem to include the words of Jesus: 'This is my body . . . this is my blood'. The account of the Last Supper given in the Gospels of St. Matthew and St. Mark—which has a decidedly liturgical character—provides the same kind of indication. The first Epistle to the Corinthians is equally suggestive, that the 'tradition' (or 'handing on') [the author uses the French word 'transmission' here; in the Latin of the Epistle, St. Paul says: '*tradidi* vobis', translated in the *Westminster Version of the Sacred Scriptures* as 'I have *delivered* to you'] which St. Paul made of the recital of the institution of the Eucharist was not only in preaching but also in the words of the liturgy."

The writer continues: "Nevertheless, it is not impossible that the Words of our Lord *were omitted during a certain period in some places.*" (Italics mine; see *La Maison Dieu: Cahiers de Pastorale Liturgique* (Les Editions du Cerf: No. 18. 29, Boulevard Latour-Maubourg, Paris-7e; also obtainable in England from Blackfriars, Oxford).) The author points out in a footnote that the Council of Trent did not define the nature of the sacramental form by means of which Our Lord consecrated the bread and wine at the Supper, and that during the Middle Ages a certain number of theologians held that Christ consecrated the elements by means of a special 'blessing' before His words: "this is my body", etc., the latter words being used in order to declare to the disciples that the consecration had taken place. This opinion was also held by Alphonsus Salmeron, one of St. Ignatius Loyola's first companions and one of the best-known theologians at the Council of Trent. The writer of this article goes on to say that apparently the regular and indispensable use of the words of institution as the form of consecration was due to Pope Alexander (A.D. 107–16), and that he inserted into the canon the full account of the Last Supper. This last assertion is made by a writer in the *Liber Pontificalis* in the sixth century.[1] The author of this article says that the writer of the *Liber Pontificalis* would hardly have *invented* such a statement at a period in which the words of Our Saviour at the Supper were regarded as absolutely necessary, and had been so regarded for ages past. Thus his statement must have been derived from a more ancient source. It is a matter for theologians to discuss and for the authority of the Church to define fully. But it is difficult to reconcile this statement with the traditional teaching of the Church. (See article: 'L'Eucharistie et L'Agape: de leur union a leur disjonction', by H. Chirat in *La Maison Dieu*, No. 18, as above, pp. 48–60, especially pp. 56 and 57.)

EUCHARISTIC MEALS NOT THE EUCHARISTIC SACRIFICE: Fr. Crichton quotes from an article ("the brilliant essay", he calls

---

[1] The *Liber Pontificalis* is composed of a series of biographies of the Popes—in the first part, from St. Peter to Felix III; in the second part, down to the fifteenth-century Popes. The first part was probably written by one writer—about 530; the second by a series of unknown persons. (See *Liber Pontificalis: Texte, Introduction et Commentaire*, by L. Duchesne, 2 vols. (Paris, 1886–92).)

it) written by Canon E. C. Ratcliff in the *Journal of Theological Studies*, vol. xxx, pp. 23 *et seq.*, on the possibility that the Liturgy of SS. Addai and Mari, the normal Nestorian Liturgy, referred to farther back in these pages, was originally a 'eucharistic meal' in memory of the Holy Eucharist, but not the Eucharistic Sacrifice itself.

This "eucharistic meal," says Canon Ratcliff, "was a commemoration *not in words but in act*, that is, an imitating of Christ's example, for the *eucharistia* is said over bread and wine (perhaps only over bread at one time)"; and Fr. Crichton adds: "in other words this form of 'eucharist', according to Canon Ratcliff, was independent from the real Eucharist as regards time, occasions, etc.; it was an attempt to connect *all* Christian meals more closely with the sacrificial meal instituted at the Last Supper". Following this, Fr. Crichton suggests further that this 'eucharist-meal' is, perhaps, the real explanation of the much-discussed *Didache* (see *ante*, p. 14)—that the *Didache*, in fact, was not a Eucharistic liturgy at all in the true sense. Dix, however, considers that chaps. ix and x of the *Didache* give an early description of the agape, but that in chap. xiv the full Eucharist is given and under "quite different terms" (Dix, pp. 90 *et seq.*).

Finally, it is difficult to see why a simple reference to the Last Supper should not have been included in the series of thanksgivings, and so have formed part of the undivided Eucharistic Prayer in early times—as it actually does in Hippolytus' Liturgy. The same applies to the recital of the Words of Institution.

THE WESTERN PREFACE AND CANON: The variable preface is special to the Western Church. While the Canon (except for the change of the prayer *Communicantes* and *Hanc igitur*—sometimes, only the first—on certain great feasts, such as Easter and Pentecost) is invariable, the preface—that is, the part before and leading up to the *Sanctus*—changes according to the feast or the season. The Roman preface, too, has lost the whole of the thanksgiving series at the beginning, and the opening words: *Vere dignum et iustum est, æquum et salutare, nos tibi semper et ubique gratias agere* ('Right, indeed, it is and just, proper and for our welfare that we should always and everywhere give thanks to

Thee, Holy Lord, almighty Father, eternal God') are the only reference to thanksgiving in it, besides the *Sanctus*. Neither the Gallican nor the Mozarabic rites nor the Ambrosian have any such series, although all begin the preface (called in the Gallican and Spanish rites *immolatio*—'offering' or 'sacrifice'; *illatio* —'like the Greek title, *anaphora*—'raise up', that is 'offer'; *contestatio*—'earnest request') with the same type of opening words as in the Roman—*Vere dignum*, etc.

Both the Roman rite and all these rites go on at once to a commemoration of the feast or season of the year. It is not possible to state the exact date of this change in the Western Eucharistic Prayer, as there is no actual evidence—that is, it was not 'noted down' in any liturgical manuscript. But as already pointed out, neither St. Ambrose at Milan in his work, *De Sacramentis*, iv, 4, 14, written just before A.D. 400, in which he treats specially of the Mass; nor, again, St. Augustine in Africa (*d*. A.D. 430) in his sermons or other works, say anything at all about preface or *Sanctus*—though each treats of the actual part of the rite in which they now occur. St. Ambrose, it is true, in treating of the canon, says that in the earlier part of it "praises are offered to God" (*laudes Deo deferuntur*). But these 'praises' are, he tells us, 'said by the priest', and there is no suggestion that the people join in them, as they always did in the *Sanctus* when first introduced, and which they continued to do even during the Middle Ages. The above words seem to refer to the 'thanksgiving series', then still standing at the opening of the Western Eucharistic Prayer (in A.D. 400). It was precisely in this way that Justin had spoken of the series at the opening of the Roman Eucharistic Prayer, in A.D. 150: the bishop "sends up praise and glory to the Father" (*Apologia*, i. 65: cf. Dix, p. 222). St. Augustine, too, while he often reminds his people in his sermons of the opening dialogue between priest and people in the Eucharistic Prayer (that is, *Sursum corda*)_ and quotes its exact words, never once gives the idea that the prayer led up to a chant sung by all together. If such a chant had existed in his time in the African rite, he could hardly have failed to at least refer to it (e.g. *Serm.* liii, 14).

We have discussed (on p. 98 to p. 101) the two Italian Eucharistic Prayers discovered by Cardinal Mai. The texts of these prayers, as already noted, show a Eucharistic Prayer without the *Sanctus* or any reference to it at all. The longer of the two also leads straight on to what would now be called the 'Canon', and there is a close analogy between it and the concluding part of the *Te igitur* section in the actual Roman Canon. This analogy continues as far as the words *sacrificia illibata* (inclusive) in the Roman Canon. Both the texts also still possess at least remnants of the thanksgiving series of the earliest Eucharistic Prayers.

DATE OF THE INTRODUCTION OF THE SANCTUS AT MILAN: This may be gathered, says Dix, from a tradition in the church of Milan that its bishop, Eusebius (A.D. 451–65) was the author of the "Milanese 'proper' prefaces for the greatest feasts of the year". The arguments are not absolutely decisive, says the writer of the above—and, in fact, this could hardly have been expected. Nevertheless, Eusebius really seems to have been the author of the most ancient of the Milanese prefaces. We are told, also, by Ennodius[1] (who knew him) that he was a Greek from Syria (Ennodius, *Carmina*, ii, 86). So again we find Syria in connection with the Western Liturgy—as "the source of the Western preface and *Sanctus* and about the middle of the fifth century as the date of its introduction" (Dix, p. 541). As there was always close connection between Milan and Rome, and the former was always inclined to follow the customs of the latter, it is possible that the introduction of the preface and *Sanctus* at Milan followed soon after their admission at Rome. Perhaps, on the other hand, Eusebius in this case showed Rome the way.

THE SANCTUS IN THE WEST ON FESTAL OCCASIONS ONLY: This fact may have been the cause of the substitution of a commemoration of the particular feast or season in the place of the older thanksgiving series. The proper prefaces are older than the common preface, since it was only on special feast-days that the *Sanctus* and its introduction the preface were admitted into the Eucharistic Prayer. It was the use of the preface and

[1] Magnus Felix Ennodius, born in Gaul A.D. 474; Bishop of Pavia soon after A.D. 513.

Sanctus in all Masses about A.D. 529 (cf. the Council of Vaison in France) that probably led to the need of a 'common preface'. Although there is no special commemoration to replace the thanksgiving series, as in the case of a feast, the old thanksgiving series is absent and the preface leads directly to the *Sanctus*. But in the Gallican and Mozarabic rites, the problem was solved by actually providing a special preface for every day or occasion of the Liturgical Year. Rome—quite characteristically —provided, as above, a *single* preface for all ordinary days on which no particular feast was observed. This common preface, too, consists merely in "a simplified and abbreviated version of the single invariable introduction to the *Sanctus* in the Syrian rite, from which the use of the *Sanctus* had originally been borrowed in the West" (Dix, as above). In the Leonine and Gelasian Sacramentaries there are a large number of proper prefaces, but these seem to have been used in parts of Italy outside Rome.

PREFACE AND SANCTUS FROM SYRIA: It was in Egypt, as we have seen, that the preface and *Sanctus* originally started, and spread all over Christendom during the fifth century, so that it soon came to be regarded as a universal, and even an Apostolic, custom, and up till quite recent times, too. Nevertheless, it was from the *Syrian* rite (which had borrowed the Egyptian usage) that Rome and the other Western Churches adopted this chant directly, and, moreover, adapted it to their own special way and spirit. In the East, too, it is the Syrian form, not the original Egyptian form, that is preserved—and preserved as it was when taken over. The great importance of this question of the probable origin and introduction of preface and *Sanctus* into the Eucharistic Prayer justifies the number of pages taken up with explaining it. It is really necessary to obtain as clear and distinct a notion as possible of the process if we are to understand the development of this part of the liturgy.

THE CONSECRATORY SECTION OF THE EUCHARISTIC PRAYER: The section of the prayer which follows the *Sanctus* is called the 'canon' in the West; in the East 'anaphora' is the title of the *whole* prayer, including both sections. This latter word is

Greek and means 'raising up' or 'carrying up'; that is, 'offering' something; it might be translated as 'prayer of offering' or 'oblation'. The word 'canon' is also Greek, although, from its use in the West, it has become a Western word. It means a ruler, a straight rod, and so a 'rule' or 'standard' of either faith or practice. Dix calls the canon the 'second part' of the Eucharistic Prayer, and a part which has been *added* to it in later times, a later development of the original simple 'thanksgiving prayer'. We have seen already that there has undoubtedly been considerable development in the whole of the early form of the prayer, and especially, perhaps, in this second section; but it would seem to have been a 'development' not of additions from outside but of what already was virtually present—e.g. the reference to the Last Supper and the recitation of the Words of Institution now 'enlarged' and insisted upon, rendered clear and outwardly more important. The author of *The Shape of the Liturgy*, in connection with all this, seems to be influenced by his (surely quite personal and unusual) insistence upon the nature of the Last Supper as "not strictly a eucharist" (Dix, pp. 75 *et seq.*)—not the 'first-Mass', as a Catholic would say—but merely a kind of 'rehearsal' of what Christ wished His Church to do *after* His crucifixion. It is here quite clearly declared that there could not have been any 'memorial sacrifice' of that offered upon the cross until the latter *had actually been offered*. This seems to imply setting restrictions upon the actions of Our Saviour, as though He (who is God as well as man) were bound down by the limitations of human life and of time. Without question, God had arranged in the Divine plan of our Redemption that it should be effected in time, in the conditions of human life, by the physical shedding of the blood of His Son—the complete *physical* surrender of His human life upon the cross. But this truth in no sense excludes the real, sacramental offering of that life in anticipation at the Last Supper —any more than it excludes the real, sacramental offering of it in *memory* in the Mass, on the altars of the Church. As the Mass is *now*, the Last Supper was *then*—the very Sacrifice of the cross itself, 'differing only in the manner of offering', as the Council of Trent so clearly puts it. From the human point of view and in time the Sacrifice offered at the Last Supper looked *forward* to the Sacrifice to be offered on the cross. From the same point of view, the Sacrifice of the Mass now looks *back* to that same Sacrifice. But in the sight of God and in itself, Last Supper, Cross and Mass form *one eternal Act*. Catholic tradition, too, has always regarded the Last Supper, from the human aspect, as the 'First Mass'.

DEVELOPMENTS OR ADDITIONS TO THE PRAYER: In maintaining that the original simplicity of the undivided 'Prayer of Thanksgiving' was added to and a 'second half' introduced, Dom Gregory Dix admits that the real difficulty is to lay down exactly where this 'second half' begins. He suggests that it lies between the mention of the Last Supper (either a full account of the institution of the Holy Eucharist or a mere reference to it) and the concluding doxology. This latter appears to be universal and to belong to the primitive nucleus of the prayer, but Dix thinks that it is difficult to judge whether or not any reference to the Last Supper can be found in the early prayer.

The chief difficulty, according to him, is that: "In all the traditions, the reference to the Last Supper is separated from the thanksgiving series by a sort of intervening clause or 'link'. . . . And this link is not the same in any two of them, either in substance or expression." He points out, too, that the link never seems to be at all closely connected with the series of thanksgivings at the beginning of the prayer and that the reference to the Last Supper is never in the form of a 'thanksgiving' but in that of a 'statement'. In the case of the Egyptian preface and *Sanctus* in which the "original 'glorifying of the Name' has survived in its primitive position . . . the allusion to the last supper comes *after* this". All the same, he makes it clear that the reference to the Last Supper and Institution occurs in some form in all the traditions and—what is both interesting and significant—that the form of thanksgivings used in Jewish meals, called the *berakah*, provides in its final thanksgiving for the earthly food "wherewith thou feedest us continually". This Jewish thanksgiving, says Dix, might easily have suggested a thanksgiving for the heavenly food of the Eucharist. and, further, he shows that St. Justin, in his *Apologia* (i, 66).

speaks of the 'word of prayer which comes from' Jesus Himself, and that would seem to point to the fact that something of the sort existed in the Eucharistic Prayer in his time (Dix, pp. 225–30). In his review of *The Shape of the Liturgy* in *Magnificat*, Fr. Crichton mentions the, no doubt, quite unconscious "writing to a thesis" which is apparent from time to time in the author's attitude, and the consequent tendency on his part to 'bend' certain facts in order to make them fit in with that thesis. In the above case, for instance, he seems almost to have made up his mind that the earliest form of the Eucharistic Prayer was 'eucharistic' in the strictest sense, and did not admit any other element than that of thanksgiving. And yet in his edition of *The Apostolic Tradition of St. Hippolytus* he says that "Hippolytus' Canon is, so far as form goes, modelled strictly on those old Jewish 'eucharistic prayers' ", that "The outline of such prayers is always the same", and that it consisted in a series of thanksgivings to God (or as we should regard them now, acts of 'blessing God'—the same thing for the ancient Jews) for His mercies towards man and that these thanksgivings lead up to and *justify* certain petitions, usually introduced by some word as 'now therefore'. The scheme was: "having thanked Thee as in duty bound, for Thy gifts and mercies, 'we therefore' —or 'we now'—proceed to ask for other gifts."

In *The Shape of the Liturgy*, Dom Gregory Dix speaks of the reference to the Last Supper as preceded by a " '*statement* of Christ's purpose in instituting the eucharist' " and of being itself the " 'Statement of His Institution of the eucharist' " (Dix, pp. 158 and 159). Surely the 'statement' is included in the 'thanksgiving' and to completely separate the two notions seems to be merely 'splitting hairs'. Perhaps the character of the reference to the Last Supper and Institution as a 'statement' rather than an 'act of thanksgiving' in the developed liturgies is the result of the discussions that arose later on as to the actual 'moment of consecration' in the Eucharistic Prayer and the controversy between the Words of Institution and the Epiclesis; that is, the Invocation of the Holy Ghost. In consequence of all this, it may be that the thanksgiving for the Institution at the Last Supper became the statement of the Words of Institution as an 'action'—whether, as in the West itself, action of consecration, or as later in the East, *leading up* to the action of the Invocation.

THE LINK IN THE VARIOUS LITURGIES: The need of a link binding together the thanksgiving portion of the prayer with the consecratory part marks *development* in the Eucharistic Prayer, but not necessarily *additions from outside*; that is, any introduction of elements which were not in the prayer before. In Hippolytus, the link between thanksgivings and consecration seems very close (Dix, *The Shape of the Liturgy*, pp. 157–62; *The Apostolic Tradition of St. Hippolytus*, pp. 7–9). In Sarapion, the link is connected with the final words of the *Tersanctus*—'full is the heaven', etc., and so in the later Egyptian Liturgy, where it is, too, practically an 'invocation' of the Holy Ghost (somewhat 'watered down') *before* the consecration. In the liturgies of SS. James, Basil and Chrysostom the link is connected with the actual words of the *Tersanctus*, 'Holy, holy, holy'. This is found also in the Western liturgies in the Gallican and Spanish rites, in which the 'link' nearly always begins with the words *Vere sanctus, vere benedictus*. In the Ambrosian rite, the link is a prayer leading directly to the Words of Institution, which begin with the characteristic Western form, *Qui pridie quam pateretur* ('Who on the day before he suffered'); the Roman rite also has a 'link-prayer' leading up to the words *Qui pridie*, and of the same type as the Ambrosian but slightly different in form. The Roman 'link-prayer' is as follows: *Quam oblationem tu, Deus, in omnibus quæsumus, benedictam, adscriptam, ratam, rationabilem acceptabilemque facere digneris* ('Which same offering we pray thee, O God, be pleased to make wholly blessed, to consecrate and approve it, making it reasonable and acceptable'). This form begins with a relative clause: *Quam oblationem* —which now connects it with the preceding prayer: *Hanc igitur oblationem servitutis nostræ . . . quæsumus, Domine, ut placatus accipias* ('And so, Lord, we thy servants . . . beseech thee to accept this offering as pleasing to thee'). The Ambrosian prayer is: *Fac nobis, hanc oblationem adscriptam, ratam, rationabilem, acceptabilem: quod figura est corporis et sanguinis Domini nostri Jesu Christi. Qui pridie* ('Make this offering for us, Lord, consecrated, approved, acceptable: for it is the figure of the body and blood of our Lord, Jesus Christ: Who the day before' .... etc.). This is the form of the prayer found in the treatise *De Sacramentis*, written by St. Ambrose (*De Sacramentis*, iv, 5, 21–3, 26, 27), and what he describes therein of the then existing Milanese rite probably also provides a more ancient form of that of Rome, or, at any rate, shows a close connection between the two rites. The Ambrosian prayer is not 'relative' like the Roman, and St. Ambrose does not speak of any preceding prayer like the Roman *Hanc igitur*. Of course, the introduction of preface and *Sanctus* has considerably confused the whole question of the Eucharistic Prayer and its development and, in the case of the Roman and Ambrosian rites, the 'oneness' of the prayer has been obscured by what looks like a collection of short prayers connected with one another, but nevertheless each complete in itself.

CHAPTER VI

THE ROMAN CANON

THE later Roman Canon needs a chapter to itself, for it has always been a difficulty above all the many other difficulties in the history of the Liturgy. Theories concerning its origin and development are almost without end, and few of them agree on many points. That great liturgical scholar, Mr. Edmund Bishop, was the first to deprecate this confusion, and in particular, theories which involve the continual disarrangement of the order of prayers in the canon. In some cases, for instance, it is stated that some of the prayers have been moved from a position *before* the consecration to one after it; sometimes prayers originally *after* the consecration have been arbitrarily placed before it. For all this Mr. Bishop maintained there was no evidence at all, and he considered that, on the contrary, the Roman Canon was in many ways more 'primitive' in its construction than any other existing liturgy. Nevertheless, it is certainly true that it is quite *sui generis* in its general make-up; entirely different in form from even that of the other Western rites. As we have already seen, it consists of a series of distinct, though connected, prayers both before and after the consecration. The Eastern anaphora, although the original one long prayer is now divided by the *Sanctus* into two sections as in the West and, moreover, the section after the *Sanctus* interrupted by the insertion of diptychs and intercessions, has, nevertheless, preserved the outward appearance of unity better than the Western rites. In the Gallican and Mozarabic rites there is usually only one short prayer after the *Sanctus*, before consecration, and another similar prayer after consecration. All the same, Edmund Bishop always maintained the more 'primitive' character of the Roman Canon, and the possibility of one day being able to explain the apparent difficulties and differences. In *The Shape of the Liturgy*, Dom Gregory Dix fully agrees with Bishop's views, which are, indeed, confirmed by the real advance in liturgical studies since his day. Like Bishop, Dom Gregory Dix considers that, as regards the *contents* of the early Eucharistic Prayer, the Western rites in general have kept the old idea of one prayer more faithfully in some things than those of the East, which underwent some radical changes in the fourth century. As regards the other two Western rites, Gallican and Mozarabic, it is evident that these, as they stand in the manuscripts of sixth-century date, have been influenced by the introduction of the preface and *Sanctus*, and by the developed liturgical year with its changing prayers, Scripture lessons and so on. Both *Sanctus* and liturgical year appear in the West only in the fifth century. Hence, the fidelity of these two rites to ancient tradition consists simply "in arranging their new contents on the old Western scheme" (Dix, p. 557, long footnote and p. 558).

To turn directly to the Roman Canon: the question of the real significance of the puzzling phrase *Te igitur* has been dealt with in discussing the general form of the Eucharistic Prayer.[1] The words mark the transition from thanksgiving to petition and declare the justification of the latter as flowing from the former—*igitur* ('therefore'). The special petition of this part of the prayer is concerned with the offerings of bread and wine: *hæc dona, hæc munera, hæc sancta sacrificia illibata* ('these gifts, these official debts,[2] these unspotted sacrificial offerings') which God is asked to accept and bless through His Son, Our Lord. So far, the *Te igitur* section follows more or less closely the end part of the second of Cardinal Mai's old Italian Eucharistic Prayers —some of the words, as we have seen, used in both the Roman Canon and this prayer are almost identical. The Roman Canon then goes on to what may be called 'truncated intercessions'—the prayers for the Church, the Pope, local bishop and originally, probably, for all orthodox bishops in general. The old Italian prayer ends with the words: *Per Iesum Xstum . . . per quem petimus et rogamus* ('Through Jesus Christ . . . through Whom we pray and beseech'), but stops short after *rogamus*.

---

[1] Dom B. Botte, however, omits the *igitur* altogether in his new translation of the canon (in French), declaring that the word, in the Latin of the fourth century, had no greater force than the Greek conjunctive particle '*de*'—which can be rendered 'and further' (*La Maison Dieu*, 23, p. 38, 1950).

[2] "*Dona*," says Dom Dix, "are 'free gifts', *munera* are payments"—which are the due of some office—"exactly 'liturgies' in the old sense" (Dix, p. 500, footnote 3).

PRAYERS FOR CHURCH AND POPE: Whether these words were followed by prayers for Church and Pope as in the Roman Canon, or whether they led on at once to the 'link' connecting the first part of the prayer with the Last Supper and Institution, it is impossible to say, but as the old Italian prayer gives us the more ancient form, with its relic of the thanksgiving series and absence of the *Sanctus*, it may at least be suggested that at that date such intercessions had not yet been introduced into the Eucharistic Prayer. In the case of the Roman Canon itself, these truncated intercessions were almost certainly introduced after the old intercessory collects (the 'solemn collects' of Good Friday) had been dropped from regular use at the end of the preliminary service. It is worth noting that the words of the prayer for the Church are actually the same as the *Præfatio* of exhortation to the people, recited by the celebrant before the collect for the Church, still used on Good Friday: *In primis, quæ tibi offerimus pro Ecclesia tua* ('which we offer Thee in the first place for Thy holy Catholic Church') . . . *una cum famulo tuo papa nostro N., et antistite nostro N., et omnibus orthodoxis atque Catholicæ et Apostolicæ fidei cultoribus* ('together with thy servant, our Pope N., and our Bishop N., and with all orthodox believers and professors of the Catholic and Apostolic Faith'). These last words are always translated now as though they applied to all Catholics in general. They are not found in the earliest manuscripts of the Roman Canon, and Edmund Bishop considered them to be interpolations of a later date. But the Abbot of Mont César in Belgium, Dom Bernard Capelle, maintains, on the contrary, that they belong to the original text—with the exception of the word *Catholicæ*. The other words: *omnibus orthodoxis atque Apostolicæ fidei cultoribus* ('for all orthodox professors of the Apostolic faith') did not, according to Dom Capelle, refer to the members of the Church in general, who had already been mentioned in the words *Ecclesia tua sancta Catholica* ('Thy holy Catholic Church'). The word *orthodoxis* referred to all other *bishops* who were 'orthodox' Catholic bishops. Dom Capelle adds that there is probably a word understood here, such as *papis* (the dative plural of *papa* —literally 'father'). The Latin title *papa*, which we translate 'pope', was not at first reserved exclusively to the Bishop of

Rome, but was given to all bishops—each of whom was the *papa* ('father') of all those in his church—or diocese, as we say now. The words *antistite nostro* ('for our Bishop'), used in other places than Rome, as well as the prayer for the Pope—who in Rome is also the 'local Bishop'—are later additions which came in after *papa* had become the special title of the latter alone.[1] It was adopted only when the original meaning of the words *orthodoxis (papis)* had been forgotten. In his own edition of the Roman Sacramentary, St. Gregory the Great (*c.* A.D. 600) omitted the words *et omnibus orthodoxis atque apostolicæ fidei cultoribus* altogether, almost certainly because he considered them to be superfluous, since, according to the then generally accepted idea, they referred to the ordinary members of the Church, already included in the prayer for the whole Church. As we know that St. Gregory rearranged the text of the canon drawn up by St. Gelasius in other ways, and himself probably added the words *diesque nostros in tua pace disponas* ('order our days in Thy peace') to the *Hanc igitur*, the above act of the holy Pope will not seem strange. After this come four distinct (though connected) prayers, beginning respectively with the words: *Memento Domine famulorum famularumque tuarum* ('be mindful, O Lord, of Thy servants and handmaids'); *Communicantes et memoriam venerantes* ('in communion with and reverencing'—the prayer goes on to mention Our Lady, Apostles and saints); *Hanc igitur oblationem* ('This offering, therefore'); *Quam oblationem* ('which offering do thou, O Lord, vouchsafe to bless'). We shall discuss the first three of these prayers (*Memento, Communicantes, Hanc igitur*) in the next chapter. We merely state here that none of the three represents the Roman intercessions or 'diptychs' (the latter word is correctly used only as the title of a custom observed in the Eastern liturgies—the "Roman 'diptychs' are a myth" (Dix, p. 507). But these three prayers are certainly *connected* with the notion of 'intercessions' and with the notion *underlying* the Eastern diptychs.

---

[1] The Patriarch of Alexandria still has the right to use the title 'Pope': he is 'Pope of Alexandria'. In the Russian Orthodox Church even 'simple priests' are commonly called 'popes', and in Greece *pappas*.

THE ELUSIVE TERM 'IGITUR': This is used again in the prayer beginning *Hanc igitur*. In this prayer *igitur* indicates a return to the preliminary offering of the gifts in the earlier part of the *Te igitur*—preliminary, that is, to the solemn sacrificial offering which takes place at the consecration. The preliminary offering comes after the above prayers for Church, Pope, special persons, the saints and so on.

THE LINK: QUAM OBLATIONEM: To turn now to the fourth prayer—*Quam oblationem*: this prayer is the 'link' between the earlier parts of the Eucharistic Prayer and the account of the Last Supper and Institution. The final words are: *ut nobis corpus et sanguis fiat dilectissimi Filii tui Domini nostri Jesu Christi* ('that it [the offering] may become *to*—or *for*—us the body and blood of thy most dearly beloved Son, our Lord Jesus Christ'). The words *ut 'nobis' corpus et sanguis fiat* ('that it [this oblation of bread and wine] may become "to us" the Body and Blood') do not imply that the change is merely subjective or symbolical. The request in this prayer is that the real objective change which the Words of Institution effect may act on us as the body and blood of Christ. In the same way, in the analogous prayer in the Ambrosian rite the oblation is described as the 'figure' of the Body and Blood of Our Lord, and the prayer begins: 'make this oblation approved... *for us*'. The explanation is the same as in the case of the Roman *Hanc igitur*. The expression 'figure' (in Latin, *figura*) does not mean that after consecration the bread and wine are only 'figures' or symbols of the Body and Blood of Our Saviour; it refers to the outward forms or 'species' of bread and wine which remain, even after transubstantiation has taken place—the 'accidents', as theologians call them. The accidents are, in fact, the outward signs or indications—'figures'—of the real objective but inward presence of the Body and Blood (*De Sacramentis* iv, 4, 14).

THE ANAMNESIS: After the consecration come three prayers beginning, respectively: *Unde et memores*; *Supra quæ propitio*; *Supplices te rogamus*: the first of these is known technically as the *anamnesis*, a Greek word meaning 'memorial'; 'calling to mind'; 'recollection', since it recalls to mind the Passion, Resurrection and Ascension of Our Saviour—but it is also a solemn expression of the Church's share in the oblation of the 'Holy Bread of eternal life and the Cup of everlasting salvation' (*Roman Missal*, edited by the Rev. J. B. O'Connell). The memorial of the Passion, Resurrection and Ascension at this point in the liturgy seems to have started in Rome and to have spread thence into other rites, but all liturgies have a prayer of oblation after the consecration. This prayer is followed by two more, one asking for God's acceptance of the sacrifice as offered on earth—as He deigned to accept the sacrifices of the Old Law beginning with that offered by Abel. The second— which has always been considered as of great importance and especial sanctity—begs for the ratification in heaven of the sacrifice offered on earth asking that it be "carried up by the hands of Thy holy angel to Thine altar on high". The prayer then closes with the request "that those of us who by partaking of this altar shall have received the sacred body and blood of Thy Son, may be filled with heavenly blessing and grace". This prayer is, then, also a prayer for the communicants, and such a prayer is found in this position in all liturgies. It is probable, too, that this part of the *Supplices te rogamus* was, in earlier times, much fuller and longer than it is now.

MEMENTO OF THE DEAD: In every Mass, according to the Roman rite, a prayer for the dead follows immediately, beginning *Memento etiam* ('remember also') of the same type as the *Memento*—for the living, before consecration. This prayer for the dead will also be considered in the next chapter, together with the first *Memento*. The second *Memento* is followed by a prayer beginning with the words: *Nobis quoque peccatoribus famulis tuis* ('and to us, also, Thy sinful servants'). The first three words are said aloud by the celebrant, although the rest of the text is recited secretly. Besides being a supplication for 'Thy sinful servants' (most probably these words referred originally to the celebrant himself and his concelebrating bishops and priests), the text includes the names of certain of the apostles and martyrs and asks for union with them—much as in the *Communicantes*. It seems that it was introduced by Pope

Gelasius I, together with that prayer and for the same reason
—to bring the names of the saints into the Eucharistic Prayer.
It is possible, however, that Gelasius introduced only the names
of the saints, and that the prayer itself (for celebrant and concelebrants) already existed in the Canon before the *Memento
etiam*. There is no real connection between it and the prayer
for the dead (Dix, p. 557; see the long footnote and the reference therein to P. B. Whitehead's article, 'The Acts of the
Council of 499', and the date of the prayers, *Communicantes*
and *Nobis Quoque*, etc., *Speculum* (1928), iii, 152 *et seq*.). The
Nobis quoque seems to follow quite naturally after the *Supplices
te rogamus*, without either the *Memento etiam* or the names of the
saints. The words *per quem hæc omnia, Domine, semper bona creas,
sanctificas vivificas, benedicis et præstas nobis* ('By whom, Lord, thou
dost ever create, sanctify, quicken, bless and bestow all these
good things upon us'), which carry on the final words of the
Nobis quoque—that is, the *per Christum*, etc., are usually explained
as a relic of the blessing of fruit, milk and other offerings
brought to the altar, together with the sacrificial bread and
wine, by the offerers at Mass and which are found as early as
the Liturgy in *The Apostolic Tradition* (p. 10, v and vi). The
words, however, probably referred *originally* primarily to the
consecrated Bread and Wine. The words immediately connected with these—*per ipsum et cum ipso et in ipso* ('through Him
and with Him and in Him')—and which are at the very end of
the Canon, form the doxology of the Eucharistic Prayer, and
they express the whole meaning and significance of Christian
worship.[1]

To sum up: apart from a few revisions and additions by
Gelasius and Gregory the Great, the Western rite, as it had
developed in the fourth century, still survives in the Roman
Mass, in spite of the 'improvers' of all the centuries—and the
above account of its history "can be substantiated from the
evidence, though this has not yet been done" (Dix, p. 557
footnote). This no doubt is true, but it is generally admitted
that the earlier form of liturgy, given in *The Apostolic Tradition*
and described in these pages, represents more or less roughly the

---

[1] The complete text is: "*through* Him and *with* Him and *in* Him is given to Thee,
O God almighty Father, in unity with the Holy Spirit, all honour and glory."

type of Liturgy in use by the Latin groups in Rome and round about the city at that period, and it still remains an unanswered difficulty as to how and when exactly the later type first came into being.

Two Recent Books on the Canon: The latest work on the history of the Roman Canon is set out in two recently published books: the first in Germany and entitled, *Missarum Solemnia (Eine Genetische Erklärung der Römischen Messe)*, by Josef Andreas Jungmann, S.J. (2 vols., Wien (Herder), 1948).[1] This book has recently been translated into English and French (Duckett, 140 Strand, London, W.C.2). It was highly praised by Dom Louis Brou of Quarr Abbey in a long article in the *Downside Review* (Spring 1949, pp. 215 *et seq.*). The author, a learned German Jesuit, confines himself to the Roman Mass, merely touching on the Eastern rites in connection with the Roman. His work, says his reviewer, will be of lasting value for all interested in the study of liturgical history. The translations (English and French) have not yet been completed.[2]

The second work is *The Canon of the Mass: Its History, Theology and Art*, by Dom Jerome Gassner, O.S.B. (Monk of Seitenstetten in Austria), now in Rome and appointed Postulator General in causes of beatification and Prosynodal Judge at the Roman Curia in 1949. His book is published by the B. Herder Book Coy., 15 & 17 South Broadway, St. Louis 2, Mo. (and 33 Queen Square, London, W.C.1), with a Foreword by the Abbot of St. Gregory's Abbey, Shawnee, Oklahoma. Dom Gassner had been lecturing at this abbey for six years, and this entitles his book to be spoken of as 'American'. It has also been reviewed in the *Downside Review*, Autumn 1950, in 'Shorter Notices', pp. 105 and 106. The reviewer says of it that, in spite of being at first sight "unattractive . . . being written in very clumsy English" and containing many misprints and an incomplete index, it would, nevertheless, be a mistake to disregard it; for the author has put an immense amount of work into the study of the sources of the Roman Canon, and the result is undoubtedly of great value.

We may say here that in general Dom Gassner holds views

See p. xvii. Note at end.   [2] February 1952.

very similar to those expressed in these pages regarding the early forms of the Eucharistic Prayer, the original position of the intercessions and 'names' (diptychs), etc. He believes, however, that the *Sanctus* was part of the prayer from the earliest times, deriving from the use of the Jewish Liturgy, the Christian prayer being founded upon the Jewish *Hallel*. He speaks, too, of the preface as a relic of the original 'Eucharistic Prayer-form', although the series of thanksgivings at the beginning have been much reduced. The preface is not, therefore, in Dom Gassner's view a preface to the *Sanctus*, as Dom Gregory Dix calls it, but, as usually understood, it is the preface to the Canon; that is, the consecratory portion of the Eucharistic Prayer which later came to be regarded as composed of two parts, united but distinct. Dom Jerome Gassner's chief contribution to a newer way of regarding the nature of the Roman Canon is found in his decidedly interesting explanation of the *two* objects of the prayer—namely, thanksgiving and invocation. This may be summed up as follows:

SUMMARY OF DOM GASSNER'S VIEWS: The earliest form of the Roman Eucharistic Prayer was that of one, undivided prayer beginning with a series of thanksgivings to God for various expressed reasons, and leading up to the account of the Last Supper, the institution of the Eucharistic Sacrifice by Christ; the offering by Him of the Sacrifice and the communion of the disciples present. This form appears in the second and early third centuries, in the Liturgy described by St. Justin, martyr, in his *Apologia*, and in the liturgical text given in *The Apostolic Tradition*. During the course of the second century this prayer was divided into two parts; the first being the 'preface' leading up to the three-fold *Sanctus*, now a distinct chant in itself sung by choir and people; the second being the 'canon', the consecratory part, beginning immediately after the *Sanctus*. This portion consists of three 'pre-consecratory invocations' (the *Te igitur*—as far as *pro Ecclesia tua*; the *Hanc igitur* and the *Quam oblationem*). These three 'pre-consecratory invocations' ask for the sacrificial blessing of the offerings of bread and wine by Our Lord (through His priest), and for the full result of that blessing, the consecration. After the consecration there are

again three invocations ('post-consecratory'), which look *back*
to the consecration as the 'pre-consecratory invocations' look
forward to it, and ask for the results of the consecration in the
communion of those taking part in the Sacrifice.

These 'invocations', according to Dom Gassner, were introduced into the early form of the Eucharistic Prayer by the
Church—or rather, were developed by her out of the early
form of the prayer. They are founded on the later (non-
Jewish) Christian distinction between the ideas of 'thanksgiving' and 'blessing' as expressed in the words of institution in
the Roman and other Canons: *Tibi gratias agens, benedixit*
('when He had *given thanks*, He *blessed*' or 'giving thanks, He
blessed'). These two words were identical for a Jew—to
bless God meant to *thank* Him and vice versa—but for Westerns
there is a subtle difference between them. In the scriptural
accounts of the Last Supper, these two expressions are never
found together; it is always either 'giving thanks' or 'blessing'
alone—since these two words for the Evangelists meant one and
the same. (See Matt. xxvi. 26 and 27; Mark xiv. 22, 23; Luke
xxii. 19; 1 Cor. xi. 24; Matt. xiv. 19 and xv. 36; 1. Cor. x. 16—
for this use of one or the other phrase.) In Hippolytus' liturgy
only the words 'giving thanks' are used; for this liturgy, as we
have seen already, is still impregnated with the original Jewish
thanksgiving-prayer character. But in the Roman rite of later
date (sixth, seventh, eighth centuries) we find both expressions.
The reason of this introduction by the Church of both terms in
the phrase: 'giving thanks, He blessed', says Dom Gassner, was
first, in order to commemorate and carry out *everything* said and
done by Our Lord at the Last Supper and to hand on each
expression used by the different Evangelists respectively. Both
expressions were combined in one in the Roman rite, and this
combination is found also in the Ambrosian rite as given in the
De Sacramentis, and in both cases repeated at the consecration of
the wine as well as of the bread. Both words are used also in
the Byzantine and other Eastern rites. The second reason for
the adoption of the double phrase was to make it clear that the
words 'giving thanks', while signifiying directly the act of
thanksgiving, signified also indirectly the invocation of blessing.
Vice versa, the term 'to bless' signifies directly the act of bless-

ing and indirectly that of thanksgiving. In the term 'giving thanks He blessed', the two notions are combined.

The three 'post-consecratory' invocations are according to Dom Gassner: the *Supra quæ*, *Supplices te rogamus*, and also the words *Per quem hæc omnia, Domine, semper bona creas*. With regard to the nature and significance of these 'invocations', the author's views seem to be a trifle confused—hesitating between an invocation *for* consecration and one merely for the *effects* of consecration in communion—partly, no doubt, owing to the lack of agreement among authors on the question and also its extreme intricacy. He seems ready, nevertheless, to admit the presence originally of an invocation of the Holy Ghost for consecration, and placed *after* the institution-narrative in the Roman Mass.

Our author, it is interesting to find, holds practically the same views regarding the use of the word *igitur* in the *Te igitur* and *Hanc igitur* as are expressed in these pages, and he also considers the prayers for Church and Pope in the *Te igitur* to be a relic of the old intercessory prayers after the Gospel originally recited in every Mass. He quotes, too, the authority of the Rev. V. L. Kennedy, to whom we have referred earlier. This book certainly deserves careful reading, in spite of its irritating style.

CHAPTER VII

THE MEMENTO OF LIVING AND DEAD; INTERCESSIONS; DIPTYCHS; NAMES

In order to really grasp the meaning and significance of the two prayers in the Roman Canon entitled *Memento*, it is necessary to know and remember that, during the early fourth century, a new form of intercessory prayer found its way into the Eucharistic Liturgy itself—formerly 'intercessions' existed only in the preliminary service, the *synaxis*. The old intercessions at the end of the service consisted of a long series of prayers for various *classes* of people; the new intercessions consisted of a mere list of the *names* of certain *individuals* which were recited aloud by a deacon during the Liturgy. This recital of individual names cannot itself be looked upon as an 'intercession' or 'prayer'; it was, rather, a 'call to prayer' addressed to clergy and congregation, inviting their personal prayer during the Liturgy for those whose names were thus announced. Except that the list of names formed an actual element of the Liturgy, it was of much the same nature as the 'notices' read out in these days, at the parish Mass, after the Gospel.

The Names in the East: It is in the East that this form of intercession is first heard of during the fourth century, being found in the *Euchologion* of Sarapion, Bishop of Thmuis, of which we have already spoken. In this liturgy, the recital of the names takes place in the anaphora after the Invocation—in this rite, of the *Word*, not the Holy Spirit. There is a prayer here for the dead in general, during which a pause is made to read out the names of certain individuals. The prayer is closely connected with the preceding prayer for the communicants— 'these people'; that is, the people actually taking part in the Liturgy as offerers and communicants. But both the prayer for the dead and the names of the departed members of 'this people' are quite evidently later interpolations in Sarapion's rite, and it seems most probable that they were brought from the

Church of Jerusalem, where the custom of praying for the dead and reading out their names during the anaphora had been introduced about this period. The custom spread gradually elsewhere in the Eastern Churches. Any intercession in Sarapion's rite during the anaphora cannot be a 'native' element, for the old form of general intercessions for all classes is still in use and in the original place at the end of the preliminary synaxis. There is even a special 'rubric' laying down that these prayers (of the old 'collect' type) are to be recited *before* the prayer of offering'—that is, the anaphora. The prayer for the 'offerer-communicants' after the Invocation is, however, an early element of the Eucharistic Prayer in all liturgies. It is possible that prayer for the dead and the mention of the names of certain individuals grew out of, and developed from, this latter prayer for the living members of the local Church. There is also a reason for such prayers, for both living and dead, in this position which is put forward by St. Cyril of Jerusalem[1] —namely, the special efficacy of prayer made in the very presence of the Divine Victim upon the altar. This reason also suggested or supported the move of the Intercessions for the living from the end of the preliminary service to the anaphora —usually after the Invocation.

EXCEPTIONS TO THIS POSITION: While the custom of reading out the names of the dead during the anaphora and after the Invocation is found in most of the Eastern rites, there are at least two exceptions. The later Alexandrian Liturgy, although it kept to the names of the dead only, as in Sarapion's *Euchologion*, has moved them back to the first part of the anaphora, adding them to the general intercessions which are found in the very middle of that part of the anaphora leading up to the *Sanctus*. This position is interesting, as it is analogous to the position of the much shortened intercession and recital of names in the *Memento* of the Roman Canon, and this provides another case of close connection between the Roman and Alexandrian rites. Secondly, the Alexandrian position of the intercessions and the diptychs of the dead shows fairly clearly that these are interpolations, for they have no direct con-

---

[1] Cyril of Jerusalem, *catech.*, xxiii. 9 (quoted by Dix, p. 499).

nection with this part of the anaphora, and, in fact, completely interrupt it. The second exception is found in the East Syrian (Nestorian) rite, in which the diptychs of both living and dead are recited *at the offertory*—and the general intercessions— formerly a long series of biddings but now in litany form—are also still in the old place; as follows:

(i) The intercessions—as described above.

(ii) The dismissals—that is, simply the formulæ—no one is really dismissed now.

(iii) The offertory-ceremonies—placing the elements on the altar—taking them from a kind of 'credence-table' near the altar. They are prepared before the synaxis.

(iv) Recital of the Creed.

(v) The diptychs of both living and dead—formerly, most probably, only the latter.

It is true that now there are short intercessions immediately after the *Sanctus*, but these are very slight and the *main* intercession is that before the offertory. This position—most unusual in an Eastern rite—which is analogous to the position of the shortened intercession in the *Te igitur* clause of the Roman Canon, shows that, as Mr. Norman says in his *Handbook to the Christian Liturgy*,[1] "the petitions in the *Anaphora* were evidently inserted at a later date, about the tenth or eleventh century". It is possible that in the Coptic rite the diptychs were also formerly recited at the offertory, since there is still a relic of the offerings made by the people at this part of the liturgy. The deacon calls on the people three times to bring up their offerings of bread and wine before the offertory-prayer, saying: "Offer, offer, offer," although the first part of the offertory takes place now as in the Byzantine rite, before the liturgy begins. When the people really *did* bring up their offerings at the offertory, it would seem only natural that the names of the dead should have been recited also in that place, as in the East Syrian rite. In Sarapion, as we have just seen, the prayer for and the recital of the names of the dead are connected with the prayer for the people as *communicants*. It came, no doubt, to be considered natural to pray here for former communicants

[1] London: S.P.C.K., 1944, p. 266.

now departed. In the East Syrian rite (and, perhaps, the Coptic as well) the connection was between the departed and the living as *offerers*. At that period offerers and communicants were closely united, even inseparable, ideas.

DEVELOPMENT OF THE DIPTYCHS: Originally the Eastern diptychs were mere lists of the names of those dead persons (later on, of the living also) for whom prayer was to be made during the liturgy. But, according to *The Shape of the Liturgy*, these lists came "into sudden prominence at Constantinople *c.* A.D. 420", and this eminence was brought about by the disputes which arose as to whether the name of St. John Chrysostom, who had been deposed from the bishopric of that city and who had died in exile in A.D. 407, should be inserted into the diptychs or not. From all this it appears that the diptychs at Constantinople then consisted of separate lists of the living and the dead, and that each list was arranged according to ecclesiastical precedence: bishops, clergy, laity—headed by the names of dead emperors. The diptychs, as Edmund Bishop also pointed out (in his Appendix III, 'The Diptychs', in *The Liturgical Homilies of Narsai*, pp. 97–117), "were to be made a test and touchstone of orthodoxy". They became actually a part of the text of the liturgy and developed liturgical formulæ and prayers. In this form, says Dix: "the West never had any 'diptychs' properly so-called at all". It is, then, a pity to use an Eastern technical term like the word 'diptych' in the case of the Western rites, and this and the constant confusion between 'intercessions', 'names' and 'diptychs'—all three really distinct *types* at least—leads to continual misunderstanding and mistake (Dix, pp. 506 and 507).

THE NAMES IN THE WEST: The 'names' always remained the 'names' and never developed into 'diptychs' in the Eastern sense, even though the 'thing' called diptych which gave the title to the lists of names inscribed upon it—that is, the twofold writing-tablet of wood or ivory—*was* used in the West for the purpose.

In the West the earliest evidence for the 'names' is found in the Spanish or Mozarabic rite, and is mentioned in the Council of Elvira, in its twenty-ninth canon (*c.* A.D. 305), as a custom already in existence. Possibly this custom was in use even in the third century (Dix, pp. 499 and 501; see also Appendix III, 'The Diptychs', in *The Liturgical Homilies of Narsai*, p. 113). On p. 115 Bishop refers to the later Council of Mâcon (A.D. 585), which orders the continuance of, or rather return to, the practice of offering the bread and wine at the offertory, as this custom had fallen into disuse. From all this we find that in the West the names followed a course exactly opposite to that of the East. The names in the Western rites were those of the *living* only and, moreover, of a *particular section* of the living; that is, of those persons who brought offerings of bread and wine for the Holy Sacrifice and presented them at the offertory of the Mass. In the Spanish rite, in that of Gaul and, as we shall see, in the Italian rites apart from that of Rome itself, the names of the living 'offerer-communicants' were recited aloud (probably by the deacon) either singly, as each person made his offering, or all together immediately after all the offerings had been presented—a kind of 'roll-call' of the faithful, in fact (Dix, p. 499).

IN THE AMBROSIAN RITE: At Milan, St. Ambrose tells us in his *De Sacramentis* (iv, 4, c. A.D. 395), that "prayers are asked for kings, for the people and the others". In these words St. Ambrose is considered by some writers to be speaking of the names, and that these were recited at an early point of the Eucharistic Prayer itself—more or less the same place, in fact, as that of the *Memento* in the Roman Canon. But the above words sound much more like the 'prayers of the faithful' or great intercession—e.g. in the mention of kings. It would seem, too, that St. Ambrose is not giving the strict *order* of the prayers here, and so he is possibly referring to these intercessions recited after the Gospel, as they had not yet, at this date, been removed from the ordinary Mass liturgy. St. Ambrose is concerned here, not about the exact *place* of the prayers, but as to whether what the celebrant says is said as a man or in the Person of Christ Himself. The former type belong to the earlier parts of the liturgy; the latter to the part with which he is immediately concerned—the consecratory portion. (See *The Early History of the Liturgy*, 1947, p. 156.)

IN THE ROMAN RITE: The first mention of the names is to be found in the famous letter from Pope Innocent I, in A.D. 416, to Decentius, Bishop of Eugubium (now Gubbio), in Central Italy. The latter, finding that the customs in use in his own diocese differed considerably from those in use in the Mother Church of Rome, had asked the Pope what ought to be done about it. Chief among these customs was that of the position of the names at Mass. This was before the offertory-prayer very much as in Gaul and Spain, though the order was not exactly the same in detail.[1] In his answer the Pope objected to this position as too early, the recital of the offerers' names taking place before the offerings had been 'commended to God'— that is, before any offertory-prayer had been said. Innocent wishes Decentius to adopt the Roman usage in this respect, as also in the other points mentioned in the letter. But in these changes which he desired Decentius to make it is most probable that the Pope was not (as has been taken for granted perhaps too easily) insisting upon a return to older customs which had been preserved in Rome, but was striving to introduce *new* customs which had been adopted there only fairly recently—perhaps by the authority of Innocent himself. It is much more likely that in provincial Churches, such as Gubbio, the more ancient customs had been kept up and that these had also continued in other Western countries—e.g. Gaul and Spain. As Dix says: "The letter of Innocent I has been strangely misunderstood by modern commentators" (Dix, p. 109). But the letter seems to have been strangely misunderstood on another point by Dix himself, as well as by other writers. This misunderstanding concerns the real meaning of the last few words of the letter, and it (the misunderstanding) is irrespective of the view held by the writer about the exact position of the 'Names' which the Pope is

[1] In the Gubbio rite the order was as follows: (i) Kiss of Peace; (ii) names recited—presumably after the persons named had presented their offerings; (iii) offertory-prayer—*after* both Pax and 'Names'.

In the Gallican-Spanish rites the order was: (i) 'Names'; (ii) the *Oratio post nomina* ('prayer after the names')—originally the 'preface' to the following prayer; (iii) *Oratio ad pacem* ('prayer for peace')—both this latter and the preceding prayer were divided between the 'Names', the Kiss and the offerings; (iv) Kiss of Peace. It will be noticed that, at Gubbio, the order followed the primitive arrangement much more closely.

insisting upon. The meaning of these last words is certainly not clear.

TEXT OF THE LETTER TO DECENTIUS: *De nominibus vero recitandis antequan precem* [or—*preces*] *sacerdos faciat atque eorum oblationes quorum nomina recitanda sunt, sua oratione commendet; quam superfluum sit et ipse pro tua prudentia recognoscis; ut cuius hostiam necdum Deo offeres, eius ante nomen insinues, quamvis illi incognitum sit nihil. Prius ergo oblationes sunt commendandæ, ac tunc eorum nomina quorum sunt edicenda ut inter sacra mysteria nominentur, non inter alia quæ ante præmittimus 'ut ipsis mysteriis viam futuris precibus aperiamus'* (Innocent I, *Ad Decentium, Epist.* xxv; *P. L.,* t. xx, col. 553). The usual translation is as follows: 'concerning the recitation of the names before the priest says the prayer [or—"prayers"] and before he commends in his own prayer the offerings of those whose names are to be recited: your own prudence[or more probably—"wisdom"] will show how superfluous[1] it is to introduce the name of one whose offering you have not yet presented to God [that is, by some prayer of oblation— either the *Secreta* or *Oratio super oblata* or, perhaps, the *Te igitur* with its reference to the *dona, munera, sacrificia illibata*], since to Him nothing is unknown. The offerings, then, should first be commended [i.e. offered verbally] and afterwards the names of those whose offerings they are, should be recited. They should be recited during the sacred mysteries and not among the things which we place before, *so that by the mysteries themselves we may open the way for the prayers that are to come.*' The first part of the letter—as far as 'and afterwards the names of those whose offerings they are, should be recited'—might be understood as referring merely to the difference between the custom at Gubbio of reciting the 'Names' immediately after the Kiss of Peace was given at the very beginning of the Mass of the Faithful before any prayer had been said; and the use in Spain and Gaul of reciting them *after* a prayer, 'commending' the offerings to God. But it is the words which follow that are the cause of difficulty and misunderstanding, namely: 'They [the 'Names']

---

[1] The word 'superfluous' (*superfluum*) used above seems hardly to be the right word in this connection; probably the Pope really meant something like 'unfitting' or 'unnecessary'.

should be recited *during the sacred mysteries* and not among the things which we place before, so that by the mysteries themselves we may open the way for the *prayers that are to come.*' (See *Epist. Pontificum*, ed. Constant I (Paris, 1721); *Catholic Encyclopædia*, Innocent I; *The Shape of the Liturgy*, p. 500.) In an article in the *Journal of Theological Studies* (April 1919), xx, 215 ff., entitled 'Pope Innocent I—"De nominibus recitandis",' the late Dom R. Hugh Connolly of Downside Abbey pointed out the absurdity of the above translation of these last words. But his own translation does not really solve the difficulty. Dom Connolly prefers to consider the word 'future' or 'to come' (*futuris*) as applying not to 'prayers' (*precibus*) but to 'the mysteries' (*mysteriis*). His translation is then: "That by the prayers we may open up the way for the mysteries themselves which are to follow." In his fairly recent work on liturgical history referred to above, the Rev. James Norman, M.A., criticises the above translation, and suggests in its place one in keeping with his own view that Innocent had no intention of ordering the 'move' of the offerers' names from offertory to canon, but simply a 'move' from before the offertory prayer to after it, as he considered that the Gubbio position was too early, since it was in the Mass of the Catechumens—and even before the dismissal of the latter—rather than in that of the Faithful. As paraphrased by Mr. Norman, the whole letter runs as follows: " 'Now about reciting the names before the priest says the prayers' [i.e. the 'prayers of the faithful', the 'intercessions'; Mr. Norman accepts the plural form *preces*—'prayers'] 'and commends in his own prayer' [i.e. the equivalent of the Roman *Secreta* or *Oratio super oblata*] 'their oblation . . . . the names ought to be mentioned . . . within the Mass of the Faithful, and not as with you, in the Mass of the Catechumens, and thus the most sacred part of the rite (*futuris precibus*) may be prepared for by that portion of the service which is reserved for the faithful' " (*Handbook to the Christian Liturgy*, p. 61). This writer says that the Latin words *prex* and *mysteria* ('prayer'; 'mystery') had not yet become technical terms for the Canon of the Mass. He shows, too, that Dom Connolly himself "takes the words of Boniface I, [*c.* A.D. 420] *inter ipsa mysteria* ['during the mysteries themselves'] as including the Prayers of the Faithful, though he says that [in this particular case] 'Innocent certainly employs *mysteria* to describe the canon', on the grounds that he is dealing expressly with the different parts of the Mass''. This—as Mr. Norman puts it—is a little arbitrary! Mr. Norman's own exposition of this difficult matter seems to be the best and clearest expression of the view that the 'Names' were still recited at the offertory in the Roman rite in Innocent's time. Dom Gregory Dix, however, although he considers that the offerers' names were *originally* recited in this early position in the Roman Mass as well as everywhere else in the West, nevertheless believes that a change had been made about Innocent's time— and perhaps by the Pope himself! He says that whether Innocent meant by the 'commendation' to God of the offerings a special prayer (*Secreta* or *Oratio super oblata*) recited at the offertory, or whether (that prayer not yet being introduced) he was referring to the early part of the *Te igitur* (in which there really *is* a 'commendation' of the offerings)—"there can be no doubt that *c.* A.D. 400 the 'Naming' of the offerers at Rome comes in approximately the same place as in Milan, in the Eucharistic Prayer itself'' (Dix, p. 500). As for the *reason* for such a change, we can only guess that perhaps the Pope (or whoever it was who brought it about) thought that the important mention of the people's gifts at the beginning of the Eucharistic Prayer—itself so near to the moment of consecration which would change these earthly gifts into the heavenly gifts of Christ's Body and Blood—was the most fitting time to 'commend' the offerers themselves. Probably, too, the example of the Eastern rites transferring the intercessions from the early part of the Liturgy of the Faithful to the anaphora and the fact that the diptychs were also recited in the anaphora (and in their case probably from the first) had some influence on it all. But Dix's translation of the difficult passage of Pope Innocent's letter to Decentius does not really make it clearer than any of the other translations. His translation is: ". . . 'So one should first commend the offerings and afterwards name them who have made them. One should *name them during the divine mysteries and not in the part of the rite which precedes*, so that the mysteries themselves lead up to the prayers to be offered' '' (Dix, p. 500, italics are mine). What does this sentence—the part italicised—mean? The same question may be asked about Dom Connolly's translation given on p. 139.

THE 'CORRECT' TRANSLATION: The only satisfactory translation of this difficult passage in Innocent's letter to Decentius—in fact, it would not be an exaggeration to say the *only one that makes any sense at all*—is that given by the Rev. V. L. Kennedy, C.S.B., in his book *The Saints of the Canon of the Mass* (Roma, 1938, p. 22). Fr. Kennedy says: "the first part of this statement is clear. In substance the Pope says that it is wrong to recite the names of the offerers before the priest says the prayer by which the offerings are commended to God . . . the second part is more difficult and it is usually interpreted to mean that the names are to be recited in the course of the sacred mysteries, so that [i.e. 'in order that'] by the mysteries themselves we may open the way for the prayers [that are] to come. . . . [but] the mysteries, the canon with its consecration, *is the 'all important thing'*. We do not prepare for certain prayers *by* the canon; we prepare *for* the canon by the [other] prayers. The mere *order* of the words [in the letter] is not decisive; the whole clause *ut ipsis mysteriis viam futuris precibus aperiamus* is directly connected with what precedes it—*quæ antea præmittimus* ('those things which we place before'). The meaning then is: the offerings are first to be commended, and then the names of those, whose offerings they are, to be recited: and this is to be done within the sacred mysteries and not in the course of those other things which we place before, that we may [*in order* that we may] open the way for *the coming mysteries themselves by our prayers.*" This is the exact opposite to the usual translation—but at least it makes Innocent talk sense! Instead of declaring that the mysteries were to open the way 'for other prayers to come'—one might well ask *what* prayers these could be—the Pope really says that 'the other things'—that is, the earlier portions of the Mass preliminary to the Eucharistic Prayer—were put first in order to prepare the way for 'the mysteries' in that prayer. In other words that the names are to be recited *during the Canon*, and not during that part which precedes the Canon and prepares the way for it. This translation of Innocent's last words in his famous letter 'makes

sense' as a translation and also shows clearly that he wished
the names to be recited within the Canon. Any attempt to
make him a supporter of the earlier position in his own period
at Rome leads to endless difficulties and practically forces into
his words a meaning which they do not really bear. Finally, it
may be said that such an attempt makes the whole meaning of
the last part of the letter almost impossible to understand. Fr.
Kennedy agrees with Dom Hugh Connolly in coupling *futuris*
with *mysteriis* and not with *precibus*, but does not agree with his
conclusion—that it was the later position of the 'Names' which
prepared the way for the 'mysteries'.

FURTHER CONFUSION ABOUT THE LETTER: This confusion is
the result of the common tendency to confuse the 'Names' with
the 'Intercessions', and both with the 'Diptychs', of which
something has already been said. In his letter, Innocent is not
talking about either intercessions or diptychs but simply and
solely about the Western custom of reciting the names of those
who offered the bread and wine at Mass. As for the Intercessions, these prayers still existed and were recited after the
Gospel at Mass as a regular part of the Holy Sacrifice in
Innocent's time (A.D. 417 is the date of his death—his birth
date is unknown). They are actually mentioned—in the old
form of collects—and at the old time after the Gospel, and in
the ordinary Mass up till the time of Pope Gelasius I. After that
time, however, they disappear as a regular element of the
Roman Mass, and their place is taken, first by the litany (introduced by Gelasius at the beginning of the service), secondly—
perhaps—by the prayer for Church and Pope in the *Te igitur*.
   The very wording of the *Memento* shows clearly the original
object of the prayer: 'Be mindful, Lord, of thy servants and
handmaids, N. & N., and of all here present . . . [for whom we
offer, or] who offer unto thee this sacrifice of praise, for themselves, for all their kinsfolk (*suisque omnibus*)'. After the *Memento*
comes the prayer beginning *Communicantes*. This latter prayer
may possibly be the earliest mention of the dead in the Western
Eucharistic Liturgy—that is, the names of the 'Blessed Dead',
Our Lady and the Saints. It was, in any case, the only reference
to any dead persons in the Roman rite until the late intro-

duction of the *Memento etiam* (of which we shall speak presently) after the consecration. The *Communicantes* is not easy to translate; the word *communicantes* itself is the present participle— meaning 'communicating' or 'joining with'—without any subject or subjects with which to agree or any principal verb, and the same may be said of the word *venerantes* ('reverencing'). This curious character of the prayer is perhaps the result of its being a late interpolation from elsewhere by Gelasius (A.D. 492–6). In general the two participles no doubt agree with a subject like *nos* ('we'), meaning the celebrant, his concelebrants and ministers and members of the congregation. This word may be again the subject of *offerimus* or *qui offerunt* ('we offer' or 'who offer') in the *Memento*, or perhaps these participles hark back to the words *rogamus ac petimus* or *tibi offerimus* ('we humbly pray and beseech' or 'we offer unto thee') in the *Te igitur*. In any case, the *Communicantes* is not an original element of the Canon. It is followed by the *Hanc igitur*. This prayer was also originally connected with the names, but those of certain special persons or those belonging to special classes (religious men and women, the newly baptised and so on) or of those who were unable, for some reason, to bring offerings themselves. According to Dix, the fact that this prayer is one of the two prayers of the Canon still changeable on certain occasions,[1] shows that it belongs to the fifth century, when variable prayers were brought into the Liturgy. In the Leonine and Gelasian Sacramentaries many interchangeable forms of this prayer are found. In the Leonine Sacramentary, in the Mass entitled *In Pentecosten ascendentibus a fonte* ('On [the Day of] Pentecost, for those rising up from the font'—i.e. the newly baptised), the *Hanc igitur* is placed immediately after the *Memento* between that prayer and the *Communicantes*. In his edition of the Leonine Sacramentary, Mr. Feltoe says of this: "In one instance [pp. 24 and 25] the natural order of the *Hanc igitur* and *Communicantes* is inverted, but this is probably due to the transcriber's carelessness and to nothing else" (*The Leonine Sacramentary*, edited Feltoe, 1896, p. xvi, footnote). This assertion, however, may be due simply to what Mr. Feltoe, and no doubt most people, *consider* to be the natural order of the two prayers. Dom Gregory Dix, on the other hand,

---

[1] The other is the *Communicantes*.

thinks it quite probable that the Leonine order was the original order and, moreover, the more natural one. For if the original order were *Memento; Hanc igitur; Communicantes*—it would have meant the recital of the names first of the usual offerers (*Memento*)—and also, in that prayer, the names of certain persons for whom offerings were made if, for some reason, unable to offer themselves (mention is still made of these in the *Memento*: *pro quibus tibi offerimus vel qui tibi offerunt*; 'for whom we offer *or* who themselves offer', etc.); then of particular persons, on particular occasions (*Hanc igitur*), and finally the recital of the names of the 'Blessed Dead' (*Communicantes*). As to who were the particular persons whose names were mentioned in the *Hanc igitur*, we find in the Leonine and Gelasian Sacramentaries a large number of special forms of the prayer which, instead of the request to God to accept the offering, as in the form now in use: *Hanc igitur oblationem . . . quæsumus, Domine, ut placatus accipias* ('We therefore beseech Thee, O Lord, to be appeased and to accept this oblation'), expresses the direct action of offering, and the verb is sometimes in the singular, instead of the more usual plural. Occasionally it is in the third person (singular or plural), or even, again, in the *first person singular* ('I offer'—*offero*). Sometimes this was the celebrant himself.

Possibly it was St. Gregory the Great who included the *Hanc igitur* as a regular feature in the canon, and who arranged the present form. He is at least the traditional author of its final words: *diesque nostros in tua pace disponas* ('do Thou order our days in Thy peace'), which remain unchanged, even when the first part varies on certain feasts. The original connection with the recital of the names has been lost, but it still existed in the sixth century on certain occasions. (See *Gelasian Sacramentary,* edited Wilson, p. 34.) Dix suggests that besides adding the clause *diesque nostros,* St. Gregory was also responsible for changing the position of the prayer to *after* instead of *before* the *Communicantes*—and that he probably expanded and re-arranged the lists of saints in both *Communicantes* and *Nobis quoque.* In the days when the *Hanc igitur* admitted the names, on certain occasions, of particular persons; when, too, instead of the words *hanc igitur,* the prayer began with *hanc etiam* or *itaque* ('again' or 'and so')—and once, in the *Gelasian Sacramentary, hanc quoque* ('also')—its position immediately after the *Memento* and before the *Communicantes* would have been the more natural position.

THE NAMES OF THE DEAD IN THE WEST: In the East, as we have seen, the earliest evidence of the recital of 'Names' in the Liturgy is that of the dead; in the West the contrary is true—only the names of the living, and of a special section of the living, were recited in early times.

IN GAUL AND SPAIN: The earliest evidence of the names of the dead is found in the seventh–eighth centuries. Here the names of the dead were added to those of the living which were recited at the offertory. This development of the Western 'Names' was partly due to the Gallican and Spanish tendency, which has already been noticed, to adopt elements of the Eastern rites. Thus the Gaulish and Spanish 'Names' became much more like the Eastern Diptychs than those of the Roman rite. The Mozarabic rite, in the later MSS., declares explicitly that the 'Names' are those *offerentium et pausantium* ('of the offerers and the departed ones'[1]—i.e. the dead). Gregory Dix says that it is *possible* that the dead were mentioned by name together with the living in the Gallican and Spanish rites even in pre-Nicene times, and that the relatives or some representatives of the dead offered in " 'the name of' those departed from that church in its peace and communion"; but he adds that if this idea is "not contradicted by the evidence, it is not explicitly supported by it" (Dix, pp. 499 and 500).

IN ROME: In the Roman Mass the General Intercession, while it continued to be a part of the everyday rite, did not include in its long series of prayers any mention of the dead.[2] When the 'Names' came into fashion in the West, we find at first only those of the offerers at Mass—at Rome this was in the *Memento* before consecration. The first evidence in Rome for the recital at Mass of the names of ordinary dead persons (apart,

[1] Literally 'the waiting' or 'resting ones'.
[2] This is true also of the intercessions in Sarapion's *Euchologion*, which resemble the Roman prayers so closely.

that is, from the 'Blessed Dead') *as an item of the regular service*, occurs only in the ninth–tenth centuries. This custom was adopted from France, where it had become the regular custom in the eighth–ninth centuries. Both in France and Rome, before that time, the 'Names' of dead persons were recited only in Masses celebrated *for* the dead and at funerals. There are several MSS. of the Roman Canon in which there is no reference to the ordinary dead at all.

In the later Roman Canon the names of the dead are mentioned in a short prayer beginning *Memento etiam* ('Be mindful also'). This prayer was evidently intended to correspond with the *Memento* (of the living) before the consecration, although introduced into the canon at a much later date and *after* the consecration. According to Mr. Edmund Bishop, the *Memento etiam* is really ancient in style and undoubtedly of Roman composition; but it is an open question as to the date of its introduction into the Roman rite—even as an element only of the Requiem Mass. As we have seen already, while the souls of her departed children were not forgotten by Mother Church, they were not prayed for publicly and liturgically in the earliest period, the Liturgy being primarily and externally concerned with the living members of each local church and, in general, of the Church throughout the world.

In both the *Memento* of the living and that of the dead, the place in the prayer in which the 'Names' were to be recited, was indicated by the letters *N. et N.* (for *nomen*—'name'). In the *Memento* of the living, the names of those for whom the celebrant wishes and has been asked to pray are still actually mentioned (secretly) at this point. But in the *Memento etiam*, although *N. et N.* are still printed in every missal, the mention of the 'Names' is put off till after the words *qui . . . dormiunt in somno pacis* ('who . . . rest in the sleep of peace'). Edmund Bishop says that this arrangement is "a middle term that does not belong to either use, Roman or Gallican, but shows a compromise between the two. . . . The rubric 'nomina' in spite of grammar is made part of the text, and the recitation of the names is deferred and intercalated between the two clauses of which the Memento consists, i.e. between the words '. . . in somno pacis' and 'Ipsis Domine et omnibus . . .';

this, again, is a compromise which will allow either of the silent recital of the names by the celebrant, or of the insertion of 'the diptychs' " . . . the latter alternative "has, in derogation of its ancient practice still evidenced by the words of the Memento themselves, been by-and-by adopted by the Roman Church" (The *Journal of Theological Studies*, July 1903, 'On the Early Texts of the Roman Canon', pp. 555–77). In this article Mr. Bishop goes into the question of the *Memento etiam*, and shows that it was a late interpolation into the Canon, and at first only for use in Masses for the dead, and he gives for his authority in this the Lyons deacon, Florus (died *c.* A.D. 860). (See *Journal of Theological Studies*, p. 572 and p. 573 and footnotes.) Florus speaks of this early temporary use of the *Memento etiam* as being the ancient custom still (in his own day) observed by the Roman Church. It would seem to be most likely that it was the introduction of special Masses offered for the dead (*special* dead persons particularly) which gave rise to the custom of mentioning individual names in the Mass, and it was no doubt started and brought about by the Franco-Irish and Spanish communities, for whom prayer for and mention by name of their departed 'dear ones' was a matter of personal love and devotion. As Bishop says in the above article: "It is no accident that All Souls Day originated in France" (*Journal of Theological Studies*, July 1903, p. 575).

POSSIBLE EXCEPTION TO THIS DATE: Some liturgical authorities consider that in Africa, as early as the third century, we have evidence of a 'naming' of dead persons in the Liturgy—and, moreover, within the Eucharistic Prayer itself. This evidence is said to be provided by St. Cyprian of Carthage (A.D. 240) in two passages in Ep. xvi. (ix.), 2, and in Ep. i. (lxvi.), 2. The first passage objects to the reception of lapsed persons to communion and speaks of their 'name being offered'. But the reading of the passage in Latin, says Dr. Srawley: "appears to be faulty, and the more recent editors give the correction 'offering is made in their name' " and in a footnote: Reading: *offertur nomine eorum* (Hartel), (Srawley, 1947, pp. 126 and 127). The second passage from St. Cyprian refers to the decision of an earlier African Council that those bishops

who appointed clerics as executors, in their wills, are to have
no offerings made for them, nor is the Sacrifice to be celebrated for the repose of their souls. But Dr. Srawley again
considers that in this decision the Council is speaking of offering the Mass for the dead and of a yearly commemoration of
the dead in general—he says that "this is probably all that is
meant in this passage. It is *inadequate evidence* of the existence of
a public recitation of the *names* of the dead in the normal
Eucharists of the Church" (italics mine). He points out that St.
Augustine, speaking of this commemoration of the dead, says
distinctly that there is *no* mention of their names (*etiam tacitis
nominibus eorum sub generali commemoratione suscipit ecclesia*; 'The
Church admits [the remembrance of the dead] although their
names are not mentioned'). Dix, however, thinks that, on the
contrary, these words *etiam tacitis nominibus eorum* ('although
their names are not mentioned') imply that there *was* usually
an individual 'naming' as well as the general mention. (See, for
St. Augustine's words, his *De cura pro mortuis gerenda* ('Of the
solicitude to be shown for the dead'), § 6. Migne, *P.L.* 40, 596;
as in 'The Liturgical Homilies of Narsai', p. 112, footnote 2,
in Appendix III, by E. Bishop). Dr. Srawley shows that Augustine makes a distinction between the ordinary dead for whom
prayer was offered and the martyrs whose prayers were asked
for, and that nuns were included as sharing in their martyrdom.
The distinction between martyrs and ordinary dead persons is
found also in the Mozarabic rite—but in the Gallican rite only
the latter's names were recited. In the Roman rite, on the contrary, only the names of Our Lady and the saints (the 'Blessed
Dead') were recited at first, and even these were introduced
fairly late into the Canon, and the prayer for the ordinary dead
(*Memento etiam*), as we have seen above, did not appear till very
late—comparatively speaking—and at first only in Requiem
Masses. The conclusion to be drawn from all these differences,
thinks Dr. Srawley following Mr. E. Bishop, is "that this diver-
gence of custom in the West with regard to the recital of the
names of the dead 'points to a later and independent adoption
of a practice imported or suggested from elsewhere' ". (Srawley, p. 206 and quotation in footnote from article by E. Bishop
in *Journal of Theological Studies*, xii, 392, see also iv, 371 f.)

METHOD OF RECITING THE NAMES: Innocent says nothing in his letter to Decentius of Gubbio as to *how* the 'Names' were recited in the Roman rite—that is, whether aloud or secretly. At Gubbio and elsewhere in other parts of Italy, as in Gaul and Spain, the names of the living were recited aloud—probably by the deacon. If they had been recited secretly in Rome, as in the present use of the *Memento*, Innocent would surely have drawn Decentius' attention to so striking a difference from the custom at Gubbio, and also have insisted upon its adoption there, together with the other points of which he (the Pope) had spoken. St. Jerome, in an earlier period, tells us "that in his day the names of persons who had made offerings to the church funds were publicly read out in church. . . . Although he does not expressly say so, yet from all analogy, and from the use by him of the specific term *offerentes*, it is only reasonable to conclude that this recitation of names was made at the time of the mass. . . . That this . . . custom prevailed also in Rome and in Upper Italy appears also from the famous letter of Innocent I to Decentius, bishop of Gubbio of the year 416". In neither the Spanish Council of Elvira in A.D. 305 or 306— which speaks of the recitation of the names of the offerers in connection with the oblation at the altar—nor in the above letter is it stated that the names were said aloud and publicly; "this must be a matter of inference from Jerome's words and later usage" (Edmund Bishop, in Appendix III: 'The Diptychs', in *The Liturgical Homilies of Narsai*, pp. 98 and 99).

It seems probable that the Eucharistic Prayer at Rome, and everywhere at that time, was still *one* prayer, undivided as yet by the *Sanctus* into two sections, and that the whole prayer was still chanted aloud as far as and including the Words of Institution and continuing thus up till the end. The silent recitation of the section after the *Sanctus* (the Canon) in the West and of the whole Prayer (the anaphora in the East—except the Words of Institution, which are *chanted* aloud) seems to have become customary during the sixth century. It apparently was brought about owing to the influence of the East Syrian Churches at that date. (See *The Liturgical Homilies of Narsai*, Appendix V, 'Silent Recital of the Mass of the Faithful', by Edmund Bishop, pp. 121–6). The names of the dead in Gaul, and of the saints

as well in Spain, were recited aloud (when they were introduced), like the names of the living offerers, as they were recited
like the latter, at the offertory. But in Rome the late date of
their introduction into the Canon brought them into the silent
recitation of that part of the Eucharistic Prayer.

THE NAMES OF THE SAINTS: Connected with the diptychs are
the lists of names of the saints (preceded by that of Our Lady,
Queen of saints) which are found in all later liturgies, Eastern
and Western. At first local martyrs' names alone were recited;
but later those of patriarchs, prophets and apostles were added.
This innovation was started by St. Cyril of Jerusalem in his
Catecheses (A.D. 348), and it was adopted everywhere—together
with other innovations introduced by that saint. In Rome the
list of saints was rather haphazard, and it never lost altogether
its local character. The present arrangement in the Roman
missal is, it seems, due to Gregory the Great, *c.* A.D. 595.
Among the men-saints there are still only four non-Roman
martyrs among the whole sixteen, and one of the four—St.
Ignatius of Antioch—was actually martyred at Rome. Again,
among women-martyrs there are only four out of seven
who were not Roman—two of them (Agatha and Lucy were
Sicilians) were almost certainly added by St. Gregory.[1] Besides
these there is St. Anastasia from the Balkans, whose cultus was
due chiefly to Greek settlers in Rome. Her name was introduced
into the Canon apparently from confusion with the lady also
called Anastasia, who built an old parish church in Rome
which became known as the *Titulus Anastasiæ*. This word *titulus*
('title'—literally a 'label' on which the names or 'titles' of persons or places were written) was given to the early parish
churches in Rome served by those priests of the local Roman
church, progenitors of the later 'cardinal-priests of the Holy
Roman Church' (i.e. again the *local* church of Rome).

---

[1] See, for the names of the saints in the Canon, the brochure by the Rev. V. L.
Kennedy, C.S.B., in *Antichità Cristiana*, etc., Rome, 1938—referred to on p. 141.

CHAPTER VIII

THE INVOCATION OF THE HOLY GHOST AND THE 'MOMENT' OF CONSECRATION

IMMEDIATELY after the consecration in the Roman Canon come the three prayers, beginning respectively: *Unde et memores* ('Wherefore . . . mindful'); *Supra quæ propitio ac sereno vultu* ('Upon which [vouchsafe to look] with a favourable and gracious countenance'); *Supplices te rogamus . . . jube hæc preferri . . . in sublime altare tuum* ('We humbly beseech thee . . . to command that these [offerings] be carried . . . to thine altar on high'). The first is officially called the *Anamnesis*—from a Greek word meaning a 'memorial'—as it commemorates the Passion, Resurrection and Ascension of Our Lord and is, in fact, a development of His words to the disciples at the Last Supper: 'Do this for a commemoration of me' (Luke xxii. 19). In this full form the prayer seems to be a special feature of the Roman rite; in the other developed rites, while there was always a solemn prayer of oblation after the consecration, only the Roman rite commemorated also the Passion, Resurrection and Ascension—which all together make up the Sacrifice of our Redemption. But this 'Roman type' soon spread elsewhere—not necessarily in a copy of the exact words, but in the underlying idea—and in the East as well as in the West. It was not adopted *everywhere*, however, even in the West—for example, it is not found in either the Gallican or the Spanish rites. In Hippolytus' canon there is the initial form which was fully developed in the later Roman Mass—'when ye do this [ye] do my memorial (*anamnesis*); doing therefore the memorial (*anamnesis*) of His death and resurrection, we offer to Thee the bread and the cup' (*Apostolic Tradition*, pp. 7 and 8). In this Liturgy, as a whole, we really have all the elements of the later Roman Canon—except its 'interpolations': there is the thanksgiving-series of the Eucharistic Prayer (most of which was lost when the threefold *Sanctus* and its preface were introduced), leading up to the account of the Last Supper and the Institution of the

Eucharist; then comes the 'Therefore-section', as it might be called—corresponding to the *Te igitur* in the Roman Canon, but in Hippolytus occurring later in the prayer and connected with the carrying out of the 'Memorial' (*anamnesis*) of the Redemption and with the prayer for the offerers and communicants. (*Apostolic Tradition*, pp. 8 and 9.)

THE 'EPIKLESIS', OR INVOCATION, OF THE HOLY GHOST: In the Eastern liturgies another type of prayer is found in this part of the anaphora—its precise position differs in different rites— known as the *Epiklesis*: this is the Greek title which means 'invocation', 'calling upon'. In this prayer the Holy Ghost is invoked to come down upon the offerings of bread and wine, and to change them into the Body and Blood of Our Lord. In the Orthodox Eastern Church the prayer is considered to be the 'form' or 'moment' of consecration, the Words of Institution being the historical 'statement' of what Christ did at the Last Supper and of the commands He gave to His disciples regarding His actions. But in its earlier forms this prayer calls upon the Holy Spirit to come down—not upon the offerings, but upon *those who have offered them*, upon the people present and about to communicate—in order to sanctify them and make them worthy of the Holy Food. Whether the Invocation, even in this earlier form, was a 'primitive' element of the Holy Sacrifice is still a much-discussed question. Its primitive and essential element is usually supported by Anglicans, but some Catholic writers are of this opinion also. It is still a question among liturgical writers, too, as to whether or not the Roman Canon originally possessed an Invocation of the Holy Ghost. That it possesses an 'invocation' for the consecration of the bread and wine but *before* the Words of Institution and without special mention of the Holy Spirit, is a fact that cannot be denied. What is called by Dix the 'link-prayer' (the prayer *Quam oblationem*) is certainly an 'invocation' in this wider sense. In the Egyptian Liturgy (and in its earliest form the Liturgy of Sarapion) there is an Invocation (of the Holy Ghost) before the Words of Institution and in the MSS. of the Egyptian Liturgy which were discovered at 'der Balyzeh', there is a *fully developed* Invocation of the Holy Ghost for the consecration of the elements, after the *Sanctus* and well before the Words of Institution. Again (as seems to be inevitable in all such cases!) the MSS. stop short at the important moment, and we are left ignorant as to whether or not there was another epiklesis as well, *after* the Words of Institution—as in Sarapion's Liturgy and in the later Alexandrian rite.

THE EPIKLESIS IN THE APOSTOLIC TRADITION: In Hippolytus' Liturgy there is an epiklesis of the Holy Ghost after the Words of Institution: "And we pray Thee that [Thou wouldest send Thy Holy Spirit upon the oblation of Thy holy Church] Thou wouldest grant to all [Thy saints] who partake to be made one that they be fulfilled with [the] Holy Spirit, for the confirmation of [their] faith in truth". We have taken this translation from the edition of *The Apostolic Tradition* by Dom Gregory Dix. It is he who prints the actual epiklesis in square brackets, as he maintains that this apparent example of an epiklesis in the early third century is almost certainly a late Eastern interpolation. It is not found in the text which he entitles 'T' in 'The Textual Materials' of his edition of *The Apostolic Tradition* (p. lxvi, No. iii *et seq.*). This is the text of the Testament of Our Lord, which is a seventh-century Syrian translation of a lost fourth-century—or early fifth-century—extension and adaptation of *The Apostolic Tradition*. Dom Gregory Dix points out that it is important to remember here that the writer of 'T' made use of a very good codex of the *Tradition*, and that he "also succeeded in treating his source with remarkable respect" (p. lxvii). He adds that an Eastern of the late fourth or fifth century might have been expected to be particularly careful to insist upon the epiklesis—if such a thing existed in the original text of the *Tradition*—or, if it was not in it, to have himself inserted it into his own edition of the text, especially as he has followed Hippolytus' text *word for word* right up to this particular point! Moreover, in 'T' alone, the clause which follows the part given above in square brackets is really a 'coherent text'. But there are other liturgical scholars who do not agree with this view, and who regard the Invocation of the Holy Ghost in the other texts of *The Apostolic Tradition* as genuine and as a striking example of its early introduction into the Eucharistic

Prayer. For example, Dr. Srawley declares that "the reading [containing the Invocation] is fully supported by both the Latin and the Ethiopic versions which are direct translations". He adds that "the words contain no petition for the conversion of the elements as in the later Greek forms. The whole emphasis is on the action of the Holy Spirit on the minds and hearts of the faithful, 'to bring God's people together in one', and 'the oblation of holy Church', while it includes the gifts, would seem to suggest the whole action of the Church in offering. It is, in fact, a prayer for communicants" (*The Early History of the Liturgy*, Cambridge, 1947, p. 70). While this shows that the Invocation in *The Apostolic Tradition* is of the early form, it does not thereby prove that it was in the original text.

Dom Bernard Botte, O.S.B., of the Abbey of Mont César, in Belgium, also disagrees with Dom Gregory Dix's view. In his recent brochure—*Hippolyte de Rome: La Tradition Apostolique*, 1946 (Blackfriars' Publications, agents for Les Editions du Cerf, Oxford, pp. 22 and 23)—he says: "I believe that Fr. Dix is mistaken." He himself considers that the absence of the Invocation in *The Testament of Our Lord* is of much less importance than the agreement about its presence found in *other* texts— quite independently of each other. As a matter of fact Dom Botte really *denies* that the Invocation is absent in the text of *The Testament*. He says that although the Invocation does not appear in exactly the same part of the Prayer as in the particular MS. of *The Apostolic Tradition*, quoted by Dom G. Dix, it is found, nevertheless, only a little farther on—"In an equivalent form". But what Dom Botte considers to be an equivalent form of epiklesis in *The Testament of Our Lord* is simply the last part of the prayer in Hippolytus' Liturgy, in which the *actual epiklesis* was inserted in later times (according to Dix), and runs as follows: 'And we pray Thee that . . . Thou wouldest grant to all [Thy Saints] who partake, to be united [to Thee] that they may be fulfilled with the Holy Spirit for the confirmation of [their] faith in truth' (*Apostolic Tradition*, p. 9). This is hardly an 'epiklesis', i.e. an *invocation* of the Holy Spirit, asking Him to come down upon either the communicants or the offerings. There is, in fact, no *invocation* of the Holy Ghost at all—although He is *mentioned* in the prayer which asks that the communicants be 'fulfilled with the Holy Spirit for the confirmation of their faith, in truth'. Finally, Dom Botte does not touch at all upon the long and detailed discussion of the general question of the epiklesis of the Holy Spirit; its introduction into the Liturgy; its significance and so on—which is given by Dix in *The Apostolic Tradition*, pp. 75–80; iv, 11–12; nor does he explain why—if the epiklesis was really an original part of Hippolytus' text—it was not copied, *as it stands*, in the text of *The Testament*!

In an article in *Theology* (an Anglican review), xxviii, 1934, No. 166, pp. 189 *et seq*.) Dom Gregory Dix shows that outside Syria the Invocation of the Holy Ghost in the Liturgy "cannot be traced farther back than *c*. A.D. 330". He sums up: "the explanation which best suits *all* the facts is that of interpolation [of the epiklesis] in L.E." L is a "fragmentary Latin version" of the Apostolic Tradition of the late fourth or early fifth century; E is an "Ethiopic version of the whole treatise" of a fifth-century text of *The Apostolic Tradition*. (See *The Apostolic Tradition of St. Hippolytus*, edited Dix, 'Textual Materials', p. iii, and 'Textual Notes', p. 79.)

THE INVOCATION IN THE WEST: In *The Liturgical Homilies of Narsai*—already spoken of in these pages—Mr. Edmund Bishop inclines, like Dom Dix, to the view of the comparative lateness of the epiklesis of the Holy Ghost as a feature of the Liturgy, and also of the comparative lateness in the explicit development of theology about the Holy Spirit. Even in its earlier form, invoking the Holy Spirit to sanctify the communicants and to enable them to profit by their reception of the Divine Food, the Invocation of the Holy Ghost seems to have been a fairly late introduction into the Eucharistic Liturgy. As for its presence in the Western rite: a direct Invocation of the Holy Ghost is found—*occasionally* only—in the Gallican and Spanish MSS.—which are of sixth-century date, be it remembered. In the Roman rite, apart from the epiklesis found in Hippolytus—which may or may not be genuine—the only other 'clue' is found in two writings of Pope Gelasius I (A.D. 492–6). The first is a treatise on the two natures of Our Lord written against the Monophysites; the second occurs in a letter to Elpidius (Bishop of

Volterra in Tuscany), dealing with the administration of the Sacraments by criminal members of the clergy. In the first the Pope says that "the image and likeness of the body and blood of Christ are celebrated in the performance of the mysteries", and that "they pass into this, that is the divine substance, by the operation of the Holy Spirit" (Thiel, *Epp. Rom. Pontif.*, l, 5.4.1). In the second, Gelasius asks "how will the heavenly Spirit (*cælestis spiritus*) come [when] called (*invocatus*) to consecrate the divine mystery, if the priest who prays for His coming be rejected as full of criminous deeds?" (Thiel l, 486). In the recent re-edition of his book, *The Early History of the Liturgy*, Dr. Srawley says, after giving the above quotations, that these words of Gelasius "give no indication as to how the Holy Spirit's action in the Eucharist found expression", and that the first of the two passages could be regarded as referring to "a general recognition of the Holy Spirit's ministry in the Eucharistic rite", while in the second passage, the "vague phrase . . . (*cælestis spiritus*) is consistent with something little more than the phrase used in the *Epistle to Cæsarius*, which speaks of 'the divine grace sanctifying the bread at the mediation of the priest' "—in Latin, *divina autem sanctificante gratia, mediante sacerdote, liberatus est ab appellatione panis* (*P.G.*, lii, 758). He adds that it has been argued that the original epiklesis "has been whittled down in the Roman and other Western rites under the influence of the idea that the words of Christ constitute the real consecration. But the evidence produced *is inadequate to support this conclusion*" (p. 178, italics mine). Had there been such an epiklesis in the Roman Canon, it is incredible that it should have left not a trace behind in any of the MSS., nor any reference to it in any ancient liturgical or other writings, except the above uncertain passages in Gelasius' letters and treatise. Cardinal Schuster, in his Sacramentary (Vol. I, p. 270. English translation. Burns, Oates & Washbourne, Ltd., 1904), while he considers that the words of Gelasius refer to a '*pre-consecratory* epiklesis' (although he does not explain *why* or *how* the words of the Pope imply this latter fact), admits that the passage is not absolutely conclusive, for the Pope in writing to Elpidius may very well have been using an argument *ad hominem* and basing his reasoning on the anaphora of his correspondent.

THE QUAM OBLATIONEM—AN EPIKLESIS: We have seen that some writers look on the *Quam oblationem* as a relic of a former pre-consecratory *full* epiklesis of the Holy Ghost, reduced later to a vaguer form—here again even the possible 'why' and 'how' are not explained, apart from the supposed more recent influence of the Words of Institution. The fact that there is a considerable amount of resemblance between the Roman Canon and the anaphora of the Egyptian rite and, especially, that the latter has, besides the usual Eastern epiklesis after the Words of Institution, an epiklesis before them—just after the 'tersanctus'—certainly strengthens the opinion that the *Quam oblationem* is a pre-consecratory invocation, asking for the Divine act of consecration, but not necessarily ever an Invocation of the Holy Spirit in the technical sense, as in the Eastern rites.

THE ORIGINAL ROMAN EPIKLESIS: Some consider that the *Supplices*—which is in the same *position* as the epiklesis in most Eastern rites—is a 'watered down' relic of the original Roman epiklesis. But not only is the epiklesis 'watered down' in this prayer—its nature is completely *reversed*. The Roman prayer, instead of asking for the descent of the Holy Ghost upon the oblations, asks that the oblations may be "borne by the hands of thy Holy Angel to thine altar on high". The late Mr. Codrington, speaking of the above view of the *Supplices* as the Roman epiklesis, says, first, that in certain Egyptian anaphoras translated into Syriac, there is an epiklesis of the Holy Ghost conjoined with a prayer asking God to receive the sacrifice upon His heavenly altar (as in the Roman prayer), and he gives as examples the anaphora of Timothy of Alexandria (British Museum, Add. 14520); the anaphora of Severus (alias Timothy as above), translated into Latin by Renaudot, *Litt. Orien. Coll.* ii, 321 ff.; Syriac original (Paris, Bibliothèque Nationale, MS. 75); Syriac anaphora of S. John Chrysostom (Renaudot, ii, 242 ff.). In the Greek Liturgy of St. Mark this prayer is found as the 'prayer of the offerers', i.e. *before* consecration. This latter position and object of the prayer is of late date and is contrary to the genuine Egyptian use. Mr. Codrington shows also that these two prayers—the prayer invoking the Holy Spirit to consecrate gifts upon the *earthly* altar and the prayer asking that they be taken up to the *heavenly* altar —are two quite incompatible types and represent two quite different notions. In this respect, as in others, the Egyptian Liturgy agrees with that of Rome (*Journal of Theological Studies*, April 1938, No. 154, xxxix, 141–50). From Mr. Codrington's article it appears that the earlier Egyptian Liturgy (that is, of the date when the epiklesis was introduced) possessed a 'full-blown' epiklesis *before* consecration, and a prayer corresponding to the Roman *Supplices* (perhaps, rather to its earlier form in the *De Sacramentis*) *after* consecration. This provides again further resemblances between the Roman and Egyptian rites.

CHAPTER IX

FINAL PRAYERS OF THE CANON AND DOXOLOGY

AT the end of the prayer *Nobis quoque* there are two formulæ of special interest. The first runs as follows: *per quem hæc omnia, Domine, semper bona creas, sanctificas, vivificas, benedicis et præstas nobis* ('through whom [Jesus Christ], O Lord, thou dost always create all these things good [i.e. 'create them *as* good', '*make* them good'], dost hallow, enliven (or 'vivify'), bless and bestow them upon us'. (See Genesis i. 31; Wisdom xi. 25.)). The above words are usually explained as referring to the blessings of other gifts, presented, together with the offerings of bread and wine, by the faithful at Mass. For example, in the Liturgy of Hippolytus offerings of oil, cheese and olives were presented, and the form of the blessings of these objects is given in the text. We have, too, an actual example in our own times: the solemn Blessing of the Holy Oil of the sick on Maundy Thursday by every bishop in his own cathedral, which takes place, moreover, at this very moment in the canon.

ABOVE EXPLANATION UNSATISFACTORY: According to the Rev. J. B. O'Connell, author of several important books on the ceremonial of the Roman rite and editor of the recently published Missal in Latin and English (London: Burns, Oates & Washbourne, Ltd., 1949)[1] and other liturgical authorities, the words in question refer *primarily* to the consecrated Gifts themselves, and can be so applied quite satisfactorily. If we remember that the consecrated Elements each retain after consecration the outward appearances and characteristics of bread and wine—the 'accidents' as the theologians say—we shall see that the word *creas* ('thou dost create') can certainly be used of them. Then the words *sanctificas, vivificas, benedicis* ('Thou dost hallow, enliven'—i.e. 'fill with life', bless) all

---

[1] His other works are: *The Ceremonies of the Roman Rite*, by Adrian Fortescue, re-edited and corrected; there have been seven editions (Burns, Oates & Washbourne, Ltd.); *The Celebration of Mass*. 3 vols. (Bruce Publishing Company, Milwaukee, U.S.A.; Burns, Oates & Washbourne, Ltd., 1940, and second edition, 1948-9). The second work is entirely his own.

imply the act of consecration which in a very true sense
sanctifies, fills with life and blesses the material offerings of
bread and wine by changing them *substantially* into the Body
and Blood of Christ Himself. The final words *præstas nobis*
('Thou dost bestow upon us') refer to the communion of celebrant, concelebrants and people—upon all of whom God
bestows this 'Bread of Life' and 'Chalice of salvation'. Fr.
O'Connell points out that the words *per quem* ('through whom'
—i.e. Our Lord) which follow the conclusion of the *Nobis
quoque* (after which come the words discussed above) are
closely connected with the prayers that precede the *Nobis quoque*.
First, the *Unde et memores . . . offerimus . . . de tuis donis et datis,
hostiam puram . . . panem sanctum vitæ æternæ et calicem salutis per-
petuæ* ('. . . we offer . . . from the Gifts given us by Thee, a pure
Victim . . . the holy Bread of everlasting life and the cup of
never-ending salvation'), and the following words *supra quæ*
('upon which' [Gifts]) and *supplices te rogamus . . . iube hæc* ('we
humbly beseech Thee . . . command that these [Gifts] be taken
up by Thy Holy Angel, to Thine altar on high') leading up to
per eumdem Christum Dominum nostrum ('through the same Christ,
Our Lord'), after which the words *per quem hæc omnia* no doubt
originally followed at once; that is, before the addition of the
memento etiam and *nobis quoque*. If, however, the latter prayer
formed part of the developed Canon from the first, the *per
quem hæc omnia* would still have followed on quite well. It may
be that the word *creas* led to the notion that the whole set of
expressions used here could not refer to the consecrated Elements. On the contrary, it would seem that the whole 'set' describes what we may call the 'evolution' of the Divine action
with regard to the Sacred Gifts of the Holy Eucharist.

Another objection might be made, on account of the plural
words—*hæc omnia* ('all these things') being applied to the Mass
as celebrated to-day—normally with only one large host and
one chalice. We must remember, however, that in the days when
these words were written, the small square altars of the Roman
basilicas were often 'heaped up' (as one of the Mass-secrets puts
it)[1] with a large number of small *loaves*—not thin wafers—and

---

[1] Mass of All Hallows' Eve—i.e. The Vigil of All Saints on October 31st,
Hallow-e'en, in Scotland.

several chalices of wine. All these loaves and all the wine were offered during the Mass by the members of the congregation, who all normally received communion at the Mass, in both kinds.

THE WORDS DUE TO POPE ST. LEO I: It has been suggested to the writer by the Rev. J. B. O'Connell in a private letter, that the clause in question may have been introduced into the Roman Canon owing to the opposition of St. Leo I to the Manichæan heretics in the fifth century. In Sermon xlii (for Lent) occurs the phrase: *Omnia bona bonus Auctor instituit et unus est universorum rerum Auctor* ('All good things their good Maker hath appointed and the Maker of all things is *One*') (*P.L.*, t. liv.).

THE WORDS OF THE DOXOLOGY: These are—*per ipsum et cum ipso* etc. ('through Him and with Him'); which follow *per quem hæc omnia*, and are more fittingly united with the preceding words if these refer to the consecrated gifts, as suggested above. The *amen* in reply to the doxology was originally chanted by the whole congregation, and it is still sung by the choir—which represents the congregation. The words themselves of the doxology sum up the meaning and significance of the Holy Sacrifice: "*through, with,* and *in* [the Divine Victim] is offered to God the Father all honour and glory in unity with the Holy Spirit". Very similar words are found in an example taken from the *Missale Gothicum* given by Duchesne in his book on Christian worship, and it forms the conclusion of the prayer called *Post Secreta*, after the consecration; sometimes also called *Post Pridie*[1] or *Post Mysterium*. The words are as follows: *Hæc nos, Domine, instituta et præcepta retinentes, suppliciter oramus . . . ut fiat nobis eucharistia legitima . . . in transformationem corporis ac sanguinis Domini Dei nostri Jesu Christi Unigeniti tui, per quem omnia creas creata benedicis, benedicta sanctificas et sanctificata largiris Deus, qui in Trinitate perfecta vivis et regnas in sæcula sæculorum* ('holding fast, O Lord, to these institutions and precepts, we humbly pray Thee . . . that a legitimate Eucharist be made for us . . . in the transformation of the body and blood of our Lord

[1] A witness to the original use of the form *Qui pridie quam pateretur* in the Gallican rite.

and God Jesus Christ, Thine only-begotten Son through whom Thou dost create all things; created Thou dost bless them; blessed, Thou dost sanctify and sanctified, dost bestow [upon us], O God, Who in perfect Trinity livest and reignest world without end'). This will be found in *Christian Worship: Its Origin and Evolution* (London: S.P.C.K., 1903, pp. 217, 218). In a footnote on p. 217 the author says that the words *Ut fiat nobis eucharistia legitima* "are a sort of customary phrase, characteristic of the Gallican Epiclesis". The Mozarabic rite has: *Hæc omnia nobis indignis servis tuis valde bona creas, sanctificas* ('All these things Thou dost create exceeding good for us thine unworthy servants, dost sanctify'). The *Missale Gothicum*, as above, omits *hæc*, and *omnia* is not found in all the MSS. With regard to this word, cf. Coloss. i. 15–17; 1 Cor. viii. 6.

The 'Our Father', or Lord's Prayer: Its position in the Roman rite, after the doxology of the Canon, is apparently due to St. Gregory the Great. That saint was considered by liturgical authorities until fairly lately to have merely *moved* the Lord's Prayer from the original position just before communion (as in the African rite) back to the end of the Canon after the doxology. The present tendency, however, is to consider that St. Gregory did not only move the prayer, but actually *introduced* it into the Canon. The view that the Lord's Prayer is a primitive and universal element of the Eucharistic Liturgy is no longer held by the authorities, since there are early examples in which it is not found at all. St. Justin, for example, does not mention it, and it is not in Hippolytus' *Apostolic Tradition*. Again, in the East it is not in the Apostolic Constitutions or 'Clementine Liturgy', as this document is often called. It is true that the Clementine Liturgy was never *in use* as a Liturgy; it was merely a composition of liturgical formulæ put together by a learned writer of the fourth century who is generally believed to have been the same as the interpolator of the Epistles of St. Ignatius of Antioch. The fact that this writer made use of the 'Epistle to the Corinthians' written by St. Clement of Rome is the reason for the title 'Clementine Liturgy'. But although, as said above, this Liturgy was never in practical use, it is, nevertheless, founded upon the Syrian liturgical type of the end of the fourth or beginning of the fifth centuries, and it is the earliest description of that liturgy in writing.

First Evidence for the Use of the Lord's Prayer: Its position at the end of the Eucharistic Prayer in the East is declared by St. Cyril of Jerusalem (A.D. 348); St. John Chrysostom, a generation later, does not mention it, however, at Antioch—so apparently it was not a widespread custom in Syria in Cyril's time (Dix, p. 130). It is absent in the earlier form of the Egyptian rite represented by the *Euchologion* of Sarapion.

In the West, St. Ambrose—about A.D. 395—speaks of the Lord's Prayer in his work *De Sacramentis* (*iv*, 24—not *vi*, as given on p. 131 in the 1945 edition of *The Shape of the Liturgy*), as in use at Milan. St. Augustine, early in the fifth century, speaks of the *Pater noster* in the Liturgy in Africa—he says: 'the whole of this petition [that is, the Eucharistic Prayer] as the Saint puts it: 'the prayers made when the elements are blessed and consecrated and broken [for distribution] *almost* the whole Church concludes with the Lord's Prayer' (Aug. *Ep.* 59; *Ep.* 149, 16; see Dix, p. 131; see, too, Srawley, p. 143, italics mine). Notice that the Saint says: '*almost* the whole Church'—not 'the *whole*' Church, absolutely. It is possible that the exception St. Augustine had in mind was the Church of Rome—where Dix tells us that "the innovation does not seem to have been accepted until the time of St. Gregory I" (*c.* A.D. 595, Dix, p. 131 in footnote 3; a reference to St. Gregory the Great, *Epist.* ix. 12—in which Gregory speaks of the Lord's Prayer at Mass. See also: 'John the Deacon', *Vita Greg.* ii. 20); in his epistle to John, Bishop of Syracuse, he speaks of the *Alleluia*, the *Kyrie eleison*, the vestments of the subdeacon and the Lord's Prayer. The holy Pope says of this latter—*Orationem autem Dominicam idcirco mox post precem dicimus, quia mos apostolorum fuit ut ad ipsam solummodo orationem oblationis hostiam consecrarent; et valde mihi inconveniens visum est ut precem quam scholasticus composuerat super oblationem diceremus et ipsam traditionem quam Redemptor noster composuit super eius corpus et sanguinem non diceremus.* The usual translation runs as follows: 'But we say the Lord's Prayer (*orationem . . . Dominicam*) immediately after the canon [*precem*—i.e. 'the

Prayer' *par excellence*] because it was the custom of the apostles to consecrate the victim (*hostiam*) of the sacrifice (*oblationis*) by that Prayer [i.e. the 'Lord's Prayer'] itself only. And it seems to me very unfitting (*valde inconveniens*) that we should say over the sacrifice a prayer which some learned man [*scholasticus*—perhaps merely 'some *student*'] had composed, and that we should not say over His body and blood that [prayer] which is handed down as our Redeemer's own composition.'

ANOTHER POSSIBLE TRANSLATION: The words—*quia mos apostolorum fuit ut ad ipsam solummodo orationem oblationis hostiam consecrarent*—may be translated thus: 'because it was the custom of the apostles to consecrate the victim with the *prayer of oblation* itself only'—that is, with what we now call the Canon alone, and without any other prayer! The usual translation is the result of taking the words *oblationis* and *hostiam* together as meaning the *victim* (*hostiam*) of the *sacrifice* (*oblationis*); the suggested translation here, however, takes the words *orationem* and *oblationis* together as meaning, 'the *prayer* of oblation'—the 'sacrificial prayer', the Canon. St. Gregory, according to this translation, instead of saying that the apostles used in consecrating only the Lord's Prayer, says, on the contrary, that they did not use it at all, but only the 'Prayer of Oblation'. This seems more likely to be the real explanation of his words, for it can hardly be true that St. Gregory really believed that the apostles consecrated by means of the Our Father alone—even if the Words of Institution were included as well. What he would seem to have found 'unfitting' (*inconveniens*) was that Our Lord's own Prayer was not used *at all* in His own Sacrifice—even though this was the custom of the apostles themselves. No doubt, also, he knew that the Lord's Prayer *was* used in Africa and some other places. But quite in accordance with the usual way of the Roman Church, when adopting usages from elsewhere, the holy Pope preferred to place the Our Father immediately after the doxology of the Canon, and so in closer connection with it rather than in connection with the communion as in Africa.

AFTER THE LORD'S PRAYER, THE FRACTION: The fraction was the breaking of the bread for communion—an action which gave a title to the whole Eucharistic Sacrifice itself. Justin does not mention the fraction; the first description of it is found in Hippolytus' Liturgy in *The Apostolic Tradition* (see Dix's edition, already quoted, pp. 41 and 44). The chief celebrant (the bishop) broke the bread for his own communion and that of the concelebrating clergy around him; the deacons broke those loaves consecrated by the bishop for the general communion. The concelebrating priests also broke the consecrated loaves held before them by the deacons upon a 'vessel' (probably, as later on at Rome, a paten; this was still later changed, a corporal being used instead). The original reason for breaking bread at Jewish meals—and, indeed, at those of all ancient peoples—was simply to have a practical way for the host to distribute the bread to a number of people. But it soon became symbolic in Christianity, and was looked upon even in apostolic times as a sign of unity between all sharing in a common meal, that all should eat the same bread, the pieces being all broken from one loaf. This was naturally especially insisted upon in the Holy Eucharist (1 Cor. x. 17; St. Ignatius—of Antioch— xx. 1). Later on, but before the end of the second century, another symbolism arose: the breaking of Our Lord's body upon the cross. This symbolism may have been due to the later use of many loaves instead of only one from which all received their portions. This development—necessary because of the ever-increasing number of communicants—lessened the external evidence of the 'one mystical Body' feeding upon the 'One Bread'. This increase in numbers also led to the preparation of small portions of the Eucharistic bread for consecration, and this no doubt was the reason of the fraction losing some of its primitive importance. Much the same ceremonial was used for both fraction and administration of communion in the *Ordo Romanus Primus*, as in *The Apostolic Tradition* (p. 40, No. xxiii, and p. 43, No. xxiv).

IN THE ROMAN MASS TO-DAY: This part of the rite consists of six elements as follows:

(*a*) The 'little elevation', of Host and Chalice together, so-called to distinguish it from the more solemn elevations of Host and Chalice (each separately) which were introduced during the Middle Ages—that of the Chalice not until the fourteenth century. The 'little elevation' takes place during the words *omnis honor et gloria* ('all honour and glory'), which are the last words in the doxology of the Canon.

(*b*) The chant or recitation of the *Pater noster* and the 'embolism' (the prayer beginning *Libera nos*—'Deliver us, we beseech thee, O Lord, from all evils') now recited secretly after the *Pater noster*.[1]

(*c*) The *Fraction*: first of the Host into two halves; secondly, by detaching a small particle from the left-hand half (the right-hand half being first laid upon the paten). The first of the two fractions takes place during the first words of the conclusion of the *Libera* (*per eumdem Dominum nostrum*—'through the same our Lord' etc.); the second during the words: *Qui tecum vivit et regnat in unitate Spiritus sancti Deus* ('Who liveth and reigneth with thee in the unity of the Holy Ghost, one God').

(*d*) *Three signs of the cross* made with the small particle over the Chalice, during the words: *Pax Domini sit semper vobiscum* ('May the peace of the Lord be ever with you').

(*e*) *The Commixture*—that is, the mingling of the sacred Body and Blood by dropping the small particle into the Chalice with the words: *Hæc commixtio et consecratio corporis et sanguinis Domini nostri Jesu Christi fiat accipientibus nobis in vitam æternam* ('May this mingling and hallowing of the Body and Blood of our Lord Jesus Christ avail us receiving them, unto life everlasting'). At High Mass the chant of the *Agnus Dei* is carried out after the commixture; at Low Mass the celebrant recites it also after that rite.

(*f*) THE KISS OF PEACE: this follows after the first of the three prayers said in preparation for his communion by the celebrant, which is actually a prayer for peace; all three prayers are of mediæval introduction into the Mass.

From all this it can be seen that the fraction might easily pass unnoticed or, if noticed, might appear to be connected with the commixture rather than with the communion.[2] The

---

[1] From late Greek *embolismos* (from the verb *emballo*—'to throw in; insert; add'. The embolism is 'added to' the *Pater noster*. It is found in all Western rites and in many Eastern liturgies, but not in those of St. Basil and St. John Chrysostom.

[2] The use of small Hosts made for the communion of the congregation (and usually taken from the tabernacle for that purpose) is one reason for the fraction being reduced to a mere formality.

fraction as we now have it is, in fact, really that carried out originally for this purpose (the commixture), and distinct from the solemn fraction for the communion of all present.

AN EXPLANATION OF THIS DEVELOPMENT: This is given in a learned article in the *Revue Bénédictine*, by Dom B. Capelle, O.S.B., Abbot of Mont-César, Louvain. Dom Capelle works out in this article the original series of the above actions of the Mass as shown in the *Ordo Romanus Primus* (*P.L.*, t. lxxviii), which is the earliest account of this section of the Mass after the description given in the Eucharistic Liturgy of St. Hippolytus' *Apostolic Tradition*. The series in the *Ordo* is as follows: (*a*) the Little Elevation (then the only one in the Mass); (*b*) Fraction; (*c*) Commixture. This is the normal series found in practically all liturgies Eastern and Western. (See 'Le Rite de la Fraction dans la Messe Romaine', in *Revue Bénédictine*, t. liii, Nos. 1–4, 1941, pp. 5–40; see, especially, for above, p. 6.) Dom Capelle explains the series of the rites and the meaning in both Eastern and Western liturgies.

The words: *ta hagia tois hagiois* ('holy things for the holy') are found in all Eastern rites,[1] although there is not always an accompanying elevation. In the case of both words and elevation, the intention is to remind the communicants of what they are about to receive and the need of fitting preparation and reverence. (*b*) *Fraction*: This is found in all Eastern rites before the communion as in the West, but in the Coptic rite of Egypt there is, besides, a preliminary fraction when the celebrant says while reciting the words of institution: "He [Our Lord] brake it [the bread] and gave it to his saintly disciples and holy apostles." At these words the celebrant breaks the bread into three parts but without separating them—the full fraction being made at the usual place. The Eucharistic fraction was an attempt to reproduce Our Lord's own action at the Last Supper—the breaking of bread common in all Jewish meals as among all ancient nations. (*c*) *Commixture*: This is not found in all Eastern rites. Where it is practised, its object is to declare that the broken Bread and the Wine poured out,

---

[1] *The Rites of Eastern Christendom*, by Archdale A. King (first volume, pp. 547 *et seq.*).

though externally distinct and separate, are not in truth separated but are One. In the Syrian Liturgy of St. James (Brightman, *Liturgies Eastern and Western*, p. 62), a small particle is broken from one of the large halves (into which the consecrated Bread has been divided), and is dropped into the Chalice with words similar to the *Agnus Dei* of the Roman Mass, which latter words were, in fact, introduced into that rite by the Syrian Pope, Sergius I, in A.D. 700.

THE FRACTION (IN THE WESTERN RITES): In the Gallican and Mozarabic (Spanish) rites the order was: (*a*) The chant of the words 'holy things for the holy' (in Latin), but without any elevation. (*b*) *Fraction and Commixture*: The Pseudo-Germanus of Paris explains the fraction as representing or recalling a miracle which had been 'described by the holy Fathers, of old' (*declarata antiquitus sanctis patribus fuit*). According to this story, a priest, while breaking the bread during the liturgy, saw an angel cutting the members of a glorious child in pieces. This miracle is taken from the *Vitæ Patrum*—translated from the Greek in Rome about A.D. 550 (*Revue Bénéd.*, t. liii, pp. 7 and 8). In Spain, however, the fraction kept its original importance as the preparation for communion, following the example of Our Lord at the Last Supper. In the formula accompanying the commixture, the words *Sancta sanctis* ('holy things for the holy') were used as an introduction to the rest of the formula as follows: *Sancta sanctis: et commixtio corporis et sanguinis Domini nostri Jesu Christi edentibus et bibentibus sit in vitam æternam* ('holy things for the holy: and may the mingling of the body and blood of our Lord Jesus Christ avail those who eat and drink unto everlasting life'). In the Milanese rite the formula used in this place is derived—like other elements in this rite—from Gallican sources. It is practically the same as the above Spanish formula, but adds the word *consecrati* to *corporis et sanguinis D.N.I.C.*—in English it would run: 'May the mingling of the *consecrated* body and blood.' This word '*consecrati*' is evidently an adaptation of the Roman formula: *Hæc commixtio et consecratio corporis et sanguinis* ('may this mingling and hallowing'—or 'consecration'—'of the body and blood'). The Roman form speaks of *consecration* at this moment, whereas the Milanese form uses the word in the past tense and passive form—the *conse-crated* body and blood'. This would seem to be due to an attempt to solve the theological difficulty caused by the use in the Roman rite of the word 'consecration' in connection with what is already consecrated, while the latter use in the Roman Mass seems to be a relic of the earlier custom (no longer admitted as valid) of consecrating unconsecrated wine by dropping a particle of consecrated Bread or pouring consecrated Wine into it.

The fraction at Milan is accompanied by the words: *Corpus tuum frangitur, Christe; calix benedicitur* ('Thy body is broken, O Christ; the chalice is blessed')—which, as Dom Capelle points out, is a mere statement of fact! He goes on to show that the series of acts and prayers in this part of the Mass, as in the earlier arrangement—elevation, fraction, commixture—is in keeping with the most ancient usage, and, too, the meaning expressed in the series is perfectly clear. Thus, the Host and Chalice are elevated to show and to remind the communicants what they are about to receive as the Food and Drink of their souls—in the words (probably in the Roman rite, too, originally, as in the other Western rites as well as in the Eastern rites): 'holy things for the holy.' By these words the communicants were reminded of the need to prepare themselves as worthily as they could. The consecrated Bread is then broken so that It may be distributed among all—that all may be 'made one' in the 'one Bread'. The Bread is mingled with the consecrated Wine, to show that the sacred Body and Blood, separated in the Sacrifice of the Cross, were reunited at the Resurrection, and that the two 'kinds' in the Eucharistic Sacrifice, although they are *dis-tinct* from each other, do not imply any real *separation*—for in each kind the whole Christ is present. As we have seen above, the *Ordo Romanus Primus*, in which is given a full description of the Roman solemn Mass in the eighth century—and probably in earlier centuries, at least in part—we have a picture of the earlier and simpler form of the three rites: elevation, fraction and commixture. But Dom Capelle warns us that we cannot always depend upon the edition usually quoted, as it was edited in the seventeenth century by Dom Mabillon, who based his edition upon a mediocre text. Dom Capelle himself makes use here of a number of MSS. of the two earlier recensions of the *Ordo* (*Revue Bénédictine*, pp. 9–38).

THE 'FERMENTUM' AND 'SANCTA': The above-mentioned difficulty concerning the *Ordo Romanus Primus* is connected chiefly with two rites in the solemn Mass, known as the *fermentum* ('leaven') and the *Sancta* ('the Holy'—which may be either in the singular number, agreeing with *Hostia*, the 'Victim'; or in the plural, meaning simply 'the holy things', the offerings of bread).

It may be said at once that in the *fermentum* we are dealing with a well-attested historical *fact*, but in the case of the *Sancta* there is no real certainty, for it rests apparently upon the authority of Mabillon alone, in his commentary on *Ordo Romanus Primus* (cf. *P.L.*, t. lxxviii, 869–70; cf. also *Revue Bénéd.*, t. liii, pp. 16 ff.). The learned Benedictine himself, says Dom Capelle, "put forward this explanation with great care: *meo quidem iudicio . . . ut quidem opinor . . .*" ('according to my judgment at least . . . as I at least think'). What, then, are these two rites?

THE FERMENTUM: This rite, which took place in both Eastern and Western liturgies, is, in the eyes of Dom Gregory Dix, the earliest example of official reservation of the Blessed Sacrament —though for only a very short time. The name *fermentum* ('leaven') was given to particles broken from the loaves consecrated by the Pope at the solemn or stational Mass in Rome (and by other bishops in their episcopal cities), and 'reserved', that is, probably, kept upon the altar till near the end of the Mass, when the various particles were carried by acolytes to the titular churches, where Solemn Mass was being celebrated the same day as the Papal Mass for those of the faithful unable to assist at the latter. These particles were put into the Chalice by the celebrants in the titular churches at the time of the fraction. The rite of the *fermentum* symbolised the fact insisted upon by St. Ignatius of Antioch (A.D. 50 to between A.D. 98 and 117): 'Let that be accounted a valid Eucharist which is either under the bishop or under one to whom the bishop has assigned this' (*Epist. Smyrn*, viii, 1). The *fermentum* showed, too, the 'oneness' of the Sacrifice, although offered by many ministers in many places. The title *fermentum*, 'leaven' indicated that the portion of the Pope's or bishop's *oblata* consecrated by him, 'leavened' (spiritually) the *oblata* of the other celebrations of the Mass, permeating them, so to speak, with the authority of the High Priest of the whole Christian Priesthood. When the stational Mass was not celebrated by the Pope in person, a *fermentum* was sent by him from his own offering of the Holy Sacrifice to his deputy in the stational church. The *fermentum* is of very early origin, dating from the second century. It is first mentioned by St. Irenæus of Lyons in a letter to Pope Victor I—in A.D. 195 (Dix, pp. 21, 134, 285; and see *A Detection of Aumbries*, by the same author, 1942, pp. 16 *et seq.*; also published by Dacre Press, Westminster). The *fermentum* is mentioned also, later on in A.D. 416, by Pope Innocent I in his letter to Bishop Decentius of Gubbio. The Pope lays down that the *fermentum* must not be carried out to far-off country churches—to avoid irreverence to the Blessed Sacrament; in Rome it was carried only to the titular churches or in other cities to the more important parish churches, not to the lesser places such as the oratories in cemeteries, etc. (*Epist.* xxv, *ad Decentium ep. Eugubinum*: Migne, *P.L.*, xx. 553).

The *fermentum* continued in practice in Rome up till the eighth or ninth centuries; in the East, however, it was probably dropped during the fourth century.

THE SANCTA: Although this title is used in the *Ordo Romanus Primus* in a quite general sense, upholders of the 'rite of the *Sancta*' consider that it is a *title*, in a technical sense, analogous to the term *fermentum*. According to the explanation given by Dom Mabillon and his followers, the *Sancta* was another particle (like the *fermentum*) broken by the Pope from one of his *oblata*, and left upon the altar till the end of the Mass. It was then reserved—wherever it was customary to reserve the Most Holy— until the next Mass celebrated by the Pope. During this Mass it was dropped into the Chalice before communion, another particle having been broken from the consecrated Bread to serve as the *Sancta* for the next Mass again. The object of this rite, it is said, was to symbolise the oneness of the Sacrifice *in time*, as that of the *fermentum* did with regard to *place*; the Sacrifice offered by the Pontiff yesterday was thus shown to be identical with that offered to-day.

Dom Gregory Dix, in *The Shape of the Liturgy*, considers that the *Sancta* was introduced into the Roman rite only during the sixth century, and that it came from the Gallican rite. In Gaul the ceremony seems to have been mentioned first by St. Gregory of Tours, in his *de Gloria Martyrum*, 86 (*c.* A.D. 580; Dix, p. 134 and footnotes 2 and 4). In the Gallican ceremony the Blessed Sacrament was carried in procession into the church at the offertory. In his description of the Gallican Mass in the eighth century, the Pseudo-Germanus of Paris (*c.* A.D. 700) speaks of the Body of the Lord carried in procession in vessels shaped like towers (*in turribus*) at the moment of the offertory. Duchesne, in his *Christian Worship*, explains this as referring to the oblations of bread and wine to be consecrated at Mass and which were brought into the church in this solemn manner, and to which, by anticipation, the same honour was shown as they received after consecration—much as happens to this day in the ceremony of the 'Great Entrance' at the offertory in the Byzantine Liturgy. (*Christian Worship: Its Origin and Evolution*, etc. (London: S.P.C.K., 1903, p. 203).) On p. 205 of this book, Monseigneur Duchesne quotes from the writings of St. Gregory of Tours, which we have mentioned above, where St. Gregory speaks of the deacon "accepting the *tower* in which the Mystery of the Lord's body was contained" and which he was taking into the church "that he might place it upon the altar". The Lord's Body, however, escaped from his hands and *placed Itself* upon the altar—a miracle which was believed by those present to have indicated the unworthiness of the deacon in question! In common with most liturgical authorities in his day, Duchesne believed that the above description of the Gallican rite ascribed to St. Germanus of Paris (*c.* A.D. 496–576), was actually written by him, and that the Gallican rite in general was of Eastern origin.

In the *Ordo Romanus Primus* a similar 'procession of the Blessed Sacrament' is described, which, however, takes place, not at the offertory but at the very beginning of the Mass, as the Pontiff and his ministers were entering the basilica during the chant of the introit-psalm with its repeated antiphon. As they entered the sanctuary, two acolytes approached each bearing a *capsa* (a kind of pyx or box of metal) containing the *Sancta*—the term is used here in the plural—a *number* of consecrated particles. The subdeacon, coming forward, opened each *capsa* to show the sacred particles to the Pontiff. The latter adored the Blessed Sacrament and inspected the contents of the *capsæ* to see if there were too many particles, in which case he ordered some to be put in the usual place of reservation—in *conditorio*, says the text. Among these particles, it is maintained, was one which had been consecrated by the Pope in the preceding Mass and re-served as the *Sancta* (in the official sense) to be placed in the Chalice at the end of the actual celebration. Nothing is said in the *Ordo* as to the destiny of the two *capsæ*, but it is supposed that they were held, or at least one of them was held, by one of the acolytes in the sanctuary until the special *Sancta* was taken to the altar. Some think that this *Sancta* was taken out of the *capsa* and held by the acolyte upon the paten. It has long been a difficulty to explain why the subdeacon (formerly an acolyte) at High Mass holds the *empty* paten wrapped in a humeral veil and held up with such reverence, from the offertory till the end of the *Pater noster*. The paten is, it is true, a consecrated vessel of the altar; nevertheless, it is not easy to see why it should be treated with such almost excessive reverence, and not simply laid down (on the credence, for example) till wanted at the altar. If, however, it was originally the Blessed Sacrament that was held thus on the paten, the difficulty is overcome at once. In the *Ordo Romanus Primus* the writer, after speaking of the Canon as far as the little elevation, suddenly remembers that he has omitted to say what is to be done with the paten. He says: *Nam, quod intermissimus de patena* ('we have, by the way, omitted something about the paten'), and he goes on to describe the very complicated ceremonial of trans-ferring the paten from acolyte, subdeacon, deacon and so on, until it is received by the second deacon from the archdeacon and presented by him to the Pontiff himself. The paten, the writer explains first in this delayed description, was taken by an acolyte and held—wrapped in a linen veil—before his breast from the beginning to the middle of the Canon. Then follows

the above-mentioned complicated description of its 'journey' to
the altar. When the Pontiff said *Pax Domini sit semper vobiscum*
('The peace of the Lord be ever with you'), he made the sign
of the cross three times with his hand over the Chalice, and then
dropped the particle of the consecrated Host into it. In the
text the words are: *mittit sancta in eum*—'he drops the Holy'—or
'the Holies'—'into it'—the Chalice. Here the word *sancta* would
seem to be the neuter *plural* accusative of *sanctum*, and so to
mean *several* particles and not only one. *The Ordo* gives no
further explanation, but many think that this is the *Sancta* in the
special sense of that term. The writer of the *Ordo*, after speaking
of the Kiss of Peace, goes on to say that the Pope breaks off a
portion from one of the two loaves, which he had offered himself, on the right side of the loaf and leaves the broken portion
upon the altar when he goes to the throne to assist at the general
fraction by the concelebrating bishops and priests and deacons. The *Ordo* explains that the consecrated fragment is thus
left upon the altar: "so that while the solemnities of the
Mass are celebrated, the altar may never be left without the
sacrifice". Nothing is said about the final disposition of the
particle. Dom Capelle, in his article in the *Revue Bénédictine*,
t. liii, treating of this part of the *Ordo*, shows that the threefold
sign of the cross over the Chalice and the act of dropping a consecrated particle into it are later interpolations in the original
text; he admits the breaking of the other particle which was
left upon the altar by the Pontiff, but declares that the explanation given for thus leaving it upon the altar is also a later
interpolation and evidently the work of one not altogether at
home with Roman rites and observances.

*Dom Capelle, in short, does not believe in the existence of any such
rite as that of the* Sancta: He points out that the text of the *Ordo*
contains no indication of it. With regard to the adoration of the
reserved particles of the Blessed Sacrament borne by the two
acolytes at the beginning of the ceremony, this seems to be
partly in preparation for offering the Holy Sacrifice, but
principally (as the text itself declares) in order to supervise the
condition of the reserved Sacrament. There is no mention at all
of any special *Sancta* contained in the *capsa* since the preceding
Mass, and now brought to the sanctuary to be consumed at the

Mass about to take place. If there had been, surely the *Ordo* (which goes into such detail in laying down the different ceremonies of the Papal Mass) would have carefully explained one of such importance as this? Again, while there is (as we have seen above) a long and complicated description of the transfer of the paten from one official to another—and just at the moment of the Mass at which the supposed rite of the *Sancta* ought to take place—no *suggestion* even is given of a consecrated particle actually upon the paten. On the contrary, as Dom Capelle says: "this paten which is kissed and passed on, is evidently empty" (*Revue Bénéd.*, t. liii, pp. 14 ff.). Farther on in his article the Abbot says that while "the need to underline the hierarchical idea in the *tituli* [the parish churches in Rome] in which the priest celebrated only in the name and in the place of the Bishop of Rome, is easy to understand, the desire to unite the sacrifice of to-day with that of yesterday seems less natural —even rather far-fetched"; and he adds: "In the description of the ceremonies of our *Ordo* everything is minutely laid down and the various duties clearly portioned out between acolytes, subdeacons and deacons"—why, then, should the passage concerning the (supposed) rite of the *Sancta* be such a complete exception? Dom Capelle concludes: "This idea [of the *Sancta*] does not go back further than Mabillon's brain!" (*Revue Bénéd.*, t. liii, pp. 17–22). Dom Capelle considers that the portion broken by the Pope from one of his own *oblata* and left upon the altar, as described in the *Ordo*, was the *fermentum* which, as we have seen, was a consecrated particle to be sent from his own Mass to the Mass celebrated the same day in the titular churches. It was at the *Pax Domini* that the Pope put this particle aside; it was at the *Pax Domini* that it would be dropped by the celebrant of the titular church into his own Chalice: the two acts correspond. Dom Capelle considers that the fragment thus reserved till this moment of the Mass was placed in one of the *capsæ* entrusted to the '*subdeacon-oblationer*',[1] who took it to the titular church (*Revue Bénéd.*, t. liii, p. 16). It must be confessed that the above explanations are not much clearer, at

---

[1] This official was a member of the papal cortège; his title indicates that he was the bearer of the Pope's personal offerings of two loaves from the Lateran, and that he offered these in the Pope's name at the stational Mass. (See Atchley. *Ordo Romanus Primus.* (London, 1905, p. 137).)

first sight, than those put forward by upholders of the *Sancta*—as far at least as the text of the *Ordo* is concerned. The word *fermentum* is not used at all in connection with the particle left upon the altar and, as we have already seen, nothing is said as to its final destination. From the text, too, it would seem that only *one* particle was broken off by the Pontiff—and yet, as we know, several Masses were celebrated at about the same time as the Papal stational Mass, in the various titular churches in the city. The ceremony of the *fermentum* consisted in sending a *corresponding number* of particles, thus broken by the Pope from his own *oblata*, to be distributed among the titular churches at more or less the same time. No doubt the answer to this would be that the rite of the *fermentum* was so well known, and so constantly in practice, that minute explanations were considered unnecessary. Moreover, as a matter of fact, the ceremony *is* fully described in the first of two *supplements* to the *Ordo Romanus Primus* (of which Dom Capelle speaks), and this description lays down certain changes in the rubrics required when the Pope was not himself the celebrant of the stational Mass. Such an occasion demanded a *fermentum* brought from the Pope's own Mass, celebrated elsewhere. The text of this supplement is of ninth-century date: ". . . when he [the Pope's deputy] is about to say *Pax . . . vobiscum*, the particle of the *fermentum* consecrated by the Apostolic [Lord—that is, the Pope] is brought by the subdeacon-oblationer and given to the archdeacon, who offers it to the bishop. The latter, making three signs [of the cross] and saying *Pax . . . vobiscum*, drops it into the chalice" (*P.L.*, t. lxxviii. 948; cf. *Revue Bénéd.*, t. liii, p. 22).

When the Pope did not celebrate Mass at all and there was therefore no *fermentum* for the deputy-bishop in the stational Mass, the following rubrics are given; these are the same as the directions laid down in the *Ordo* for the Papal Mass, up to the breaking of the particle to be left on the altar. The supplement orders that when the celebrant says *Per omnia sæcula sæculorum*, he breaks the oblation on the right side, and the portion thus detached is *put into the Chalice*. This is evidently an adaptation of the *fermentum* ceremony—from mere habit, for there was no real *reason* to put the particle in the Chalice, in this case, as in the case of the *fermentum* sent by the Pope. This rubric for a

Solemn Mass without the *fermentum* seems to have reacted upon that of the Papal Mass itself. According to one text of the *Ordo Romanus Primus*, fraction and commixture are made in this way by the Pope—*at the altar*, not at the throne. But this is a later interpolation, as Dom Capelle shows. In the original text there was a fraction simply in order to obtain the particle which was to be left on the altar, and there was no commixture.[1] Dom Capelle presumes—conjecturally, as he himself declares—that this interpolation was put into the *Ordo* elsewhere than in Rome, and also that the special edition of the *Ordo* in which it is found was likewise brought out elsewhere than in Rome. (*Revue Bénéd.*, t. liii, pp. 24 ff.)

THE SANCTA AND THE PATEN: One unfortunate result, if the *Sancta* be rejected, will be that the satisfactory explanation which it provided for the subdeacon holding the paten so solemnly at High Mass must be rejected also, and so that ceremony still remains a puzzle! Perhaps it will be necessary to return to the explanation generally accepted—that in those days the altar being very small and the 'altar-breads' being large and thick—little loaves, in fact—there was not enough room to place the paten on the altar. In those days, too, there was probably no 'credence-table',[2] and so the acolyte held the paten wrapped in a 'humeral veil' (the scarf worn round the shoulders—hence the name 'humeral' from the Latin *humerus*— 'a shoulder'), since all sacred vessels were held thus and not in the bare hands. But probably this was done without the elaborate ceremony we see nowadays in the case of the subdeacon, who replaced the acolyte during the Middle Ages. Dom Capelle sums up the facts and the conclusions at which he has arrived as follows:

---

[1] The real fraction—a long and complicated ceremony in which the Pope did not take part himself—was carried out when the Pontiff went to his throne, and it was at the throne, too, that the commixture took place.

[2] 'Credence' from Italian 'credenza' (in Latin, *credentia*—from *credere*, 'to believe' or 'trust'). The primary use of the credence was to hold the vessels for the ceremony of the *prægustatio* ('preliminary tasting'); to ensure the absence of poison in either the bread or the wine. This ceremony is still observed at the Papal Pontifical Mass and also prescribed for Pontifical Mass celebrated by the Diocesan. But usually the credence is used simply to support the chalice, paten and cruets for High Mass.

GENERAL CONCLUSIONS: (i) According to the earliest known series of rubrics in the Papal *Ordo* in Rome, the various ceremonies of the fraction did not begin until *after* the words *Pax Domini* had been chanted by the Pontiff. These words were, then, the signal for the Kiss of Peace to be given among clergy and laity; it seems that the Pope himself did not give the Kiss to any person—although he probably kissed the altar or the paten.

(ii) *The fraction* as it is now found in the Roman Mass is in reality derived from the *first* fraction—in the *Ordo Rom. Primus* —necessary, in order to obtain the *fermentum* which was left upon the altar. When the rite of the *fermentum* was given up, the particle thus broken off, instead of being left upon the altar, was dropped at once into the Chalice and so a commixture at the altar was introduced into *every* Mass. This led finally to the suppression of the ancient and most impressive ceremony of the fraction carried out by all the assistant clergy for the communion of all taking part in the Sacrifice.

(iii) *The Chant of the Agnus Dei:* this was originally instituted to be sung during the fraction—which took a considerable time. It was then altogether separated from it, and is now separated also from the short fraction which replaces the original ceremony.

(iv) It may be asked why the Host is now broken into three portions—first into two halves, and then a small particle is detached from the left-hand half? Originally the Pope offered for himself two loaves of bread. From one of these loaves he broke off the portion to be left upon the altar. This fraction left *three* portions of bread—one entire loaf, the broken loaf and the portion broken from it. In later times a mystical meaning was given to this number three. According to Amalarius of Metz (later Bishop of Trêves, died A.D. 850), a great liturgical writer of the ninth century and especially interested in the Roman rite, the three portions of the Host represent three states of Our Lord: the particle dropped into the Chalice represents the body of Christ risen from the dead (the Body and Blood being united again); the portion received in communion represents the Body still upon this earth; the third portion left upon the altar represents the Body of Our Saviour in the sepulchre. In Amalarius' time this latter particle was used no longer for the *fermentum*, but served for the Viaticum of the dying (*P.L.*, t. cv, 1154; cf. *Revue Bénéd.*, t. liii, pp. 29 and 30). Dom Capelle concludes this long and interesting study with a suggestion of the possible restoration of the earlier series of actions in this part of the Mass—a restoration which could be effected without any great disturbance of the existing rubrics—as follows:

1. After the *amen* of the embolism (*Libera nos*) which follows the Lord's Prayer, and which itself might be chanted or recited aloud (as on Good Friday in the Mass of the Presanctified and in every Mass in the Milanese rite), the celebrant would say secretly the first of the three prayers now said just before communion. This is actually a prayer for peace: *Domine Iesu Christe qui dixisti: pacem relinquo vobis* ('Lord Jesus Christ who didst say . . . peace I leave you'), and so ought to be said before the Kiss of Peace, whether in act, as at High Mass, or only in word, as at Low Mass. The 'word' is the phrase: *Pax Domini sit semper vobiscum* ('May the peace of the Lord be ever with you') —an invitation to receive the Kiss, and at High Mass the Kiss would follow immediately after the invitation.

2. Having crossed himself with the paten and kissed it, the celebrant would carry out the rites of the fraction and commixture as prescribed to-day—but in *silence* as on Good Friday. At High Mass the *Agnus Dei* would be sung during the fraction; at Low Mass the celebrant would continue to recite it after the fraction, as is the actual rule.

3. Immediately after all this, the celebrant would recite secretly the two remaining prayers before communion (*Revue Bénéd.*, t. liii, pp. 39 and 40).

THE COMMUNION OF THE CELEBRANT AND ALL PRESENT: Communion was regarded as the climax and completion of the Eucharistic Sacrifice by all pre-Nicene writers. It seems that in early times it was distributed in both kinds by the deacons, not by the celebrant or his assistant priests—this is clear from St. Justin. But St. Hippolytus in his *Apostolic Tradition* insists more than once that the bishop shall, if possible, give the Bread 'to all with his own hand', assisted by the concelebrating priests. These latter also administer the Chalice—'or, if there are not enough of them, the deacons' (*Apostolic Tradition*, pp. 43 and 44).

In later times this function accorded to the deacons had to be restricted to a certain extent, as the deacons were inclined to 'promote' themselves above the priests and so to administer communion in both kinds and even to priests! The administration of the Chalice to the faithful laity, however, continued to be the deacon's duty in Rome until a comparatively late date. Deacons were also sometimes allowed to administer communion in the species of bread from the reserved Sacrament, but they were ordered to receive communion themselves from the bishop or concelebrating priests and *after* the latter had received their own communion. In the early period communion was received by all (lay-folk as well) standing, and by the clergy first. It appears, also, that the communicants moved from one 'minister' to another—to receive both kinds—and the latter remained standing before the altar. In the present usage, the communicants kneel at a rail or at the steps of the sanctuary, and the celebrant passes along the row.

Second Half of the Eucharistic Prayer: All this part of the Mass is composed of what the author of *The Shape of the Liturgy* calls the 'second halves' of the Eucharistic Prayer, and which he regards as later additions belonging to the fully developed forms of the Eucharistic Liturgy. This he considers is evidenced by the "great diversity" found in the different rites; he even looks on the words of institution as part of the 'second half', and not (in primitive ages at least) as essential elements. Dom Gregory Dix himself, however, gives us a proof of the *importance* of the words of institution, when he says (speaking of the words used in the administration of communion) that those who consider that the words of Our Lord at the Last Supper were really 'words of administration' "find no support in the practice of the primitive church. On the contrary, that church . . . places the words of institution as the *central thing* in the eucharistic prayer"; and on another page he says: "For this much is certain. Whether the reference to the last supper belongs to the primitive nucleus or not, it is *the centre or pivot* of all the developed traditions of the prayer" (Dix, pp. 137 and 227 —italics mine.) There is really no difficulty about these diversities in the development of liturgical forms—even in the case of the words of institution. The diversity in form, development in expression and clearness of intention are not proofs that entirely new additions have been made—in the sense of new *teaching* or *doctrine*. In spite of diversity in *form*, both the words of institution and the 'links' joining the earlier part of the Eucharistic Prayer with the account of the Last Supper or the above words of institution are all at one in the underlying and essential 'sameness' of meaning and intention—which is all that really matters.

No Formal, Corporate Thanksgiving: There was no 'postcommunion' prayer and no blessing was given. The only ceremony following the communion was the *dismissal*. This was a pronouncement—made probably by the deacon—that the service was ended and that all might retire. In the actual Roman Mass we have the words: *Ite missa est*—the word *missa* is late Latin for *missio*,[1] and the whole may be translated as: 'Go, it is the dismissal'—literally, 'the sending away'. After this came the cleansing of the Chalice (the 'ablutions', as we say now) and the removal of the altar-cloth—which was what we should now call the 'corporal'[2]; the service had begun with 'laying the cloth' and placing the Chalice and paten with their contents (wine and water and small loaves of bread) upon it. When during the fourth century a formal, public act of thanksgiving was added, the ablutions still usually took place at the same moment, and so *before* the thanksgiving. But later on, in the Eastern Churches (in Syria, before the end of the fourth century), a custom was brought in of removing to the sacristy the particles of consecrated Bread that remained over from communion. These consecrated particles were consumed in the sacristy, and the Chalice cleansed there also afterwards. Dix thinks it possible that this removal of the consecrated Bread to the sacristy, before the prayers of thanksgiving, was due to the custom of reservation—which was then usually in the sacristy and more or less secret. The feeling then was that the sacred elements should not be on the altar "except during the vital sacramental action itself, from the offertory to the communion"

---

[1] From this word, as we have seen, comes the title 'Mass', for the Holy Sacrifice.
[2] But it then covered the whole altar; now it is only large enough for the Chalice and Host to be placed upon it. It is a kind of square napkin.

(Dix, p. 140). In the present Roman Mass the ablutions still take place at the early moment of the rite and before the thanksgiving prayer. The celebrant now drinks these ablutions from the Chalice; formerly they were poured away—in the Middle Ages, down the 'piscina'—that is, the drain made for that purpose in the wall, usually on the south side of the altar, and having above it a shelf on which the cruets of wine and water can be placed; the name 'piscina' literally means a fishpond—from the Latin word *piscis*—a fish. It was at this moment of the Liturgy that, according to St. Justin, some of the consecrated Bread was given to the deacons for them to take to the sick and to those in any way prevented from communicating during the Liturgy. The faithful present also received consecrated particles to take with them, to be reserved in their own homes for communion on those days of the week on which the Liturgy was not celebrated.

SUMMARY: (i) The present Roman preface and canon formed originally but one long prayer—the 'Eucharistic Prayer'—of which the first part consisted of a series of thanksgivings to God the Father for all His mercies—especially for the Incarnation and the Redemption of His Son. The second part was concerned with certain petitions justified by the acknowledgment of the above-mentioned Divine mercies; and by the duty of thanksgiving for these fulfilled in the first part.

(ii) The original Eucharistic Prayer was probably not at first divided into two by the chant of the threefold *Sanctus*. This chant seems to have been introduced into the prayer fairly late in its history, and, moreover, when it was introduced (apparently in the Egyptian rite) it was probably at first placed at the *end* of the Eucharistic Prayer, forming the climax of the doxology. The chant of the *Sanctus* seems to have spread from Egypt all over the Church, both in the East and in the West.

(iii) The two early Italian Eucharistic Prayers spoken of on pp. 98 provide—especially the longer of the two—an idea of how the original Roman prayer was formed, and they have relics of the series of thanksgivings which originally comprised the first part of the prayer. They show, too, the connection between the thanksgivings of the first part and the petitions of the second part. The longer of the two prayers turns from thanksgiving to petition, because—"we cannot worthily give thanks to Thy great mercy" . . . therefore . . . "we pray Thee of Thy great and merciful love to hold accepted this sacrifice which we offer unto Thee . . . through Jesus Christ our Lord and God; through Whom we pray and beseech" (in Latin, *per quem petimus et rogamus*). Unfortunately this prayer stops short at the most important point, but it goes far enough to show, by comparison with the present Roman canon, that it is an equivalent of the *Te igitur* section, but without any 'preface' (in the later sense) or *Sanctus*. (See Dix, p. 541.) It is clear that the resemblances between the early Italian and the later Roman prayers are fairly close. Both ask for the acceptance of the Sacrifice by God, and both use almost identical words in connection with Our Lord—e.g. "Through Jesus Christ our Lord and God, through Whom we *pray* and *beseech*" (Italian prayer); "Through Jesus Christ Thy Son, our Lord, we humbly *pray* and *beseech* Thee" (Roman Canon). The words *underlined* are the same, in Latin, in both cases— *petimus/et rogamus*, or *rogamus ac petimus*.

(iv) The 'puzzle' of the Roman Eucharistic Prayer is to a great extent due to the reduction of the original thanksgiving series to a mere statement that: "it is meet and right to give thanks to God in all places and at all times", the position of the series, stating the various reasons for this, being taken up with other matters, or leading up directly to the *Sanctus*. Thus, the original use of the word *igitur* to indicate the transition from thanksgiving to petition (as in the Eucharistic Prayer for the consecration of the Chrism) was obscured and the *igitur* became a 'mystery'!

(v) Before the prayers for the Church and the Pope, the *Memento* of the living and the *Communicantes* all became parts of the Canon, the words *quæ tibi offerimus* ('which we offer unto Thee'—omitting the *in primis*, 'in the first place'), which come after *hæc dona, hæc munera, hæc sancta sacrificia illibata* ('these gifts, these duties, these holy, unspotted sacrificial offerings') were probably the last words of the *Te igitur* clause, which would then have been followed immediately by the prayer leading to Our Lord's words and action at the Last Supper (the consecration of the gifts) introduced by the words *Qui pridie quam pateretur* ('Who, on the day before He suffered'). This prayer is called, by Dix, the 'link' between both the preliminary thanksgivings and petitions and the account of the Last Supper. The Roman 'link' begins: *Quam oblationem* ('which offering'), following immediately after the *Hanc igitur* ('This offering'), and so connected with it by the relative *quam* ('which'). Perhaps this prayer began, originally, not with the relative form *Quam oblationem*, but with one more like the direct form in the Ambrosian rite—*Fac hanc oblationem* ('make *this* offering' etc., instead of 'which offering'). As we have seen, the Roman *Hanc igitur* prayer is of later date, and at first was used only occasionally.

THE ROMAN CANON IN GENERAL: It can be said that, apart from a few revisions made by the two Popes, Gelasius and Gregory the Great, the Western type of Liturgy (as developed during the fourth century) still survives in the Roman Canon in use to-day—in spite of the "'improvers' of all the centuries", as Dix says on p. 557 of *The Shape of the Liturgy*. This page (except for barely five lines at the top) is taken up with two long and most helpful footnotes on what has been, up till now, a very complicated question.

In the first of the two notes the author gives the following useful summary; he says: "The history of the Roman canon does not seem very difficult to make out in its main lines, *once we discard theories about 'dislocation' and 'diptychs' and the 'primitive Roman epiclesis'* " (italics mine). Then comes the summary:

(i) Preface and *Sanctus* took the place of the ancient series of thanksgivings in the fifth century, leaving, practically, merely the words declaring that it "is meet, right and our bounden duty at all times and in all places to give thanks", etc.

(ii) The second part of the *Te igitur*, following after the mention of the offerings—namely the prayers for the Church, the Pope, local bishop and probably, originally, of all orthodox bishops—is connected, like the *Hanc igitur*, with the 'naming' of those who presented offerings of bread and wine at Mass which was introduced at this point in the Canon in the fourth century.

The first part of the *Te igitur*, however, belongs to the old

Eucharistic Prayer. The opening words lead on to the petitions which—as the word *igitur* ('therefore') indicates—were justified by the dutiful acts of thanksgiving at the beginning of the Eucharistic Prayer.

(iii) *Communicantes* was introduced by Gelasius (A.D. 492–6)—the idea being derived from the Jerusalem rite, in which the Saints were 'named' as well as ordinary persons.

(iv) *Quam oblationem* is the survival of the pre-Nicene 'link' between the first part of the Eucharistic Prayer (thanksgivings and petitions) and the account of the Last Supper, consecration, etc.

(v) After the Institution comes the prayer known technically as the *anamnesis*—that is, the memorial of the Passion, Resurrection and Ascension of Our Saviour (which appears to have been at first special to Rome, but to have spread thence all over the East and West); two prayers follow—for the acceptance of the Sacrifice by God—as He had accepted the sacrifices of the Old Law (*Supra quæ propitio*) and for the ratification of the Sacrifice offered on earth, upon the heavenly Altar (*Supplices te rogamus*). These three prayers are perhaps later developments of the one short prayer in the Ambrosian rite which expresses the ideas of each. The *Supplices* includes prayers for the communicants, which part was probably fuller and more explicit in earlier times.

(vi) *The Memento etiam*—commemoration of the dead—was originally inserted only in Requiem and funeral Masses and, even thus, is of fairly late introduction into the Roman Mass.

(vii) *Nobis quoque* was introduced by Gelasius at the same time as the *Communicantes*, and for the same reason. It is possible, however, that Gelasius introduced only the names of the saints in this place, and that the rest of the prayer was actually in the Canon already, and apart from the *Memento etiam*; it follows on quite well from the preceding prayer, *Supplices*, and would seem to have been a prayer for the celebrant and his concelebrants ('we also, Thy sinful servants').

(viii) *Per quem hæc omnia* ('through Whom all these [good things]') is the old blessing of fruits and other such things offered at Mass and found as early as the Liturgy described in *The Apostolic Tradition of Hippolytus* (pp. 10 and 11 of Dix's edition, 1937). But it seems very probable that these words referred originally (and still refer primarily) to the Body and Blood of Our Lord under the sacramental species. *Per ipsum* is the closing doxology of the Canon. It appears, then, that the *variable* prayers in the Canon are fifth-century additions when the 'fashion' of variable prayers was coming in, in the West, and which nearly carried the day at Rome as in Gaul. Dom Gregory Dix concludes: "I believe that this account of the matter can be fully substantiated from the evidence, though it has not yet been done" (p. 557, footnote 1).

PART II

PRAYER: THE DIVINE OFFICE

CHAPTER I

THE CHARACTER OF CHRISTIAN WORSHIP

THE Divine Office is the solemn public prayer of the whole Church, just as the Holy Mass is the solemn public sacrifice of the whole Church. In both cases the solemnity and the public character remain intact no matter what the circumstances or the method of celebration; for example—Low Mass celebrated in the presence of the server alone or the Divine Office recited (by one bound to that recitation) in private.

THE TITLE 'OFFICE': This is derived from the Latin word *officium*, meaning 'duty' or 'obligation'—or, again, 'service'. This duty, obligation or service is 'divine' because it is owed to God Himself. In his Holy Rule, St. Benedict calls it 'the *Work* of God' (*Opus Dei*), and declares that it is the principal work of the monastic life, underlying and influencing all other work that may be undertaken by the monks, and which must never be 'preferred' to the Office—never 'put in its place' (*nihil praeponatur Operi Dei*; 'let nothing be put before the Work of God'). (*The Rule of St. Benedict*, chap. xliii: 'Of those who come late to the Work of God, or to table'.)

The Prayer of the Church was fully developed only in the fourth century, but the *elements* probably existed long before that date—even from the very beginning of the Church herself. It was, however, in the fourth century that Christian worship came forth from the obscurity of the earlier ages, the ages of persecution. It ceased to be the private worship of what was, in the eyes of the pagan world, merely one among many other 'secret societies' for the service of some god unknown to the ordinary Roman citizen, and became the corporate worship of the Christian Church recognised and respected in the civilised world of the day. This change in the idea of Christian worship—in the minds of those outside Christianity and of Christians themselves—was the cause of another change, especially concerned with the Eucharistic Sacrifice, then as

always the very centre of that worship. This was the change
from what is called the 'eschatological' view of the Holy
Sacrifice and of Christian worship in general, to a view affected
by the process of time. (See Dix, pp. 305, 306.) This change
does not mean that the eschatological emphasis was or ever
could be entirely lost sight of. It still had, and has, its importance,
and that importance is being recognised more and more at the
present day. This is noticeable in the striking tendency of so
many quite different and independent writers on the Holy
Sacrifice to return to the more ancient point of view regarding the exact nature of its sacrificial character and of its connection with the Sacrifice of the Cross, which also involves a
return to the eschatological emphasis to which we have referred
above.

A FEW WORDS ON ESCHATOLOGY: This term is derived from
the Greek *eschaton*, which means 'the end'. In the eyes of the
Jews and in those of the Christians (who adapted it from the
Jewish point of view), the beginning and end of all life was to
be found in God and His will. The end especially (the 'eschaton') was known as 'the Day of the Lord' to which everything
in history leads up, and in which all history would be summed
up, in spite of all the efforts of evil to upset the Divine plan.
This 'End' is at once *in* History and *beyond* it; the summing up
of time and its transformation to what is beyond and above
time. Early Christianity, which had developed out of Judaism,
saw the 'End' or purpose of all history, of all life, in Jesus
Christ, in Whom it was at once proclaimed as *about to come* and
as *already accomplished*. In His death upon the Cross, in His
resurrection from that death, and in His ascension into heaven,
the End, the 'Age to come' was proclaimed and realised. His
Church, which is His Mystical Body, is, too, the proclamation
and the realisation of the 'Eschaton'—for the Church *is* Christ.
At the same time history continues; so that in the idea of the
End, the Eschaton, we have both time and eternity.

THE IMPORTANCE OF ESCHATOLOGY—for us moderns, very
difficult to grasp—lies first in the fact that it concerns very
closely the nature of the Eucharistic Sacrifice, and can be of

immense help in understanding that 'Mystery of faith', as far, that is, as such a mystery may be understood. To most of us the words of our Saviour to His disciples at the Last Supper: "Do this for a commemoration of Me" (or 'memorial of Me'— in Greek, *anamnesis*—Luke xxii. 19, etc.) means that the Mass is the commemoration in *our times* of the Sacrifice offered upon the Cross in *past times*—many centuries ago. This is, of course, perfectly true and correct as far as it goes, and from the merely human point of view. But there is *more* than this (much as it is in itself) in the significance of the 'Mystery of faith'. From the point of view of eternity, of God Himself—the Mass is not only the memorial of the Cross in the ordinary meaning of that word —simply the reminder by means of a symbolical act, of something that actually took place many ages ago—it *is*, here and now, the Sacrifice offered upon the Cross, and, in fact, the *whole* of the Redeemer's work on earth; His resurrection, ascension and entrance into the heavenly Sanctuary, for in the sight of God all is 'now'—time is swallowed up in eternity.[1] In passing, we may remark that it seems strange that the author of *The Shape of the Liturgy*, although he explains the whole notion of Jewish and Christian eschatology so clearly and applies it so effectively to the question of the connection between the *Mass* and the Cross, should, nevertheless, apparently find it difficult to apply it to the *Last Supper* and the Cross. He prefers to consider the Last Supper as only a 're-hearsal' (as he himself puts it) of what Our Lord wished His disciples to do—*after* His death upon the Cross—on the grounds that the 'memorial Sacrifice' could not be offered until the Sacrifice it commemorated had itself been offered. But why should Our Saviour be thus restricted by the exigencies of time *before* the Offering upon the Cross, but not *after* it? To quote the author's own words: "The same eternal fact can touch the process of history *at more than one point*, and if there is an apparent difference in the effects of such contacts,

---

[1] See *The Sacrifice of Christ our Head*, by Canon Eugène Masure; translated by Dom Illtyd Trethowan, Monk of Downside (London: Burns, Oates & Washbourne, Ltd., 1943)—especially Book III: 'The Sacrifice of the Mass'; see also *Downside Review*, July 1947, 'The Mass: Sacramental Immolation'—article by Canon Masure (pp. 195–210); *Theology and Sanity*, by F. J. Sheed, p. 190 (London: Sheed & Ward, 1947)—a quotation from this excellent exposition of the Mass and of sacrifice in general is given in *Appendix I*.

that difference is entirely on the side of the temporal process, *for eternity knows no 'difference' and no 'before' or 'after'* (Dix, p. 263, italics mine).[1]

[1] With regard to this—see 'Some Flaws in the Shape of the Liturgy', by Maurice Bévenot, S.J., in *The Month*, January–February 1946, No. 949, lxxxii, 50–7.

CHAPTER II

THE ORIGIN OF THE DIVINE OFFICE

THE custom of public prayer distinct from public sacrifice also comes under the influence of the changed ideas in Christian worship which came into being during the fourth century. It has been maintained by Dix that such a custom *began* only in the fourth century, and that in pre-Nicene days, and up to that century, there was no regular system of corporate prayer except an occasional use of the service, which generally preceded the celebration of the Eucharistic Sacrifice, used *apart* from the Sacrifice. The existence even of a regular vigil-service on Saturday evenings in preparation for Sunday is denied, and it is maintained that the only vigils were that of Easter on the eve of the great Day (Holy Saturday, as we call it now), and perhaps that also on the eve of Pentecost.[1] Later on there were, besides these vigils, the 'station-days' on which the service of readings from Holy Scripture, psalms and intercessory prayers was celebrated. In some places (probably at Rome and Alexandria, for example) these station services did not include the Eucharist, but in other places (e.g. in North Africa) it followed the synaxis, as can be gathered from the writings of Tertullian.

Dom Gregory Dix considers that the regular 'Divine Office' is entirely due to the monks, and that it was adopted by the Church as a whole only during the course of the fourth century. His reason against any corporate daily prayer-service in the early Church—besides the lack of direct evidence—is the contention that the early Christian life of worship was incompatible with the life of the pagan world in any *public* manner; there could be no open intermingling of daily life and worship. In other words, Christians had to practise their religion in secret—or, at least, apart from those of their fellow-men who were not of their own faith. But in the case of the monks, daily worship

---

[1] Possibly, but not *certainly*, it is said, there were also vigil-services at the tombs of the martyrs on their feast-days; the day of martyrdom.

could be carried out in full, since the monk left the world in order to give himself up to a life of worship and prayer in the monastery, and so to carry out literally, as far as possible, the exhortation of Our Lord: "we ought always to pray and not to faint" (Luke xviii. 1). Christian worship, then, was realised *fully* only in monastic life. Nevertheless, as time went on the Church was influenced to a great extent by the monastic form of prayer throughout the day, and gradually adopted this scheme of continual prayer.

THE HOURS OF THE DIVINE OFFICE: Since it is impossible for human beings—even monks—to pray always in the absolutely literal sense (there must be time to eat, sleep, study, work), the public or 'family' prayer of the monks was spread out over the day by means of the various 'Hours', during the night, at dawn, at the three most important moments of the working day—the third, sixth and ninth hours (our nine, twelve midday and three o'clock), the time in ordinary life to start work or occupation, to eat the midday meal and to stop work[1] till after the siesta or afternoon rest—and finally at sunset and before retiring to rest. In this way, too, the words of the Psalter quoted in his Rule by St. Benedict, when speaking of the Work of God: 'Seven times a day I have given praise to thee' (Psalm cxviii. 164), in connection with the Day Hours; and: 'I rose at midnight to give praise to thee' (Psalm cxviii. 62) are fulfilled. (See *Rule of St. Benedict*, chap. xvi.) In pre-Nicene times, prayer in the morning and evening, and also at the above times during the day (the *third* and *ninth* hours were, too, the times at which the Jewish daily sacrifices were offered), was undoubtedly practised by both clergy and laity apart from the monks, but as private devotions, not corporate worship. This notion that the origin and development of the Divine Office was the work almost entirely of monks has been much criticised in a number of reviews (otherwise favourable) of *The Shape of the Liturgy*.

THE DEVELOPMENT OF THE OFFICE: While it is granted willingly that the early monastic communities gave great impetus to the development of the Office during the fourth

---

[1] On account of the heat of the day just beginning.

century, and that the 'Little Hours' (Prime, Terce, Sext, None and Compline) are almost certainly 'monastic inventions'— that is, as elements of the *public* Office, for, as we have seen, prayer at the third, sixth and ninth hours was practised, at least privately, in early times—"all the weight of evidence is that Vespers and Matins-Lauds grew out of the . . . vigil, which was *the* public liturgy of the Church at which everyone assisted" (*The Shape of the Liturgy*, a review by the Rev. J. D. Crichton, in *Magnificat*, Spring 1946, iv, No. 3, 1–7). This reviewer makes the same criticisms in an article entitled 'The Divine Office', in *Liturgy: The Quarterly of the Society of St. Gregory*, January 1949, pp. 1–10. The whole of this article is well worth careful reading for all who love the Divine Office —and also for those who do not know enough about it. In other words, there was an ecclesiastical office—or at least a *beginning* of it—in early times, distinct from the later monastic office by which, however, its final development was influenced considerably. In the *Eastern Churches Quarterly* (October–December 1945, pp. 170–200), a reviewer writing under the initials A. v. d. M., although in general he writes of the author of *The Shape of the Liturgy* very favourably indeed, does not hesitate to point out what he considers mistakes or inaccuracies—especially with regard to the Eastern liturgies and ceremonial. He upholds strongly the early and ecclesiastical character of the vigil-service, and also the frequency of its celebration in the early Church. This reviewer denies the correctness of the statement that in Rome, and in the West generally, the Paschal Vigil was the only one held in the year. He asks where such a rite could have come from—as he puts it in his, not always quite correct but often amusing, English diction: the idea of the uniqueness of the Paschal Vigil "would require an explanation of the why and the where such an isolated instance would happen to exist . . . where did the *ordo* or structure of such an unique vigil come from? Or, alternatively, who built it up out of the blue *c.* 360?" (p. 186).

Finally, in a book entitled *The Influence of the Synagogue upon the Divine Office* (Oxford University Press, 1945), Mr. C. W. Dugmore, B.D. (sometime James Mew Rabbinical Hebrew Scholar in the University of Oxford) maintains and brings forward much argument in its favour, that from the earliest times the Christian Church possessed two daily public services of morning and evening 'praise', which it had inherited and adapted from the example of the Synagogue.

MORNING AND EVENING PRAYER: In the regular 'Divine Service' not only were there two public services on the Sabbath day (Saturday) and on Monday and Thursday (fast-days), but there were also evening and morning services on every day of the week. On Sabbath days and also on the Mondays and Thursdays, the service consisted of readings from the Scriptures (especially the Law and the Prophets), of the chanting of certain psalms, a sermon and prayers; but on the other days, apparently, only psalms and prayers were recited; there were no lessons from Holy Scripture, and there was no sermon. It is a generally accepted view, as we have seen earlier, that the first part of the Mass-Liturgy (which is quite evidently in itself a complete service) was derived from the Sabbath-service of the Synagogue. According to Mr. Dugmore—in summing up all his arguments: "It has been suggested that the Christian week included worship not only on the Lord's Day but on every day as well." He says that on Saturdays "in the East not the West—and Sundays—the Holy Eucharist was celebrated from the beginning as well as the Pro-Anaphora", and that in some local churches this double service was celebrated also on the Wednesday and Friday station days,[1] but in other places probably the Pro-Anaphora alone. The Pro-Anaphora[2] alone was, too, the normal service everywhere on weekdays. But here again there may have been differences in practice. It is certain that at Rome and Alexandria, and in most other places, Scripture lections and instructions on them were of daily occurrence. In some churches, however, the service may have been confined to prayer and praise. He concludes that "there can be no doubt that public worship at dawn and at sunset was the tradition of the early Church" (p. 112). The author finds his evidence for this daily

---

[1] Which days formed the Christian counterpart to the Jewish weekly fast-days, on Monday and Thursday.

[2] That is, the service preceding the Holy Eucharist—*anaphora* ('offering') is the Greek name for the Eucharistic Prayer.

public service of prayer and praise morning and evening, first of all in the likelihood, even certainty (as far as that is possible without actual *proof*) that the early Church, composed at first entirely of Jews, must have been influenced by and attached to the observances of the Religion in which her children had been brought up and which was the Divine preparation for the Religion to which they now belonged (Dugmore, pp. 43 *et seq.*).

EUCHARISTIC AND NON-EUCHARISTIC WORSHIP: Secondly, Mr. Dugmore relies on certain of the early Christian writers— e.g. Tertullian and Origen, both of second-century date. The former says explicitly: *Aut sacrificium offertur, aut Dei verbum administratur*—'either the sacrifice is offered, or the Word of God is set forth' (*De Cult. Fem.*, 11. xi.; *P.L.*, i. 1445). All these writers at least *refer* to what may be legitimately considered to be daily public services of prayer, although word-for-word proof cannot be asserted. At the end of chap. III ('The Christian Week') Mr. Dugmore says that we may conclude from all that he has written that daily services modelled upon those of the Synagogue had existed in the Church from the very beginning, apart from the celebration of the Holy Eucharist. The latter was usually (though by no means always) preceded by a similar service—the pro-anaphora or synaxis—but this service had existed as a distinct service in itself from the earliest times, and was recited without the Eucharist on weekdays, both in the East and in the West. In the latter a daily celebration of the Eucharist became habitual (introduced possibly in Rome or in North Africa) at the beginning of the third century, and this custom was found also in certain isolated districts in the East; but it never became universal there. With the growth in the West of the daily Mass and the rise of monasticism in both East and West, the daily non-Eucharistic services became part of the developed monastic Hours and influenced the already existing distinct monastic services of the morning and evening, later known as 'Matins' and 'Vespers' (this morning office, later still, was given the name of 'Lauds', see Dugmore, pp. 57 and 58). In the following chapter, 'The Growth of the Canonical Hours', Mr. Dugmore fully admits the monastic origin of the Little Hours and the fusion which came about,

probably during the fourth century, between the old ecclesiastical 'morning' and 'evening praise' and the monastic '*Laus
perennis*' ('perpetual praise')—perpetual, that is, in the wide
sense, being celebrated *throughout the day*, and not only morning
and evening.

THE VIGIL-SERVICE: Monasticism was accountable not only
for the Day-Hours, but also for the nightly vigil-service which
had been celebrated only on Saturdays in the ecclesiastical
office. With regard to the vigil in general, Mr. Dugmore tells
us that it is not till Tertullian's time that we have definite news
of the weekly vigil. No doubt the Easter Vigil was the first in
use and, just as the Christian week was formed on the model of
what we now call Holy Week, so the weekly vigil was an adaptation of the great Paschal Vigil. But, again as in the case of
the week itself, the weekly vigil came into being quite early.
Mr. Dugmore says that this vigil every week was held probably
on the Sunday—that is, on the evening of Saturday, or, as the
Hebrew method of time put it, 'between the evenings'. This
means that the sabbath ended in the evening, and the first day
of the week—our Sunday—began and lasted till the following
evening. The vigils on the anniversaries of the martyrs' 'witness' to Christ Our Lord were of somewhat later date than the
weekly vigil—in accordance with the development of their
'cultus' in the Church. Tertullian speaks of regular vigils which
he calls *nocturnæ convocationes* (lit. 'nightly callings together')
(*Ad Uxor.* 11, xiii; *P.L.*, i, 1406). It seems from the context that
these '*convocations*' took place on the station-days. The vigil
properly so-called was a very late service—about midnight—
and in preparation (like the Paschal Vigil) for the Holy
Eucharist; hence it would have been celebrated only in those
places in which the Eucharist itself was offered on the station-
day. Where this was not the usage, the ordinary pro-anaphora
office would have been observed (Dugmore, pp. 41 and 42).

TWO TYPES OF OFFICE: Not only were the two types of office
(ecclesiastical and monastic) distinguished by the different
number of services in each, they were also distinguished by the
difference in the *intention* for which such acts of worship were

celebrated. The public service of prayer and praise offered by the Church was based upon that of the Jewish Liturgy from which it was derived. The idea among the Jews underlying the two services of 'morning' and 'evening' praise was to 'bless' (that is, to 'thank') God, for His gift of light to man. In the morning God was blessed for the light of the sun—His immediate creation; in the evening He was blessed for the light which He had given man the power to produce himself, in the lighting of the evening lamp. This idea was kept on in the Christian Church, with the addition of thanksgiving for the spiritual light of the soul given to the members of His Mystical Body by Our Lord in His resurrection, which was especially honoured in the morning office of praise. In the Synagogue morning service there was at the beginning a benediction for the gift of light. In the Christian Church we have the text of such a benediction, in the form of a hymn, in the *Testament of Our Lord* (probably a Syrian liturgical document of about A.D. 350). This document is derived from the much older *Apostolic Tradition* of St. Hippolytus of Rome, and the text of the morning hymn is no doubt an example of an earlier tradition. With regard to the blessing of the lamp in the evening, St. Basil the Great, in the same century, speaks of it as being of immemorial antiquity. He says: "I will now add what perhaps would be otherwise too insignificant to adduce, but on account of *its antiquity* is required for the refutation of him who accuses us of novelty. It seemed good to our fathers not to receive in silence the gift of light at eventide, but as soon as it appeared, to return thanks." What the Saint says next is of special interest: "Who was the author of these words of thanksgiving at the lighting of the lamps we are unable to say: the people, however, use the old form, and no one ever thought them guilty of impiety for saying, 'We praise Father, Son and God's Holy Spirit'." (*De Spirit. Sanct.*, xxix. 73; *P.G.*, xxxii. 205; see Dugmore, p. 46.) In time the evening service came to be known in Latin as the *lucernarium* (from *lucerna*, 'a lamp'), which might be translated as 'the lamp-service'. A striking survival of this service remains in the Roman rite, in the Blessing of the Paschal Candle by the deacon on Holy Saturday. The special blessing of the fire which precedes that of the candle, however, is a late addition to the Roman rite, dating only from the eleventh century and coming from Gallican sources. The ceremony of the candle itself—apart from this special form—was an ancient one, for it was in use in Jerusalem before the end of the fourth century. The original Roman ceremony would have been—as the author of the *Shape of the Liturgy* puts it: "the practical one of getting a light to hold the service by" (Dix, pp. 23 and 24, footnote 3).

In the fourth century we have a very interesting and very living account of the public services in preparation for Easter in the local church of Jerusalem.

ÆTHERIA AND JERUSALEM: This account—which incidentally shows the two types of service, ecclesiastical and monastic, closely united but not yet entirely fused into one—is provided in the letters written by a Spanish abbess, called Etheria or Ætheria, to her nuns describing her journey to the Holy Land in A.D. 385–8. These letters were discovered by Signor G. F. Gamurrini in 1887, and published under the title *Peregrinatio Silviæ*, because at first this lady was believed to be Silvia, sister of the celebrated Imperial minister in Aquitaine, Rufinus. But her true name and personality were established in recent discussions on the matter (Srawley: *The Early History of the Liturgy*, Cambridge, 1947, p. 73).[1]

In these letters of the Spanish nun, which are referred to by both Dom Dix and Mr. Dugmore in their respective works, Ætheria (this is apparently the most favoured form of her name) describes in detail the daily offices in the church of the Anastasis (that is, 'Resurrection'), and shows very clearly the distinction between the ecclesiastical and monastic services of which we have spoken. She describes the evening service at the 'tenth hour'—about our (natural) 4 p.m.—which service she calls 'licinicon' (the correct form is *luchnicon*—the Greek translation of the Latin *lucernarium*). Ætheria tells us, too, that there is also an office at dawn: "when it begins to get light (*lucescere*)". These two hours are ecclesiastical; other hours of which Ætheria speaks, which are celebrated during the course of the

[1] The most recent account of Etheria and her journeys is: *Éthérie, Journal de Voyage*: Latin text. Introduction and Translation. By Hélène Pétré. *Sources Chrétiennes*, Editions du Cerf, 1949; see *Downside Review*, Spring 1949, pp. 196–8.

day, are monastic offices at which the *monazontes* and *parthenæ* —monks and nuns (literally 'solitaries' and 'virgins') assist regularly. The clergy and lay-folk were also present at all these hours, but they were present *officially* only at the morning and evening offices, which were strictly ecclesiastical.

THE MONASTIC NIGHTLY VIGIL: At the 'nocturn'[1] as it was called only monks and nuns were *officially* present, although a few 'devout' members of clergy and laity also assisted. Mr. Dugmore says: "The special importance attached to these times of prayer [that is, the early morning and evening services] is best explained on the hypothesis that they represent the tradition of the primitive Church at Jerusalem derived directly from the Synagogue practice and continued throughout that obscure period of which we have few, if any, records, until they became incorporated in the monastic Hours of prayer, some time in the fourth century." The chief object of these monastic Hours, as we have seen, was to fulfil—as far as is possible under the ordinary conditions of human life—the admonition of Our Lord to 'pray *always*'. The Divine Office became, in fact, the external mark of and witness to the monastic vocation; that is, a life dedicated to continual worship and prayer. The second example of the difference between the early ecclesiastical and the monastic services lies in the methods of using the psalter. In the ecclesiastical services, the psalms chanted were specially selected for the circumstances, as devotional 'comments' on the lessons of Holy Scripture that had just been read aloud. The author of *The Shape of the Liturgy* points out as a good example of a 'devotional comment': "the use of Ps. xc. [lxxxix] 1–12 as a comment on Hos. vi. [Osee in the Douai Bible] at the paschal vigil, which was the Roman use in the third and probably in the second century" (Dix, p. 39 and footnote 3). Later on the Lesson from Osee became the first of the two lessons before the Passion in the Good Friday service, when—as we shall see was the case—the twelve prophecies were introduced (together with other additions) into the Holy Saturday vigil-service. But on Good Friday a tract taken from the Prophecy of Habacuc (chap. iii) now took the place of Psalm xc. [lxxxix] 1–12.

[1] In Latin, *Nocturnus* ('nightly, by night', 'nocturnal'—from *nox, noctis*—'night').

The underlying object of the monastic hours of prayer was the chant of the whole Psalter of 150 psalms distributed throughout each Hour, so that the whole would be completed in the week—this is the express desire of St. Benedict, who says in his Rule that "those monks would show themselves very slothful in the service of their devotion ['devotion' in the sense of the 'consecrated duty' of their state of life] who said in the course of a week less than the entire Psalter . . . since we read that our holy fathers resolutely fulfilled in a single day what I would that we tepid monks may achieve in a whole week" (*The Rule of St. Benedict*, chap. xviii, 'In what order the psalms are to be said'). The psalms were the private as well as the family prayers of the monks, and they had been the prayers of the solitaries of the desert and elsewhere before these were united in communities in the cenobitical way of life.

THE DOUBLE OFFICE AT JERUSALEM: In Ætheria's time the morning and evening praise of the clergy followed the morning and evening office of the ascetics. When the ecclesiastical vigil-service took place on Saturday, the bishop and the greater number of clergy and laity left the church while the ascetics chanted their own vigil-office, or 'night-office'; those of the clergy and laity who stayed on for it doing so as a private devotion. As for the day-hours Terce, Sext and None (at 9 a.m., midday and 3 p.m. of our time respectively), these hours were hardly more than private devotions even at this period. In Jerusalem, according to Ætheria, Terce was recited only during Lent, although the other two hours were celebrated every day. In a very interesting article on the origin and constitution of the Divine Office in *La Maison Dieu*,[1] I. H. Dalmais, O.P., lays down practically the same historical outline as given above, but, like Dix, he considers that the Saturday vigil of the ecclesiastical office was a much later development, and he agrees in thinking that at first the only vigils in existence were the original Easter Vigil (perhaps also at Pentecost), and those at the tombs of the martyrs on the anniversaries of their martyrdom, although these

[1] *La Maison Dieu* (Les Editions du Cerf, Cahier No. 21, 29, Boulevard Latour-Mauborg, Paris-7e. 1950), *Origine et Constitution de l'Office*, by I. H. Dalmais, O.P., pp. 21–39, especially p. 31.

latter are not absolutely certain. He warns us, too, not to rely upon the descriptions of the Office at Jerusalem by Ætheria as examples of the Divine Office and its development in general. "This usage," he says, "is purely local and an example of the unique character of the church in which it was celebrated." Père Dalmais, however, fully admits that early texts in Africa and Egypt supply the principles of the later development of the Office during the fourth century—for both the clergy and the monks. He says, too, that in the Acts of the Apostles we find mention of the steadfastness of the Christian community at Jerusalem in the practice of prayer. This prayer was then 'community prayer'. We have also made mention of the special times for daily prayer—at the third, sixth and ninth hours (that is, the later offices of Terce, Sext and None), although these hours were then private devotions, not liturgical offices. According to Père Dalmais, even the ecclesiastical offices of morning and evening praise are of fairly late date in the history of the Liturgy. He does, however, admit the possibility that they were established, in some places at least, soon after the time of Hippolytus of Rome. The latter—in the third century—mentions the same series of 'hours' of prayer (Terce, Sext and None) spoken of above, although even in his time they were not yet part of an established liturgical Office.

THE ROMAN OFFICE MONASTIC: Père Dalmais also tells us the interesting fact that at Rome, quite differently from the other Western rites and from those of the East, the monastic type of Office seems to have prevailed entirely over the ecclesiastical type—if, indeed, the latter ever existed at all in the Roman Church. He says: "As far back as we can go, the Roman Office appears as a monastic office of the Western type, combining the usages of both Egypt and the East, but in rather a heavy and rough and ready manner" (Dalmais, *La Maison Dieu*, pp. 36–8).

A DOUBLE TRADITION: Père Dalmais says that the whole question of the history of the Divine Office lies in the fact that there is everywhere *a double tradition*; ecclesiastical and monastic. The first is concerned with the sanctification of the morn-

ing and evening hours, perhaps influenced by the daily morning and evening sacrifices in the Temple of Jerusalem; lessons
from Holy Scripture "for the instruction of the Christian people were added" to the chant of psalms "at least at the evening
office" (Dalmais, p. 38). He says, too, that the Paschal Vigil
was a most ancient tradition, which was copied in later times
more or less for all Sundays of the year, and which influenced,
too, the 'funeral-vigils' at the martyrs' tombs. Finally, it was
the influence of the monks which in the service of the basilicas—
that of the Holy Sepulchre in Jerusalem in A.D. 340, and perhaps
at Antioch and Constantinople towards the end of the fourth
century, and certainly at Rome and in Gaul during the fifth
century—which started the intermingling of the two traditions;
and nowhere else as much as at Rome, did the monastic use
prevail over the ecclesiastical to such an extent (Dalmais,
p. 39).

THE FULLY DEVELOPED OFFICE: Two other day hours besides those of Terce, Sext and None are found in later times.
These are: 'Prime' (*prima hora*—the first hour of the day after
dawn, about 6 a.m. of our time, at the equinoxes) and 'Compline' (*completorium*—from *complēre*—'to end', 'complete'), the
last office of the day before retiring to rest.

THE OFFICE OF PRIME: In the fourth century, Cassian—that
great authority on monastic life and himself a monk[1]—describing the psalmody of the Egyptian monks of his day in the
second and third books of his *Institutiones*, and comparing it
with that of his own monastery at Bethlehem, speaks of a
morning office which had recently been introduced. The reason
for this new office was to remedy an abuse that had crept into
the observance, namely that of the monks returning to their
beds after the night-office and resting there as late as the hour
of Terce. Until recently the introduction of this new office was
considered by most liturgical authorities to mark the origin of
the above-mentioned office of Prime. But some now consider
this to be mistaken, and that the new office was that called

---

[1] John Cassian (*Ioannes Cassianus*) of Southern Gaul (A.D. *c.* 360–435). Became
a monk at Bethlehem. Visited many monasteries and wrote on monastic life.

Matins by St. Benedict, which in later times was known as
Lauds. Prime, say these writers, was unheard of until the time
of St. Benedict—that is, during the sixth century. This view is
upheld by the Rev. Fr. John Morson, O.C.R., in *Pax*, the
quarterly review of the Benedictines of Prinknash. If it is true
(and there seem to be serious reasons in support of it), the
adoption of an office of morning praise by the monks was not
a mere *adaptation* of the similar office celebrated by the clergy
from the earliest times, but an independent institution—
although it was probably influenced and helped on by the
ecclesiastical service. In any case, the fairly late adoption of the
morning office by the monks is no argument against the earlier
origin of the ecclesiastical office.[1] Quite recently a book on the
origin of the office of Prime has appeared—*Les Origines de
Prime*, by Dom Jacques Froger, monk of Solesmes. Dom Froger,
too, considers that the Bethlehem office was Matins—that is,
Lauds as it is now called—and that Prime is almost contemporary with St. Benedict himself.[2] The principal argument in
favour of this office at Bethlehem being Lauds rather than
Prime is the fact that Cassian speaks of it under the title of
matutina solemnitas ('morning solemnity'); and this is almost the
exact title used by St. Benedict in speaking of the morning
office which follows the vigil- or night-office; the Saint calls it
matutinorum solemnitas ('the solemnity of the mornings')—
sometimes simply *matutina* ('morning'). There is very little
difference or significance between these terms used by St.
Benedict and Cassian. The word *matutinum* (in English, 'matins')
was later on given to the night-office, formerly known as vigils
or nocturns, when it came to be celebrated habitually in the
early morning instead of during the night. The title of *Laudes*
('Lauds'), now given to the morning praise, was so given on

---

[1] See *Pax*; Spring, Autumn and Winter numbers 1945 and Spring–Winter 1946:
'Origins of Monastic Liturgy', by the Rev. Fr. John Morson, O.C.R., of Mount
St. Bernard's Abbey, Leicester. See, especially, Summer 1945, pp. 69 and 70.

[2] *Les Origines de Prime*, par Dom Jacques Froger, moine de Solesmes (Rome:
Edizione Liturgiche (1946)). But see a long review of the above by O. Chadwick
in the *Journal of Theological Studies* (July–October 1948, pp. 178–82). Mr. Chadwick
criticises Dom Froger's view, in spite of the fact that in the *J.T.S.* of the preceding
year (July–October 1947) there is a very favourable review of the book by the
well-known liturgical scholar, Dom Louis Brou, of Quarr Abbey, who considers
Dom Froger's arguments to be conclusive. Mr. Chadwick, nevertheless, maintains
that the question cannot be regarded as finally settled.

account of the three psalms of praise (Psalms cxlviii, cxlix, and cl), of which the first and third begin with *Laudate* ('praise ye'), becoming 'lauds' in English. These psalms, however, did not form part of the morning office at Bethlehem, which, says Fr. Morson, "began in Cassian's youth, *but not as an entirely new office* . . . as formerly . . . it was completed *together with Vigils*" (*Pax*, Summer 1945, p. 70, italics mine); but they *did* form part of St. Benedict's *matutinorum solemnitas*, and from the above their connection with some form of 'morning praise' is fairly evident.

If Fr. Morson is right in saying that the Bethlehem *matutina solemnitas* was the origin of Lauds, and not Prime, the latter office still remains an 'unknown quantity': when, where and how did it arise? The author of *Les Origines de Prime* says that the exact date of its origin is uncertain; but that it was certainly not earlier than the sixth century. The reviewer of his book, however, in *The Journal of Theological Studies* argues that Cassian, speaking of this 'new office' as he calls it in his *Inst.* iii. 4, says that its introduction completes the number seven in the liturgical prayer of the monks. In previous chapters Cassian speaks of the series of 'hours' as follows: 'Nocturns', that is, the night-office; a morning office; Terce, Sext, None and Vespers (*lucernaris hora*), and this latter he qualifies as *ad extremum*—'at the end'. This seems to suggest that there was no other office in the day after vespers.

THE OFFICE OF COMPLINE: In chap. 4 Cassian describes the institution of the new 'morning office' at Bethlehem, ending with the above statement that this new addition to the 'hours' makes up the sacred number of seven—in accordance with the words in Psalm cxviii. 164: "seven times a day I have given praise to thee, for the judgments of thy justice". Dom Froger considers that there *was* another office after Vespers (analogous to the later fuller office of Compline) in Cassian's time, and that this office is mentioned by him in *Inst.* iv. 19; his words are: "the brethren having met together in one place in order to chant the psalms, which they sing habitually when about to retire to rest" (*convenientibus in unum fratribus ad concinendos psalmos quos quieturi ex more decantant*)—a "text", says the reviewer, "whence the majority of modern liturgiologists has decided that a formal Compline office cannot be deduced". He thinks that this psalmody before retiring for the night meant merely the singing of a few psalms as an 'evening devotion', though no doubt the formal office grew out of it later on. There is no other reference in Cassian's works to any other evening office after Vespers. Dom Froger gets out of the difficulty of Cassian's description of his vesper-office as *ad extremum* ('the end') by translating the Latin into 'after that' (*après cela*) which, says his reviewer Mr. Chadwick, is "rather free"! Compline as well as Prime has a very uncertain origin, which is still the subject of discussion. Dom Froger says that it was not earlier than the sixth century—that is, in St. Benedict's time, but it is no longer generally held that it was the saint himself who introduced it. In the Holy Rule, St. Benedict speaks of Compline (*completorium*)—and is the first to call it by that name —but without any *explanation* of the office or its name (as though it were something already well known); he speaks only of the number of psalms that are to be said in the office (*Rule of St. Benedict*, chaps. xvi, xvii, xviii).

THE UNIFICATION OF THE DOUBLE OFFICE: This was effected by the combination of the ecclesiastical and monastic hours of prayer. The organisation of these two elements at Jerusalem, as described by Ætheria, seems to have been the work of St. Cyril, Bishop of Jerusalem, in A.D. 350. Some even consider that he 'invented' the ecclesiastical office himself, but it seems more likely that he only organised it, adopting his ideas from the monastic 'family' prayer, and thus preparing the way for this latter to become also the corporate prayer of the whole Church. The as yet partial union between the two types of office found at Jerusalem in Cyril's time is also evident in both the Mozarabic (Spanish) and the Ambrosian rites in the West, and is still, moreover, quite noticeable in both rites. In an interesting little book on the subject,[1] Mr. W. C. Bishop says that: "In the services of the ancient Ambrosian and Mozarabic rites we find a survival of genuine examples of the ancient

[1] *The Mozarabic and Ambrosian Rites: Alcuin Club Tracts, XV*, by W. C. Bishop, M.A. Edited from his papers by C. L. Feltoe. D.D. (A. R. Mowbray & Co., Ltd., London, 1924, p. 57).

secular services of the Western Church from which inconsistent accretions can readily be separated, leaving the original form and order of the services practically intact and complete." The "inconsistent accretions" are the additions introduced into the old ecclesiastical office, consisting originally of only two daily services (morning and evening) and a weekly vigil-service, from the monastic *cursus* which extended over the whole of each day.

In the office of Vespers, in both the Ambrosian and Mozarabic rites, there is a reference to the *lucernarium*—the ritual lighting of the evening lamp which was the chief characteristic of the earlier service of evening praise. The psalms used were originally specially selected psalms. In the monastic *cursus*, however, the whole Psalter was arranged to be recited during a certain period of time. The same is true of the other office of 'nocturns'. This office was made up of the elements of what are now treated as two distinct offices—matins and lauds—but which, in the Ambrosian and Mozarabic rites, formed only one. According to Mr. Bishop, there is evidence that the original Vespers and Nocturns of the Spanish and Ambrosian rites were not daily services, but occurred only on those days on which Mass was celebrated. This shows, perhaps, the original identity of the two offices with the weekly vigil-service of the old ecclesiastical *cursus*.

The Byzantine Rite: On p. 57 Mr. Bishop speaks of the Byzantine rite and says: "The Byzantine rite is used by both monks and seculars . . . and in its present shape the rite is evidently monastic, though it is probable that some parts of these services are derived from earlier secular sources; and I believe the same can be said of the present Coptic, Jacobite and Persian-hour services." Père Dalmais mentions this book by W. C. Bishop and C. L. Feltoe on *The Mozarabic and Ambrosian Rites*, and agrees with the authors' statements. But there is another possible example of this partial fusion of the two offices (ecclesiastical and monastic) in the Byzantine rite to which the present writer has so far failed to find any reference or even any recognition of its existence, in any literature about the Eastern offices.

MIDNIGHT OFFICE AND GREAT VESPERS: The Byzantine Office possesses, besides the usual system of 'Hours', two other offices which are not found in any other liturgical system. These are: (*a*) an office known as the 'Midnight Office' (in Greek, *Mesonyktikon*) and (*b*) the office known as 'Great Vespers' (*Megalos Hesperinos*). The first of these two is quite distinct from the office called 'Daybreak Office'—*Orthros*, which is equivalent to the two Western offices of Matins and Lauds joined together, although the Midnight Office is often spoken of as though it corresponded to the Western Matins, and the Daybreak Office to Lauds. 'Great Vespers' is, however, really distinct from 'Little Vespers', this latter being celebrated on ordinary days, while the former is celebrated only on Saturdays and on days when there is a long vigil-service known as 'Pannychis' (that is, 'All-night-service'). Strictly speaking, the Vigil or Solemn Office should start with 'Little Vespers' on Saturday evening, and this office should be followed immediately by 'Great Vespers'; then, in monasteries, the monks' supper—with a solemnly chanted grace—and after supper, *Apodeipnon*—that is, the 'after-supper' service corresponding to the Western Compline. Next should come the Midnight Office and the Daybreak Office. After Compline the monks would ordinarily retire to rest till the Midnight Office unless there were a 'Whole-night vigil' (*pannychis*, referred to above). This latter is also called the *Agrypnia*, i.e. 'Watch-service' (from the Greek *agrypnein*—'to be wakeful' or 'watchful'). The Pannychis really fulfils its name and lasts the *entire* night, the service going on without cessation through all the hours of the Divine Office up till Sext—after which follows the Divine Liturgy. It seems that nowadays, when Great Vespers is sung, even though there is no all-night vigil, Little Vespers is usually omitted and both Compline and the Midnight Office as well. The fact that only Great Vespers is recited is no doubt the reason why its true character of a separate office (and, perhaps, of a relic of the early ecclesiastical vigil) has been lost sight of, and it has become merely a more solemn form of ordinary Vespers. It is, however, of quite a distinct type from the ordinary monastic Vesper-office and is much longer. Great Vespers consists of the so-called 'vesper-psalms'; that is, Psalms cxl, clxi, cxxviii and cxxxiii—these are always used though there are other changeable psalms also. Psalm cxl is the 'vesper-psalm' *par excellence*, and is found in all rites. In the West nowadays, besides the use of the whole psalm in ferial Vespers on Friday in the Roman rite, the second verse—*Dirigatur, Domine, oratio mea, sicut incensum in conspectu tuo* ('Let my prayer arise, O Lord, like incense in thy sight')—is always used as a 'versicle' and 'respond' just before the Magnificat antiphon both at Vespers on ordinary Sundays and ferias—except Saturday, when the verse is *Vespertina oratio ascendat ad te, Domine. Et descendat super nos misericordia tua* ('Let the evening prayer go up to thee, Lord, and let thy mercy come down upon us'). These 'Vesper-psalms' are perhaps survivals of the selected psalms formerly used in the primitive ecclesiastical office; the same would apply in the case of the *Laudate* psalms, always recited at the Morning Office in both East and West, as they still are. It seems, then, to be at least probable that 'Great Vespers' is not really vespers at all in the monastic sense of the term, but is a survival of the ancient Saturday and festal vigil. Whether this vigil existed in the earliest days of Christianity or was a later development does not really matter.

Besides psalms and prayers, a number of lessons are read during 'Great Vespers'.[1] This is another example of its character of vigil rather than vespers.

On ordinary Saturdays and lesser feasts there is no 'All-night service'. Little Vespers is followed by Great Vespers (in practice, as we have said already, Little Vespers is usually omitted), Compline and the Midnight and Morning Offices follow later, and the usual time-intervals between them and the Little Hours and the Liturgy are observed.

SUMMARY: In the probable development of the Byzantine Office, the Midnight Office is a relic of the monastic *daily* vigil-service—somewhat reduced in form and length; the Morning—or Dawn—Office and Little Vespers represent the old eccle-

---

[1] See, with regard to Great Vespers and the omission of Little Vespers: *The Byzantine Office*, by John Bannerman Wainewright (London: Cope and Fenwick, 1909, especially p. 23, footnote). In the Orthros Office, the section in which the *Laudate* psalms are recited is called *Ainoi* ('Praise' or 'Lauds'). But this 'Lauds' is not itself a separate office.

siastical 'Morning' and 'Evening' Praise' now combined with the monastic forms of services at the same time. Perhaps these latter are derived from the ecclesiastical services, but also, perhaps, they may be independent 'inventions'. Great Vespers is a relic of the ecclesiastical weekly and festal vigil.

The Little Hours (Prime, *Proté*—Terce, *Trité*—Sext, *Hekté*—None, *Ennaté* and Compline, *Apodeipnon*) are all monastic in character. In passing, we must note that there are two forms of Compline—'Little Compline' and 'Great Compline' (*Mikron Apodeipnon; Megalon Apodeipnon*). But the analogy with Great and Little Vespers goes no farther than the names, for Great Compline is really only a more solemn form of the office than Little Compline, and takes its place entirely on certain occasions. It appears that Great Compline is possibly an older form. It is chanted on the Mondays, Tuesdays, Wednesdays and Thursdays of each week in Lent up till Wednesday in Holy Week. It may also be recited on the Wednesdays and Fridays of the 'Lents' before Christmas and 'The Apostles'—that is, the Feast of SS. Peter and Paul. Besides these days, it is recited on the Vigils of Christmas and Epiphany—these vigils actually *beginning* with this Office. In other vigils, as we have seen, Compline—that is, *Little* Compline—is omitted altogether.

THE WEEKLY VIGIL IN THE WEST: This seems to have been combined with the monastic daily vigil to form the daily Night-Office, the 'Nocturns' as it was also often called. This combination is perhaps most evident in the Benedictine Office as laid down for his monks by St. Benedict in the Holy Rule. In this office there are always the twelve psalms which are spoken of as especially sacred by Cassian, who even declares that that number was introduced into the night-office of the Pachomian monks by an angel.[1] St. Benedict himself insists very strongly that this 'sacred number' of twelve be adhered to always in the Nocturns, whether there are three or only two of the latter. The saint, however, always anxious to avoid over-taxing the strength of his monks, divided the twelve psalms into

---

[1] Cassian, *Institutiones*, II, v.

two sets of six—each forming a 'nocturn'.[1] On certain feasts, instead of only two nocturns and three lessons as on weekdays, there are three nocturns (the third being composed of three canticles from the Scripture Prophets) and twelve lessons. In summer, as the nights in Italy are very short, there was only one short lesson, to be recited by heart. The twelve lessons on the feasts when these occur are divided into three sets of four lessons each—four for each nocturn. In the solemn Easter Vigil on Holy Saturday (formerly celebrated during the night of Saturday in preparation for Easter Day), there are twelve lessons from the Prophets, and these are divided into two sets of four each by two of the three 'tracts' (the fourth and the eighth), the third tract being sung after the *eleventh* Prophecy, as the twelfth is followed immediately by the blessing of the font[2] or by the litany, where there is no font. Whether this arrangement implies any real connection between the Holy Saturday Vigil and the Benedictine vigils or not, it is impossible to say definitely, but it is at least worth mentioning. It must, however, be remembered that the Holy Saturday vigil with the twelve prophecies is probably not the original Roman form of the vigil, but comes partly from Gaul, partly from Jerusalem.

POSSIBLE SURVIVAL OF OLD VIGIL: There is one case, at least, in the West, of an actual vigil-service distinct from the night-office, which, however, was celebrated as well. This case is mentioned in the writings of Cassiodorus (A.D. 490–583), a contemporary of St. Benedict, and like him the founder of a monastic community, at Vivarium on his own property. In his description of the liturgical offices in his monastery, Cassiodorus speaks of two forms of night-office, which he calls, respectively, nocturns and vigils—as we have seen, St. Benedict uses both names for the same office. According to Cassiodorus, nocturns was the name of the normal night-office, while vigils was that of a special office on Sundays and certain great feasts—which lasted all night. (See an article on 'St. Benedict

---

[1] This word is used by St. Benedict also in the case of the night-office as a whole; it is synonymous with 'vigils' and both words were originally military, the name for the soldiers' night-watch. Two or three nocturns does not imply that originally they were each a distinct *office*; there was only one office during the night.

[2] The tract, *Sicut Cervus* (Ps. xli. 2–4), is sung during the procession to the font.

and the Eremitical Life', by Adrian Hastings in the *Downside Review*, Spring 1950, pp. 191–211; on Cassiodorus and the vigils, see p. 208. The reference to these two offices in the writings of Cassiodorus is found in Migne, *P.L.*, t. lxx.)

The vigil-office, which lasted all night and was celebrated only on Sundays and certain feasts, sounds remarkably like the *Pannychis* of the Byzantine rite.

CHAPTER III

THE LITURGICAL YEAR

THE eschatological emphasis of the early Liturgy, of which something has already been said, was also affected by the development of the Liturgical Year—which the author of *The Shape of the Liturgy* calls "the sanctification of time" (pp. 303–96—and see especially pp. 333 *et seq.*). During the second half of the fourth century, besides the development of the daily Prayer of the Church, another development was taking place—that of the calendar or 'guide' to the cycle of the Liturgy during the whole year—dedicated now in the Christian ideal to the memory of the redemptive work of Christ our Lord upon earth. The fully worked out Office enabled the Church to sanctify human life within the bounds of time. This was effected by means of the different 'Hours' of prayer, consecrating the chief parts of every day: the 'watches' of the night; the early dawn; the time for beginning the day's work; the midday rest during the heat of the day (in Italy and in Eastern countries); the return to work in the afternoon; the hour of sunset; and, finally, the time for retiring to rest at the end of the day. These were: the Vigils or Night Office; Matins or Lauds; Prime; Terce; Sext; None; Vespers; Compline. In the same way the Liturgical Year, when its main outline had been worked out, effected the sanctification of all seasons of the year. In this way nature itself, and social life which rested upon it, were marked out by Christian ideas and provided with a Christian outlook.

DEVELOPMENT OF DIVINE OFFICE AND LITURGICAL YEAR: These went on side by side, but each was at first carried out, to some extent, independently and under more or less different influences. As already pointed out, the development of the Divine Office seems to have been the result of a combination of the two ecclesiastical daily services of public worship (morning and evening) and the various hours of prayer during each day, introduced by the monks. While some do not agree with Dix's statement that the Office *originated* with the monks and devout laity, it certainly seems to be true that monks and laity had a good deal to do with the later development and organisation of the Divine Office. That, on the other hand, the Liturgical Year was worked out chiefly by the bishops and the secular clergy seems certainly to be the case. (See Dix, p. 334.) This latter development introduced a different process in both Office and Eucharistic service (as regards the lessons from Scripture and the prayers), bringing in as the basis of both the year instead of the day and the week. The official organisation of the Office and the calendar was beginning, more or less, in the year A.D. 350, but all this did not take place at once or quite smoothly everywhere. The use of the psalms, too, as already remarked, differed in the old ecclesiastical Office from that in the monastic daily round of prayer. In the former, certain psalms were chosen on account of their fitness for various reasons. But in the monastic Office, the underlying intention was the recitation of the psalter as a whole in a certain fixed period of time and apportioned to the various hours, days, etc. In the time of St. Benedict, the intention laid down by the saint in his *Rule* was that the whole psalter should be recited in the course of the week; he says that if his own arrangement "be displeasing to anyone"—that is, to anyone in authority, not to any one in general, in the community—"he should, if he think fit, order otherwise, taking care in any case that the whole psalter of a hundred and fifty psalms be recited every week . . . for those monks would show themselves very slothful in the divine service who said less than the entire psalter . . . since we read that our holy fathers resolutely performed in a single day what I pray we tepid monks may achieve in a whole week" (*The Rule of St. Benedict*, chap. xviii). It is true that, speaking of the Office on saints' days in chap. xiv, the Patriarch of monks lays down that it is to "be ordered . . . as prescribed for Sundays: except that the psalms, antiphons and lessons *suitable to the day* are to be said". But according to Dom Delatte and other commentators on the Holy Rule, St. Benedict almost certainly means the psalms and other elements of the Office apportioned for each feria (weekday), not specially chosen for the feasts—

otherwise his command that the whole psalter was to be recited every week would have been impossible to fulfil.

'PROPER' PSALMS AT JERUSALEM: In A.D. 385, when Ætheria paid her famous visit to the Holy Land, she describes—as something quite new to her—the custom at Jerusalem according to which, on feast-days of Our Lord and of the saints, the psalms and other parts of the Office were not those of the ordinary weekly cycle, but were specially chosen as more appropriate to the feast being celebrated. In connection with this, according to Dix, it appears very probable that we owe to Jerusalem and to its "liturgically minded Bishop St. Cyril", not only the organisation of the daily Office in the Church, but also the introduction of the 'proper' of the saints, and, to a great extent, that of the liturgical seasons as well (Dix, pp. 349 ff.). In other local churches, and especially in those of the West, the notion of thus varying the use of the psalms on feast-days came in more slowly.[1] None of these changes—nor even the 'ordering' of the Divine Office, of the calendar or of the Liturgical Year—was directly brought about by ecclesiastical authority. All took place gradually and naturally, as it were. As Edmund Bishop was so fond of saying, it was popular devotion that had so much to do with the growth of the Liturgy. Rubrical decrees and such matters are of fairly modern date in its history.

(I) PRE-NICENE AND POST-NICENE: Before the fourth century the Liturgical Year was of extreme simplicity, and it was governed, like its centre—the Eucharistic Sacrifice—by the eschatological aspect, in which historical commemorations of events, taking place at special periods, had practically no place. The liturgical cycle consisted originally, all over the Christian world, of just two annual feasts: (i) the Paschal feast and (ii) the feast of Pentecost, and besides these, the observance of the Sunday—the 'Lord's Day'—which was a weekly continuation

---

[1] This no doubt is the explanation of the use in St. Benedict's own day of ferial psalms even on feasts in the Benedictine office (that is, if Dom Delatte and others are right). Even now, neither psalms nor hymns are changed in the Little Hours (except on Sunday and Monday); and in the reformed Benedictine breviary, the use of ferial psalms has been restored on lesser doubles. On Whitsunday and during the Octave, the *Veni Creator* is said at Terce, instead of the usual hymn.

of the Paschal feast, the 'setting forth' of the mystery of the resurrection of our Saviour from the dead—or, rather, of the mystery of the Redemption as a whole.[1] In Rome in Hippolytus' day, and in Africa in Tertullian's (early third century), the calendar was still of this simple formation, and even twenty years after that, in Origen's time in Egypt, it was still the same. At first the 'Liturgical Week' was the guiding principle of Christian worship. Then, the spread of the Christian faith beyond the Holy Land and its gradual freedom from persecution led to the development of the Liturgical Year. In the week, the 'first day'—in time known as 'Sunday' or the 'Lord's Day'—was set apart for corporate worship. Sunday, like the Paschal feast, was not so much the memorial of a past event, but rather *the manifestation in time of the eternal Act of Redemption in Christ.* The title 'sunday' is originally pagan and Roman; the first day of the week was dedicated to the sun-god—the *dies solis* ('day of the sun'). In English all the other days of the week are also dedicated to pagan gods, but to those of the Scandinavian theogony—except Saturday and Monday. Thus, we have Tuesday dedicated to the god Tiu; Wednesday to Woden (or Odin); Thursday to Thor; Friday to the goddess Freya; while Saturday, like Sunday, is dedicated to a Roman god, Saturn, and Monday ('moon's day') to the god of the moon .The ecclesiastical Latin title of Sunday is *Dies Dominica*, the 'Lord's Day' (which becomes 'Dimanche' in French), as it was and is the day especially consecrated to the Lord's work among mankind. During the first three centuries, the 'manifestation' of the Redemption effected by Our Saviour on the cross, and certified, so to speak, in His resurrection and ascension, was the sole reason for the observance of Sunday. Only during the fourth century did it come to be considered as also the Christian substitute for the Hebrew Sabbath—the 'Day of rest', in memory of the seventh day upon which God rested, after the work of creation. In the Jewish Sabbath it was the avoidance of all work rather than the attendance at public worship that was in-

---

[1] It seems that, historically, Sunday (the weekly feast of the Resurrection) existed before the yearly feast—the Paschal Feast. Nevertheless, the latter came into use very early, in Apostolic times. (See *Dimanche et Vie pascale*, by D. Jean Hild, O.S.B. (Éditions Brepols, S.A., Turnhout (Belgique); Paris, 28, Rue d'Assas, VIe, 1949) (p. 39, footnote 1).

sisted upon by the Pharisees—and from this rigid and narrow point of view was derived the Puritan and early Presbyterian observance of Sunday. But in the early Church it seems that her children did not hesitate to carry on their usual daily work, just like their pagan neighbours—once they had worshipped God by taking part in the Eucharistic Sacrifice at the meeting of the local church. It was this act which was, above all else, the Christian duty—the weekly gathering together of the whole Body of Christ in union with its Head. This obligation, of course, still remains the supreme and primary obligation of the Catholic Church in the Sunday Mass, at which she demands the assistance of all the faithful—unless prevented by some sufficient reason. The words used in this connection by the author of *The Shape of the Liturgy* deserve special note here. The object, he says, of "the weekly gathering of the whole Body of Christ to its Head" was in order "to *become* what it really *is*, His Body" (Dix, p. 336). In every Mass, no matter under what circumstances it be celebrated—whether in a cathedral, in the presence of a vast crowd or in a little chapel with the server alone—is the offering of the whole Body of Christ throughout the world united in its Head. But in those early days this truth was more evident *outwardly* than it is in these—although the 'liturgical movement' is slowly but surely succeeding in helping the faithful to realise their part in the offering of the Holy Sacrifice and in arousing the desire to carry it out more completely and thoroughly.[1]

A DIVINE PARADOX: We have already noticed the existence of this paradox in the eschatological outlook of the whole of Our Lord's work in and through His Church, which is at once actually *present* here and now, in each period of life, but nevertheless continually waits for *fulfilment*. The 'Kingdom of God' has 'come', and yet we must, by Our Lord's own command, always pray—'Thy Kingdom come' (that is, 'that Thy Kingdom may come'). The Paschal feast is primarily of eschatological significance; it represents the completion and con-

---

[1] The 'Day of the Sun' was chosen as 'the Lord's Day', since Our Lord is in truth the 'Sun of Justice', the 'Light of the World'—the 'unconquered Sun' (*sol invictus*). See again Hild, pp. 32 and ff.

tinuation or—perhaps better—the 'actuality' of the Redemption. It is only secondarily a 'looking back' to the fact of the resurrection taking place at one particular moment of time. By His resurrection and ascension, the followers of Jesus have in reality—in a spiritual manner—been taken up into the heavenly Kingdom and shown thus to all men in the unity of His Church on earth.

JEWISH SABBATH AND CHRISTIAN SUNDAY: In the earliest period of the Church, the Jewish Sabbath was sometimes observed as well as the Christian Sunday—especially in the case of the 'Jewish Christians' who, as long as the sect lasted, endeavoured to combine the Jewish and Christian religions in one. In the Eastern Churches even now, the idea of the Sabbath is kept up to a certain extent in the solemnity of the Saturday liturgy. And it is certainly true that the Sabbath did have an effect upon the Sunday, and probably the notion of the regular observance of the first day of the week was suggested by that of the seventh day.

TWO FOUNDATION FEASTS: The Pasch and Pentecost of the Christian year seem, like the weekly feast on Sunday, to have come down from Apostolic times. Both are Christian adaptations of Jewish feasts—or rather they are the *reality* foreshadowed by the Jewish days, and the second has handed on its Greek name to its successor. But in the Church these feasts, which among the Jews were not confined to any particular day of the week, were fixed always on Sunday, and this arrangement was probably brought about within the first century—if not actually in Apostolic times.

PASCH AND PASSOVER: The word 'Pasch' (*Pascha*) is the Greek form of the Hebrew word *pesach*, which is translated 'passover'. The name refers to the occasion when the Angel of the Lord 'passed over' the threshold of those houses marked with the sacrificial blood of the passover lamb (Exod. xii.— see especially verses 12 and 13 and 21–3). But the word translated 'I will *pass* over' (in Latin, *transibo*) should really be '*cross* over'—the true meaning of the Hebrew word. That word does

not mean to 'pass *by*' (as it has usually been understood to do),
but on the contrary to 'pass *in*'—to cross over the threshold in
order to enter the house—and not to punish those dwelling in
it, but as a visitor, an honoured guest.

PASSOVER AND THRESHOLD SACRIFICE: In fact, the passover
sacrifice of the Israelites was probably the adaptation of a very
ancient form of sacrifice among Semitic peoples, known as the
'threshold sacrifice'. In order to show due honour to guests of
dignity—especially if they were believed to be of *divine* dignity
—a victim was sacrificed at the entrance of the house or
tent, the blood being poured out on the threshold so that the
guest 'crossed over' the blood in entering the dwelling. The
sacrificial blood thus poured out testified to the host's intention
to pay the highest honour to his guest, symbolising, as it did,
that his own life, like that of the victim's 'in the blood' (Levit.
xvii. 11), belonged to or was subject to the guest, human or
divine. The latter, by thus 'crossing over' the blood, accepted
the act of supreme honour officially.

THE CHRISTIAN VIGIL: The Jewish feast was celebrated in
the evening, and the Christian counterpart was held also at
dawn, after the solemn Saturday vigil. As usual, the vigil began with the blessing of the evening lamp, which was the duty of
the deacon; then came a series of Scripture lessons, between each
of which a responsory psalm was chanted—as in the ordinary
liturgical or 'aliturgical' service. But it seems that the original
Roman Paschal vigil did not consist of the long series of twelve
prophecies—or even of only four as in the Gregorian Sacramentary (sixth century), and still in the Carthusian and
Dominican rites to-day, but merely of the two prophecies and
the Gospel of St. John, which are now found in the Good
Friday service. (The prophecies are Osee vi.—an allusion to the
resurrection of the body, and Exod. xii.—the account of the
Passover.) This seems to have been the case in A.D. 200. The
chant of the Twelve Prophecies—now such an outstanding
feature of the Holy Saturday service—is a later development
derived from Jerusalem during the fourth century. In the
Jerusalem rite it appears, too, from a recently discovered

homily on the Passion by Melito, Bishop of Sardis (*c.* A.D. 190), that the Paschal Liturgy in Asia Minor contained the same lesson from Exodus as in Rome.[1]

GOOD FRIDAY AND HOLY SATURDAY: Since Rome and Jerusalem differed strongly all during the second century regarding the date of the Paschal feast, it seems probable that the agreements between their respective Paschal rites are "independent survivals of a rite drawn up at a very early date indeed" (Dix, p. 338). In the earlier form, after the above two lessons, followed a lesson from the Gospel of St. John, as on Good Friday later on, but originally on the Saturday, continuing right on to the account of the resurrection, with "its hint of an ascension, on Easter Day itself" (Dix, as above; see John xx. 17). On Good Friday the Passion-lesson stops at xix. 42. After the Gospel and a sermon by the bishop came the baptism and confirmation of the catechumens, who then were able for the first time, as full members of Christ's Body, to join in the 'People's Prayers' (the intercessory collects still recited on Good Friday); to take part as offerers in the Eucharistic Sacrifice and to receive the Body and Blood of their risen Saviour in communion. The twelve prophecies, which seem to have originated at Jerusalem, appear in almost every Liturgy for the Paschal vigil. But this extension of what was at first only local does not seem to be earlier than the fourth century, since, as a matter of fact, the recital of these prophecies started in Jerusalem itself only in that century.

The Paschal feast was considered from the first as the most suitable time for conferring the sacraments of Baptism and Confirmation through which the Redemption and its effects are applied to each individual: Baptism being 'into Christ's death and resurrection', and Confirmation being the 'confirming', that is, *ensuring* or *fixing*, the effects of Baptism through the indwelling of the Holy Spirit in each. So in the beginning of the Church, the Paschal feast was not, as now, primarily the commemoration of the historical fact of the resurrection of Our Lord 'in time'. It was, primarily, the 'Liturgy of the Redemption'. The early Christians did not make a clear dis-

---

[1] See Dix, pp. 338 *et seq.*

tinction between the death, resurrection and ascension as complete acts in themselves. All three acts were not only *connected* with the Sacrifice offered by Christ on the Cross; they were each a *part* of the Sacrifice. The latter was not reserved—and should never be reserved—to the death of Our Lord on the Cross alone. Thus, at first there were no special commemorations of either the Last Supper or the Crucifixion apart from that of the Resurrection and Ascension. The whole 'Mystery of Redemption' was included in the solemn Vigil of the Eve, and especially in the Eucharistic Sacrifice for which the Vigil prepared the way. This is continued in every offering of the Holy Sacrifice. As at the Paschal feast, the followers of the Redeemer are incorporated into Christ's Mystical Body by Baptism, so at every celebration of the 'Sacrifice of the Redemption' this incorporation is intensified, for in each oblation of the One Sacrifice 'the work of our Redemption is carried on' (Secret of the ninth Sunday after Pentecost).

PREPARATION FOR EASTER: Nowadays, and for many centuries past, we have been accustomed to a time of preparation for the coming of Easter, the central feast of the Liturgical Year. The forty days' fast of Lent and the period of special services lead up to the last days and acts of Our Saviour on earth in 'Holy Week', as it is always called. But this species of 'public retreat' for all is of fairly late origin and development in liturgical history. In the second century, all Christians prepared for the Paschal feast by fasting, but only for a short time just before the feast. Some fasted for only one day, some for forty hours continuously; some again for a week—according to each one's devotion. After the Great Day, and especially during the fifty days between Easter Day and Pentecost, all fasting was forbidden, as it was also forbidden on all Sundays. The fifty days formed the period of special rejoicing in the 'glad tidings' of the Paschal feast, and were a continuation of it; and the Sunday was its weekly memorial. As a matter of fact, fasting was at first a 'private mortification'; it was not laid down by the Church as a *law*—although approved and often suggested by ecclesiastical authority. The time before the Paschal feast was generally considered as a natural occasion for such mortification, and it became obligatory about the end of the fourth century. Although Tertullian wrote a treatise on fasting (*De Jejunio*, ii.; *P.L.*, ii. 1007), he nowhere speaks of *public* and *general* fasting nor do any other early Fathers of the Church. Even the full development of the Lenten fast, as Mgr. Myers shows us in his learned and helpful pamphlet, *Lent and The Liturgy*, does not mean that fasting is the *primary* object of the holy season. He goes on to say that "The only authentic exposition of the purpose of Lent to be found in the Liturgy is set before us in the lessons of the second nocturn of the first Sunday of Lent . . . from the fourth Lenten Sermon of St. Leo the Great, who was Pope from 440–61. The forty days of Lent are intended to be forty days of intense spiritual activity in order to prepare us for taking part in the solemn commemoration of the outstanding fact in the history of the human race—our Redemption." (*Lent and the Liturgy*, by the Right Reverend Edward Myers, Bishop of Lamus, published by the *Grail*, 58, Sloane Street, London, S.W.1, pp. 1 and 2.) As the author says later on, prayer and good works have their place as well as mortification. Lent, as remarked above, is the great yearly 'retreat' for *all* Christians, to enable them to realise more practically the meaning of the Christian Life, and to encourage them to greater efforts in fulfilling it in their own individual lives. In his book, *The Influence of the Synagogue upon the Divine Office*[1] (pp. 37–41), Mr. Dugmore says that among the Jews in Our Lord's time, Monday and Thursday were for public fasting on certain occasions but that there is no evidence that these days of the week were kept as regular public fasts during the year, and he continues: "There does not appear to have been any corresponding custom among the Christians of the first century in the West" (pp. 37 and 38). In the East—as in the case of the Sabbath and its influence on the solemnity of the Christian Saturday—Jewish usage had its influence, too, on the weekly fast-days, and, at first, some even continued to keep the fast on the Mondays and Thursdays, until these were replaced by the Wednesday and Friday fasts enjoined as follows in the *Didache*: "Let not your fasts coincide with those of the hypocrites, for they fast on the second and fifth days of the week [that

1 Oxford U.P., 1944.

is, Monday and Thursday]; but fast ye on the fourth day [Wednesday] and on the preparation day [Friday—the preparation—in Greek, *parasceve*—for the Sabbath]" (*Didache*, viii, 1; edited Lightfoot, in *Apostolic Fathers* (1891). This is quoted, too, by Dugmore in his book, p. 38, footnote 4).

JEWISH AND CHRISTIAN FAST-DAYS: These days (Wednesday and Friday) were kept as public fast-days, some time during the second century and at first only in the East. On these fast-days—that is, on Monday and Thursday in the Jewish use—the regular weekly evening and morning services were held in the synagogue, but while of a simpler character than on the Sabbath-day, they were more elaborate than on the other days of the week. Wednesday was chosen instead of Monday by the Church because—according to the *Didascalia Apostolorum* (xxi; edited R. H. Connolly; Oxford, 1929, p. 184, quoted by Dugmore, p. 39): "The 'custom of the former people' was to be eschewed, while Wednesdays and Fridays were marked as fast-days throughout the year 'because on the fourth day of the week they began to destroy their souls' by apprehending Christ, and Friday was the day on which they crucified Him." In the West these days became known as 'station-days' (*dies stationis*), from the Latin *statio* meaning a 'watch'—that is, a turn or period of military duty, literally a 'standing still'. At first even these fast-days were not regarded either in Rome or in the Church in general as obligatory for all. According to Tertullian, the fast before the Paschal feast—a fast of merely a few days or even of only one day—"is the only one of obligation on all Christians" (*De Jejunio*, 10). This obligation, however, was introduced by his own followers, the Montanist heretics. On the Christian station-days there was a special service, as with the Jews on their weekly fast-days. In some places (e.g. Rome and Alexandria) the service consisted of the preliminary service without the Liturgy; in others the service was followed by the Eucharist. The station-days seem to have entered the Western Church from the East and to have been accepted at first, rather reluctantly—according, again, to Tertullian (*De Jejunio*, 10).[1]

[1] *De Jejunio* 10, 14.; *P.L.*, ii. 1017, 1024.

THE MASS OF THE PRE-SANCTIFIED: In the West the only existing survival of the introductory service without the Eucharist is the 'Mass of the Pre-sanctified' on Good Friday[1]—that is, as far as the solemn intercessory collects after the Passion inclusive. The communion (now of the celebrant alone), although it is itself probably a survival of the ancient Roman manner of receiving communion apart from Mass, is a later addition to the simple service of lessons and prayers; and the Adoration of the Cross, the procession from the 'Altar of Repose' and the rest, are mediæval additions. In the East, in the Byzantine rite, a survival of the pro-Anaphora, without the Eucharistic Liturgy itself or even communion, is still in regular use. This is:

THE SERVICE OF THE TYPICA: The original meaning of this Greek word is apparently unknown; the service consists of the two psalms of praise (Psalms ciii. and cxlv.—beginning: 'bless' or 'Praise the Lord, O my soul'); certain other chants; the epistle and gospel of the day and final chants of thanksgiving. All this suggests the old synaxis that is the first part of the Liturgy. The *typica* "is still a very normal feature on 'aliturgical days' "— that is, days on which the Liturgy is not celebrated. (See 'Concerning the Shape of the Liturgy: Some Mistaken Measurements in the Shape of the Liturgy', by A. v. d. M., in *The Eastern Churches Quarterly*, October–December 1945, pp. 170–200.) In a book entitled, *Handbook to the Christian Liturgy*,[2] the author, the Ven. James Norman, M.A., Archdeacon of The Herbert, North Queensland, says, speaking of the *typica*: "Its structure suggests that it was formed on days on which the liturgy was not celebrated, and as a substitute for it; later the portions which were not already in the liturgy were placed there at the beginning . . . the *typica* is, indeed, almost the liturgy without the Anaphora" (p. 129).

THE EMBER DAYS: While the Roman Church, according to Tertullian when a Montanist, accepted the weekly station-days only reluctantly, she did, as a matter of fact, introduce just about the same period (third century) her own system of

---

[1] At Milan, also on all Fridays in Lent.   [2] S.P.C.K., London, 1944.

obligatory fast-days in what are known as the 'Ember Days'. But these fast-days are held only quarterly—not every week. They occur, respectively, in the course of the four seasons of the astronomical year—that is, in winter (in December, after the third Sunday of Advent); in spring (in March or April, after the First Sunday in Lent); in summer (in May or June, after Whitsunday); in autumn (in September, after the Feast of the Uplifting of the Holy Cross, September 14th). Thus, these fasts were observed when the chief agricultural work of the year was being undertaken in Italy. Dix considers that they were introduced as "a deliberate counter-observance to the licence of the pagan harvest festivals" (Dix, pp. 342 and 343). These fast-days were kept on Wednesday and Friday, like the station-days. But in the case of the Ember Days, Saturday was added as well as Wednesday and Friday. On these two days the ser-vice consisted originally, no doubt, of the synaxis without the Eucharist—while on the Saturday a vigil was held in preparation for the Holy Sacrifice on the Sunday. The fast on the Saturday was not considered to be a separate fast in itself, but merely a prolongation of that on Friday. The service on Saturday originally took place in the evening of that day, which was re-garded as the beginning of Sunday. In actual usage, Mass is celebrated on all three days; but the preliminary service on Wednesday shows the older form, having a lesson from the Old Testament before the epistle. On the Saturday, too, the vigil is still apparent in the six lessons (including the epistle) before the Gospel. The title 'Ember Day' has nothing to do with the embers of a fire! The word as used here is probably a corruption of the Latin words *quatuor tempora* ('quarter times'), reduced first to 'quatember', and then, by dropping the 'quator'—or rather 'quat', and also the 't' of 'tember'—reduced to 'ember' *tout court*. Down to the sixth century the Ember Days were observed only in the Roman Church. They were introduced into England by the Anglo-Saxon mission-aries and monks, who had received the usage through St. Augustine of Canterbury, the Roman monk. Through these missionaries the Ember Days were also introduced into Gaul and Germany, but they reached Spain only during the eleventh century. Although the West adopted the Eastern station-days, the East never accepted the Western Ember Days; in any case, there is never any fasting on Saturdays in the East, for, as already pointed out, that day still keeps something of the sanctity of the Jewish Sabbath in the Eastern Churches. During Lent, for example, on weekdays only the Pre-sanctified Liturgy is celebrated. The full Liturgy, however, is always celebrated on Saturday, as on Sunday.

THE DEVELOPMENT OF LENT: This period of preparation for the Paschal Mystery by prayer, fasting and good works was of gradual development, as already noted. At first consisting of only one day, it was lengthened, before the end of the second century, to two days (see *The Apostolic Tradition*, xxix. 2), a week or even two weeks, and what we now know as 'Holy Week'—that is, the last days before the Paschal feast—became a specially strict period of fasting. According to Dix, the fuller development of Lent seems to be derived, not so much from the above, as from the special discipline of the catechumens in preparation for their baptism (which they received normally on the Feast of the Redemption) in the latter half of the second century, between the times of St. Justin and Hippolytus. During the fourth century, owing to the ascetic influence of monasticism, all the faithful began to take part in the fast before baptism, and the preparations of the catechumens and the instructions given them by the clergy. Towards the middle of this century, the time of preparation and fasting was extended to six weeks. Then came the idea of identifying this period of fasting with the forty days' fast of Our Lord in the desert— another step in the development of the historical aspect of the Liturgy. Next arose the difficulty of obtaining a full forty days' fast, and various means of arriving at this were made use of, the difficulty being chiefly due to the fact that Sundays were never fast-days, and in the East, Saturdays were never fast-days either. Finally—in the seventh century—the difficulty was overcome by the addition of four days before the first Sunday of Lent— Ash Wednesday and the three following days. But it is interesting to note that, *liturgically*, the Lenten fast, in the full sense, does not start until the first Saturday. Up till then the fast lasts only till after None (formerly about 3 p.m.). But after the first Friday it lasts till after Vespers (formerly in the evening). For long past, however, the Offices of None or Vespers are recited (in choir or privately) *before* the 'one meal' of the fast-day—taken at the usual time.[1] The imposition of ashes on the Wednesday is a Gallican ceremony of sixth-century date, adopted in Rome; it is not a native Roman rite. In much the same way as the fast of Lent was at first confined to the catechumens and then extended to all members of the Church, the penitential rite of the ashes, originally imposed only upon public penitents, was extended to all Christians.

According to the author of *The Shape of the Liturgy*, the development of the historical aspect of the Liturgy and of the various special occasions of commemorating the different events of Our Lord's life and work for our Redemption is due to Jerusalem not Rome, and particularly to the personality of its Bishop, St. Cyril of Jerusalem. The fact that it was in the Holy Land, and especially in Jerusalem itself, that the actions of the last days of Our Lord's life took place made this a natural development. We have a very full and 'lively' description of it all in the letters of the Spanish Abbess Ætheria to her nuns in A.D. 385, and she gives us a clear account of the Holy Week observances in Jerusalem. The 'Pilgrimage of Ætheria' is, in fact, a mine of knowledge not only, as we have already seen, for the development of the Divine Office in general, but for that of Holy Week in particular. Her description begins with Passion Sunday; leads on to Palm Sunday, and describes the procession from the Mount of Olives to Jerusalem bearing palm branches; on Maundy Thursday, the special Mass in the morning and another in the evening; on Good Friday, the veneration of the True Cross in the morning and a solemn watch from noon till 3 p.m. on Golgotha. Then, on Holy Saturday, the Paschal Vigil and the baptisms, followed by the first Mass of Easter at which the neophytes receive their first Communion. It is also worthy of note that the Holy Sacrifice was not offered on either Good Friday or Holy Saturday.

---

[1] Since this relic of past usage really disturbs the order of the Hours of the Divine Office, some Benedictine monasteries have obtained permission from Rome to chant each Hour of the Office always at the correct time—even in Lent.

ASH WEDNESDAY AND DAYS TILL FIRST SUNDAY IN LENT: Another addition to Lent—or rather a preparation for it—was added during the seventh century in the three weeks preceding Ash Wednesday; that is, the Wednesday after the *third* of the three Sundays. These three are called respectively, 'Septuagesima', 'Sexagesima' and 'Quinquagesima'—the seventieth, sixtieth and fiftieth Sundays before Easter Sunday—in reference to the Latin name for the Lenten season, *Quadragesima*. These titles are, however, only symbolic—the three Sundays are not literally the seventieth, sixtieth and fiftieth dates before Easter.

THE TITLES 'LENT' AND 'EASTER': Lent is derived from a Saxon word meaning spring-time—it is the 'Spring-fast'. In most other languages the title is a translation of the Latin word *quadragesima*, that is, the fortieth date *before* Easter, as Pentecost is the fiftieth date *after* Easter, e.g. in French we have 'Carême'. The title 'Easter' is of very uncertain origin. According to the Venerable Bede it is derived from 'Eostre', the name of a Teutonic goddess of spring, or worshipped at the beginning of spring. Nothing, however, is known about this goddess—nor is any reference at all made to her anywhere else. It has been suggested that 'Easter' may possibly be a corruption of the Greek word 'pascha' (in its latinised form). In most languages other than English, the title of the Feast is taken from '*pascha*'; for example, again, the French 'Pâques', and in some Teutonic languages and in types derived from Teutonic sources also, the title is a form of '*pascha*'—in Lowland Scots, for instance, we get 'Paska'. A further English difference from other languages in the question of festal titles is the use of 'Whitsunday' for Pentecost, and 'Whitsuntide' for the week following that Sunday. This word seems to be simply a corruption of '*white* Sunday'—in allusion to the white robes put on by the newly baptised on the preceding Saturday—as on Holy Saturday. In this connection, the Saturday and Sunday immediately following Easter Sunday are both known in Latin as *in albis*. On the Saturday—*in albis deponendis* ('the white robes *to be laid aside*')—the white garments given to the newly baptised and worn by them all during Easter week were then taken off. The Sunday—*in albis depositis* ('the white robes *laid aside*')—was

so-called because it was the first day after this laying aside of
the baptismal robes. But all this belongs to a somewhat later
period of liturgical history.[1]

To return to pre-Nicene days and developments thereafter:
as we have seen already, in the fourth century in accordance
with the new historical emphasis which came to the fore in the
manner of regarding the liturgy, the 'oneness' of the redeeming
Sacrifice of Christ Our Lord was 'divided' in keeping with the
various distinct historical events. First, the institution of the
Holy Eucharist at the Last Supper; then the Crucifixion; next
the Resurrection—each celebrated on its particular day—the
Thursday, Friday and Sunday of the 'Great Week' as it was
often called. The result of all this was a certain loss in the
deeper spiritual union with Our Lord which, however, is being
restored more and more in these days, in Catholic devotion.
Until the uprise of this historical aspect of things, the Christian
Pasch absorbed the whole process of the redemptive work of
Christ, which was summed up in the one Sacrifice anticipated
at the Last Supper, actually *carried out* on the Cross and *carried
on* in continual renewal in that mysterious sacrifice in the
Mass. This does not mean that there was, or could be at any
time, any indifference or lack of interest in, and due observance
of, the historical aspect of the Redemption, of the life of Our
Lord, of His Mother or of His disciples. A return to the eschatological way of regarding it all means simply a fuller recognition and use of the 'oneness' that underlies the surface varia-
tions, and the distinct acts brought about by the conditions
and limitations of human life in time.

HOLY WEEK IN ROME: In Rome the observance of Holy
Week, even after development, was at first extremely simple
compared to that of Jerusalem and elsewhere. It consisted in a
strict fast every day, and (on the Wednesday and Friday) in
the celebration of the aliturgical service—that is, without the
Holy Eucharist. On both these days the service ended with the
long series of intercessory collects now recited only on Good
Friday. There was no Adoration of the Cross nor any 'Mass of

[1] The English name for *Dominica in albis* is 'Low Sunday'; the origin of this title
is uncertain, but it is probably in contradistinction to Easter Day, 'High Sunday'
—the 'Sunday of Sundays'.

the Pre-sanctified' on Friday, nor any Mass or memorial of the institution of the Holy Eucharist on Thursday. On Saturday there was no service until the night Vigil of the Paschal feast, during which baptism and confirmation were conferred and the first Mass of the Paschal Day was offered at dawn. There was no blessing of the New Fire—but the deacon solemnly blessed the Paschal candle—originally simply the light required for the night-office. As above noted, too, there would probably have been only three lessons with the responsories between. This was the Holy Week of the fifth–sixth centuries.

BLESSING AND PROCESSION OF PALMS, ETC.: The dramatic chant of the Passion, the special offering of the Holy Sacrifice and the Communion on Maundy Thursday in memory of the Institution at the Last Supper, with the procession and placing of the reserved Sacrament in the 'Chapel of Repose'; the chant of the Reproaches and Adoration of the Cross on Good Friday and bringing back the Blessed Sacrament to the altar for the Mass of the Pre-sanctified; the blessing of the New Fire and the Twelve Prophecies on Holy Saturday—all these, says Dix, are: "demonstrably foreign accretions from Syrian, Spanish and French sources, only slowly and reluctantly accepted into the Papal rite between the seventh and the fourteenth centuries" (Dix, p. 440, footnote 5).

Apparently the Mass of the Pre-sanctified had been established in the parish churches of Rome long before it was officially accepted in the Papal rite for Holy Week. We have seen already that it was a survival of the reception of communion in their own homes by the faithful—by means of the sacred Hosts which they themselves were allowed to reserve there—on those days on which there was no celebration of the Holy Sacrifice. This custom was transferred to the parish churches when reservation in private houses was given up—perhaps in the fifth century.

We have seen that, besides the aliturgical service, there were also occasions on which the Eucharist was celebrated without the former preliminary service. We have already noted examples of this, both in St. Justin's description of the Mass in his time and in the text of the Liturgy in *The Apostolic Tradition of*

St. Hippolytus. Although this form of celebrating the Holy Sacrifice came to an end in the Eastern Churches about A.D. 500, it lasted longer in some places in the West on Maundy Thursday.

THE THREE MASSES OF MAUNDY THURSDAY: On that day, in some Western local churches, there were three Masses: one for the reconciliation of the penitents who had been sent out of the church during the afternoon Liturgy, on Ash Wednesday; one for the consecration of the chrism and other holy oils at midday, and one in the evening, in commemoration of the Last Supper. There was no preliminary service at the first Mass—its place being taken by the long ceremony of reconciliation. The second Mass was preceded by the service as usual; the third Mass began at the offertory—like the first Mass—without any preliminary service. After the ninth century this evening Mass disappeared; the two Masses (of the catechumens and of the faithful) had become one indivisible service before A.D. 800. It is worth remembering that this welding together of the two Masses came about just at the time that assistance at Mass began to be *mere* assistance—that is, without a regular general communion and without really active participation in the chant and ceremonial. It is quite likely that there was a connection between the two, and that one led to the other. In the earliest days, as a matter of fact, there could not have been any active participation of the people in carrying out the preliminary service—they could only have listened while the reader read the lessons, the cantor chanted the responsory psalms and while the homily was preached. At the most they would have joined in the psalmody, repeating the respond after every verse or two verses, and in the responses to the intercessory prayers. Their own participation, strictly so-called in the latter, was in the *silent* prayer preceding the collect.

When these prayers were transferred to the Holy Eucharist itself—at first before the offertory, later on (in the East) within the anaphora, the people's share was reduced to listening. This passive assistance at the Liturgy moved on, so to speak, from the first part to the second—by a sort of natural 'procession' (Dix, p. 443).

When the Mass of the Pre-sanctified became normal on

Good Friday in the Roman rite, it was necessary to consecrate at the Mass on Maundy Thursday, not only *one* Host as now, but a sufficient number for the—probably many—communicants. These consecrated Hosts were reserved in an urn or coffer till the service on Good Friday. It is not clear where exactly in the basilica the urn containing the reserved Hosts was kept; perhaps in the *secretarium*, that is, the sacristy, or in a side chapel. Anyway, there was very little ceremony about it all: the urn or *capsa* containing the Most Holy was carried, reverently and with a certain solemnity no doubt, to the place of reservation, but there was nothing like the elaborate procession with singing, as in later times. On Good Friday, again, the *capsa* was simply carried from the place of reservation to the altar. A chalice with wine and water in it was placed thereon (no doubt *several* chalices for the people, as well), and then, after the chant of the Lord's Prayer and the following prayer *Libera nos* aloud, all received communion, drank the ablution from the chalice and then left the basilica.

During the Middle Ages this simple ceremony grew into a rite symbolising the burial and resurrection of Our Lord. Instead of only the one Host now necessary for the communion of the celebrant alone on Good Friday, two were consecrated; one of these was used on Good Friday, the other was reserved till Easter Sunday. Both were placed in what was known as the 'Easter Sepulchre' in England—an aumbry or niche in the north wall (Gospel side) of the chancel—of which many beautiful examples with carvings or paintings still remain. On Easter Day, in the early morning, the second Host was borne in triumph from the sepulchre to the High Altar, where it was exposed in a form of monstrance—sometimes in the shape of a gold or silver figure of the Risen Saviour—till the High Mass of the Feast. This ceremony is still observed in some places abroad, and in the Dominican rite also, but it was never introduced into the Roman rite. The elaborate procession of the Blessed Sacrament on Maundy Thursday, and the reservation at a specially decorated 'altar of repose', came in there, however, in time, and the name 'sepulchre' is often (quite incorrectly) given to the altar of repose. The whole ceremony was more or less influenced by the sepulchre rite, but the two rites are utterly different; the Most Holy, in the Roman rite, is reserved only till the Mass of the Pre-sanctified on Good Friday and so the reservation is not symbolic of the burial or resurrection at all. During the fifth century the consecration of the chrism and other holy oils was introduced into the Roman rite on this day. This takes place during the Canon —after the words *per quem hæc omnia*. As already stated, these words probably referred originally and directly to the sacred species, but were extended to include certain material offerings, such as milk, oil and so forth. Even as early as *The Apostolic Tradition* of Hippolytus, offerings were made, not only of oil, but also of cheese and olives, and, at the Paschal Mass, of milk and honey 'mingled together in fulfilment of the promise which was made to the Fathers, wherein He said: "I will give you a land flowing with milk and honey" (*The Apostolic Tradition of St. Hippolytus*, pp. 10 and 40). In the sixth century a ceremony was introduced which has given the name 'Maundy Thursday' to this day in English,[1] the word 'maundy' being derived from the Latin word *mandatum* ('commandment') in the words of Our Lord to His disciples at the Last Supper, after washing their feet (John xiii. 34). In memory of this act of humility on the part of Our Lord, thirteen persons have their feet washed on Maundy Thursday in cathedral, collegiate and monastic churches, by the bishop, provost, abbot or prior, as the case may be. The number thirteen is chosen in memory of the story told of St. Gregory the Great who, when washing the feet of twelve poor men chosen for the ceremony, found that there was a thirteenth—Our Lord Himself—present. During the Middle Ages, emperors, kings and princes, as well as bishops and other ecclesiastics, used to perform the Maundy. In England the actual washing of the feet by the King has been replaced by a gift of money publicly delivered to as many poor old men and women as the years of the Sovereign's age. The ceremony is carried out in Westminster Abbey, and by the Sovereign in person, if possible. Both King George V and his successor, King George VI, presented the maundy-money in person, and

---

[1] In French this day is called 'Jeudi saint'—Holy Thursday—the English title is the only one that stresses the act of washing the feet of His disciples by Our Saviour.

the present Queen, Elizabeth II, made the recent presentation. The original washing is, as it were, 'commemorated' by wearing an apron while distributing the gifts! The last English King who fulfilled this act of Christian humility and charity in the complete sense was the last Catholic (and much misunderstood) King of England, James II.

LATER CUSTOMS AND WAYS OF LIFE: These have led to various changes in the time of day at which the Holy Week services are carried out. In this there has been a continual tendency to put back to an earlier hour in the day services originally intended for the late afternoon or evening. On Maundy Thursday and Good Friday, for example, the ceremonies of the Mass with its special consecrations on the first day, and of the Mass of the Pre-sanctified on the second, were originally celebrated after the Office of None (about 3 p.m. or after). These services, and the Offices also, have been pushed back to the early morning of each day. More noticeable, perhaps, is the case of Holy Saturday: this Saturday has no special service proper to the day itself beyond the Hours of the Divine Office, when that had been fully organised. Formerly there was nothing special until the late evening, when the Paschal Vigil began with the lighting of the 'evening lamp', the chant of the Scripture lessons and their responsorial psalmody; and the baptisms and confirmations— leading up to the first Mass of Easter Day. As in the case of Good Friday, this vigil-service and its later additions and changes have been pushed back to the early morning of Saturday, leaving nothing at all during the day, till the joyful Compline office in the evening. This has led also to the curious arrangement of a very reduced form of 'First Vespers of Easter Day', fitted into the Mass itself and practically forming part of it. There is only one short psalm—*Laudate Dominum omnes gentes* (Psalm cxvi)—sung with an *alleluia* as antiphon (repeated three times) and the *Magnificat* with its own antiphon taken from Matt. xxviii. 1. All this is sung after the celebrant's communion, the postcommunion of the Mass serving as the collect of Vespers as well.[1] This arrangement

---

[1] The *Alleluia* verse after the epistle is solemnly sung three times by the celebrant and choir—introduced in a Pontifical celebration by a special announcement made by the subdeacon.

really upsets the ancient sequence of the service: the Vigil thus pushed back precedes not only the Mass (which is correct) but also the first Vespers of Easter—which belong to Saturday afternoon and should be recited before, as a preliminary to the Vigil. As a matter of fact, this 'First Vespers' itself really belongs to the fully developed system of the daily Office. In the earliest period there would either have been no vespers at all or else a very simple form of 'evening praise' connected not with Easter but with Saturday evening, followed by the vigil-service. The latter would, perhaps, have been the much shorter service later relegated to Good Friday in order to make way for the long Jerusalem type of vigil.

THE ANTICIPATED EASTER VIGIL: The relegation of the vigil to Saturday morning has also resulted in the introduction of the Office of Matins and Lauds for Easter Day—no doubt at first celebrated at midnight on Saturday, and later in the early morning of Easter Sunday.[1]

The later developments of Holy Week have given a special character to the whole week.

PALM SUNDAY, FROM JERUSALEM: This came about in the fourth century; but at Rome the Blessing of the palms at first involved the celebration of two Masses, each celebrated in a different basilica. At the first Mass the palm branches were blessed and distributed; this was followed by the procession in which the blessed branches were carried to another basilica, where the second Mass was celebrated. The former celebration of two Masses on this day is still quite evident in the Blessing of the palms as now carried out. There is a complete 'skeleton' of a Mass, with introit, collect, epistle followed by a responsory-psalm, and gospel. It is especially interesting to note that the gospel is followed by a prayer (beginning with the words *Auge fidem*—'increase' or 'strengthen faith'), which holds exactly the place of the prayer after the gospel, known at Milan as the *Oratio super sindonem*, which probably existed originally in

---

[1] In the *Acta Apostolicæ Sedis*, February 9th, 1951, the Sacred Congregation of Rites proclaimed that the Holy See had authorised a restored Paschal Vigil, which may be used by bishops and other ecclesiastical superiors in places under their own jurisdiction on Holy Saturday night, as in early days. See Appendix VI, p. 273.

the Roman Mass also, but was ousted by the prayer before the epistle in later times. After this prayer there is a preface and *Sanctus*, and this is followed by the five prayers of blessing. Then comes the distribution of the palms and the procession, ending with the actual Mass of the Sunday. During this Mass the Passion according to St. Matthew is chanted. On Tuesday the Passion according to St. Mark is chanted at Mass, and on Wednesday and Good Friday respectively those according to St. Luke and St. John. Where possible these accounts of the Passion are chanted by three deacons in a manner that is practically a form of 'mystery play'. One of the deacons takes the part of *chronista* ('chronicler'), chanting the substance of the Gospel narrative; another takes the part of Our Lord, and chants His words only; the third takes the part of the Synagogue —of the priests and pharisees, etc.—and also of the disciples. The part of the *turba* ('crowd') is usually taken by a number of those present in the church—in a monastery by those of the community in choir. All is sung to special and very beautiful tones; the ceremony is of mediæval origin.

TENEBRÆ: ANOTHER ADDITION TO HOLY WEEK: This is the Office of Matins and Lauds (in the later developed form of the Divine Office) for the last three days of the Great Week. These offices—at first celebrated about midnight on Wednesday, Thursday and Friday, then in the early morning of Thursday, Friday and Saturday, are now always anticipated early in the afternoon of the Wednesday, Thursday and Friday, so that the faithful as well as the clergy may assist at them. They have come to be looked on as practically funeral services in memory of the suffering and death of Our Saviour. The title *tenebræ* (a Latin word meaning 'darkness') is given to the Office on account of the custom (which, it seems, dates back to the fifth century) of gradually extinguishing the lights till the church or oratory is plunged in darkness. This gradual extinction probably took place originally only on Good Friday. Later still comes the regulation of the number of candles to fifteen on the *Tenebræ* 'Hearse'; that is, the triangular candlestick. In mediæval times this candlestick was called 'hearse' (from the late Latin *hericia*, itself derived from the word *herpex*), meaning a harrow, owing to the little spikes on the candlestick on which the candles were fixed.

TENEBRÆ AMONG CARTHUSIAN AND CISTERCIAN MONKS: The office of *Tenebræ* is chanted during the night—at midnight and at 2 a.m. respectively—that is, at the usual time for the night office. Although *Tenebræ* belongs to the developed form of the Divine Office, it has preserved some very ancient features: the introductory words—*Deus in adjutorium meum intende* ('O God, come to my assistance') and *Domine ad adjuvandum me festina* ('O Lord, make haste to aid me') are not said; there is no *Gloria Patri* after the psalms, neither absolution[1] nor blessing before the lessons, and no *Tu autem, Domine, miserere nobis* ('but Thou, O Lord, have mercy on us') after their recitation. In chanting the lessons themselves, the titles are not given out, as is usually done.

THE CHRISTIAN PENTECOST: Fifty days after Easter comes the second great feast of the early Christian year—that of *Pentecost*. This is derived from the Jewish feast, which has the same name in Greek and was celebrated at the same time of year. The Hebrew name of the feast means 'The Feast of Weeks'; the Greek name 'Pentecost' (from *penteconta*, fifty) was given to this feast because it was celebrated fifty days after the Passover-feast. After Biblical times, the feast, besides being agricultural in character, celebrated at the close of the harvest, came to be connected with the giving of the Law on Mount Sinai and the setting apart of 'The People of God', and this now forms its special attribution among modern Jews. In the Old Testament days the agricultural aspect was connected with the end of the harvest, which had begun at the Passover and lasted fifty days; and special sacrifices in accordance with the occasion were offered. (Levit. xxiii. 15–21; Deut. xvi. 9–22; see especially verse 16.) In the Christian Church this feast celebrates the coming of the Holy Ghost to confirm the work of Christ and

---

[1] The word 'absolution' means, in this place, simply the *concluding prayer* of each nocturn—the Latin words *absolvere, absolutio* mean 'to complete', 'the completion' —as well as to 'acquit'; to 'free' (as in the use of the word—to 'forgive sins'). In the above case the 'absolution' is the name of the collect which concludes the psalmody.

to establish the Church as the union of the People of God in the New Covenant. Any catechumens who, for some reason, had not received baptism on the Paschal feast, received it now on that of Pentecost. This Sacrament was administered at other times only in case of grave illness or in other danger of death— e.g. from persecution and possible martyrdom. The feast of Pentecost, like the Paschal feast, is preceded by a vigil on the Saturday—'Whitsun Eve', as it is usually called in English. The Mass, as on 'Easter Eve' (the old mediæval title still used by Anglicans for Holy Saturday), is preceded on Whitsun Eve by a series of 'prophecies', but there are only six, not twelve. These six lessons complete the number independently. They are separated from the epistle of the Mass which follows, as the prophecies on Holy Saturday are separated from the epistle on that day by the Blessing of the font or at least by the litany. Again, as on Holy Saturday, these so-called 'prophecies' are not all taken from the Old Testament prophets.

THE WHITSUNTIDE EMBER DAYS: These stand out among the other three: in the first place the joyful *Gloria in excelsis* is sung or said at Mass, but, instead of coming at the beginning after the *Kyrie eleison*, it is not chanted until after the *Alleluia* verse— on Wednesday, after the first of the two lessons from the Acts of the Apostles; on Saturday, after the verse which follows the fifth 'prophecy', that is, the prophecy of Daniel (Daniel iii. 47–51). In both cases the *Gloria* is followed by *Dominus vobiscum oremus* and the collect which precedes the epistle of the Mass. This curious arrangement is, it seems, the result of the union in one of two distinct sets of Masses: that of the days within the octave of Pentecost and that of the Ember Days. The chant of the *Gloria* belongs to the first set of Masses; the prophecies to the second set.

(II) LATER FEASTS: The oldest of the later feasts are Ascension, Christmas and Epiphany, and they were beginning to spread all over the Church, both in the East and in the West, by the end of the fourth century. After these come the feast now known as the Exaltation (uplifting) of the Cross on September 14th. This feast began as "the feast of the dedication of Constantine's basilica at Jerusalem on September 14th . . . Rome seems . . . to have accepted it only in the eighth century" (Dix, p. 358). The feast of the Ascension—that is, as a distinct feast apart from that of the Resurrection—seems to be due to the use of Jerusalem, like so many other developments of the Liturgy. Ætheria, in her letter describing her pilgrimage there, speaks of forty days after Easter—although she does not connect them directly with the Ascension. Formerly, the Ascension was included together with the Resurrection and the Passion as being the Redemptive Sacrifice of Christ in its fullness: the whole Work of Redemption. Ætheria also mentions the Exaltation of the Holy Cross. Now that Holy Week and Easter had become a strictly historical commemoration of those events of Our Lord's life, His Passion and death, His Resurrection and Ascension—other events of His life also began to receive similar commemorations in the Liturgy.

CHRISTMAS AND EPIPHANY: This feast is first mentioned at Rome in A.D. 354, but it seems to have been kept fairly widely in the West before this date, perhaps, in some places, before the end of the third century. It is thus probably not of Roman origin. Ætheria does not speak of it at Jerusalem in 385, but it was beginning to be observed elsewhere in the East about that time. From the third century, the Eastern Churches in some cases had already introduced a feast of Our Lord's birth on January 6th, calling it the 'Epiphany'—the feast of His 'Manifestation'—from the Greek word *epiphainein* ('to show forth, display'). In some places the origin of this feast may go back as far as the late second century. Later on, in the fourth century, East and West began to keep both these feasts, Christmas and Epiphany, successively. Christmas remained the birthday feast; the Epiphany becoming the commemoration of other manifestations of Our Lord, e.g. to the Magi, at His baptism and in the Miracle at Cana of Galilee. Rome adopted the Epiphany before A.D. 450; as always, she was slow in adopting new observances. In the East the Armenian Church still keeps the birthday of Our Lord on the date of our Epiphany, and has never adopted that of December 25th. In Scotland, too, the Scots Presbyterians refuse—officially, at least—to keep

Christmas Day (December 25th), and recognise January 6th as Our Lord's birthday, calling that day 'Old Christmas'. Of late, however, a 'High Church' movement has taken place in Presbyterianism, and December 25th and other feasts of the Church (observed also in Anglicanism and by other religious bodies) are recognised and have been admitted into her liturgy. Neither of these two dates of Our Lord's birthday were chosen as being the actual—or even the traditional—dates; they were chosen chiefly to counteract the influence of two pagan feasts of the sun-god. These were, on December 25th, the winter solstice and the birthday of the god of the sun—*Natalis Invicti*, it was called—that is, 'the birthday of the Unconquered One', the glorious source of light and warmth unconquered by the enemy of darkness and cold. On January 6th there was also a 'solstice feast' dedicated to another sun-god. The choice of this latter date in the East for the commemoration of the baptism of Our Lord as well as of His birth seems to have been influenced by a desire to counteract the pagan belief, in certain places, that on that day rivers and springs acquired miraculous qualities and even had the taste of wine. But the true date of Our Lord's birthday into this world—the actual day, month and year—is unknown. The name 'Christmas' is the old English title of this feast, and is simply 'Christ's Mass'—since the principal act on all feasts was (as it still is in the Catholic Church) the celebration of the Holy Sacrifice of the Mass. The same use of the word 'Mass' is found in certain other feasts— e.g. Michaelmas (the chief feast of the Archangel Michael, on September 29th), Martinmas (the feast of St. Martin of Tours, on November 11th) and Lammas—a corruption of 'loaf-mass', the harvest-festival on August 1st, when loaves of bread were blessed at Mass. In French the title of the feast of Our Lord's birth is 'Noël', derived from the Latin word 'natalis'—a birthday or birth-place—e.g. in the title (spoken of above) of *Natalis Invicti* given by the Romans to the winter solstice.

IN THE AFRICAN CHURCH: The feast of Christmas existed before that of the Epiphany, exactly as at Rome—with which Church that of Africa agrees in so many other cases. In Gaul the opposite is the case: the Epiphany was, as in the East, the feast of Christ's birth until the introduction of Christmas from Rome, and then the miracle of Cana became the prominent feature of the Epiphany. In both these feasts the object was always principally to *establish* the mystery and dogma of the Incarnation, not merely to record the actual date of Christ's birth.

THE SEASON OF ADVENT: Like Easter, Christmas is now preceded by a period of preparation called Advent, in which a certain element of penance is included. It is followed—again, as at Easter—by a period of rejoicing: *Christmastide*. The latter lasts up till the Feast of the Purification or 'Candlemas Day'— on February 2nd. This latter title is another example of the use of the term 'Mass' to express the significance of the day—in this case the Blessing of candles, which takes place just before Mass.

The name 'Advent' comes from the Latin *adventus* (from *advenio-ire*, 'to come'); this season prepares for the 'Coming' of the Messiah into this world in the flesh. Nothing is known of it before the fifth century, and it was first heard of then, in Gaul. From Gaul it spread, in the following century, to Italy, and from there throughout the Western Church. Advent is referred to at the Councils of Tours (A.D. 563) and Macon (A.D. 581) as the 'Winter Lent', and was of forty days' duration, from Martinmas (November 11th) till Christmas, with fasting on Mondays, Wednesdays and Fridays. There were six, five or four 'Sundays of Advent', according to the usage of different places; the number was fixed at four under Gregory VII (eleventh century). Advent was, in fact, a mitigated Lent. Several of these 'Lents' were observed in both Eastern and Western Churches in the eighth century. But originally the character of Advent was not penitential: it was a joyful preparation for the birth of Our Saviour. White vestments were used and the *Gloria* and *Alleluia* were sung at Mass, and this was the use at Rome up till the twelfth century. Since the Middle Ages the character of Advent has developed into a mingling of joy and penance—both expressed in the Mass at which *Alleluia* is sung or said, but violet vestments are used. Advent became in time a preparation as well for the *Second* Coming of Our Lord at the end of the world, and this is, perhaps, the chief cause of the penitential character. Even at His first Coming, for that matter, the fact that Our Saviour came in order to die as the Lamb of God on the Cross, 'to take away the sin of the world', would suggest the penitential aspect, too (John i. 29).

THE MONASTIC LENT: This special season was analogous to Lent rather than to Advent, for it involved a fast every day, till after None, i.e. till after 3 p.m. It lasted from September 14th till the beginning of the ecclesiastical Lent. In the Eastern Church there were, and still are, several 'Lents' during the course of the year. The strict Lenten fast lasted till after Vespers—fairly late in the evening. During the Middle Ages, on account of the growing difficulties with regard to fasting, the hour of None was pushed back earlier and earlier, until it became the custom to chant that Office at twelve o'clock midday —hence our English term afternoon, that is—'after None'—for the period of the day from twelve o'clock midday till evening, and of forenoon ('before None'), used in Scotland and elsewhere, for the morning hours up till twelve midday. For the same reasons, Vespers during Lent were in time pushed back to midday.

ADVENT THE BEGINNING OF THE LITURGICAL YEAR: The first Sunday of Advent is that nearest to November 30th—feast of St. Andrew, Apostle. Originally, Christmas Day itself, or March 25th—the Annunciation ('Lady Day')—was the beginning of the Liturgical Year, and even now Papal Briefs are dated: a die Nativitatis ('From the day of the Birth'), and Bulls: ab anno Incarnationis ('From the year of the Incarnation'). Some liturgical scholars hold that the fixing of a liturgical 'New Year's Day', and even of the whole of the Advent season, was due to the desire to wean recent converts to the faith from the pagan practices connected with the first day of the civil year; that is, the first day of the month January (in Latin, Januarius). This name was given to the month as it 'opened' the new year, and the word januarius indicated that the month was dedicated to the god Janus, originally the 'family-god' who looked after the door (in Latin, janus) of each Roman house; later, the god of the State who opened and closed the year, and who was represented with two faces looking in opposite directions.

Advent may also be considered as the liturgical 'month of Mary': Our Lady is in special prominence all through this season, and in the Advent Ember Wednesday we have what is practically a feast of the Virgin Mother. In some places—for instance, in Spain—the Annunication was at first kept during Advent.

St. Bernard points out a third 'coming' of Our Lord commemorated in Advent, which lies between the first and second. This is Christ's coming into the souls of the members of His Mystical Body—a purely spiritual and interior 'coming', which is the gradual growth and development of the Mystical Christ, who is 'born' within our souls and into whom we are incorporated (that is, made one Body with Him) in baptism.

ADVENT WESTERN IN ORIGIN: It originated probably in Gaul or Spain. In the Eastern Churches there is no liturgical Advent, though a fast of six weeks' duration is kept from November 14th till Christmas Day. In practice, this fast is not much observed outside the monasteries. Fasting existed also during the period in the Gallican Churches from November 11th. In the Roman rite, fasting twice a week (on Wednesdays and Saturdays) was observed during Advent till fairly recent times.

Instead of the six Sundays of Advent in the Gallican rite, the Roman Advent had at first only five, reduced later to four.

Christmas Day is specially marked out by the custom of celebrating three Masses—at night, at dawn and 'in the day' (*in die*). In cathedrals, collegiate churches and monasteries the last two of the three Masses are celebrated, respectively, 'after Prime', the first of the day-hours, and 'after Terce' (the office of the 'third Hour'; that is, about 9 a.m.). But the custom of three Masses is now less distinctive of Christmas since Pope Benedict XV gave permission, during the Great War, for three Requiem Masses to be said always on All Souls' Day. This was an extension of a custom which already existed in Spain. The three Christmas Masses were in existence in Rome at the end of the sixth century—St. Gregory the Great speaks of them in one of his homilies (viii. 1). At the beginning of the fifth century, however, there was only one Mass—in the morning of Christmas Day at St. Peter's. Pope Xystus III (A.D. 435–40) rebuilt the Liberian Basilica, and dedicated it to Our Lady under the title of *Santa Maria Maggiore* (St. Mary Major). From that date, a nocturnal 'station' and Mass at Christmas are spoken of in this church. Probably this was derived from the custom of the Church of Jerusalem, where there was a nocturnal 'station' at Bethlehem on Christmas night and a Mass on the day itself in Jerusalem. St. Mary Major was considered to be an equivalent of Bethlehem, and later on the relic of the Manger was placed there.

The second Mass at dawn had, at first, no special connection with Christmas, but was in honour of St. Anastasia, a martyr of Sirmium in Slavonia, whose cultus was very popular at Constantinople in the period 458–71. The date of her martyrdom was December 25th, and this date had not then been adopted at Constantinople as the feast of Our Lord's Birthday. The cult of St. Anastasia was introduced into Rome by the Byzantine colony which existed there in the middle of the sixth century, and she was honoured in a church at the foot of the Palatine Hill,[1] which formed a kind of metropolitan church for the Greek quarter of Rome. The saint's stational Mass continued to be observed by the Greek colony even after the establishment of December 25th as the feast of Christmas.

The three Masses—at night, dawn and later morning— were also celebrated in other parts of Rome, but as there was not the same reason in these places for the cultus of St. Anastasia, as in the Greek colony, the Mass at dawn was offered, like the other two, in memory of Christ's birth, and St. Anastasia was only commemorated—as she is to this day. The three Masses are now offered for the following intentions: the night Mass, in honour of the earthly birth at Bethlehem; the Mass at dawn, in honour of the spiritual birth of Our Lord in the souls of members of His Mystical Body; the Mass of the day, in honour of the eternal generation of the Second Person of the Blessed Trinity.

---

[1] This church was already known in Rome as *ecclesia* (or *basilica*) *Anastasiæ*; but whether this referred to the Saint or to a Roman lady who had built the church— or whether it was really *Anastasis* ('Resurrection')—is unknown.

OTHER LATER FEASTS OF OUR LORD: Some were introduced during the Middle Ages and soon after—in the seventeenth century; for example, the feast of the Sacred Heart, after the revelations of St. Margaret Mary Alacoque,[1] and in our own times the feast of Christ the King, established by Pius XI in 1925.

FEASTS OF THE SAINTS: During the second century, festivals of saints began to be kept. At first these were confined to martyrs, on the dates of their martyrdom, which were looked on as their *dies natalis* ('birthday') in heaven. The earliest record comes to us from Asia Minor in a letter written by the Church of Smyrna in A.D. 156 to the Church of Philomelium near by, describing the recent martyrdom of the Bishop of Smyrna, St. Polycarp (*Martyrium Polycarpi*). (See Lightfoot's *Apostolic Fathers*, Part II, 'Ignatius and Polycarp'. 3 vols., 2nd edit., London, 1889.) Of this, Dom Gregory Dix writes that: "Nothing could better illustrate the unprimitive character of much in protestant polemic against the cultus of the saints and their relics which was sincerely put forward in the sixteenth century as a return to 'apostolic' christianity" (Dix, pp. 343 and 344). In the earliest days of Christianity, 'the saints' meant all the members of Christ's Mystical Body—all still full of the Good News of Our Saviour's life and teaching, and of their own share in the Sacrifice of Redemption. But later on—in the second century—the newness of Christian life began to fade, and contact with worldly and, to a great extent still, pagan life and spirit led to the realisation that the mere fact of believing in Christ and His Church is not enough to make saints—His life and teaching must be actively *followed* and *practised* by His members. Even when this is duly realised and sincere effort is made to follow it out, the weakness of human nature and its liability to fall into sin after baptism still remains—in spite of the help of the Sacrament of Penance. This led to the clearer development of the doctrine of Purgatory with the realisation of the need of due punishment, even after death, for sins of which the *guilt* had been forgiven. So the term 'saint' was reserved first of all for those who had washed away the guilt of sin and

---

[1] This feast was granted to the whole Church by Pius IX in 1856.

any need for punishment, in their blood shed for Christ (the martyrs); then gradually extended to those Christians who, without actually giving up their lives, had in one way or another fulfilled the perfect ideal of Christianity. There is early mention, in the writings of Tertullian and other Christian writers, of the special offering of the Holy Sacrifice for the souls of the dead on their anniversaries. But the martyrs were not thus prayed *for*—they were prayed *to*—for their 'witness' to Christ (the word 'martyr' is derived from the Greek word meaning 'witness') ensured for them immediate entry into His Kingdom. Hence, as we have seen, the day of their physical death was looked upon as the day of the spiritual birthday into their true life. This seeking of the martyrs' help and prayers led on to the full development of the cultus of the saints in general, and this becomes more evident in post-Nicene days. In the fourth century the cultus was systematised; feasts were established and so on. But during this period a difference in regarding the day of the martyrdom or holy death of the saints began to come in. Instead of the terms *natale, natalitia*—or in Greek, *genethlion* (all meaning 'birthday')—the death of the martyrs and other saints were now called their 'burials' (*depositiones*); the end of earthly life took the place of the beginning of heavenly life: the eschatological aspect of the Christian life was lost in the historical; time rather than eternity now occupied attention. The author of *The Shape of the Liturgy* points out the even more striking fact that while the old word *natale* is used once in the calendar of this period, it is in a quite different sense. The feast of St. Peter's Chair on February 22nd is spoken of as *Natale Petri de Cathedra*—'The Birthday', that is the 'inauguration' of 'Peter's Chair'.[1] This use of the word *natale* commemorates an event which took place upon earth and so is temporal and historical, though of perpetual importance. (See Dix, p. 370.)

During the third century the cultus of confessors came into being. These were persons who had confessed their faith like the martyrs, but had been punished by tortures and scourging—not condemned to death. Such people were looked on as 'living

---

[1] The commemoration of St. Peter's position as the 'Foundation-stone' of Christ's Church.

martyrs'. In the early days of the cultus of the saints—of all grades—the choice was for a long time effected by their connection with some particular place. For example, at Rome at first only feasts of SS. Peter and Paul, who had been martyred in that city, were observed, and in Gaul, at Tours, that of St. Martin, who was the first of those not martyrs to be considered a saint from the very moment of his death. In the case of the first two saints the date—June 29th—does not commemorate the day of their death, but of the removal of their bodies from their tombs on the Vatican hill and along the road to Ostia, to the catacombs of St. Sebastian, as a safer hiding-place during the Decian persecution of the third century. Thus it was especially the *place* of burial that was considered important.

FEASTS OF OUR LADY: The calendar of feasts and the whole development of the Liturgical Year was not a long-thought-out, deliberate arrangement; it was a natural growth: it 'came about'. The above facts, too, explain the, to us in these days, surprising slowness in the development of feasts in honour of Our Lady. It was the existence of *relics* of the martyrs and confessors, of their bodies or what remained of them, which gave rise to the observance of the feast in the place where the body was buried or where the relics were preserved. But there were no such relics of Our Lady. Two of her great feasts, the Purification and the Annunciation, were at first feasts of Our Lord; of His Presentation in the Temple and His conception in His Mother's womb, respectively. In connection with this idea of relics of the saints as the basis of their feasts, it is interesting to know that the feast of the Blessed Virgin, known now as the Visitation, was originally the feast of the relic of her veil in the church of Blachernae at Constantinople, which was 'deposited' there in A.D. 69 (Dix, p. 376). In Rome none of the great feasts of Our Lady were adopted before A.D. 700. The feasts of the Purification, the Annunciation, Assumption and Nativity come from the Byzantine Church, and were taken over by Pope Sergius I, who was himself an Eastern.

THE FEAST AND DOCTRINE OF THE IMMACULATE CONCEPTION: It is interesting for English Catholics to know that this feast first grew up and developed in Anglo-Saxon England[1] at the beginning of the eleventh century. Dom Gregory Dix says that the feast was "on an older and rather different Byzantine basis" (Dix, p. 377). The "older and rather different basis" of this feast in the East consists in this, that it was not the sinlessness of the Conception in itself that was the basis of the feast, but rather the dignity of the Blessed Virgin as the future Mother of God which made the very beginning of her existence a glorious fact for the whole Church. The Conception was even sometimes connected with St. Anne, the mother of Our Lady, rather than with Our Lady herself, and so the feast was called 'The Conception of St. Anne'; no clear distinction being made between the active and passive aspects. The same applies to the feast of 'the Conception of St. John the Baptist'. This latter feast probably helped towards the establishment of that of the Virgin Mother. The doctrine of Mary's Immaculate Conception was *defined* as of faith for the whole Catholic Church only in 1854 by Pope Pius IX, but its full development had come about long before that date in the general belief of the Church. The fact that it was publicly accepted and allowed as a liturgical feast by ecclesiastical authority (though not accepted by Rome before A.D. 1477) shows at least what was 'in the mind' of the Church. The year of grace, 1950, saw a further development of the cultus of the Mother of God, in the solemn definition by the reigning Holy Father, Pope Pius XII, of another dogma about Our Lady also long accepted and approved by ecclesiastical authority. This is the doctrine of the bodily Assumption of the Blessed Virgin into heaven, her share in the Resurrection of her Son: since she had shared so fully in His Passion and Death.

The Feasts of Apostles and Evangelists: These are not of very ancient origin either. The oldest is that of St. Andrew on November 30th, which goes back to the fifth century and was kept early in Rome. In the Roman Mass the saint's name is always mentioned together with SS. Peter and Paul in the

---

[1] But there is evidence of a feast of Our Lady's Conception in Ireland in the ninth century. This is found in the Martyrology of the monastery of Tallaght, and in a MS. calendar, written in verse by a monk called Œngus. (See *Dictionnaire de Théologie*, vol. 7 (i), col. 987. (Paris, 1927).)

Canon, in the prayer *Libera nos*. St. Andrew is the chief Patron of Russia and of Scotland.[1]

THE SAINTS AND THEIR RELICS: The close connection between the cultus of the saints and their relics—or parts of them, or even of other objects which had contained them or had only *touched* them—led to the frequent habit of 'translating' many of them from one place to another. The so-called 'translations' were sometimes practically 'pious robberies'! This was not merely in order to get possession of the relic of some saint, but also as a means of justifying the cultus in some particular place. Gradually the full organisation of the various classes of saints and their feasts—apostles, martyrs, confessors (both bishops and non-bishops), of virgins (martyrs or simple virgins) and holy women not virgins who were either martyrs or not—was completed. Besides the historical feasts (that is, those commemorating events in the life of Our Lord, Our Lady and the saints), feasts connected with other events were introduced—for example, the dedication of important churches. Again, feasts founded upon certain aspects of Our Lord, His Mother and His saints arose: as, for instance, the feast of Corpus Christi —the feast of 'Christ's Body' in the Blessed Sacrament, which was introduced in the fourteenth century; that of the Sacred Heart—in the seventeenth—feast of the human love of God the Son symbolised in the Heart of flesh which, as part of His sacred Body, is an object of worship in itself. A very recent example of this type of feast is that of 'Christ the King' established by Pope Pius XI in 1925. In the case of Our Lady, there is the feast of the Compassion or Seven Sorrows[2] and, much later, that of the Holy Rosary (October 7th). But it was the idea of 'historical commemoration'—virtually an invention of the

---

[1] The choice of St. Andrew as Patron of Scotland is said to be due to relics of the saint brought from Patras (the traditional place of his martyrdom) by a monk called Regulus, to Kilrymont in Fife, which in time came to be known as 'St. Andrews' and was made the Primatial See of Scotland. (See *The Church Year and Kalendar*, by John Dowden, D.D., Bishop of Edinburgh, in *The Cambridge Handbooks of Liturgical Study*. (Cambridge, 1910. p. 64.) See also *A Procession of Saints*, by James Brodrick, S.J. (London: Burns, Oates & Washbourne, Ltd., 1949, p. 65, footnote 1).)

[2] There are two such feasts—one on the Friday after Passion Sunday and the other on September 15th. The first is, strictly speaking, the Feast of Our Lady's 'Compassion'—her share, that is, in the Passion of her Son.

fourth century—which first brought about the organisation of the Liturgical Year and of the Liturgical Calendar.

THE COMPLETED MISSAL AND BREVIARY: In these we find the divisions of feasts under the titles: the 'Proper of the Time', 'Proper of the Saints' and 'Common of the Saints'. The first concerns the arrangement of the different liturgical seasons—Advent, Lent, Christmas-tide, Paschal-tide; the second concerns those saints who have a special Mass and Office—the feasts of Our Lord and His Mother stand by themselves—Our Lady, however, has a 'common' for her Mass and Office in the case of her less-important feasts, and a 'Votive' Mass and Office (*several* Masses, in fact, according to the season) for Saturdays on which there is no special feast. Finally, the third—the 'Common of the Saints'—is divided into the various classes referred to above—for those saints who have no 'proper' Mass or Office.

In its complete development, the Liturgical Year leads us all through the Life of Our Lord on earth up to His Ascension into heaven—and with Him are included His Blessed Mother and His perfect disciples, the saints. "It is no wonder if the liturgy—*the supreme expression of the Church's life*—has ever since borne the marks of its grasp on human living, to the partial obscuring of its earlier character. Yet the liturgy remained then and has remained since what it always had been, *the worshipping act of the Body of Christ towards God*, by which His eternal kingdom 'comes' in time". (*The Shape of the Liturgy*, p. 393, italics mine.)

SACRIFICE AND THE MASS

(*Theology and Sanity*, by F. J. Sheed.)[1]

"RESURRECTION and Ascension belong organically to the Sacrifice He offered for us. The Sacrifice, in so far as it is the offering of a victim slain, was complete upon Calvary. But in the total conception of sacrifice, it is not sufficient—as Cain found long before—that a victim be offered to God; it is essential that the offering *be accepted by God*: and given that the nature of man requires that sacrifice be an action externally visible, it belongs to the perfection of sacrifice, that God's acceptance should be as externally visible as humanity's offering.

"It is in this sense that Resurrection and Ascension belong organically to the Sacrifice. By the miracle of the Resurrection, God at once shows his acceptance of the Priest as a true priest of a true sacrifice and perfects the Victim offered to Him, so that whereas it is offered mortal and corruptible, it has gained immortality and incorruptibility.

"By the Ascension God accepts the offered Victim by actually taking it to Himself. Humanity, offered to God in Christ the Victim, is now for ever at the right hand of the Father."

[1] From chap. xviii, 'The Redeeming Sacrifice', iv, 'Resurrection and Ascension', pp. 189–90. (London: Sheed & Ward, 1947.)

RESERVATION OF THE BLESSED SACRAMENT[1]

IT has been generally supposed that, in the earliest days of the Church, reservation of the Blessed Sacrament was practised only in order to provide for the communion of the sick and viaticum in the case of the dying. But this, it seems, is not altogether correct. In his description of the Western rite in his day, St. Justin Martyr tells us that at the end of the Holy Sacrifice, deacons took from the altar particles of the Sacred Host consecrated during the Mass, and carried them to any of the faithful who (for any just reason) had been unable to take part in the Mass. This custom did not mean reservation as we now understand it; the Most Holy was reserved only during the length of time necessary for the deacons to carry It to the persons concerned and to administer communion to them. But besides this practice, during the worst periods of persecution, when it was likely to become either very difficult or even impossible at times to celebrate the Holy Eucharist, the faithful were allowed to take a sufficient number of consecrated particles away from the last Mass at which they were able to assist, to keep in their own houses and to communicate themselves there. Not only priests, but even the laity were allowed also to carry the Most Holy on their persons when on a journey. Priests, too, like the laity as described above, often kept the Blessed Sacrament in their own houses to provide for emergencies. This very free manner of treating the Blessed Sacrament seems almost like a lack of reverence in these days, but it was not really so, nor did it mean any absence of belief in or realisation of the Real Presence of Our Lord; it was the result of very different circumstances, and due to special needs and to the constant danger of persecution. In his pamphlet, *A Detection of Aumbries* (a most useful work in connection with this question), Dom Gregory Dix speaks of what he calls (and, it seems, with justice) the first *official* example of reservation of the Blessed Sacrament, and points out that it occurs as early as the second century.

This example is found in what is known as the rite of the 'fermentum', the latter being a particle (or, rather, a number of particles) of the Sacred Host consecrated during the Papal Solemn Mass

---

[1] The most recent work on reservation is: *La Réservation Eucharistique jusqu'à la Renaissance*, par E. Maffei, 1942.

to be taken by acolytes towards the end of the ceremony, and distributed by them among the celebrants of the Solemn Masses taking
place the same day in the various 'parish churches' of Rome.
The celebrants of these Masses dropped the 'fermentum' sent from
the Pope's Mass into their chalices just before communion, and thus
expressed their union with the Vicar of Christ in the One Sacrifice;
the 'fermentum' ceremony is described in detail in this book, p. 170
to p. 177. Here, again, we have a form of 'reservation' of the same
type as those described above; that is, reservation in a wide sense of
the word and for only a very short time. At any rate, the 'fermentum'
is an example of a 'use' of the Blessed Sacrament distinct from
(though certainly closely connected with) the Holy Sacrifice.

The Place of Reservation: This question arises in connection with
reservation of the Blessed Sacrament in the later sense—as we know
it now. In the early ages of the Church, the only places for reservation for any length of time were either in the houses of both clergy
and laity as mentioned above or else on the persons of those on a
journey. Up till the ninth century, in fact, no laws or regulations
were laid down on this matter. But after the fourth century it seems
that the church gradually became the most usual place in which to
keep the Most Holy reserved for the communion of the sick, the
viaticum of the dying or for those in any way prevented from
actually taking part in the Sacrifice. As to the exact place in the
church for this reservation, nothing is laid down. But it seems probable that it was in the *secretarium* (the sacristy, as we should call it
now); later on, in the sanctuary, apart from the altar, or, again, in
a special chapel. From somewhat later usage it appears that the
vessels containing the Sacred Host were kept in what is known as an
'aumbry'. This was a small cupboard sunk into one of the walls;
the name is derived from the Latin *armarium*—literally, a chest in
which tools or implements, arms (*arma*) were kept. This cupboard
was closed with a strong door which could be locked. In this later
period, in fact, we find existing—more or less at the same time in
both Western and Eastern Churches—three chief methods of
reservation: (i) in a locked aumbry—as described above; (ii) in a
pyx or other vessel either *upon* or *above* the high altar; (iii) in a box
or casket on the altar, known as the 'tabernacle' in the West; the
artophorion ('Bread-bearer') in the East (Byzantine). In Rome, in
the decree *Sane* of Innocent III in 1215, the Pope orders 'that in all
churches the Chrism and the Eucharist be kept with strict care
under lock and key'. (See *A Detection of Aumbries*, p. 30.) The Pope
does not make it clear exactly where in the church the Most Holy
and the Holy Oils were to be kept 'under lock and key', but the most

usual Italian and Roman custom in his time was to place them in an aumbry. The aumbry could be, and often was, in the north wall (or Gospel side) of the high altar, but this varied from place to place. In Portugal and Spain, and in some parts of France, we find the aumbry in use also.[1] In Germany later on there was a special development of the aumbry. Instead of a little cupboard made in the wall, there arose a great tower-like structure, standing clear of the wall and usually on the north side of the sanctuary, but near the division between it and the nave, so that it could be seen clearly by the people. This structure is known as the 'sacrament-house' (from the German *sakrament-hausen*). In Scotland there is at least *one* mention of a hanging pyx. This occurs in an old poem about the destruction of Melrose Abbey in the Reformation period. The ruthless 're-forming' soldiers, so says the poem, dragged down the pyx from above the altar 'without any reverence'. This pyx is called by the poet the 'Eucharist', and this seems to have been the old Scottish name for the pyx and also for the 'monstrance' in which the Blessed Sacrament was exposed. But the more usual method of reservation in Scotland in the fifteenth and sixteenth centuries was in a 'sacrament-house'. No doubt this name was adopted from Germany while that country and Scotland were allies against England. Only the *name*, however, was so adopted, for the Scots sacrament-house was not a great tower-like structure as in Germany; it was simply an aumbry in the wall, which was generally adorned with carvings representing the exposed Sacrament with censing angels adoring and so on. A number of these 'sacrament-houses' are still to be found in Scotland. There are two well-known examples quite close together—namely, in the Greyfriars' church (now belonging to Sisters of Mercy) in Elgin (Moray), and in the ruined church of Pluscarden Priory, about seven or eight miles from that town. Greyfriars' church was presented to the Sisters of Mercy by the third Marquess of Bute, by whom it had been restored, and who also restored a part of Pluscarden Priory. In 1943, his son, Lord Colum Crichton-Stuart (who had inherited the Priory from his father in 1900) presented it to the Benedictine monks of Prinknash Abbey, near Gloucester, and there is a small community in residence there now. The Pluscarden sacrament-house (like that in Greyfriars' church) is quite intact, except the door, and still has its carvings of the monstrance and censing angels. Greyfriars' church is in actual use by the Sisters, but the sacrament-house is not used for reservation now.

---

[1] Sometimes the aumbry is found in the middle of the altar reredos; there are mediæval (fourteenth-century) and later (sixteenth-century) examples. The aumbry is also found in the east wall of the church, behind the altar.

In France and England the aumbry was hardly used at all. In the first of these countries, not only was the Blessed Sacrament reserved in a hanging pyx, but for a time at least it was kept in a pyx standing actually upon the altar. During the ninth century a Gallican council ordered that: "nothing be placed upon the altar except a *capsa* and the relics" (that is, a *capsa* containing the relics; by *capsa* is meant a covered vessel of metal, ivory or even wood) "or perhaps the four holy gospels of God and a pyx containing the Lord's Body for the viaticum of the sick".

This decree, says Dix in *A Detection of Aumbries*, was for a long time attributed to Pope Leo IV (A.D. 847-55), but it is really a Gallican production, probably issued at a council during the reign of the Emperor Charlemagne. (See *A Detection of Aumbries*, p. 27.) This decree does not lay down any *law* about placing the pyx on the altar, but merely suggests it as a fitting place for the reserved Sacrament. But to leave the Blessed Sacrament on the altar, openly and in an unprotected vessel like this, would easily lead to all kinds of irreverence and to danger as well. It may be, then, that the disadvantages of this use gave rise to the interesting fact that it is in France, and at a much earlier period than is generally believed, that we find the first mention of the 'tabernacle' and of its position on the altar. This is in 1198, in prescriptions issued by Eudes de Sully, Bishop of Paris. There is, too, an existing example of a French tabernacle at Senanques near Nevers, which is the oldest known tabernacle (in the accepted sense). This tabernacle is made of wood and enamelled. The use of a tabernacle of this kind was preferred to the aumbry in France in those places (not very many) where the hanging pyx was not in use. The name 'tabernacle' is at first sight rather a puzzle: the word is derived from the Latin *tabernaculum*, which means a tent. The Latin word itself, as a matter of fact, is derived from *taberna*—a 'hut' or 'shed'—something more durable than a mere tent of canvas or other stuff, and so it may be that the title tabernacle was given to the casket itself in the sense of *taberna*— a 'little house' rather than a 'tent'. Certainly it is the case that in the Middle Ages the word 'tabernacle' was often applied to objects such as the *ostensorium*—or monstrance, as we say now—in which the Most Holy was exposed on certain occasions, and even to niches in stone or wooden screens, altar-retables, etc., in which statues were placed. But in England we find a more natural explanation. In this country the most usual, almost in fact the *only*, method of reserving the Blessed Sacrament (from the twelfth century at least and probably much earlier) was in a hanging pyx. This pyx was sometimes— as was often the case in France—shaped like a dove, but in England more often in the form of a covered chalice, or a little box or casket made of silver, gold, ivory or wood. The pyx containing the Most Holy was hung up over the principal altar, and it was veiled with a square of fine-drawn linen with tassels of red and gold at each of the four corners. The pyx thus veiled was suspended from a miniature canopy of silk or some rich material, shaped either like a bell-tent—that is, a complete cone—or like a tent with a cone-shaped roof and straight sides. This little canopy generally had a metal crown round the cone—that is, round the edge of the 'roof' of the tent—or in the case of the 'bell-tent' form, round the base. Sometimes there were three crowns round the latter form, and at the Reformation the reformers called it, derisively, 'the Pope's hatt', as it resembled the papal triple-crown.

The canopy was itself suspended from the 'tester' or large canopy of silk or wood which nearly always covered the altar and altar-pace. Sometimes, instead of a separate canopy hanging from the roof by chains or cords, the altar-canopy consisted of the roof of the sanctuary just over the altar, which was made much lower than the rest of the roof. It seems that in England the little tent-shaped canopy immediately over the pyx was actually called the 'taber-nacle'. In his *English Church Furniture: The Antiquary's Books*, 'Pyxes', p. 40 (Methuen: 1907), Dr. Charles Cox says: "The general English usage was undoubtedly to place it [the reserved Sacrament] in a pyx or box of wood, metal or ivory which was then suspended in front of [*sic*—more correctly 'above'] the altar in a hanging receptacle *usually termed the tabernacle*, and sometimes only the canopy" (italics mine).[1] In this case the word 'tabernacle' evidently meant 'tent' in the original sense. Perhaps it was the idea of the 'Tabernacle of the Testimony' in the Old Testament, in which God was present in a special manner, which originated this title. Later, however, the name seems to have been transferred from the little tent over the pyx to the receptacle itself; that is, when it became general to place the pyx in a casket or receptacle on the altar. In the present Roman use (we shall see the details of this use presently) the taber-nacle, a cupboard or casket of wood, marble or metal, is (or *should* be) covered with a veil called *conopeum* (literally, a mosquito-net), which should cover the tabernacle all over 'in the form of a tent' (*ad instar tentorii*; Sacred Congregation of Rites: N. 3035, N. 1617. ad 7). This seems to suggest the idea that the Roman taber-nacle is simply the hanging pyx brought down on to the altar, the

[1] Pictures of the various types of the hanging pyx will be found in *Churches, Their Plan and Furnishing*, by Peter F. Anson (The Bruce Publishing Company, Milwaukee, 1948, p. 87). These pictures, like all the illustrations in this very interesting book, are the work of the author himself.

conopeum being the tent-canopy (originally, as we have just seen, called 'tabernacle'), which in its turn has 'come down' and has been placed over the casket or little cupboard to which it has also given the name 'tabernacle'. In the tabernacle thus placed on the altar, the principle laid down by Pope Innocent III, that the Body of Our Lord should be 'kept with strict care under lock and key', could be observed, and at the same time the reserved Sacrament kept in touch with the altar. But in England the use of the hanging pyx continued up to the eve of the Reformation—in spite of the continual attempts of ecclesiastical authority in the thirteenth century and onwards to impose the use of the aumbry in the wall as a safer method. Even when the Church was restored in England in the reign of Queen Mary Tudor, and Cardinal Pole tried to introduce the tabernacle on the altar—"fixed in a raised place in the midst of the altar"—the hanging pyx was restored everywhere, regardless of his orders (Dix, *A Detection of Aumbries*, p. 42). The tabernacle upon the altar, however, did become more or less general during the sixteenth and seventeenth centuries in the different Western Churches —chiefly owing to the increase in the number of communions of the laity at the time of the Counter-Reformation. For this, reservation in a tabernacle on the altar was found to be more convenient than in a hanging pyx, which allowed only sufficient for the communion of the sick and dying. No *order* concerning this, however, was given by Rome until as late as 1863—when "there remained probably not half a dozen exceptions to the custom of reservation in a tabernacle throughout the whole Roman communion", and "the Sacred Congregation of Rites felt it safe to make it a rule" (Dix, *A Detection of Aumbries*, p. 72). One well-known exception to the rule still in actual use may be mentioned here. In the Benedictine Abbey of Solesmes in France the Blessed Sacrament is reserved in a silver dove, standing on a dish, the whole hanging by chains under a little tent-canopy of white and gold embroidered silk, the straight sides of which hang down (hiding the dove) from the little conical 'roof' of gold material; they open in front, however, and can be drawn back. The dove and canopy do not hang from a larger canopy or from the roof of the church, but from a tall wooden standard rising behind the altar. This method is in keeping with the French mediæval custom of suspending the pyx from a standard in this position—usually in the form of an episcopal or abbatial crosier.[1]

[1] Another well-known example of the dove-pyx is in Amiens cathedral. There is a golden dove with outspread wings suspended over the altar and still used for reservation. The effect, however, is somewhat spoiled by the huge baroque reredos (eighteenth century), erected behind the altar, with clouds and rays of glory depicted on it.

There are a few examples of an analogous method of suspension in mediæval England—e.g. at Durham and Winchester Cathedrals. In both cases the veiled pyx was suspended from a little canopy fixed to a 'branch' or rod of iron gilded and projecting from the middle of the great altar-screen, which stretched across the whole sanctuary immediately behind the altar. The author of *The Rites of Durham*, who was probably one of the former monks, tells us that: "within the said quire, over the high altar, did hange a rich canapie for the Blessed Sacrament to hange within it . . . whereon did stand [that is, on the top of the canopy] a pelican all of silver, verye finely gilded, giving hir bloud to hir younge ones [this is a widespread symbol of the Holy Eucharist] and a marveilous faire pix that the holy Sacrament did hange in, which was of most pure gold, most curiously wrought of gold-smith work." (*Rites of Durham*, 7, quoted by Dr. Rock in his *The Church of Our Fathers*, iv. 239 and 240, edited by G. W. Hart and W. H. Frere, 1905.)

In the East, reservation has been and still is often in a pyx—usually a gold or silver dove with outspread wings—hanging from the stone baldaquin with four pillars, which usually stands over the altar. Sometimes there are two baldaquins—a small one of which the pillars rest upon the corners of the altar itself, and over this, again, a large one with pillars resting upon the floor.

Sometimes, again, the reserved Sacrament (in what seems to Westerners a not very reverent manner) is put in a little silk or velvet bag which hangs from a hook or nail in the east wall behind the free-standing altar—or else from a nail driven into the sanctuary-side of the *ikonostasis*, that is, the screen between sanctuary and nave. An aumbry or wall-cupboard is not infrequently found as the place of reservation. But the most general form is in a kind of 'tabernacle'; a small casket of precious metal (or even of plain wood) often made in the form of a little church, placed upon the altar itself which, in Byzantine churches, is without any kind of reredos or even gradines. This tabernacle is called in Greek *artophorion*, which means 'bread-carrier'.[1]

Owing to the almost complete separation between sanctuary and nave in Eastern (Byzantine) churches, due to the solid *ikonostasis* between them, there is considerable difference between the Eastern and Western attitude towards the Blessed Sacrament reserved. As Edmund Bishop has pointed out, the principal object of reservation to-day—and for long past—in the West is shown in the attitude of mind which expresses itself in the conception of the church as 'the

---

[1] The *artophorion* is often covered with a glass case, and at a distance is reminiscent of the 'drawing-room clock' of Victorian times!

Home of the Blessed Sacrament'. Besides greater convenience in administering communion, the Most Holy is also reserved in order to provide means of adoring Our Lord really and objectively present in His Sacrament—by means of 'visits', processions, Expositions and Benediction. There is nothing like this in the Eastern Churches.[1] Even in the church and when passing directly in front of the altar with its *artophorion*, no outward reverence or even attention is paid to it. In the East the Blessed Sacrament is still reserved, as in the early Church, only for the communion of sick and dying, or others prevented in some way from being present at the 'Divine Liturgy'— that is, the Holy Sacrifice. In the East, too, reservation is in both kinds, by means of 'intinction' (from the Latin *intingo-intingĕre*—'to dip'); the consecrated Bread being dipped into the consecrated Wine and then dried by fire to preserve it. As a matter of fact, it is at least doubtful if the consecrated Wine is preserved at all by this drying process. The origin of this method of reservation seems to be the fact that in the communion of the laity the faithful receive both kinds by means of particles of the consecrated Host dropped into the chalice, and both elements administered together in a spoon. While communion was still given in both kinds in the West, the two kinds were administered separately, and later on the Precious Blood was not given directly from the chalice but by means of a metal tube called, in Latin, *fistula*. This custom is still kept up in the Pope's own communion at the Solemn Papal Mass. During the thirteenth century, apparently, communion in both kinds for the laity gradually died out—though it may have lasted longer in some places. The Eastern custom of intinction was never approved in the West by Rome. In early times the consecrated Host was placed by the celebrant immediately in the communicant's hands, the right hand being laid upon the left. Placing the Host directly in the mouth came into use during the seventh century in some places, and ultimately became the universal usage in the West for lay-folk.

Reservation upon the high altar in the West did much to encourage and develop devotion towards the Blessed Sacrament in itself.[2] With regard to the greater safety and reverence resulting from the locked tabernacle fixed on the altar, it is interesting to know that the hanging pyx, as a matter of fact, was always locked. The

[1] In the various 'Uniate' Eastern Churches subject to the Holy See, Western devotions are being introduced, but adapted to Eastern ways.

[2] In cathedrals and in some monastic churches, the Blessed Sacrament is reserved on a side altar or in a special 'chapel of the Blessed Sacrament', not at the main altar (the 'high altar'). In this, Edmund Bishop was inclined to see a continuation, in developed circumstances, of reservation apart from the main altar in the *loculus in muro* ('the little place in the wall')—that is, the aumbry. (*Liturgica Historica*, 'On the History of the Christian Altar', Oxford, 1918, p. 38.)

Blessed Sacrament was placed in a smaller receptacle which fitted into the pyx itself, and the latter was then locked. But even with this precaution the whole pyx and its sacred content could easily be pulled down and carried away—as we read was done in the case of Melrose Abbey.

It was in Northern countries—in Germany and England among others—that this devotion towards the reserved Sacrament first developed, and Exposition and Benediction started in the first of these two countries. In Germany, too, although the Most Holy was not reserved upon the altar but, as we have seen, in a sacrament-house on one side of the sanctuary, this receptacle was not a little cupboard in the wall, the usual 'aumbry', but a great tower standing out conspicuously. The door of the sacrament-house, too, was generally a mere iron grille through which the Blessed Sacrament could be seen by all, and it was surrounded with lights to draw attention to it.

There are, in Italy, two interesting examples of the transition period between hanging pyx and tabernacle upon the altar. The first is in Rome itself, in the Basilica of St. Mary Major. This example is of sixteenth-century date, and is a tabernacle in the actual sense of this word, but of monumental size; a great bronze shrine in the form of a church with domed roof. In spite of its dimensions, however, this tabernacle does not stand *upon* the altar, or even upon a gradine on the altar, but is held up above it by four bronze angels standing upon the gradine. The second example is on the high altar of the Cathedral of Siena and dates from the thirteenth century. This tabernacle—if it can be called by that name—is in the form of a pyx or ciborium (to use the modern term) of gilded bronze. It is a huge covered cup, in fact, with a slender stem on a wide foot. Here we have a further 'move' than that of St. Mary Major's tabernacle. At Siena the pyx itself, greatly enlarged but still a pyx, is placed *upon* the altar instead of hanging *above* it. In the case of St. Mary Major there is a locked and solid tabernacle to contain the ciborium, but although not hanging above the altar it has not yet found its way, so to speak, upon it.[1]

Finally, we must refer to an article in *Country Life* (August 4th, 1944, p. 209), in which what the author claims to be the actual example of a hanging pyx in the parish church of Dennington in Suffolk is described. A later article by another writer, however, in the same paper (*Country Life*, December 1st, 1944, p. 957) shows that this so-called hanging pyx is really, not the pyx itself, but the little

---

[1] Drawings of both these tabernacles will be found on p. 96 of *Churches: Their Plan and Furnishing*, referred to farther back.

canopy—the 'tabernacle', in fact—which used to hang over the pyx.
The upper part of this canopy is made of wood and still has traces
of colour upon it. It is made in the form of a carved and crocketed
pinnacle, and from the lower edge the silken sides of the 'tent', no
doubt, could hang, and so veil the pyx hanging within it under the
wooden pinnacle, and itself veiled by the 'pyx-cloth' of openwork
linen. Only three of such wooden canopies are known to exist or
to have existed in England[1]; there are no examples of actual mediæval
pyxes at all. The existence of a mediæval 'tabernacle', however,
with its rather unusual roof of carved wood, is of great interest, even
without the pyx.

[1] At Wells Cathedral—formerly at Glastonbury Abbey—and at Milton
Abbey.

DEVOTION TO THE BLESSED SACRAMENT

BELIEF in the Real Sacramental Presence existed from the earliest days of the Church, after the institution of the Holy Eucharist at the Last Supper. This belief, however, has not always found *expression* in quite the same way; for all that is involved in the 'Mystery' of the Holy Eucharist was not explicitly grasped and clearly understood at the very beginning. In the first centuries, attention was directed to the *use* of the Eucharistic Presence in the Sacrifice and communion, rather than to the actual Presence in itself and as such.

The development of devotion to Our Lord in the Holy Eucharist has found expression in two forms: (i) in the Liturgy and (ii) outside the Liturgy. (See Dix, *A Detection of Aumbries*, pp. 42–64.)

The first consists of words and actions of adoration addressed directly to Our Lord really present in the sacred species during the celebration of the Liturgy—of which such words and actions form a real part; the second consists of words and actions of adoration, again like the first, addressed directly to Our Lord in His Sacramental Presence—but as *reserved*, distinct from either Mass or communion and even from the latter when received outside Mass. This form of devotion is either public or private.

(i) Devotions in the Liturgy are not found during the first four centuries. They begin, perhaps, towards the end of the fifth century and at first in the Eastern Churches—in Syria and Asia Minor. These devotions in the West are found at first only in the Northern parts of the Church.

At Rome the only directly Roman example is the *Agnus Dei* sung before the celebrant's communion—and this itself was introduced by Pope Sergius I, who was a Syrian. The prayers said secretly by the celebrant before communion (like those at the offertory) are not Roman, and, moreover, are of late mediæval introduction. There are other examples of Syrian influence in the Western Liturgy, in the Spanish or Mozarabic rite. (See *Liturgica Historica*, pp. 161 *et seqq.*, note B.)

Acts of adoration are: genuflections, bows, censing and so on, which express reverence to the sacramental species directly. None of these are 'primitive' nor even pre-Nicene; but they came into the Liturgy sooner than prayers and words, and perhaps those directly concerned with the sacramental species may be as early as the fourth century. Again, it is in Syria that the beginnings of such practices are found. At first they were signs of private devotion, and were not official liturgical actions. But such official sanction is found —once more in Syria—in *The Liturgical Homilies of Narsai* (Hom. xvii, A, p. 23: 'Texts and Studies', etc. Vol. viii, No. 1. Translated by Dom R. H. Connolly, M.A. Cambridge, etc., 1909). There is no mention of bows or genuflections to the consecrated Sacrament in the eighth-century *Ordo Romanus I*; nor are they found even in the printed Roman missals in A.D. 1474. It is possible, however, that these acts of reverence existed then as *customs*—but as free customs, not as ordered nor as general practices. Kneeling when receiving communion, too, became common in the West only during the thirteenth century, and it never came into use in the East at all, where communion is still received standing by all the communicants. In the Western Church, in the Solemn Mass of the Roman rite described in the *Ordo Romanus Primus*, the Pope communicated *sitting* on his throne to which Host and Chalice were brought to him from the altar by the deacon and subdeacon. At the present day, at the Papal Solemn Mass, the Holy Father still communicates at his throne—but he rises and kneels to adore the Most Holy, and then stands to receive It.

(ii) Devotions to the Blessed Sacrament, outside the Liturgy, are private when directed to the Blessed Sacrament in the place of reservation-prayers to and in the Presence of the reserved Sacrament, such as are in common use in our own days. Public devotions of this sort find expression in processions in which the Blessed Sacrament is carried; in *Exposition* and *Benediction*—the latter being a simplification of the former.

In these days the service of Benediction, which concludes a short Exposition, has developed into a strictly *liturgical service*—that is, it has become a public service laid down and legislated for by ecclesiastical authority. It does not, however, involve any obligation of attendance, as in the case of the Mass and Divine Office.

Extra-liturgical devotion in the West is due to the Christian spirit of the Northern races—it does not appear in the South or in Rome till very late in the sixteenth century. In the South the more ancient preoccupation with the *use* of the Holy Eucharist, in sacrifice and in communion (as part of the sacrifice, the primitive Christian attitude) was prevalent; whereas in the North and especially in Germanic countries after their conversion, the uppermost preoccupation was with the Eucharistic Presence of Our Lord in and for Itself.

The first example of exposition of the Blessed Sacrament is in

Germany, and it was in connection with the special German method
of reserving the Most Holy—namely, in the 'sacrament-house'. This
often involved a kind of perpetual exposition. As already pointed
out, the sacrament-house was merely closed by a grating through
which the pyx could be seen, and a light was even put *inside*, in
addition to the candles on the iron balustrade outside. In England
the almost universal custom of the hanging pyx over the principal
altar in that country did much to develop this devotion to the
Blessed Sacrament reserved, for It was thus visible to all entering
the Church and, in fact, dominated the whole place. But there does
not seem to have been any very clear distinction in England between public and private devotion to the reserved Sacrament.
According to Dom Gregory Dix, the earliest evidence seems to be
for the former rather than the latter; probably each practice reacted
upon the other in turn. In the case of public devotions, such as processions of the Blessed Sacrament, this ceremony was not at first
primarily intended as a special act of devotion towards the Blessed
Sacrament Itself. The earliest account of the Blessed Sacrament
carried in a procession is in connection with the procession of palms
on Palm Sunday. This first example at Canterbury was adopted by
Lanfranc about A.D. 1078 from the Rouen usages, and is laid down
in the new statutes drawn up by that Archbishop (*A Detection of
Aumbries*, pp. 55 and 56). On Corpus Christi, on the other hand,
there was no procession of the Blessed Sacrament until about fifty
years after the institution of the feast by Urban IV, although this
feast was especially in honour of the Blessed Sacrament. In much
the same way, Exposition and Benediction of the Blessed Sacrament did not arise, according to some writers, as a special act
of devotion towards the reserved Sacrament itself; it was at first a
special means of solemnising the chant after Compline of the *Salve
Regina* and other anthems in honour of the Blessed Virgin. This
fact accounts for the use of the Litany of Our Lady or other chants
in her honour often sung at Benediction nowadays, instead of other
chants more directly concerned with the Blessed Sacrament itself.
In the Eastern Churches, while such devotions in prayers and ceremonies in the Liturgy developed as in the West, there has never been
any *extra*-liturgical devotion, except in the case of those bodies
among the different Eastern rites which are in communion with the
Holy See. In these latter cases such devotions are carried out in
keeping with Eastern ideas and characteristics, and are by no
means mere 'Westernisations'. Although the Blessed Sacrament has
been reserved in the East on, above or near the altar since the ninth
or tenth centuries, no signs of reverence or devotion are shown

apart from the Liturgy. This is because, owing to the *ikonostasis*, the solid stone or wooden screen of the Byzantine rite, or the curtains or some other forms of separation between sanctuary and nave in other Eastern rites, the reserved Sacrament is not *evident* to the congregation, any more than is the altar itself. The solid screen or other separation, too, accounts for the preservation of the older type of altar—small and square and without gradines or any sort of reredos.[1] The *ikonostasis* now found in all churches of the Byzantine rite (in other Eastern rites except the Maronite there is *some* kind of separation) seems to have been of fairly late introduction; in its present form, not before the fourteenth century, and it originated in Russia. It is really a development of the *cancelli* of the early Christian churches in both the East and the West. The *cancelli* (from the Latin *cancellare*—to 'cross out' with lines) was a low screen—or rather balustrade—of trellis-work across the entrance to the sanctuary from the nave. To this balustrade were added light columns standing upon it and supporting a beam which stretched across the entrance arch, and on which were placed the crucifix, statues and lights. In the East *ikons* (that is, flat painted pictures) took the place of statues, and as devotion to the *ikons* developed and their number was increased, the spaces between the columns supporting the beam were filled up with trellis-work and panelling so as to have more space for the ikons; and so the solid screen, the *ikonostasis*, was produced. Originally, the purpose of the *cancelli*—even when they grew higher and became a screen rather than a balustrade—was not to shut off the altar in a mysterious Holy of Holies, as in the Jewish Temple, but merely to mark the separation between sanctuary and nave. Even when the screen became solid, this was brought about, as said above, simply in order to provide more room for the *ikons*; its very name—*ikonostasis*, 'picture-stand'—shows this.

[1] The Armenian and Maronite altars, however, are Western in form—and of the worst type!

FULL TEXT OF THE DEPRECATIO (LITANY) OF POPE ST. GELASIUS (A.D. 492–6)

Deprecatio quam Papa Gelasius pro universali Ecclesia constituit canendam.	Supplication (litany) which Pope Gelasius ordered to be sung for the Universal Church.
Dicamus omnes, Domine, exaudi et miserere.	Let us all cry: Lord, heed and have pity.
Patrem Unigeniti et Dei Filium genitoris ingeniti, et sanctum	We call upon the Father of the only begotten and holy Son of God the Father
Deum Spiritum fidelibus animis invocamus.	And the Holy Spirit with our minds full of faith.
Pro immaculata Dei vivi Ecclesia, sacerdotibus ac ministris, divinam bonitatis opulentiam deprecamur.	For the unspotted Church of the living God, for priests and ministers we beseech the fullness of Divine good.
Pro Dei magni sacerdotibus et ministris, cunctisque Deum verum sanctis colentibus populis, Christum Dominum supplicamus.	For priests and ministers, of the great God and for all holy people that worship the true God, we beseech the Lord Christ.
Pro universis recte tractantibus verbum veritatis, multiformem Verbi Dei Sapientiam peculiariter obsecramus.	For all rightly handling the word of truth, we especially entreat the manifold wisdom of the Word of God.
Pro his qui se mente et corpore propter cæolorum regna castificant et spiritalium labore desudant, largitorem spiritalium munerum obsecramus.	For those who mortify themselves in spirit and in body for the sake of the heavenly kingdom and who exert themselves in spiritual work, we beseech the liberal Giver of spiritual gifts.

Pro religiosis principibus, omnique militiæ eorum, qui iudicium et iustitiam diligunt, Domine potentiam obsecramus.

For God-fearing princes and for all members of their soldiery who love judgment and justice, we entreat, O Lord, power.

Pro iucunditate et serenitate pluviæ atque aurarum vitalium blandimentis ac prospero diversorum operum cursu, Rectorem mundi Dominum deprecamur.

For fine and fair weather with rain and life-giving breeze bringing comfort and the favourable progress of all work, we entreat the Lord, Ruler of the World.

Pro his quos prima Christiani nominis initiavit agnitio quos iam desiderium gratiæ celestis accendit, omnipotentis Dei misericordiam obsecramus.

For those whom the recognition of the Christian name has initiated and who are now enkindled with the longing for heavenly grace, we beseech the mercy of God all powerful.

Pro his quos humanæ infirmitatis fragilitas, et quos nequitiæ spiritalis invidia vel varius sæculi horror involvit, Redemptoris nostri misericordiam imploramus.

For those whom the frailty of human weakness and the hatred of spiritual evils or the many horrors of the age have filled with confusion, we entreat the pity of our Redeemer.

Pro his quos peregrinationis necessitas aut iniquæ potestatis impietas vel hostilis vexat ærumna, Salvatorem Dominum supplicamus.

For those whom the need of travel or the evil of wicked powers and hostility disquiets, we pray to the Lord our Saviour.

Pro *Iudiaca falsitate*[1] aut heretica pravitate, vel gentilium superstitione perfusis, veritatis Dominum deprecamur.

For those imbued with Jewish falsity or the perversity of heresy or the superstition of the pagan, we entreat the Lord of truth.

Pro operariis pietatis et his qui necessitatibus laborantum fraterna charitate subveniunt, misericordiarum Dominum deprecamur.

For workers in piety and for those who, in brotherly love, assist the needs of those who labour, we beseech the Lord of mercy.

[1] Cf. the 'Solemn Collect' for the Jews on Good Friday.

Pro omnibus intrantibus in hæc sanctæ domus Dei atria religioso corde et supplici devotione convenienter Dominum gloriæ deprecamur.

For all who enter the courts of this holy house of God with religious spirit and humble devotion, we dutifully entreat the Lord of Glory.

Pro emendatione animarum corporumque nostrorum omnium, ac venia peccatorum, clementissimum Dominum supplicamus.

For the amending of all our souls and bodies alike and for the forgiveness of sin, we entreat the most merciful Lord.

Pro refrigerio fidelium animarum, præcipue sanctorum Domini sacerdotum qui huic Ecclesiæ præfuerunt Catholicæ, Dominum spirituum et universæ carnis Iudicem deprecamur.

For the welfare of the souls of the faithful departed, above all, of those holy priests of the Lord who presided over this Catholic Church, we beseech the Lord, Judge of souls and of all flesh.

Mortificatam vitiis carnem et veram dilectionem præsta, Domine, præsta: castum timorem et veram dilectionem præsta, Domine, præsta.

Grant, O Lord, grant a body dead to vice and grant true love, grant, O Lord, grant: grant chaste fear and true love, O Lord, grant.

Benedictio et claritas et sapientia et gratiarum actio et honor et virtus et fortitudo Deo nostro, in sæcula sæculorum. Amen.

Blessing, renown, wisdom, thanksgiving, honour, strength and power unto our God for ever and ever. Amen.

('Patrologia Latina': Sæculum IX. B, Flacci Albini seu Alcuini, etc. Opera omnia, t. ii, col. 560. 89 in text.)

TEXTS OF THE TWO NORTH ITALIAN EUCHARISTIC PRAYERS

(See back, pp. 98 et seq.)

No. I

Dignum et justum est nos tibi hic et ubique gratias agere, Domine sancte, omnipotens Deus; neque est alius per quem ad te aditum habere, præcem facere, sacrificationem tibi offere posimus nisi per quem tu nobis misisti, etc. (Here the quotation breaks off.)

It is meet and right that we should here and in all places, give thanks unto Thee, O holy Lord almighty God; nor is there any other, through whom we can have access unto Thee, make prayer unto Thee, offer sacrifice unto Thee, save by him whom Thou has sent unto us, etc.

No. II

Dignum et justum est, æquum et justum est nos tibi super omnia gratias agere, Domine sancte, Pater omnipotens, æterne Deus, qui incomparabili tuæ bonitatis [luce] in tenebris fulgere dignatus es, mittens nobis Jesum Christum suspitatorem animarum nostrarum qui nostra[e] salutis causa humiliando se ad mortem usque subiecit ut nos ea quæ Adam amiserat immortalitate restitutos efficeret sibi heredes et filios. Cuius benignitatis agere gratias tuæ tantæ magnanimitati quibusque laudibus nec sufficere possumus petentes de tua magna et flexibili pietate accepto (acceptum) ferre sacrificium istud, quod tibi offerimus

It is meet and right, it is just and right that we should above all things give thanks unto Thee, O Lord, holy Father almighty, everlasting God, Who hast deigned to shine on our darkness by the incomparable light of Thy goodness, sending unto us Jesus Christ the Saviour of our souls: Who humbling Himself for the sake of our salvation, subjected Himself even unto death, that He might restore to us that immortality which Adam had forfeited (and) make us heirs and sons to Him. We cannot worthily give thanks to Thy great mercy for such loving kindness nor praise Thee; but we pray Thee of Thy great and stantes ante conspectum tuæ divinæ pietatis per I. Xtum Dominum et Deum nostrum: per quem, petimus et rogamus . . . (Here this quotation also breaks off.)

(English translation, by Dix, p. 540.)

merciful love to hold accepted this sacrifice which we offer unto Thee, standing before the face of Thy divine love, through Jesus Christ our Lord and God: through Whom we pray and beseech . . .

THE RESTORED PASCHAL VIGIL

In the *Acta Apostolicæ Sedis* of February 9th, 1951, the Sacred Congregation of Rites declared that the Holy See had granted to those bishops and other superiors who desired to avail themselves of the permission, the right to celebrate the Holy Saturday service in the late evening of that day instead of in the early morning. This is a return to the original usage, a restoration of the Paschal Vigil-service, including a 'first Mass of Easter Day' beginning at midnight.

This restoration is the result of a great number of petitions which have been addressed to the Holy See for a long time past. The restored service is not, however, to be considered obligatory at present; it is *permitted*, where desired, and as a trial for possible future arrangements.

The restored Vigil involves a few changes—on Good Friday and on Holy Saturday itself—during the day:

The Tenebræ Office celebrated in the evening of Good Friday (being the Matins and Lauds of Holy Saturday anticipated on the Friday) is now to be celebrated on Holy Saturday morning, at a suitable time: this concerns those places in which the Divine Office is carried out in choir. During the day the other Hours (in the above cases) should be recited at fitting times; Vespers being chanted *after* midday, and Compline in the evening. Certain changes are made in these hours with regard to the antiphons and collects. For example, the antiphon *Christus factus est* is omitted at Compline on Saturday and also Psalm l. (*Miserere*), and the Office ends with the collect *Visita quæsumus*, the conclusion being in secret.

The Vespers of Holy Saturday is as on Maundy Thursday except for the first antiphon and the antiphon at the *Magnificat*, which are both new. Holy Saturday day is now given up to the memory of Our Lord's burial.

The Vigil-service is to begin at a time which will allow the Mass of Easter Eve (really the first Mass of Easter Day) to start about midnight (*circa mediam noctem*). The altar is covered with its three cloths, but the candles are not lighted till the Mass begins.

Not only has the original time of the Easter Vigil been restored, the form of the service has also returned to its early conditions, partly by means of the omission of later additions; partly by the reintroduction of older elements which had dropped out. The order of the service, too, has been, to a certain extent, rearranged; for instance, the Blessing of the Paschal Candle takes place at the very beginning, together with that of the new fire, and is carried out by the celebrant. Both Blessings take place at the entrance to the church—if possible, outside in the open air. The new fire is blessed with only one prayer—the first of the original series of four, the last prayer of which is now said at the end of the Blessing of the Paschal Candle, which follows at once. In this latter Blessing an ancient rite has been restored. The celebrant cuts the outline of the cross in the Candle with a 'style' (cum stylo)—that is, a sharp-pointed instrument of metal or bone, a kind of pen used by the ancients to write on the wax tablets which served as 'note-books'. The cross is traced in the wax between the five holes already made for the insertion of the five grains of incense. Above the central line the celebrant cuts the first letter of the Greek alphabet—alpha (A)—and below the cross, the last letter—omega (Ω). Between the arms of the cross he cuts the four figures of the current year—for example, for the year 1953 the figure 1 on the left side, above the arm of the cross; the 9 on the right side; the 5 below the left arm; the 3 below the right arm. All this is accompanied by the words: Christus heri et hodie: Principium et Finis; Alpha et Omega (these letters being cut as their names are pronounced ('Christ, yesterday and to-day; the Beginning and the End; the Alpha and Omega'), and as he cuts the figures of the current year: Ipsius sunt tempora et sæcula: Ipsi gloria et imperium per universa æternitatis sæcula. Amen ('His are the times and the ages: to him be glory and authority through everlasting ages of eternity'). Next comes the insertion of five grains of incense, now brought to the celebrant by the deacon. If these are not blessed, the celebrant sprinkles them with holy water and in-censes them thrice, without any words. While he inserts the grains in the Candle, the celebrant says: (i) Per sua sancta vulnera; (ii) gloriosa; (iii) custodiat; (iv) et conservat nos; (v) Christus Dominus. Amen ('Through his holy and glorious wounds may Christ the Lord guard and preserve us. Amen.').

The deacon then gives the celebrant a small candle lighted from the new fire, and the celebrant lights the Paschal Candle with it, saying: Lumen Christi gloriose resurgentis dissipet tenebras cordis et mentis ('May the Light of Christ, gloriously risen again, disperse the dark-ness of heart and soul'). The triple candle is no longer used for lighting the Paschal Candle. The celebrant then blesses the Can-dle saying: Dominus vobiscum and the prayer Veniat, quæsumus, omni-potens Deus—the last of the four prayers formerly used in blessing the new fire and the five grains of incense. The introduction and blessing of these latter was due to a mistaken interpretation of the words *veniat quæsumus* . . . *super 'hoc incensum' larga tuæ benedictionis infusio*. The correct translation is: 'May thy blessing fall abundantly, Almighty God, we beseech thee, upon this enkindled light' (*incensum*, from *incendo, ere* to enkindle, set fire to, agreeing with *cereum* 'candle', understood), but it was wrongly translated 'upon this *incense*'. In the restored Vigil, although the five grains of incense are still admitted—as symbols of the Five Wounds—the same prayer, as now used for the blessing of the Paschal Candle, has the following terms: *hunc incensum cereum* ('this lighted candle'), and so there can no longer be any danger of misunderstanding. Similar words used in the *Exsultet* or *Præconium Pascale* ('The Paschal Chant of praise') also helped towards the introduction of the grains of incense: *Suscipe, sancte Pater, incensi huius sacrificium vespertinum*. This was translated: 'Receive, holy Father, this evening sacrifice of *incense*'. But it should read: 'Receive, holy Father, the evening sacrifice of this lighted *candle*'; the word *cerei*, 'candle', being understood.

All the lights of the church are extinguished during the Blessing of the Candle, and the deacon, now vested in a white dalmatic, takes the lighted Candle in his hands and the procession is formed: first the thurifer followed by the subdeacon carrying the processional cross; the deacon with the Paschal Candle, and after him the celebrant; then the clergy and people in order. On entering the church the deacon, raising the Candle, sings: *Lumen Christi* ('the light of Christ') to which all respond: *Deo gratias* ('thanks be to God'). The celebrant then lights his own small candle from the Paschal Candle. The deacon, arriving in the middle of the church, sings again: *Lumen Christi*, on a higher note, all responding and genuflecting as before. The clergy then light their candles and the deacon chants *Lumen Christi* a third time, on a still higher note, in the middle of the sanctuary, before the altar, the congregation also lighting their candles. The celebrant then goes to the sedilia on the epistle side; the deacon places the Paschal Candle on a low stand in the middle of the sanctuary, the subdeacon standing with the cross beside the lectern placed on the Gospel side. The deacon, taking the book and bowing before the celebrant, asks his blessing as at Mass, and the celebrant gives the special blessing prescribed for the *Exsultet*. The deacon goes to the lectern and, all standing up, he incenses the book and also the Paschal Candle—walking round it to do so. In the *Exsultet* the prayer for the Emperor—which, although it had not been chanted since the Christian Empire ceased to exist, always remained in the text of the *Exsultet*, no doubt, at first, awaiting the possible restoration of the Empire—has been replaced, in the restored Vigil-service, by a new and special prayer which asks God to look down on 'those who rule over us with power' (*Respice etiam ad eos qui nos in potestate regunt*), that is, for all governments in the world to-day. The prayer in English is as follows: 'Look down also upon those who rule over us with power and, through the ineffable gift of thy pity and mercy, direct their thoughts towards justice and peace. So that from the scene of their earthly labour, they may, together with all thy people, attain their heavenly home'.

After the *Exsultet* the deacon changes his white vestments for the violet folded chasuble again, and goes with the subdeacon to sit with the celebrant during the reading of the Prophecies. Only four Prophecies are chanted, taken from the twelve recited in the usual service for Holy Saturday—namely, the first, fourth, eighth and eleventh. This is a return to the Gregorian Sacramentary—as arranged by St. Gregory the Great.[1] The celebrant is no longer directed to read the Prophecies together privately; he merely listens to them. Each Prophecy is followed by a collect—the second, third and fourth also have, before the collect, a responsory, taken respectively from Exod. xv. 1 and 2; Isaias v. 1; Deut. xxxiii. 1–4. The collects are preceded, as formerly, by *Oremus* ('Let us pray'), followed by the deacon's admonition: *Flectamus genua* ('Let us bend the knees'). In the unrestored service (as in all cases when this admonition is used) the subdeacon chants immediately: *Levate* ('Arise'), so that the faithful only have time to genuflect, and no time at all for the silent prayer which they are called upon to make. In the restored service, however, the rubric says distinctly that when the deacon tells the people to kneel down: 'all on bended knees pray *for a certain space of time*' (*omnes flexis genibus, per aliquod temporis spatium in silentio orant*); the deacon then chants: *Levate*. So the original meaning and use of the collect-form of prayer—the silent prayer of the people summed up by the celebrant in a short but all-embracing form—has been restored. It may be that this restoration will be extended to all cases of this form of prayer.

At the end of the Prophecies the Litany is chanted by two cantors, kneeling in the middle in front of the Paschal Candle, and all alike kneel. The former prostration of celebrant and ministers during the Litany is no longer ordered, and the Litany is not 'doubled', the people's responses follow at once, after each invocation chanted by the cantors.

---

[1] St. Gregory the Great, according to Cardinal Schuster in his book—*The Sacramentary* (English translation. Burns, Oates & Washbourne, Ltd., 1925, vol. ii, p. 296) reduced the twelve prophecies to *six*. This is incorrect, however.

The Litany is chanted only up to the words: *Propitius esto* ('Be merciful'). Then, when there is a baptismal font, the Blessing of the font takes place at this moment. The canticle, *Sicut cervus desiderat ad fontes aquarum*, is sung only when the baptistery is in a building separate from the church, and it is then sung during the procession of celebrant and ministers with cross and candles and Paschal Candle, from church to baptistery. The Blessing as given in the Roman Missal follows, and after it the clergy return in silence to the church. The renewal of Baptismal Vows then takes place. When there is no font, this latter follows immediately after the pause in the Litany before the words *Propitius esto*. The celebrant, first incensing the Paschal Candle, and then standing in front of it in the middle of the sanctuary or in an ambo or pulpit, addresses the congregation upon the renewal of their baptismal vows in union with the death, burial and resurrection of Our Saviour. This address is in Latin, and the form of renewal of vows also, which is taken from the baptismal service, but put into the plural. Permission, however, is given where the partial use of the vernacular is allowed in the baptismal ceremony, for the address and form of renewal of vows to be made also in the vernacular. The Litany is then resumed and chanted as before, all kneeling, except the celebrant and ministers, who retire to the sacristy to vest for the Mass. The Paschal Candle is placed in its special candlestick on the Gospel side, and the altar is got ready for Mass.

At the end of the Litany the cantors begin the solemn ninefold *Kyries*, and the celebrant and ministers enter the church, bow or genuflect before the altar, and then—omitting the usual prayers at the foot of the altar—go up immediately to the altar itself. The celebrant kisses the altar and incenses it as usual. When the cantors have finished chanting the *Kyries*, he at once intones the *Gloria in excelsis*, during which the bells are rung. The rubric says nothing about any private recitation of either *Kyries* or *Gloria* by celebrant and ministers, and the same is true with regard to the epistle and Gospel. The celebrant then it seems, may sit down immediately with his ministers at the sedilia until the collect. But the celebrant himself still intones the *Alleluia* three times, after the epistle has been chanted by the subdeacon.

The rubric orders the usual three prayers to be said secretly by the celebrant before his communion—nothing, however, had been said about the analogous prayers said secretly in the ordinary Mass when offering paten and chalice at the offertory. Nevertheless, on the above analogy it seems that these prayers ought also to be said. In the 1951 order for the restored Vigil-service, the Mass ended with a communion anthem: *Vespere autem sabbati* ('On the night after the sabbath') and the postcommunion prayer, followed by *Dominus vobiscum, Et cum spiritu tuo* ('The Lord be with you and with thy spirit', or, in more modern English, 'And with you also'), sung by celebrant and choir; then *Ite missa est, alleluia, alleluia* and *Deo gratias, alleluia, alleluia* ('Go, it is the dismissal'—that is, the end of the service—'Thanks be to God' with the twice repeated *alleluia*— 'praise the Lord'—by the deacon and choir). The celebrant then gives the Blessing, but the Last Gospel is not recited; the cele- brant and ministers, after bowing or genuflecting before the altar, return to the sacristy.

The miniature Vespers, chanted at the end of the service when this is held in the morning of Holy Saturday, was omitted in the restored service, as full ferial Vespers of the Saturday had been re- cited in the afternoon of that day.[1] The miniature Vespers, fitted into the Mass in the morning service, was the result first of the development of an office of Vespers itself; secondly of the continual tendency to push the Vigil-office farther and farther back on the Saturday, until it arrived at the early morning. But the *Magnificat* antiphon, *Vespere autem*, was used as communion anthem. It is difficult to see why this was done, since neither introit nor offertory anthem are found in the Holy Saturday Mass. All was, however, corrected in 1952. In *The Clergy Review*, March 1952 (vol. xxxvii, pp. 166–80. Burns, Oates & Washbourne, Ltd., London), a recent document from Rome on the question of the restored Paschal Vigil was printed in full. Permission is given to celebrate the restored service for another three years on trial, before deciding finally as to the full restoration of this service. Certain new arrange- ments and changes were also announced. With regard to the Divine Office (choral), the office of Compline is now altogether omitted on Holy Saturday. No reason is actually given for this omission, but it is probably due to the fact that Compline is in the ordinary Office, the last 'hour' of the day, whereas the restored Vigil-service holds that position, being in a sense the continuation of Vespers; Com- pline, too, is a much later addition to the daily Office. It is also de- clared in the document that the restored Vigil takes the place of Matins of Easter Day (originally the 'night-office' after midnight on Saturday—a later development of the Holy Saturday Vigil), and so that office is also to be omitted, but the office of Lauds (which should follow the night-office at dawn on Sunday) is to be inserted at the end of the midnight Mass as follows: When the celebrant has re- ceived the usual 'ablutions' after his own communion and that of

---

[1] In any case, it would be much too late for Vespers—after midnight.

the congregation, the antiphon—*Alleluia* (thrice)—is chanted by the choir followed by Psalm cxvi. (cxvii.), and the threefold *Alleluia* is repeated after the psalm. The celebrant then immediately intones the antiphon of the canticle *Benedictus* (Canticle of Zachary; Luke i. 68–79): *Et valde mane una sabbatorum, veniunt ad monumentum, orto iam sole. Alleluia.* ('On the first day of the week, very early in the morning, they came to the sepulchre, the sun being now risen. *Alleluia.*' (Luke xxiv. 1)). While the Benedictus is being sung, the celebrant incenses the altar in the usual way at solemn Lauds and Vespers. The antiphon *Et valde* is repeated at the end of the canticle. The celebrant then sings *Dominus vobiscum* and the postcommunion prayer, which serves also as the collect for Lauds. The prayer is followed by *Dominus vobiscum* and *Ite missa*, etc., as already described.

This 'miniature office' of Lauds is simply an adaptation of the miniature Vespers when the service is held in the morning.

Among the *ordinationes* (regulations) laid down in the Roman document, there is one concerning the procedure permitted now on the Vigil of Pentecost ('Whitsun Eve'). In those churches in which the restored Vigil has been celebrated, the six Prophecies before the Blessing of the baptismal font and the latter ceremony itself can be entirely omitted on Whitsun Eve, and the Mass—High or Sung Mass as well as Low Mass—will then begin with the introit: *Cum sanctificatus fuero in vobis, congregabo vos de universis terris: et effundam super vos aquam mundam et mundabimini ab omnibus inquinamentis vestris: et dabo vobis spiritum novum. Alleluia. Alleluia.* (Ezech. xxxvi. 23–6), followed by Psalm xxxiii. 1: *Benedicam Dominum in omni tempore* ('When the time comes to proclaim my Majesty by delivering you, I will bring you home again from every part of the earth: and I will pour cleansing streams over you, to purge you from every stain you bear and breathe a new spirit into you. Alleluia. Alleluia.' (Psalm xxxiii. 1) 'At all times, I will bless the Lord: his praise shall be on my lips continually'). This introit is printed in the Roman Missal at the end of the Whitsun Eve Mass, for the use of individual priests celebrating Low Masses on that day.

In the *Acta Apostolicæ Sedis* of February 9th, 1951, it was said that the Service should begin at such a time as would allow the solemn Mass of Easter to start about midnight (*circa mediam noctem*. See p. 273). But in the more recent document of 1952, provision is made for certain cases in which it would be impossible or difficult, for some reason, to carry out the restored Vigil exactly as laid down. In such cases the bishop of the diocese, if he considers it to be necessary for sufficiently important reasons, may give permission for the service to start earlier in the evening, and therefore for the Mass to begin before midnight; but the service must not begin earlier than 8 p.m.

Those priests who have celebrated the midnight Mass of the restored Vigil may celebrate Mass again on Easter Sunday, and even two or three Masses if they possess the necessary indult from Rome to do this on ordinary Sundays. Those of the congregations who have received communion on Holy Saturday in the morning may also receive communion during the midnight Mass—but not if the Vigil-service is celebrated at the earlier time, as above indicated. Those who communicate during the midnight Mass may not do so again on the Sunday.

The fast in preparation for celebrating the Midnight Mass and receiving communion should begin at least at 10 p.m., and, in the case of an earlier celebration of the Vigil, at least at 7 p.m. Priests who have celebrated Mass at midnight and wish to celebrate again on the Sunday, may take something liquid (tea, coffee or soup) after the midnight Mass, keeping a complete fast from then for at least an hour before the Mass on the Sunday. Besides these thoughtful arrangements for external needs, it is clear that Papal Authority looks to the restored Vigil-service as the means of more effective, 'living' public worship; a restoration of what had to a great extent been lost for the faithful during past centuries. This is shown by the directions laid down that, in all parishes and other centres, the people are to be *prepared* for this great occasion by teaching and instructions on the matter all during Lent.[1]

[1] See an excellent article in *The Tablet*, March 8th, 1952, called 'Celebrating Easter Night: A significant Reform', by Lancelot C. Sheppard, p. 196.

BIBLIOGRAPHY

Adversus Hærreseos, St. Irenaeus.

Antiq. Eccles. Rit., Dom Martène.

Apostolic Fathers (2nd Edn.), Ed. Lightfoot (Macmillan & Co. Ltd.).

Apostolic Tradition of St. Hippolytus of Rome, Ed. Dom Gregory Dix (S.P.C.K.).

Augustine Synthesis, An, Erich Przywara, S.J. (Sheed & Ward).

Bishop Sarapion's Prayer Book, Trans. John Wordsworth (S.P.C.K.).

Bobbio Missal, The, André Wilmart and Others (Henry Bradshaw Society).

Byzantine Office, John Bannerman Wainewright (Cope & Fenwick).

Canon of the Mass : Its History, Theology & Art, Dom Jerome Gassner, O.S.B. (B. Herder).

Canon de la Messe Romaine, Le, Dom Bernard Botte, O.S.B.

Catholic Eastern Churches, The, Donald Attwater (G. E. J. Coldwell, Ltd.).

Catholic Encyclopædic Dictionary, Edited by D. Attwater (Cassell & Co. Ltd.).

Celebration of the Mass, The, J. B. O'Connell (Burns, Oates & Washbourne, Ltd.).

Ceremonies of the Roman Rite Described, A. Fortescue. Re-ed. J. B. O'Connell (Burns, Oates & Washbourne, Ltd.).

Christ in the Liturgy, Dom Illtyd Trethowan, O.S.B. (Sheed & Ward).

Christian Sacrifice, The, Canon Eugène Masure ; Trans. Dom Illtyd Trethowan, O.S.B. (Burns, Oates & Washbourne, Ltd.).

Christian Worship (Origines du Culte Chrétien), Mgr. L. Duchesne (S.P.C.K.).

Church of Our Fathers, The, Dr. Rock, Ed. G. W. Hart & W. H. Frere (London: John Murray).

Church Year and Calendar, John Dowden, D.D. (Camb. Handbooks of Liturgical Studies).

Churches, Their Planning & Furnishing, Peter F. Anson (Bruce Pub. Co.).

De Civitate Dei, St. Augustine.

De Sacramentis, St. Ambrose.

Detection of Aumbries, DOM GREGORY DIX (Dacre Press : A. & C. Black, Ltd.).

Dialogues of St. Gregory, Second Book: See *Saint Benedict by St. Gregory the Great (2nd Edn., 1951)*, (Stanbrook Abbey Press, Worcester).

Dictionnaire d'Archéologie, etc., Librairie Letouzey et Ané., Paris.

Didascalia Apostolorum, Ed. DOM R. H. CONNOLLY (Oxford University Press).

Dimanche et Vie Pascale, DOM JEAN HILD, O.S.B. (Edn. Brépols).

Dissident Eastern Churches, The, DONALD ATTWATER (G. E. J. Coldwell, Ltd.).

Early Eucharist, The, FELIX L. CIRLOT (S.P.C.K.).

Early Euchologion, An, Ed. C. H. ROBERTS & DOM B. CAPPELLE (Bureau du Muséon).

Early History of the Liturgy, The, J. H. SRAWLEY, D.D. (Cambridge University Press).

Eastern Churches Quarterly (G. E. J. Coldwell, Ltd.).

L'Eglise ancienne, a-t-elle connu la Messe du soir? DOM ELOI DEKKERS, O.S.B.

English Church Furniture, DR. CHARLES COX (Methuen).

Epistulae Rom. Pont. Genuinae, A. THIEL (Braunsberg).

Ethérie, Journal de Voyage, Trans. HÉLÈNE PÉTRÉ.

Etudes Bibliques, PÈRE M. J. LAGRANGE, O.P. (Lecoffre).

Eucharistic Consecration in the Primitive Church, G. A. MICHELL (S.P.C.K.).

Florilegium Patristicum, mcmcccv, Fasculum vii.

Gelasian Sacramentary, Ed. H. A. WILSON, M.A. (Oxford University Press).

Gregorian Sacramentary, Ed. H. A. WILSON, M.A. (Oxford University Press).

Handbook to the Christian Liturgy, VEN. J. NORMAN, M.A. (S.P.C.K.).

Hippolyte de Rome: La Tradition Apostolique, DOM BERNARD BOTTE, O.S.B. (Edition du Cerf: Oxford).

Influence of the Synagogue upon the Divine Office, The, C. W. DUGMORE, B.D. (Oxford University Press).

Introduction to the Study of Eastern Liturgies, PÈRE S. SALAVILLE; Trans. MGR. J. M. T. BARTON (Sands & Co. Ltd.).

'Journal of Theological Studies' (Oxford University Press).

Lent and the Liturgy, RT. REV. E. MYERS (Grail Publications).
Leonine Sacramentary, Ed. C. LETTS FELTOE, B.D.
Lesser Eastern Churches, The, ADRIAN FORTESCUE (Catholic Truth Society).
Liber Pontificalis, Ed. DUCHESNE.
Liturgica Historica, EDMUND BISHOP (Clarendon Press).
Liturgical Homilies of Narsai, Ed. DOM R. H. CONNOLLY (Cambridge University Press).
Liturgies, Eastern & Western, F. E. BRIGHTMAN (Oxford University Press).
Liturgy & Worship, Ed. W. K. LOWTHER CLARKE, D.D. (S.P.C.K.).

Maison Dieu, La Cahiers de Pastorale Liturgique No. 18 (Editions du Cerf).
Mediator Dei (Encyclical), POPE PIUS XII (Catholic Truth Society).
Mémorial du Seigneur dans la Liturgie de l'Antiquité Chrétienne, L. CUNIVERT MOHLBERG (Rome Ed. Liturgiche).
Miscellanea Liturgica, Ed. CERF. LEX ORANDI.
Missarum Solemnia, Trans. FR. J. A. JUNGMANN (Duckett).
Monumenta Liturgica, Ed. FARNBOROUGH ABBEY.
Mozarabic & Ambrosian Rites, The, W. C. BISHOP, M.A. (Alcuin Club Tracts, A. R. Mowbray & Co. Ltd.)
Mystère du Culte dans le Christianisme, Le, DOM ODO CASEL, O.S.B. (Les Editions du Cerf, Paris).

Notes on the Catholic Liturgies, ARCHDALE A. KING (Longmans, Green & Co. Ltd.).

Ordines Romani du haut moyen age, M. ANDRIEU (Louvain).
Ordo Romanus Primus: Commentary on, DOM MABILLON, O.S.B.
Origines du Culte Chrétien, DUCHESNE.
Origines de Prime, DOM JACQUES FROGER (Rome: Edn. Liturgiche).
Orthodox Eastern Church, The, A. FORTESCUE (Catholic Truth Society).

Paschal Mystery, The, LOUIS BOUYER; Trans. SR. M. BENOIT, R.S.M. (Allen & Unwin).
Peregrinatio, ETHERIA, Trans. MCCLURE & FELTOE (S.P.C.K.).
Procession of Saints, JAMES BRODRICK, S.J. (Burns, Oates & Washbourne, Ltd.).
Psalms in the Jewish Church, W. O. E. OESTERLY (London).

Religion of Earliest Man, The, W. SCHMIDT, S.V.D. (Catholic Truth Society).

Réservation Eucharistique jusqu'à la Renaissance, E. MAFFEI.

Rites of Eastern Christendom, ARCHDALE A. KING (Burns, Oates & Washbourne, Ltd.).

Rites of Western Christendom, ARCHDALE A. KING (Catholic Book Agency, Rome).

Roman Missal, Ed. J. B. O'CONNELL (Burns, Oates & Washbourne, Ltd.).

Roman Pontifical, The, DOM PIERRE DE PUNIET; Trans. by M. V. HARCOURT (Longmans, Green & Co., Ltd.).

Rule of St. Benedict (S.P.C.K.).

Sacramentary, The, CARDINAL SCHUSTER (Burns, Oates & Washbourne, Ltd.).

Sacrifice of Christ Our Head, The, CANON EUGÈNE MASURE; Trans. DOM ILLTYD TRETHOWAN (Burns, Oates & Washbourne, Ltd.).

Saints of the Canon of the Mass, The, FR. V. L. KENNEDY, C.S.B. (Antichita: Rome).

Scriptorum Veterum Nova Collectio (1828).

Shape of the Liturgy, The, DOM GREGORY DIX (Dacre Press: A. & C. Black, Ltd.).

Te Deum ou Illatio, DOM PAUL CAGIN (Solesme).

Textes et Etudes Liturgiques, ABBEY OF MONT CÉSAR (Louvain).

Theology & Sanity, F. J. SHEED (Sheed & Ward).

Uniate Eastern Churches, The, A. FORTESCUE (Burns, Oates & Washbourne, Ltd.).

Western Liturgy & Its History, The, THEODOR KLAUSER; Trans. F. L. CROSS (Mowbray).

Westminster Version of the Sacred Scriptures: (St. Paul's Epistles to the Churches), (Longmans, Green & Co., Ltd.).

INDEX

Ablutions, 49–50, 181
Addai and Mari, SS. See Liturgies
Advent, 242–5
Aetheria. See Etheria
Agape, 5, 14, 43, 46, 48, 50
Agnus Dei, 88, 178–9
Alexandrian Rite. See Liturgies—
    Egyptian
Aliturgical Services, 8, 55, 230–1
Alleluia, 34, 71, 77, 87, 163
Altar, 90
Altar of Repose, 233
Ambrosian Rite. See Liturgies
Amalarius of Metz, 178
Anamnesis. See Prayers
Anaphora. See Prayers—Eucharistic
Angelic Hymn. See *Sanctus*
Anglicans, 152
Antioch. See Liturgies
Antiphon, 72–86
Antiphonary, 28
Apostolic Constitutions, 16, 52, 162
Apostolic Tradition, 14–16, 18, 24,
    42, 53, 90–91, 95, 102, 118,
    127, 151–5, 162, 165, 167,
    179, 185, 199, 234
Ashes, Imposition of, 228
Aumbries, 254–63

Baptism, xxiv, 16, 30, 42, 221, 228,
    231 (See also Liturgies for
    Holy Saturday)
Basil, St. See Liturgies
Benedicamus Domino, 12–13
Blessed Sacrament:
    Devotion to: 264–7
    Reservation of, 55, 233, 254–63
Blessing:
    Aaronic, 9
    Before Communion, 75, 85
    Cup of, 4–5
    End of Eucharist, 75

Blessing—*continued*
    Eucharistic Offerings, 6, 44
    Jewish, 6, 46
    Of Fire, 200
    Font, 105
    Oils, 22, 30, 44, 56, 103, 105,
        159
    Palms, 231, 236
    Paschal Candle, 199, 274
Breaking of Bread, 10, 48
Byzantine Rite. See Liturgies

Calendar, 214–51
Cambrai. See Sacramentary
Canon:
    Actionis, 93
    Roman, 20, 112, 121–31, 159,
        162, 182
Catechumens, 12, 35, 42, 66, 67,
    138
Celtic Rite. See Liturgies
Ceremonies, 26–7
Chaldean Rite. See Liturgies
Chant, 34, 71–2. (See also Psalms)
Church Orders, 14, 24
Chrysostom, St. John. See Liturgies
Clement, St. See Apostolic Con-
    stitutions and Liturgies
Collects, 67–9, 77, 85–6. (See also
    Prayers)
Commixture, 166–70, 177
Communion, 9, 17, 48–9, 55, 106,
    160, 179–80
Compline. See Divine Office
Concelebration, 91
Confirmation, 16, 42, 221
Consecration in Eucharist, xx, 5,
    48–9, 106, 109, 115, 152,
    159–61, 183–4
Consecration of Bishops, 18
Coptic Rite. See Liturgies—Mono-
    physite

285